Agricultural Supply Response

Hossein Askari
John Thomas Cummings

The Praeger Special Studies program—
utilizing the most modern and efficient book
production techniques and a selective
worldwide distribution network—makes
available to the academic, government, and
business communities significant, timely
research in U.S. and international economic, social, and political development.

Agricultural Supply Response

A Survey of the Econometric Evidence

Praeger Publishers   New York   Washington   London

PRAEGER SPECIAL STUDIES IN INTERNATIONAL ECONOMICS AND DEVELOPMENT

Library of Congress Cataloging in Publication Data

Askari, Hossein.
    Agricultural supply response.

    (Praeger special studies in international economics and development)
    Bibliography: p.
    Includes indexes.
    1. Underdeveloped areas—Agriculture. 2. Underdeveloped areas—Agriculture—Mathematical models. I. Cummings, John Thomas, joint author. II. Title.
HD1417.A84   338.1'09172'4   76-23376
ISBN 0-275-23260-3

PRAEGER PUBLISHERS
111 Fourth Avenue, New York, N.Y. 10003, U.S.A.

Published in the United States of America in 1976
by Praeger Publishers, Inc.

© 1976 by Praeger Publishers, Inc.

Printed in the United States of America

The measurement and analysis of the price responsiveness of agricultural supply, particularly in developing countries, is a matter of considerable importance in a food-hungry world. Where agricultural supply responds readily to price, changes in production can be accomplished through relatively decentralized changes in market conditions and incentives. Equally, however, local agriculture will be sensitive to changes in world market conditions unless governments intervene. On the other hand, where agricultural supply is not price responsive, local agriculture, while protected from market fluctuations, will not respond readily to decentralized incentives; governments wishing to affect that supply will have to do so by changing the underlying technological or social conditions under which the crops are produced. It is thus important to know which crops in which countries are responsive to price and to measure that responsiveness. Further, it is important to understand the differences in price responsiveness over crops and countries, to understand what sort of conditions militate against it. Only with such knowledge can the effects of governmental policies on local agriculture be assessed.

Despite the importance of this question and despite the fact that it is preeminently an empirical question capable of an econometric answer, discussions of these issues remained largely theoretical until the early 1960s. It was for this reason in 1963 that I proposed to the late Max F. Millikan, director of the Center for International Studies at the Massachusetts Institute of Technology, that the center undertake the sponsorship of a series of empirical investigations into supply response in less-developed agriculture. Professor Millikan readily agreed and some (though by no means all) of the investigations summarized in the present volume were the result.

Important as detailed individual investigations are, however, it was our hope in sponsoring them that the day would come when sufficient information had been accumulated to allow both an overview and an analysis of the different results obtained for different crops under different social conditions. We hoped that such an analysis would provide a deeper understanding of the forces that lead to price responsiveness than can be afforded by the simple measurement of price elasticities in particular cases. The present volume goes a long way toward answering that need. In it the authors perform two valuable services. First, they draw together in a single place and analytically summarize the known results. Second, they provide an analysis of the intercountry, intercrop problem mentioned above, contributing to our understanding of the sorts of crops and the sorts of conditions under which price responsiveness will be high or low. If some of their conclusions are only tentative, that is because the problem is difficult indeed. Yet only with an understanding both of individual empirical results and of the effects of differing social and technical conditions on price responsiveness can governments sensibly plan agricultural policy in a developing world.

ACKNOWLEDGMENTS

This work began in 1970 as a result of encouragement from
Franklin Fisher to bring together a number of studies that were
undertaken at the Massachusetts Institute of Technology during the
1960s. All of these studies were, either directly or indirectly,
based on the Nerlovian supply response model. Given that these,
and many other studies, form the basis of our present work, we
owe great debt and appreciation to all of these authors.

During this long and seemingly endless project, the Center for
International Studies at MIT has given us financial support for
typing. In addition, Amy Leiss, the assistant director of the center,
has given us much support throughout the last two years. Many
patient people have typed various drafts of this manuscript; they
include Adele Bogden, Mrs. Frank Goodwin, Sharon Miller, and
Cindy Wimberley. In addition, Ugur Aker has done an excellent
job of indexing.

Above all, none of this would have been possible without the
interest, advice, and constant encouragement of Franklin Fisher.
There is no way that we can thank him enough for his intellectual
and moral support.

Finally, we have been able to carry this project to a conclusion
because our families have been kind and generous with both their
time and affection.

CONTENTS

LIST OF TABLES AND FIGURE

xiv

Although industrialization remains the prime goal of political and economic planners throughout the developing world, the last decade has seen a strong resurgence of interest in and concern for agriculture. The continued high population growth rates, the frequent waning of early enthusiasm generated by often unrealistically optimistic development schemes adopted with the achievement of political independence, the worldwide emigration from the country-side that has led to almost exponential growth of the urbanized areas: all these factors and more have served to intensify the problems of feeding nations that are rapidly, if somewhat uncertainly, abandoning traditional life styles in the name of modernization. Furthermore, the central role agricultural products play in the export trade of many developing countries and the always critical need in these countries for more foreign exchange to finance develop-ment projects provides additional urgency to the task of increasing agricultural output.

After World War II it looked as if the world would never again face the prospects of a large-scale famine. The enormous U.S. food surpluses in the 1940s and 1950s and later the success of the Green Revolution seemed to put the specter of hunger behind us. However, in the last decade, a combination of factors has rapidly and inexorably pushed much of the world to the brink of starvation.

In 1974 the U.S. surplus had withered away—poor harvests in both the United States and elsewhere had reduced crop output to the point that the world food reserves of grain had reached a 22-year low. World food reserves at the end of 1974 were only enough for about 30 days as compared to about 90 days in 1960-61. By December 1974 it was estimated that a worldwide minimum of 10,000 people were starving to death every week. The hardest hit areas have been

1

India, Bangladesh, Brazil, Ethiopia, and the sub-Saharan Sahelian countries of Chad, Mali, Mauritania, Senegal, Upper Volta, and Niger. In India and Bangladesh a bad harvest could kill as many as 100 million people or more in one year. Thus, over a very short period of time the world has gone from feast to famine.

The reasons behind the food shortage are many. The United States, other major exporters, the Soviet Union, and other importers have had a series of bad harvests. World population has kept pace with food output increases. Rising incomes in the Western world and Japan have also increased the demand for beef and other live-stock, which sets the stage for a very inefficient pattern of consumption. For example, it takes 20 pounds of grain to produce one pound of beef, 6.3 pounds of grain to get one pound of pork, or 4.25 pounds of grain to obtain 12 eggs. It is estimated that the grain production needed for an average American's food intake could sustain six people on a satisfactory diet in Third World countries. When such facts as these are recalled, it can be seen that the approximate constancy of food output per person hides the fact that much of the increase in production has been inefficiently used by Western consumption.

Furthermore, due to a combination of circumstances, the Green Revolution has not lived up to full expectation. Hybrid seeds need a lot of water, fertilizer, and pesticides if the promised gain is to be fully realized; if one of these is missing, yield drops sharply. This situation most recently has been dealt a sharp blow in the form of both a rapid escalation in the price of oil and the resulting increase in the cost of fertilizers. Thus many of the nations hardest hit by a food shortage are also among those being affected most adversely by the current energy crisis. As a result the short-run food problem appears very grave for many developing nations.

In the longer run the situation looks, if anything, even more bleak. The Agency for International Development estimates that by the year 2020 the world population could reach 10.5 billion, an increase of about 6.5 billion over 1970 levels; approximately 6 billion of this expansion will be in developing nations. At the same time, inputs such as fertilizers and pesticides are becoming more scarce. Furthermore, many scientists warn that the bad weather pattern may prevail for some time into the future.

All of this prompted the convening, in November 1974, of the World Food Conference in Rome. This effort, under the auspices of the United Nations, was the first international approach to the problems of world hunger. The conference faced both short-run and long-run tasks. The former were aimed at meeting any immediate emergencies and the latter were to explore ways of

increasing food availability in the future; the short-run issues could
be solved by international aid programs. On the other hand, over
the long run there are many more possibilities—increasing the
nutritional quality of food, opening up of new lands, expanding the
supply of other inputs such as fertilizer, water, and new varieties
of seed, founding and supporting agricultural research institutions
in different countries and regions, promoting the use of better
storage and distribution systems (rats and other rodents are believed
to eat some 25 percent of the world's grain output), and reducing
the rate of population increase. All these options need large investments in agriculture and its supporting infrastructure.

In essence, increasing output of food and/or reducing population
growth are the two basic ways of meeting the long-run food problem,
with the possibility of changing wasteful consumption patterns in
the prosperous nations a third possibility.

The World Food Conference seems to have made little significant
progress in solving these problems. A World Food Council was
formed to funnel food aid to needy nations and to allocate investment
funds for the development of agriculture. In addition a special
"early warning" information system was implemented that would
signal the size of harvests and possible hunger areas in the world.
But among all of these discussions only one policy was acceptable
to all—that of increasing agricultural output—but the means to achieve
this goal remain elusive.

By their very nature they require that we confront problems of
several different types: some are institutional, such as rationalizing
patterns of land ownership; some are technological, such as adapting
modern agricultural methods to small-plot farming; still others
are geographical, such as the opening of new lands to cultivation.
However, a critical assumption made by all those who hope to spur
agricultural output is that, given land reform, given availability
of fertilizers, pesticides, and irrigation techniques, given resettlement projects, and so on, farmers will in fact respond by producing
and marketing larger quantities of outputs. Furthermore, since
few countries outside the Socialist bloc have evinced any interest
in collectivizing agriculture and promoting increased output through
command techniques, this assumption is predicated on the efficacy
of the price mechanism.

The validity of this assumption has been questioned by many
observers. The objection has been made that, while farmers may
be responsive to price changes, their planting and marketing
decisions are primarily governed by traditional behavior patterns,
thereby making price response of only secondary importance in
explaining output variation. Others have postulated, indeed, that
farmers either do not respond to price changes at all or respond in

an inverse way, marketing less as prices increase. For example,
P. N. Mathur and H. Ezekiel argue that a farmer's cash requirements are relatively stable, so that the size of the marketable
surplus varies inversely with price, consumption of the produce
being the residual.[1] T. N. Krishnan argues that this is at least
not true of farmers producing at the absolute level of subsistence,
for whom consumption is fixed, not residual, but that the marketable
surplus explanation may very well be valid for those farmers who
are slightly above the subsistence level, and who thus have some
flexibility in their decision-making process: that is, to consume
more of what is produced beyond absolute subsistence needs or to
sell it in the marketplace for cash in order to increase nonagricultural consumption.[2] Together with R. O. Olson he explains variation
in marketable surplus* in terms of an income effect—that as prices
rise a peasant's real income increases, and the income effect on
the peasant's demand for consumption of the good he produces
outweighs the effect price increases might have on the amount he
brings to the marketplace.[3]

Certainly such fundamental objections to reliance on the market
mechanism as the means of feeding growing cities and of bolstering
export revenues call for an examination of whatever evidence exists
for the various explanations of peasant responses to price, particularly since most if not all of the concrete agricultural programs
undertaken by governmental agencies rely upon the assumption of
an essentially "normally operating" market mechanism. In recent
years several studies have been conducted that make available a
fairly wide, if uneven, cross-section of peasant behavior under
different conditions of geography and social structure and diverse
crop production.

In this book the authors wish first to review the more commonly
pursued governmental agricultural policies, next to summarize and
collate the results of some of the studies of peasant supply responsiveness, then to identify likely reasons for the different results
across crops and countries, and finally to discuss some of the areas
deserving further attention.

In any work such as this the authors must set some sort of
guidelines as to what studies should or should not be included; we
have done so, even if we sometimes seem to honor the guidelines
only in the breach. In 1958 Marc Nerlove published a study of the
supply responsiveness of U.S. farmers, which has since proven
to be seminal, particularly as regards the thinking of economic

---

*The question of marketable surplus is discussed in greater
detail in Chapter 5.

researchers concerned with the developing countries.[4] The Nerlove
model, hypothesizing farmer reactions based on price expectations
and/or area adjustments, has been adopted, modified, even extensively revised by many authors in the last 17 years.

Though our scope grew rapidly with our deepening realization
of the contribution made by the researchers cited below and many
others to this area of economic literature, Nerlove has remained
our boundary; his model, plus our desire in the last chapters of
this work to use elasticity estimates, have singled out for inclusion
herein studies that involve price expectation and area adjustment
models resulting in supply elasticity estimates. However, not
unnaturally, we have found rigid bounds too confining: Both non-
Nerlovian studies that present elasticity estimates and Nerlovian
works without elasticity estimates are included. Such flexibility
must be allowed to introduce comparative elements into a study of
various crops, countries, and/or time periods.

The general intention of this work, after identifying and
summarizing the principal works, is found in Chapter 10; we hope
to identify some of the factors that seriously affect supply responsiveness. Such an identification could help answer the questions:
Can the policy maker influence supply responsiveness, and if so,
how? Even perhaps more important, should supply responsiveness
to price movements prove to be small, and given that the policy
maker is willing to consider market incentives to encourage greater
output, are there identifiable policy measures that can increase the
level of responsiveness?

However, the studies examined below are area oriented, and
they mostly consider agricultural policies only incidentally and
particularly, as can be seen in Chapters 5 through 9. We begin
with the expectation that only a small fraction of these studies
(see Chapter 10) would be suitable for determination of the factors
that affect peasant responsiveness. For all these reasons we offer
only our initial intention; to clarify the directions in which future
work, in which we hope to participate, should take. There can be
no overemphasis that this work, like so many that concern the
developing economies, is tentative and hopeful. We believe this
is the spirit in which the authors we cite below have undertaken
their own studies; we know that this is the spirit under which we
have undertaken our work. We offer our results and invite further
reaction.

NOTES

1. P. N. Mathur and H. Ezekiel, "Marketable Surplus of Food
and Price Fluctuations in a Developing Economy," Kyklos 14 (1961).

2. T. N. Krishnan, "The Marketed Surplus of Foodgrains: Is It Inversely Related to Price?" Economic Weekly 17 (annual number, February 1965).

3. R. O. Olson, "The Impact and Implications of Foreign Surplus Disposal on Underdeveloped Economies," Journal of Farm Economics 42 (December 1960).

4. Marc Nerlove, The Dynamics of Supply: Estimation of Farmers' Response to Price (Baltimore: Johns Hopkins University Press, 1958).

2

AGRICULTURAL POLICIES:
A REVIEW

Before commencing our examination of peasant responsiveness
to price incentives, a brief review of governmental agricultural
policy is in order. To look at policies before discussing the underlying behavior patterns that such policies purportedly affect seems
to put the cart before the horse. However, it is a more accurate
sequence historically, if not rationally, since the systematic study
of supply response is of far more recent vintage than government
attempts to influence supply.

Our concern at this point is to enumerate the more frequently
encountered policies, pointing out their intended economic impact.
Many of the supply analyses discussed below have attempted to
account for the effects of one or more such policies by including
within the mathematical models employed variables that are postulated to measure these effects, either directly or in proxy form.*
Since these studies try, ex post facto, to gauge the roles played
by such policies in increasing (or decreasing) agricultural production,
it seems useful to discuss them in a general way, using illustrative
examples, before turning to specific supply analyses.

At the same time we will consider the possible effects on these
policies of a number of technical, social, economic, and political
factors. Some of the latter we will later hypothesize are determi-

---

*For example, Jere Behrman's inclusion of rural transportation
and malaria-control facilities, Scott Eddie's interest in railway
construction, Stephen DeCanio's concern for land-tenancy patterns,
Marcelle Arak's attempts to account for the role of a government-
controlled marketing apparatus, and measures of the extent of
irrigation systems included in several studies.

nants of supply responsiveness and we will attempt to measure the
degree to which they influence responsiveness, hoping to uncover
linkages that can be used by policy makers in order to alter the
amplitude of responsiveness in accordance with overall economic
objectives.

For discussion purposes, specific agricultural policies can be
grouped into four categories: those pertaining to land ownership
or control; those involving some degree of market management;
those affecting the rural infrastructure; and those of a technological
or research nature. Among the policies falling in the first category
are controls over rents and tenancy agreements, land redistribution,
plot consolidation schemes, resettlement projects, and agricultural
credit facilities. In the second category are price controls, crop
quantity restrictions, marketing boards, subsidies to farmers or
consumers, export campaigns, and government involvement with
agricultural imports. The third group of policies include irrigation
projects, transportation improvements, rural education, public
health projects, programs to upgrade the quantity and quality of
the agricultural bureaucracy at all levels, and facilities to publicize
and distribute at the village level such "modern" agricultural imple-
ments as fertilizer, and so on. Finally, in the fourth category are
any and all attempts both to discover new and adapt existing inputs
such as improved seed, simple tools and machines, and so on, that
are suitable for the existing environment.

LAND-CONTROL POLICIES

Agricultural policies relating to land ownership or title make
up what is popularly called "land reform." Such policies are hardly
the fruit of modern economics: Deuteronomy treats the problems
of a formerly nomadic people needing a new institutional framework
suitable for agriculturists. In more recent times the opening of
vast tracts to cultivation in the Western hemisphere required legislative guidance, such as the Homestead Act, passed by the U.S.
Congress in 1862 to regulate the settlement of the Great Plains.
The displacement, to some degree or other, of semifeudal propertied
classes in dozens of countries around the globe during the last 100
years has been in most cases at least initiated by governmental
activity.

The motivations for land reform programs are varied, including,
for example, both ethical elements of social justice (as in the case
of the restoration of stolen Indian lands in the early stages of the
Mexican Revolution) and practical political considerations (the post-

Civil War consolidation of the Republican party's power base in the
Midwestern states). But there are also many economic arguments
put forward, ranging from the strongly held, if vaguely formulated,
premise that a peasant will work harder and of course produce more
"if he is his own boss" to quite elaborate development models where
the enhancement of national savings involves the elimination of a
profligate Ricardian landlord class.

In discussing the first category of agricultural policies it is
important to stress their interdependent nature. Any substantial
program that is expected to be more than merely a legislative
facade involves systematic implementation on several fronts; the
existence of loopholes can insure a program's failure to achieve
any significant restructuring of the agricultural sector.

India

For example, the first post-Independence agricultural steps
undertaken by the Indian government involved the abolition of the
zamindari tenancy system, a relic of the colonial era which granted
zamindars (who were, in the legal sense, intermediaries) the right
to collect rents in return for paying some proportion as taxes.
Aside from removing a hateful reminder of British rule, this "reform"
achieved little of an economic nature, inasmuch as pre-Independence
legislation had long since removed the worst abuses of the system
by guaranteeing the renewal rights of the zamindars' chief tenants,
who under the post-Independence legislation received title to the
lands they previously held in tenancy. These peasants now pay in
taxes the same portion that formerly went to the zamindars; even
the social benefit of higher revenues to the state governments is
largely negated since most of these funds go to compensate the
exzamindars.

More importantly, no real redistribution of land took place,
since subtenants and agricultural workers received no land of their
own. The exzamindars, who retained title to all lands which they
personally cultivated (including those tilled by hired workers) or
for which tenants could not clearly prove occupancy rights, and the
former chief tenants who could prove their rights were the only
beneficiaries. Tax reform took place; agricultural reform did not.[1]

Legislation affecting the maximum size of holdings has been
passed in several Indian states, but without exception the allowance
of the registration of land titles in the names of individual family
members; the total exemption from the imposition of ceilings granted
to plantations growing tea, sugarcane, and several other crops; and

the generally high maximum holdings set for other lands have
rendered such legislation close to meaningless.2 On the other hand,
some states have made significant strides in furthering land consoli-
dation.3 Though the very small size of the average landowner's
total holdings and the extreme degree of subdivision in many areas
makes consolidation all the more imperative, the economic effects
of a more rational pattern of land division are limited in the long
run by the density of the agricultural population.

Egypt

A more comprehensive approach to reforms affecting land
distribution was undertaken in Egypt following the overthrow of the
monarchy in 1952. Though almost two-thirds of the Egyptian
fellaheen owned their own land prior to the revolution, most of
their holdings were very small.4 Furthermore, most peasants
found themselves in nearly perpetual debt to large landlords or
moneylenders—debt that was repaid through transference of a large
portion of each crop, usually all or most of the more valuable cotton
output, leaving the cereals to the peasant and his family.

Since the holdings of the discredited royal family were large,5
the revolutionary government began its agrarian reform program
with a respectable pool of land available for distribution. However,
the first few years of the program were disappointing because little
redistribution beyond the former royal lands took place,6 despite
provision in the enabling legislation for the seizure with compensa-
tion of all large holdings (greater than 500 feddans). Only gradually,
with the sequestration of foreign holdings after the Suez fiasco (1957),
the reduction of the maximum allowable individual holdings from
500 to 100 feddans (1961), and a general tightening of restrictions
on overall family holdings was much redistribution accomplished.
By 1962 about 1 million feddans, or about one-sixth of Egypt's
arable land, had been transferred, either directly or indirectly as
a result of the Agrarian Reform program, to small landowners
(those with total holdings of less than five feddans).

Other measures affected the peasantry almost as much, at
least in the early stages during the 1950s, as did direct redistribution. State-owned mortgage and credit banks rapidly expanded
their services among small farmers, and credit was used as an
instrument to encourage the growth of cooperative ventures. The
latter were also furthered by the methods that were employed to
redistribute lands that had previously made up the larger estates.
However, here again the effects were gradual in the 1950s, though

the spread of the cooperative movement speeded up during the 1960s.
Similarly, minimum wage legislation, introduced to protect the
poorest of the fellaheen, the agricultural workers, was honored
mostly in the breach in the first few years, with stricter enforcement awaiting the second stage of agrarian reform decreed by
President Nasser in 1961.

Generally, Egypt's two decades of effort to redistribute landholdings have been considerably more far reaching than India's.
However, the slow start Egypt made can be traced to reasons similar
to those hindering India: the retention of considerable political
influence by the middle- and upper-income agricultural classes,
and the lack on the local level of adequate (and honest) personnel
to enforce existing legislation.

Iraq

The problem of adequate personnel is one that almost all
developing countries have to contend with, in at least the first
stages of any agrarian reform program. Iraq, for example, was
no exception in this regard; yet unlike the Indian and Egyptian cases,
Iraq's reforms, undertaken after her 1958 revolution, accomplished
a rapid seizure of the larger holdings. Perhaps the factors most
responsible for this were the almost complete destruction of the
political influence of the large landholders during the early months
of the republican government, and, with the Ministry of Agrarian
Reform in the hands of communist members of President Abd al-
Karim Qasim's leftist coalition for most of his regime's five-year
existence, the landowners' inability to reestablish their sway during
the critical early period when most of the land designated as subject
to the provisions of the Agrarian Reform Law of 1958 was expropriated.[7] (All holdings in excess of about 625 acres of irrigated
land or about 1,250 acres of rain-fed land were subject to expropriation; altogether this amounted to about 3.9 million acres or about
25 percent of the privately owned land. By 1966, 3.2 million acres
had been expropriated.)

Unfortunately the redistribution of lands was far slower than
their expropriation,[8] and this fact together with the failure of the
government to fill the ancillary roles of the former landlords, such
as credit extension and the provision and maintenance of the so-vital
water pumps, contributed to a decline in agricultural output in the
early 1960s. Though Iraq's reform was genuine, even revolutionary,
the real benefits of the program to the peasantry were scant even
up to ten years after its inception. Here again the Iraqi experience

points out the strong interdependence of reforms affecting land distribution and the availability of a trained and dedicated agricultural bureaucracy.

Though most land distribution programs have been imposed from above and therefore their success or failure seems largely dependent upon factors affecting the attitudes and competence of those in the government responsible for their planning and execution, a number of rural parameters might logically be hypothesized as playing important roles in the course of such programs. For example, the availability of arable but untilled lands or of significant holdings under state domain can allow considerably more redistribution, especially in the early stages of a reform program when the resistance of the old landlord class may be strongest. These two factors were of central importance in shaping the landowning patterns in "new" countries like the United States, Canada, and Australia, and at the present time the efforts of Brazil to mitigate the poverty of her northeast region are largely dependent on the opening of the Amazon Basin to settlement and cultivation.

The extent of rural literacy should be an accurate proxy for political awareness and activity among the peasantry, although the transistor radio is fast replacing the printed word as a prime means of communication between capital city and countryside. Rural population density or mean plot size could forecast the impact of any redistribution of land on total output (as well as serve to indicate under what conditions redistribution should take place), although obviously, the high per-acre crop yields achieved in Japan or even in Egypt can at least partly overcome the demand on the land for peasant subsistence alone.

The above discussion indicates the complexity of possible tenancy-related policies and the impossibility of making wide-ranging valid generalizations across societies as diverse as those that are the subjects of the supply analyses discussed below. Nevertheless, it seems reasonable to assume that the researcher has a better chance at success in choosing a statistical measure of landholding patterns that, under application of econometric techniques, will yield reliable indications of the direction and magnitude of the links between such patterns and agricultural output in particular cases. On the level of the particular study, land reform programs, for example, that exist mainly on paper can be distinguished from those that have seen a steady implementation over a period of time. Supply analysis of a situation where the latter is true should be able, in the presence of reliable time-series information, to identify the relationships with output that are of interest. Several such studies should allow at least some restricted generalizations about the likely influence of land reform in other situations where its implementation is at least as genuine and comprehensive as in the cases for which the studies have been carried out.

MARKET MANAGEMENT POLICIES

Agricultural policies in the second category, those affecting in some way the market conditions, are hardly new. For example, attempts to regulate prices are probably as old as markets themselves; a Hittite code more than 3,800 years old not only specifies the prices of many commodities, but also, in a gesture toward urbanites, forbids charging prices in the city markets that are higher than those prevailing in the countryside.

Evasion has always been the bane of any governmental attempts to control the market, and not until the present century, with its vastly enlarged police powers of surveillance and mobility and its international trade across tightly controlled borders, have policies been possible that are both more than occasionally effective and also nation- or worldwide in their ramifications. This is particularly true of measures requiring international cooperation, such as export-price-stabilization agreements.

Brazil

Brazil, long the world's dominant supplier of coffee, first tried to exercise some control of output in the late nineteenth century. Regulations over new planting and attempts to stockpile coffee date to the first decade of this century and became permanent (and more effective) in the mid-1920s. However, attempts to reach agreements with other producing countries on export prices and quantities were fruitless until after World War II. Brazil's experience indicates considerable evasion of early planting regulations,[9] but much more success with her later export control board, which was able to fix producer prices, and, through an elaborate quota system, to control the quantity of coffee reaching the world market.

As the major world supplier of coffee, Brazil's policies have had repercussions on the policies instituted by the smaller producing nations. Uganda, for example, which prior to World War II marketed less than 1 percent of the world coffee supply, benefitted considerably from Brazil's efforts in the 1930s to stabilize prices through stockpiling; as a result, Ugandan coffee, which is primarily of less

desirable varieties, not only kept but expanded its markets during
this period.

Brazil's efforts to reach accord among the major coffee-growing
nations finally bore fruit in the postwar period with the International
Coffee Agreement (ICA), which was adhered to by both producing
and consuming nations. However, the performance of ICA has been
marred by essential policy differences between the Latin American
and African signatories. The former, particularly Brazil and
Columbia, the two largest producers, want to maintain their relative
shares of a world market that grows at about 3 percent a year, and
to do so under conditions of stable prices. The latter, whose coffee
output has increased markedly since World War II and for whom
foreign exchange earnings realized from coffee sales play a major
role in overall development schemes, prefer to continue to expand
their production rapidly, arguing that price stability is secondary
and at most only slightly affected by increases in Africa's small
market share. The ICA, though an improvement over Brazil's
unilateral stabilization efforts in the 1920s and 1930s, has hardly
proven a panacea for either Latin American or African members;
only coffee consumers, who have enjoyed stable prices considerably
lower than those of the peak in the mid-1950s, have found ICA an
unmixed blessing.

Ghana

The unpredictability of the effects of marketing controls can be
seen in the history of Ghana's Cocoa Marketing Board. Set up
during World War II the board had three main goals in its early
years: the stabilization of world prices, the reduction of the number
(and consequently of the revenue share) of middlemen between producer and exporter, and the provision of funds for general economic
development through cocoa export taxes. Of these, it was successful
only in the last, but through serendipity the marketing board seems
to have helped Ghana avoid precipitating a massive cocoa glut in the
1960s. Merrill Bateman argues that high and rising world prices
during the 1950s would have undoubtedly brought on this result, had
not the board held producer prices down in order to generate revenue
through export taxes.[10]

He also provides another example of the problems plaguing
control boards. Ghana's Coffee Marketing Board was unsuccessful
throughout the 1950s in its attempts to realize export revenues
because most of the crop was smuggled into neighboring territories
where no price controls were in effect and the then high world prices

for coffee prevailed. Not until France instituted controls in her
territories w..s Ghana's coffee board able to attract much of the crop.
Though market controls over exports can be rendered ineffective
through a combination of incentives toward smuggling and police
forces insufficient to deter the practice, at least it would seem that
even a country suffering from manpower deficiencies can be reasonably successful in exerting considerable control over export crops.
The difficulties of carrying out market control policies must increase
almost exponentially when the crop concerned is domestically consumed.

India

Such has been the case in India, where the national government
has pursued policies designed to ensure urban consumers adequate
supplies of food grains at low prices. To this end a number of
different methods have been used, including direct price controls,
subsidies, commodity procurement agencies, governmental distribution networks down to the level of village retail food outlets, and
direct rationing. No single method has been constantly applied
nationwide, with, for example, essentially free trade in foodstuffs
in the mid-1950s and a mixture of free and controlled markets for
the same commodity often coexisting. The situation is further
complicated by the fact that in keeping with the constitutional arrangements of the Indian Union, food policies are generally under the
control of the states, with the federal government acting mostly to
coordinate the activities of the states. Though the frequent parallel
existence of free and controlled markets and the sheer immensity
of the problems of policing such an admixture of programs has
obviously allowed considerable opportunity for evasion by the
peasantry of the more unpopular regulations, government involvement on the distribution level on the basis of fixed prices certainly
affects the farmer's price expectations.
Another circumstance of considerable importance is the Indian
government's consistent reliance on food imports, primarily to
assuage shortages, but concurrently to keep prices down. As a
result of the U.S. Public Law (PL) 480 program ("Food for Peace"),
India had access to the U.S. granary. During the 1960s India was
the annual destination of as much as 20 percent of the total U.S.
wheat output. While such assistance is credited with saving upwards
of 25 million lives in the famine of 1966-67, it has also lessened
the need for the Indian government to face up to the shortcomings
of its agricultural program. The possible effect on whatever price

responsiveness the Indian peasantry might show of seemingly endless
quantities of cheap U.S. grains needs no further comment.

The Food for Peace program, under PL 480, had clearly the
positive effect of adding to the recipient country's resources and
thus enhancing growth and the ability to feed the population. However,
this cheap food had a negative effect in reducing the economic incentives for increased agricultural output and/or policies for reducing
fertility in the countries receiving such food aid.[11] Currently,
however, PL 480 aid is not available since the size of American
agricultural surplus is close to zero. At the same time, India and
several other countries that formerly received American food aid
are facing chronic food shortages.

In summary, although the motivations behind a government's
adoption of agricultural policies of a market-controlling character
may range from revenue raising to keeping the urban proletariat
content, present in most of these measures is an element of a
sought-after stability—of price, quantity, or both. Since any success
will transmit this stability to the peasantry, we should find some
guidance as to the advisability of such policies if we know something
about cultivator attitudes toward risk. A conservative peasantry
might respond quite favorably (with increased output) to a well-
formulated program that offers some guarantee, at least of
subsistence income. On the other hand, a peasantry that shows
the risk-taking nature of an entrepreneurial class might react
negatively to an overly paternal package of government blandish-
ments. Obviously, peasants, whether they be conservative or daring,
would seem unlikely to be favorably impressed by market controls
that too openly tip the balance in favor of urban dwellers at the
expense of those living in the countryside.

RURAL INFRASTRUCTURE POLICIES

One might make a case that, in any economy 80 percent or
even more of whose labor force is on the land, almost any infrastructure investment will have some effect on agriculture. However,
even beyond discounting the all-too-frequent tendency for political
regimes to dignify grandiose monumental schemes like airport
terminals and soccer stadiums with the appellation of development
investment, our concern here is with programs of a definite rural
coloring.

Among the latter, perhaps the most "rural" are water-control
projects. The long history of attempts to alter nature's water
distribution network, the obvious success of modern techniques in

the more developed agricultural economies even under the most
adverse climatological conditions, and the frequent potential to
achieve simultaneously nonagricultural benefits such as the generation
of electrical power has put such projects near the top of many
countries' priority lists. However, the speckled performance
record in this area in recent years indicates a tendency to overlook,
particularly in the case of major projects, the multilevel implications of the decisions to proceed with the central features of the
project, such as dams or diversion canals.

For example, the Helmand Valley Irrigation Project—a U.S.
attempt beginning in 1952 to export the TVA experience to Afghanistan
lock, stock, and barrel—proved far too elaborate for the beneficiary's
meager manpower and capital resources. The two large dams and
the irrigation network at the heart of the project were completed
by a U.S. construction firm months ahead of schedule, but this
was about the only positive feature of the project during the 1950s.
Inadequate soil surveys resulted in the resettlement of formerly
nomadic tribes on highly saline land that requires an expertise on
the part of irrigation technicians far ahead of what was available
in the country. Under the original agreement the Afghani government committed itself to covering all the domestic currency costs,
which then promptly rose to absorb more than half its tax revenue.

Only a massive commitment on the part of the United States
to bail out the scheme, in light of the considerable U.S. loss of
face during the early phase of the Helmand project (and the extension
to Afghanistan of Soviet credits that had been sought mostly in
response to domestic economic pressures imposed by the Helmand
efforts), has achieved, in the 1960s, some promise of fulfillment
of the original vision. Should this prove ephemeral, more than
U.S. prestige will be lost: This single project has dominated
Afghan development attempts for more than two decades, absorbing
a major part of whatever scant resources beyond bare subsistence
the country has been able to spare.

Even the Egyptians, whose recorded continuous use of water
control is the planet's longest and whose Aswan High Dam has on
the balance proven to be among the most successful development
projects of the century, have not been immune to overlooking vital
aspects of new hydrological undertakings. Following the 1952
revolution, the Tahrir (Liberation) Province Autonomous Organiza-
tion was founded to reclaim more than 1,200 square miles of
semidesert land west of the Nile Delta. Ten years and £40 million
later, wells and canals had been constructed; a supporting industrial
complex including canning and pasteurizing facilities, and a considerable road network had long since been completed but remained
mostly unused: barely 5 percent of the land area involved was

actually under cultivation. Attempts to organize the land along
cooperative lines had failed, largely due to a lack of competent farm
management personnel. By 1959 large stocks of farm equipment
suitable mostly for the cultivation of large plots were on hand but
more than 40 percent was unused or inoperable.[12]

Some of the difficulties encountered in achieving the results
envisioned for irrigation projects in India are recounted by Kusum
Nair:[13] peasants in Andhra Pradesh who show little interest in
increasing yields and will take advantage of available canal water
only after the rains fail; others in Madras who draw more water
than is legally permissible, despite frequent stiff fines, in order
to increase their cultivation of water-intensive paddy because of
the prestige attached to a rice diet, rather than grow the relatively
"dry" cash crops, such as cotton, the project was supposed to
benefit; cultivators in Orissa who could not be persuaded to plant
a second crop annually of paddy, despite the unusual benificence
of the government in providing water free of charge and even
constructing the field channels, because the water had "lost its
electricity" and hence its potency in the power-generating facilities
combined with the nearby irrigation project.

Other infrastructure-type agricultural policies have had
similarly checkered performance records. Development economists
have become all too aware of the problems generated by rural
education. Higher literacy rates are supposed to open doors to
the twentieth century for the peasantry, paving the way for the
greater use of fertilizers and new seeds, a more rational land use,
family planning, and all sorts of advances calculated to build
"Nebraska in Asia in our time." Certainly greater rural literacy
does open doors to the twentieth century, but the access gained
seems to bring almost as many problems as blessings. In many
countries the dilemma can be expressed simply: How much rural
education? Is there a way to calculate just the right dosage that
can make farmers literate and yet keep them literate farmers?

The problems of rising expectations that go with education
carry over and are amplified in attempts to upgrade the competence
and effectiveness of the bureaucracy dealing with agriculture. Too
often it seems every employee of the relevant ministries, from
agronomy Ph.D.s to graduates from postprimary school institutes
designed to train "county-agent" type technicians, will be content
with nothing less than assignment to ministry offices in the capital.
Certainly no job involving direct contact with the soil or its cultivators can rate as high in prestige. One of the authors particularly
remembers a young technician employed by the Iraqi Ministry of
Agriculture and Agrarian Reform who was assigned to a small
village in the marsh country near the confluence of the Tigris and

Euphrates rivers. Although he was obviously enthusiastic about his work, which involved everything from disseminating information about improvements in rice cultivation to supervising a small clinic, and just about as obviously served as the only meaningful link between the villagers and the government in Baghdad, he confided he would serve no more than the term imposed on him as an obligation resulting from his government scholarship. The reason was simple: Neither his wife nor his children lived with him in the village. For prestige reasons her family insisted he keep them in the provincial capital, some seven hours away by boat and taxi, a trip he was lucky to make twice a month.

It is hard to see what in the way of concrete proposals can be made that would alter such situations. More often than not, agriculture stands at the very bottom rank in status. In some societies, perhaps most, prestige can be bestowed through higher income rewards, and this may be helpful (for example, through "hardship" bonuses, and so on) in encouraging trained personnel to take rural posts. However, in a society trying desperately to capture whatever surplus exists in a mostly agricultural economy, meaningful increases in income as a means to increasing status is hardly a practical suggestion regarding the occupation of farming per se.

Though no general applications are possible, programs that appeal to what might loosely be termed "patriotism," of either a national or purely local variety, have been moderately successful. Examples range from Iran's Literary Corps, which sends urban students out to the countryside as teachers, to Senegal's Animation program, which was designed to bring young men selected by their fellow villagers to rural-based training centers for short courses in elementary economic improvement. Such programs as these might not assure a supply of technically competent careerists to the villages; nonetheless, they may tip the balance for those problems whose solutions do not require continuity of service on the part of the involved bureaucrat or a very high level of expertise. A useful alternative, if not a very pleasing one to the idealistic ear, is some form of obligatory national service program, perhaps tied, as is Iraq's, to obligations incurred in return for educational assistance granted by the government.

To conclude this section on infrastructure investments, a comment is in order on two types of projects—transportation and public health—that figure prominently in Thailand's agricultural performance, according to one of the studies discussed in detail later.[14] A highway constructed into the northeast region primarily for defense purposes provided the country's first all-weather link between this area and Bangkok. Since its opening, corn, which had long been grown in the northeast as fodder for livestock, has become one of Thailand's major exports, finding a large and growing market, particularly in Japan.

In Thailand, in Afghanistan, in several Latin American countries, improved transportation facilities have sliced astronomically high shipping costs, opening export markets and enlarging domestic ones. Each project of this type is unique, yet at least one generalization seems possible: A transport project that is the first to provide a modern reliable link, at least at harvest time, to an area is a very likely candidate for notable success.[15] On the other hand, a facility that only upgrades or parallels an existing link requires particular forethought lest it prove more a frill than a benefit. For example, in the opinion of many economists, Iraq's replacement of the narrow-guage railroad between Baghdad and the port city of Basra with a standard-gauge line compatible with the rest of the nation's railway system may be a long time in paying for itself since it parallels two highways, one completely paved, the other partly paved, both of which were being upgraded simultaneously with the railroad project.

The full benefits of rural public health programs are difficult if not impossible to assess. However, even from a narrowly economic viewpoint, the elimination or control of debilitating disease can have enormous effects on agricultural output. Behrman found Thailand's antimalaria program a highly significant factor in the expansion of both corn and kenaf production.[16] Though the world-wide campaign against malaria has gone a long way toward eradication of this scourge, much more that would improve the basic agricultural input of manpower remains undone.

Again, with what we have lumped together as policies and programs affecting the rural infrastructure, we have a situation that defies sweeping generalizations with much validity or usefulness to decision-making authorities. Again, however, the specific situation may be rewarding to the researcher, as Behrman's results indicate. The effects on peasant responsiveness of several factors that are related to rural infrastructure are sought in the study recounted in the concluding chapter of this work, a study in which were encountered precisely the expected difficulties when generalization is attempted—the inability in several cases to locate comparable data series for a cross-section of countries.

SCIENTIFIC RESEARCH POLICIES
IN AGRICULTURE

Finally, let us consider briefly agricultural policies in the fourth category: those relating to scientific research. Perhaps no single area has contributed more to the staving off of the Malthusian doomsday, though only recently realized, than the immensity of the benefits gained from agricultural research in terms of investment returns. Zvi Griliches, in his pioneering study of hybrid corn in the United States, calculated a total research expenditure of more than $130 million and an almost fantastic 700 percent annual return realized on the investment.[17] Two research breakthroughs of comparable magnitude have been prominent in the last decade, and have again proven the value of such efforts. The total costs of operating the International Rice Research Institute (IRRI), a joint venture in the Philippines of the Ford and Rockefeller Foundations, from its founding in 1962 until 1968 was $15 million. By 1968-69 the Asian rice harvest was estimated to be as much as $1 billion higher because of the extensive use of new varieties developed at IRRI. Though these new strains also involve somewhat higher production costs, the return per dollar invested in research is phenomenal. Estimates of the gains realized from wheat strains developed at the International Maize and Wheat Improvement Center in Mexico were as high as 750 percent per year in Mexico alone by 1963, and by 1968, Asian acreage in the new Mexican wheats was more than seven times that planted in Mexico.

Not only do these new grains promise the world enough breathing space to get its population house in order, but perhaps even more satisfying to the development economist is the speed with which the peasantry of lands as diverse as Nepal and Turkey have switched to the high-yield seed. Here at least is one program that has succeeded in several nations, coming from the outside, spreading from agricultural ministry outward to the provinces despite all the problems of communications lags along the bureaucratic pipeline, of peasant resistance to new ideas, of insufficient local supporting technology, and of inadequate transportation facilities that we have enumerated above as barriers to rural economic development. The improvement has been exponential, with about 200 Asian acres in the new grains in 1964-65, jumping to 4.8 million acres in 1966-67, and to 34 million acres by 1968-69. Gains have continued, though at a slower pace dictated by both the natural limit of acreage suitable by virtue of soil type and climate conditions for these particular strains and the need in some areas for supporting facilities, such as fertilizer plants, whose construction has lagged, and not by all the cultural factors that so frequently frustrate social transformation.

Of particular importance regarding agricultural research is that, unlike most of the programs discussed in this chapter, it is an area where the developed countries, with their vast numbers of competent scientists and technicians, can play a vital role. While

no guarantees of success can be attached to particular projects, the
general performance of agricultural research in the last 100 years
proves its value; the spread of the new grains in the last decade
proves its practicality.

In a complementary field it would be truly amazing if societies
whose engineers can design "jeeps" for the lunar surface could not
also use their talents to devise simple cheap tools and machines
that will both raise the productivity and alleviate the drudgery of
an Asian peasant. The engineer who is the hero and title character
of The Ugly American designed a bicycle-powered irrigation pump;[18]
the major barrier to this kind of "breakthrough" is the need to invert
the Western technological psyche and to "think small."

SUMMARY

The policies enumerated above have been employed either to
spur agricultural production and efficiency, to achieve some social
goal, or both. However, most occasions of their use have been
without prior knowledge of the extent of their effect on output. As
we have already indicated, though, a number of supply analyses
among those that have been published in recent years have included
measures of specific policies or programs in the models they have
employed to identify the determinants of crop supply. These results
can be of benefit to decision makers in development-oriented bureaucracies who previously have operated in the dark, acting on hunch
or educated guess.

In the past the resulting gap between policy formulation and the
consequent changes in production levels has had serious economic
and political repercussions in numerous cases. To help bridge
this gap we propose now to outline all the recent studies of supply
response, beginning with Nerlove's seminal work. We hope such
a compilation itself can be of service in the future modification
or enlargement of traditional agricultural development policies
as well as an aid to future researchers. Furthermore, we will
attempt to use the results of some of these studies to identify a
number of underlying social, political, economic, and technological
factors that we hypothesize govern peasant responsiveness to price
incentives. If such determinants can be indicated, policy makers
will be given tools with which they can influence not merely the
output levels of particular crops but also the basic market orientation
of cultivators. This result will be very useful in increasing agricultural output in developing nations and thus reducing the problem of
hunger in the world.

NOTES

1. Doreen Warriner, Land Reform in Principle and Practice (London: Oxford University Press, 1969), chapter 6; Kusum Nair, Blossoms in the Dust (New York: Frederick A. Praeger, 1961). Both of these works cite a number of examples illustrating this point.

2. Warriner, op. cit., p. 173. In Uttar Pradesh, one of only two states where any redistribution of land had taken place during the 1960s under provisions of ceilings legislation, only 24,000 acres had been actually distributed.

3. Ibid., p. 204. In Uttar Pradesh, consolidation efforts had affected about half the cultivated land by 1964.

4. Gabriel S. Saab, The Egyptian Agrarian Reform 1952-1962 (London: Oxford University Press, 1967), table 2, p. 14. In 1950, 66 percent of the farmers owned their own land, amounting to 61 percent of the cultivated land. On the other hand, over 75 percent of the farmers held less than five feddans (1 feddan = 1.04 acres), with 21 percent having less than one feddan.

5. The royal family held over 300,000 feddans—almost half were already in state hands in 1952 due to loans and advances made to the ex-king and his family. See Gabriel Baer, A History of Land Ownership in Modern Egypt 1800-1950 (London: Oxford University Press, 1962), chapter 5; also tables 28, 32, and 35.

6. Baer, op. cit., p. 29. About 431,000 feddans had been redistributed by 1960.

7. Warriner, op. cit., pp. 86, 89, 91.

8. Ibid., p. 91. Only 600,000 acres had been redistributed by 1966.

9. Marcelle Arak, "The Supply of Brazilian Coffee," (Ph.D. dissertation, Massachusetts Institute of Technology, 1967), discussed in Chapter 7.

10. Merrill Bateman, Cocoa in the Ghanaian Economy: An Econometric Model (Amsterdam: North-Halland, 1968), discussed below in Chapter 7.

11. For a discussion of these effects, refer to Franklin Fisher, "A Theoretical Analysis of the Impact of Food Surplus Disposal on Agricultural Production in Recipient Countries," Journal of Farm Economics 45 (November 1963); and Theodore Schultz, "Value of U.S. Farm Surpluses to Underdeveloped Countries," Journal of Farm Economics 42 (December 1960).

12. Saab, op. cit., p. 157.

13. Kusum Nair, op. cit., pp. 33ff, 69ff, 141ff.

14. Jere Behrman, Supply Response in Underdeveloped Agriculture: A Case Study of Four Major Annual Crops in Thailand 1937-63 (Amsterdam: North-Holland, 1968).

15. For an interesting attempt to analyze the benefits of road construction in some detail, see Herman G. VanderTak and Jan De Weille, Reappraisal of a Road Project in Iran (Washington, D.C.: International Bank for Reconstruction and Development, 1969).

16. Behrman, op. cit., see below in Chapter 5.

17. Zvi Griliches, "Research Costs and Social Returns: Hybrid Corn and Related Innovations," Journal of Political Economy 66 (October 1958): 419-31.

18. William J. Lederer and Eugene Burdick, The Ugly American (New York: Norton, 1958).

3

THE NERLOVE SUPPLY
RESPONSE MODEL

Marc Nerlove, in his seminal study of dynamic supply response, proposed three types of output changes for consideration: (1) those in response to changes in current prices which do not portend any particular changes in expectations about future prices; (2) immediate response to changes in expected future prices; and (3) response to changes in expected and actual prices after sufficient time has passed to allow for full adjustment.[1] Though examples of the first type can be cited, for example, harvesting decisions concerning perennial crops (see discussion in Chapter 4), Nerlove restricted his attention to the two more common responses: short- and long-run responses to changes in price expectations, and to the problems of distinguishing empirically between the two.

Price expectations obviously involve uncertainty, and considerable work had been done on this problem before Nerlove. The earliest and simplest explanation of agricultural price expectations, that producers are influenced solely by the most recent season's prices and that price expectations are that this last season's price will prevail in the next period, is embodied in the so-called cobweb model. Over the years this has been proposed as illustrative of a number of economic market situations where changes in the quantity available for market occur in a discrete rather than continuous fashion. Particular crops, within a given geographic region, obviously fall into this market category, with overall supply in a single time period—the harvest—almost completely determined by planting decisions made at a point preceding the harvest that is governed by the agronomic, climatological, and other pertinent characteristics peculiar to the crop in question and the locale of its cultivation. Appreciable changes in supply cannot occur until the next harvest period. (Obviously for a few crops and in regions where

climate is fairly steady year round, crop seasons are not rigidly
tied to the solar calendar, but such situations are exceptional in
the world agricultural picture.)

Cobweb situations can involve both stable and unstable equilibria,
depending on the relative positions of the demand and supply curves.
Should demand be relatively more elastic than supply, the tendency
toward equilibrium would be one of dynamic stability. That is, in
this situation the quantity and price fluctuations are damped and
tend in the long run to equilibrium. However, if the market is
characterized by demand relatively less elastic than supply, then
a sequence of circumstances result in which quantity and price
oscillations occur about identifiable equilibrium levels; however,
these are exploding rather than damped in nature. Given the
generally found inelastic demand for most basic foodstuffs, this
latter situation seems likely to describe more commodity markets
than the dynamically stable cobweb.

Of course the cobweb model, as it stands, is naive in more than
just the formulation of price expectations, but since this is our
primary interest, we need explore the model no further. A more
sophisticated adaptive approach to expectations was suggested by
Richard Goodwin.[2] Allowing for a "learning" process on the part
of cultivators, he formulated present expected price (P_t^e) as actual
price in the last period plus (or minus) some proportion of the
change in actual price between two periods ago and the last period:

$$P_t^{\,e} = P_{t-1} + \delta(P_{t-1} - P_{t-2}) \tag{3.1}$$

Such an approach, while obviously more satisfying intellectually
than the underlying simplifications of the cobweb theorem, is
nonetheless rather naive itself: Farmers are still assumed to
have very short memories.

A more satisfactory approach to expectations has been developed
from a concept suggested by L. M. Koyck.[3] Past experience can
be allowed to be of infinite duration, while more recent information
nevertheless is weighted more heavily if output (Q) is dependent on
prices in the following way:

$$Q_t = \alpha\, P_{t-1} + \alpha\lambda\, P_{t-2} + \alpha\lambda^2\, P_{t-3} + \alpha\lambda^3\, P_{t-4} + \ldots \tag{3.2}$$

where $0 < \lambda < 1$ then:

$$Q_t - \lambda Q_{t-1} = \alpha\, P_{t-1}$$

or

$$Q_t = \alpha P_{t-1} + \lambda Q_{t-1}$$

and

$$\Delta Q_t = Q_t - Q_{t-1} = \alpha P_{t-1} + (\lambda - 1) Q_{t-1} \tag{3.3}$$

α then illustrates short-term responsiveness to prices, and $\alpha/(1 - \lambda)$ the long-term equilibrium response; λ indicates how fast the cultivators will make the adjustment process—the closer λ is to unity, the slower this takes place, while rapid adjustment would be signaled by a value of λ near to zero.

Several modifications of this basic distributed lag expression can be employed as might seem appropriate. If the weights attached to past prices are believed to be monotonically decreasing only before a certain point in time, say period t - k, then the overall distribution can be expressed as:

$$Q_t = \alpha_o P_{t-1} + \alpha_2 P_{t-2} + \ldots + \alpha_{k-1} P_{t-k+1} + \alpha_k \lambda P_{t-k}$$

$$+ \alpha_{k+1} \lambda^2 P_{t-k-1} + \ldots \tag{3.4}$$

One obvious use for such a formulation in agriculture would be in the case of crops that take more than a single season to mature, or for perennial crops where one might hypothesize, for example, the capital-stock nature of the crop might promote an approximately equal sensitivity to prices realized in each of the two or three seasons immediately preceding planting, with declining attention paid to successively earlier prices.

If n, the number of years in the past that are thought relevant to the formation of expectations, is relatively small, and if the price data involved are not collinear, estimates for the weights attached to past prices can be made using ordinary least-squares estimating techniques. Should n be large or collinearity be a problem, then estimates can be made only if restrictions are imposed upon the pattern of the values of the weights.

Such a method was suggested by Shirley Almon,[4] who used Lagrangian interpolation polynomials to generate a set of weights $W(i)$ that are assumed to be the values at $x = 0, 1, \ldots, n - 1$ of a polynomial $W(x)$ of degree $q + 1$, where n is the number of periods over which the distributed lag is postulated to extend, and where $q < n$. If $q + 2$ points on the curve illustrating the lag distribution are known, then all the values $W(i)$ can be calculated as linear combinations of these known values $(W(x_0) = a_0$, $W(x_1) = a_1$, . . . $W(x_{q+1}) = a_{q+1})$ from:

$$W(i) = \sum_{j=0}^{q+1} \Phi_j(i)\, a_j \qquad (i = 0, 1, \ldots, n - 1) \tag{3.5}$$

where the $\Phi_i(i)$ are the values of the interpolation polynomials at $x = i$. Since Almon wished no weight attached to prices before time $t = 0$ or after $t = n - 1$, she took x_0 to be -1 and x_{q+1} to be n, so that the first and last terms in 3.5, $W(-1)$ and $W(n)$ are thus zero and equation 3.5 becomes:

$$W(i) = \sum_{j=1}^{q} \Phi_j(i)\, a_j \tag{3.6}$$

With the first and last values thus specified, various lag distributions result.[5]

NERLOVE'S MODEL

In his discussion of price expectations, Nerlove referred to work by Theil, Modigliani and Sauerlender, and Eisner,[6] all based on surveys conducted in the industrial sector, to indicate a widespread tendency to underestimate actual price changes and the likelihood that better predictions could be made using some simple mechanical device such as projections of the current value of the variables to be predicted. He then asked the questions as to whether in fact entrepreneurs really attempt to forecast a particular value of an economic variable or whether they instead try to anticipate the "normal" level of future values of this variable. Entrepreneurs might increase profits if they improve the accuracy of their forecasts, but perhaps not by much over the levels realized through their acting in response to changes in expectations regarding these "normal" values—in other words, whatever extra profits might be possible might not be worth the added expense involved in significantly improving accuracy.

If then the underestimation of the magnitude of short-term changes represents entrepreneurial reactions to shifts in expected "normal" values, the question must then be asked as to what is "normal?" Nerlove begins by postulating that such expectations depend upon what prices have actually been in the past, that is, on

some present idea of what is "normal." Certainly the way past
prices effect expectations would change over time and under the
influence of specific, important shifts in the various political,
economic, and social institutions affecting the producer. Nevertheless, at any given point in time, some relationship between present
normality and future expectations, he argues, offers the most solid
conceptual starting point.

Nerlove then develops a Hicksian approach to expectation,[7]
quoting Hicks' formulation of the elasticity of expectations (of the
price of commodity X as "the ratio of the proportional rise in
expected future prices of X to the proportional rise in its current
price").[8] Hicks' limiting cases (an elasticity of zero, accompanying
no effect on expectations of changes in current prices, and a unitary
elasticity, indicating that if expected prices were currently at
their long-run equilibrium levels and thus anticipated to remain
constant, they will be expected to remain constant at present levels)
recognizes, according to Nerlove, that particular past values of
a variable have some, but not absolute, influence on what is thought
to be "normal." In other words, past prices in general and not in
particular govern expectations about "normal" price levels.

However, all past prices do not have equal influence; rationality
dictates greater weight be attached to more recent values. Some
sort of weighted moving average of past prices seems in order,
and Nerlove uses Hicks' concept of elasticity of expectation to
derive an expression of price expectations. If we assume that,
at any point in time, some kind of an expected "normal" price
exists for the producers and denote this as P_t^e, then Hicks' conception of P_t^e can be seen as last period's expected "normal" price
plus or minus some degree of adjustment depending upon the elasticity of expectation and last period's actual price.

Nerlove postulates that this adjustment can be expressed as
a fraction of the difference between last period's actual and expected
"normal" prices, or:

$$P_t^e = P_{t-1}^e + \beta(P_{t-1} - P_{t-1}^e) \tag{3.7}$$

where β, the coefficient of expectation, is constant. If β is zero,
actual prices are totally divorced from expectations, while a unitary
value implies a naive cobweb-type model where expected prices
are identical with last year's realized price. Nerlove states his
hypothesis: "Each period people revise their notion of 'normal'
price in proportion to the difference between the then current price
and their previous ideal of 'normal' price."[9]

Equation 3.7 represents a moving average of past prices with
the weights declining the farther back in time. This can be seen
if it is rewritten as:

$$P_t^{\ e} = \beta \, P_{t-1} + (1 - \beta) \, P_{t-1}^{\ e} \tag{3.7a}$$

which is a first-order difference equation that can be solved for
P_t^e as a function of time t, P_t and the coefficient β. After a few
simplifying assumptions we have:

$$P_t^{\ e} = \sum_{\lambda=0}^{t} \beta(1 - \beta)^{t-\lambda} P_{\lambda-1} \tag{3.8}$$

thus expressing people's conception of "normal" price expectations
as a weighted average of past prices. The weights assigned to each
past price will decline as we go back in time if $0 < \beta < 1$. This is
clearly of the same form as Koyck's distributed lag.

Nerlove then turns his attention from short-run to long-run
adjustments to changes in price expectations. He reviews the
conventional distinction between short- and long-run supply elasticities and the inherent conclusion that the former must be less than
or equal to the latter since the longer the time period available to
the supplier in which to make output adjustments the more options
regarding changes in inputs are available. Thus the reaction, over
time, to changes in price expectations, expressed in terms of
output (Q) takes the form of a distributed lag. But the largest
one-period shift most likely occurs in the first relevant period
following the change in expectations; and the period needed to attain
total adjustment could theoretically be infinite; even that in which
some predetermined fraction of adjustment, such as 90 percent,
could be quite lengthy.

The question of changes in output brought upon by changes in
price, Nerlove explains, is actually threefold in nature: the effect
on price expectations of changes in current prices; the effect of
changes in expectations on long-run equilibrium output; and the
effect of changes in long-run output on current output. The first
problem has already been discussed above, and the third was
mentioned in the previous paragraph: that is, actual output (Q) is
a function of long-run equilibrium output (Q^D) and time. Since
Q^D itself changes over time, we need to formulate a relationship
between Q and Q^D that is valid no matter what the time.

This relationship Nerlove expresses (analogously to equation
3.7) as:

$$Q_t - Q_{t-1} = \gamma (Q_t^{\ D} - Q_{t-1}) \tag{3.9}$$

that is, in each period, actual output is adjusted by some fraction
(γ) of the difference between long-run equilibrium output (hereafter
called desired output) and actual output in the previous period.
Like β, γ is a constant, and is termed the area adjustment coefficient.
In this stock adjustment model for agriculture, farmers do not
necessarily adjust to the desired level of output in one period; that
is, γ may not equal one. In general, there are a number of reasons
why γ may take on other values. There are, in the first place,
the uncertainties that are involved; a farmer does not know with
certainty future prices, weather, and so on. As a result he does
not adjust immediately since there are costs associated with a
wrong decision. Furthermore, it may be impossible or at least
difficult to adjust fully in one period, given physical constraints.
As such, a farmer would be likely to take time to adjust to expected
prices. Rewriting in the form of first-difference equation,

$$Q_t = \gamma Q_t^D + (1 - \gamma) Q_{t-1} \tag{3.9a}$$

and solving for Q_t, we obtain, after some manipulation:

$$Q_t = \sum_{\lambda=0}^{t} \gamma (1 - \gamma)^{t-\lambda} Q_\lambda^D \tag{3.10}$$

If $\gamma = 0$, output is unchanged from year to year; if $\gamma = 1$, area
adjustment is complete in a single time period. Again, this stock
adjustment model results in a Koyck form of a distributed lag. As
a result, one cannot distinguish between the form of equation 3.10
and 3.8.

ESTIMATION OF THE MODEL

Because neither long-run equilibrium output (Q^D) nor expected
"normal" price (P^e) are observable variables and because the
assumption of a proportional relationship between these two variables
is needed to bridge the causal gap from price changes to output
changes leads to problems of identification, it is not possible to
separate the difference between the short-run and long-run elasticities of supply from the difference between current or last period's
actual price and the expected level of future prices. But this
separation is important to make, since, depending on whether the
lag between expected "normal" and current price or the lag between
desired long-run equilibrium and current or short-run equilibrium

output predominates, the effect of past prices on current output will
be quite different for different products.

In estimating short-run elasticities of output (in terms of acreage)
with respect to expected "normal" price, difficulty arises due to the
inability to distinguish these estimates (made with the assumption
that $\beta < 1$ and $\gamma = 1$) from those that would be obtained if it were
assumed that farmers take last year's actual price as this year's
expected "normal" price but do not or cannot immediately make
full adjustment to long-run equilibrium acreage (that is, $\beta = 1$ and
$\gamma < 1$).[10] Nerlove proceeds as though the former were true and
considers a model made up of equations 3.7 and:

$$Q_t = a_o + a_1 P_t^e + u_t \tag{3.11}$$

Substituting P_t^e as in equation 3.8 yields:

$$Q_t = a_o + a_1 \sum_{\lambda=0}^{t} \beta(1 - \beta)^{t-\lambda} P_{\lambda-1} + u_t \tag{3.12}$$

Nerlove used iterative calculating procedures, estimating values
for a_o and a_1 for different values of β by means of maximum
likelihood methods, and also followed a noniterative procedure by
first transforming equation 3.11 into a relationship between actual
acreage and lagged observed price and acreage, and performing
a regression of the form:

$$Q_t = \pi_o + \pi_1 P_{t-1} + \pi_2 Q_{t-1} + v_t \tag{3.13}$$

It is possible to obtain estimates for the expectation and
adjustment coefficients that can be distinguished one from another
if there is some relevant and observable variable (Z_t) that appears
in the output equation in addition to the "normal" price, for example,

$$Q_t = a_o + a_1 P_t^e + a_2 Z_t + u_t \tag{3.14}$$

This together with:

$$P_t^e = P_{t-1}^e + \beta(P_{t-1} - P_{t-1}^e) \tag{3.7}$$

and

$$Q_t - Q_{t-1} = \gamma(Q_t^D - Q_{t-1}) \tag{3.9}$$

yields a structure that describes dynamically a supply response
model for which distinct estimates of all the parameters can be

obtained using either maximum likelihood procedures or least-squares technique on an equation of the reduced form:

$$Q_t = \pi_0 + \pi_1 P_{t-1} + \pi_2 Q_{t-1} + \pi_3 Q_{t-2} + \pi_4 Z_t + \pi_5 Z_{t-1} + v_t \quad (3.15)$$

These estimated parameters π_i are:

$$\pi_0 = a_0 \beta \gamma \qquad\qquad (3.16a)$$
$$\pi_1 = a_1 \beta \gamma \qquad\qquad (3.16b)$$
$$\pi_2 = (1 - \beta) + (1 - \gamma) \qquad (3.16c)$$
$$\pi_3 = -(1 - \beta)(1 - \gamma) \qquad (3.16d)$$
$$\pi_4 = a_2 \gamma \qquad\qquad (3.16e)$$
$$\pi_5 = a_2(1 - \beta)\gamma \qquad\qquad (3.16f)$$

The structural coefficients enter equation 3.15 asymmetrically, indicating, in principle, the possibility of distinguishing between the price expectation and area adjustment lags, provided the inclusion of a variable such as Z_t can be justified. The details of the estimation procedure of the Nerlovian model will be taken up in the next chapter.

NERLOVE'S APPLICATION

Nerlove applied his model, equations 3.14, 3.7, and 3.9, to an analysis of the supply response shown by farmers in the United States for maize, cotton, and wheat. As regards the problem of estimating values for the parameters, he was unable to distinguish the coefficient of adjustm nt from that of expectation, apparently because no suitable variable could be found that could be introduced into the output equation, as in equation 3.14 enabling identification problems to be overcome.

In computing the supply parameters for these crops during the period from 1909 to 1932, Nerlove used four different formulations of his model, three of which are reported below: (1) β, the coefficient of expectation is assumed to be equal to unity, that is, this year's expected price is last year's actual price; (2) no restriction placed on β; and (3) expected price is a weighted average of the last two years' prices, using the form:

$$P_t^e = \alpha P_{t-1} + (1 - \alpha) P_{t-2} \qquad (3.17)$$

Because the growing seasons of maize and winter wheat overlap in several states, a farmer must decide when planting wheat how much acreage he will later put in maize, and this decision often must be made before complete information about prices (that is, in year t - 1) is available, so Nerlove constructed the model for maize supply (using formulations 1 and 2) with prices lagged both one and two years.[11]

In commenting on the results, Nerlove points out the generally greater success at explaining acreage variation and the larger elasticities that are attained by using the second formulation, with coefficients of expectation for all three crops that are approximately 0.5, that is, using an expected price that is approximately equal to the average of last year's expected and average prices. In the case of maize, prices lagged two years seem to be more pertinent in explaining acreage variation than those lagged one year; similarly, inclusion of wheat prices in the maize equations results in larger values of R^2, though adding consideration of lagged maize prices to the wheat supply equations has very little effect either on the calculated parameters or on the value of R^2. Further evidence for the dependence of maize acreage in year t on maize prices in year t - 2 can be seen in the calculated values for α, the weight assigned to prices in the year t - 1 in the third formulation (0.57 for both cotton and wheat, and only 0.16 for maize).

In an early exchange on the basic Nerlove model, A. E. Brandow and Nerlove discussed the possible bias in parameter estimates as a result of misspecification of the model—in particular, the omission of an important nonprice variable.[12] As an example of such a situation, Brandow used an estimating equation containing lagged prices and acreage for barley, a crop undergoing considerable expansion in acreage after the introduction of a new variety in the mid-1920s. For the period 1909 to 1932 his regression indicated a short-run elasticity for barley of +1.32. Brandow argued this estimate was high as a result of the exclusion of any measure representing technical change. Nerlove acknowledged his basic points regarding specification bias but argued that while this effect was likely to have resulted in an underestimate of the adjustment coefficient, the estimated elasticity might well still be correct.

In a later work Nerlove further developed his hypothesis and, in the paper written with William Addison, tested its effectiveness in identifying both short- and long-run elasticities.[13] The results of interest here were obtained using a variation of equation 3.15, which included a time-trend variable (T) to represent changes in those factors not conveniently quantifiable, and incorporated into the analysis:

$$Q_t = a + b\, P_{t-1} + (1 - \gamma)\, Q_{t-1} + c\, T + u_t \qquad (3.18a)$$

then applying it to the output of 20 crops produced for the fresh
vegetable market in the United States during periods of varying
length from 1919 and 1955. These results are compared with those
obtained from a simple static supply analysis using a model of the
form:

$$Q_t = d + eP_{t-1} + fT + u_t \qquad\qquad (3.18b)$$

The difference in the results were quite startling in some respects.
The Nerlove-Addison model uniformly explains more of the output
variation than does the static model; in only a few cases are the R^2
values obtained using the latter even close to those coming from
the dynamic model. Their Durbin-Watson statistics indicated
significant positive serial correlation for 19 out of 20 vegetables
when the static model was used. On the other hand, the dynamic
analyses indicated no serial correlation in 17 out of 20 cases, with
the test being inconclusive for the remaining three. In the single
case where the dynamic approach indicates a perverse (though not
statistically significant) price to acreage relationship, for artichokes, the authors hypothesize their model was too simple for
this crop, pointing to a considerable difference that results in the
price parameter when the additional variable of lagged output is
included in the simple model.[14]

NOTES

1. Marc Nerlove, The Dynamics of Supply: Estimation of
Farmers' Response to Price (Baltimore: Johns Hopkins University
Press, 1958).

2. Richard Goodwin, "Dynamic Coupling with Special Reference
to Markets Having Production Lags," Econometrica 15 (1947).

3. L. M. Koyck, Distributed Lags and Investment Analysis
(Amsterdam: North-Holland, 1964).

4. Shirley Almon, "The Distributed Lag between Capital
Appropriations and Expenditures," Econometrica 33 (1965).

5. In a later work, Phoebus Dhrymes (Distributed Lags:
Problems of Estimation and Formulation [San Francisco: Holden-
Day, 1971]) showed that the specification of zero weights is of
crucial importance in determining the profile of the resulting
distribution. Working with the same data inputs, he obtained
"humped" distributions, as well as both monotonically increasing
and decreasing sets of weight estimates, depending upon whether
zero conditions were imposed and where they were imposed.

6. F. H. Theil, "Measuring the Accuracy of Entrepreneurial Anticipations," presented at the 17th European Meeting of the Econometric Society (September 1955); F. Modigliani and O. H. Sauerlender, "Economic Expectations and Plans of Firms in Relation to Short-Term Forecasting," in Short-Term Economic Forecasting, Studies in Income and Wealth, Vol. 16, (Princeton, N.J.: National Bureau of Economic Research, 1955); and Robert Eisner, "Expectations, Plans and Capital Expenditures: A Synthesis of Ex-Post and Ex-Ante Data," presented at the Conference on Expectations, Uncertainty and Business Behavior (October 1955).

7. John R. Hicks, Value and Output (Oxford: Oxford University Press, 1946).

8. Ibid., p. 205.

9. Nerlove, op. cit., p. 53.

10. This assumption, that one of the two coefficients is equal to unity, can, if it is unwarranted, lead to several difficulties. More than ten years after Nerlove's work, Roger Waud, "Misspecification in the 'Partial Adjustment' and 'Adaptive Expectations' Models," International Economic Review 9 (June 1968), argued that not only were estimates based on such misspecifications likely to be seriously biased, but also the estimated standard errors become noticeably larger relative to the estimated regression coefficients as the expectation coefficient becomes smaller.

11. See also Marc Nerlove, "Estimates of Supply of Selected Agricultural Commodities," Journal of Farm Economics 38 (May 1956): 496-509.

12. A. E. Brandow, "A Note on the Nerlove Estimate of Supply Elasticity," and Marc Nerlove, "On the Nerlove Estimate of Supply Elasticity: A Reply," Journal of Farm Economics 40 (August 1958).

13. Marc Nerlove, "Distributed Lags and Estimation of Long-Run Supply and Demand Elasticities: Theoretical Considerations," Journal of Farm Economics 40 (May 1958); and Marc Nerlove and William Addison, "Statistical Estimation of Long-Run Elasticities of Supply and Demand," Journal of Farm Economics 40 (November 1958).

14. Vahid Nowshirvani, "Agricultural Supply in India: Some Theoretical and Empirical Studies" (Ph.D. dissertation, Massachusetts Institute of Technology, 1962), pointed out that in Nerlove's formulation of price expectations, the disturbance term is assumed to be confined to the supply equation, this is not only an unnecessary assumption, but from the viewpoint of estimating the supply function, it is preferable if a disturbance term is also included in the demand equation. Also, John F. Muth, "Rational Expectations and the Theory of Price Movements," Econometrica 29 (July 1961) proposes

an alternative formulation; prices are represented as consisting of two components, one permanent and the other transitory.

4

A CRITIQUE OF
POST-NERLOVE EMPIRICAL
SUPPLY RESPONSE ANALYSIS

From these beginnings came applications of the basic Nerlove response model to cultivator behavior for the output of a wide variety of crops in a multitude of countries representing a cross-section of the stages of economic development.[1] Some of the studies used the same model as did Nerlove, but most depart in one or more respects from the paradigm.

Most of these distinctions can be grouped into three categories. First are elementary modifications in the Nerlove/Nerlove-Addison model; second are those variations that include measurements of particular factors of interest in the situation under investigation, corresponding to the variable Z in equation 3.14; finally come attempts to represent quantitatively situations not considered by Nerlove—primarily perennial slow-maturing (that is, more than one crop-season) crops, and/or livestock. Clearly the Nerlove model has to be altered a great deal to handle livestock as there is no acreage involved and there are also theoretical problems associated with a capital stock. In the discussions in the following chapters several dozen such varieties of the basic model are encountered and the results of the corresponding studies are presented. In hopes of minimizing later potential confusion regarding these multifarious models, we will now turn our attention to a discussion of the developments and adaptions of the Nerlove approach.

Considering the basic model, consisting of equations 3.14, 3.7, and 3.9, and setting aside for now much discussion of the variable Z, we find two concepts in the model open to some differences in statistical representation—prices (P) and output (Q)—plus one not in Nerlove's model—crop yield.

CONCEPTUAL PROBLEMS WITH THE MODEL

Let us consider some of the problems involved when a model
of this kind is used for annual crops. Whatever measure of output
is used as the dependent variable in equation 3.14, then it is plausible
to hypothesize that desired output level is a function of expected
price. But confronting the researcher immediately is the question
as to what price variable should be used in the model. Nerlove's
discussion of prices is phrased mostly in terms of current market
realizations, with normal or expected prices defined in terms of
past market prices. Not surprisingly, many researchers, beginning
with Nerlove, have inserted more realistic price formulations into
supply analyses extending over a time period of more than a few
years. Price series most frequently cited in their studies include:

- the price of the crop received by farmers;
- the ratio of the price of the crop received by farmers to some
  consumer price index;
- the ratio of the price of the crop received by farmers to some
  index of the prices of the farmers' inputs;
- the ratio of the price of the crop received by farmers to some
  index of the prices of competitive crops (or the price of the
  most competitive crop).

To leave aside for the moment the problem of choosing a deflator
(which is frequently determined by data availability), let us first
point out that, given reasonable assumptions, it is quite possible
that none of these four price formulations may be the proper one
to use in equation 3.14. To make this point we ask: Why would a
farmer produce more of a particular crop? Several possible
answers suggest themselves:

- He might produce more to increase his own consumption of
  the crop.
- He might produce more to keep his own consumption of this
  crop the same, in the face of rising input costs.
- He might produce more if he wishes to buy more of other goods.
- He might produce more in order to keep his consumption of
  other goods the same (if the relative price of such goods is
  going up).

If output is changing because of the second reason, then we could
use as our price variable the ratio of the price of the crop to an
index of input prices; alternatively, the difference between crop

and input prices, a profitability measure, could be employed. If producers are motivated by either the third or fourth reasons, on the other hand, then crop prices deflated by some index of consumer prices would be a reasonable measure of price, as would be crop price relative to that of alternative crop(s), an indication of income realized by cultivators. But should they be motivated in large part by a desire to increase their own consumption, then no price variable seems very pertinent.

Therefore, in general we can see that it is not unlikely that the price formulation used in a supply model might have little or no relevance in cultivator decisions. It seems hardly necessary to point out that in most developing nations farmers buy only a very select basket of goods (or none at all) and, as a result, deflating by some consumer price index may be of dubious value. Using the relative price of two competitive crops (in production) also encounters difficulty. For instance, if the relative price of rice to wheat goes up a great deal in a period when all other prices are constant, we might get a large increase in rice production. However, if such a sizable real increase in the relative rice-wheat price were accompanied by increases in most other prices as well, we might see a much smaller response. In this case the estimation problem might be eliminated by using the ratio of the acreage planted to rice to the acreage planted to wheat as the dependent variable. Furthermore, if the adaptive expectation model is estimated using the money price of rice, with the resulting elasticities then deflated, the results would not be the same should the model be estimated using deflated prices, though the former would be the more plausible approach if the efficacy of the money illusion is assumed. Clearly, if we wish to justify inclusion of any specific price variable, we must know why the farmer wants to alter his production.

In addition to the difficulties enumerated above that might be encountered in forming a price series at any given time, there are other not unlikely problems to be met over any extended period of time. (For example, it is hard to imagine that, in general, the expectation coefficient, B, in equation 3.7 remains constant over a long period of time.) The most appropriate price variable of ten years ago may no longer be relevant. For example, if farmers become more prosperous and educated they may well buy a much wider range of consumer products. Though it is our contention that in the early stages of development the consumer price index would not be an appropriate deflator, when might it become so?

Thus, even if one knew the correct price to use at any time, one would need a much more complicated price expectation equation because of possible changes over time. As a result the use of an inappropriate price series casts some doubt on the empirical results

and may also account for some of the response differences observed
in various studies.

Still another objection can be raised to the price expectation
equation 3.7. Imagine a situation where output has been growing
steadily, and then in one particular year the increment in output
is much larger than had been normal, leading to an actual price
decline. As a result the farmers' price expectations for the period
may have been quite far off. It only seems reasonable that farmers
would take this fact into account in calculating their expected price
for the next period. In other words, the farmers' price adjustment
process (here simply represented by the coefficient β) actually may
depend upon a number of factors, such as changes in output and any
exogenous occurrences that might influence prices.[2] To partially
remedy this situation, we might replace equation 3.7 by

$$P_t^e - P_{t-1}^e = \beta(P_{t-1} - P_{t-1}^e) + \delta(Q_t^e - Q_{t-1}) \qquad (4.1)$$

where: Q_t^e is expected output, and

Q_t is actual output

thus allowing for aberrations in output in the formation of price
expectations.

Before concluding this section let us consider some of the
practical aspects of choosing appropriate price series. Price
deflation, in the many studies discussed below, has involved almost
as many approaches as there are relevant studies. Indices have
been based on consumer retail and wholesale prices; often, in
developing countries particularly, researchers have had to content
themselves with whatever data in this regard was available. Crop
prices have also been deflated by indices designed to measure potential alternative activities—weighting the prices of competing crops
in some fashion or other to construct the index. Such measures
have two obvious, if unavoidable, limitations: the subjective evaluation made by the researcher when determining the weights to be
used, and the relevant data limitations, a problem again of particular
importance in many developing regions. The latter is notably
important when considerations of food, as opposed to cash, crops
are of interest: Is the entire output or only the marketed fraction
relevant in determining weights, and then, exactly what is the
relationship between total and marketed output?

Output statistics have also been incorporated into the supply
analyses in several versions. Most directly, output is measured
in terms of crop weight or volume produced or marketed, but in
fact the basic relationship between expected prices and cultivator
reactions seems better expressed not so much in terms of harvested
tonnage (dependent, for example, on such extraneous matters as

secular variations in weather) but rather of planted and harvested
acreage. Planted acreage is generally the best available method
of gauging how cultivators translate their price expectations into
action.

The use of such inputs as fertilizer and pesticides is also
influenced by prices. Thus a farmer instead of increasing acreage
may choose to employ more of such inputs. This may in turn
increase acreage elasticity by less (in general) than supply elasticity.

However, farmers do not really want to adjust area but output-
to-price fluctuations—equation 3.14 is framed in terms of desired
output. Area adjustment is fraught with ambiguities—for example,
if a farmer had this as his goal, he could rapidly increase his
planted acreage with sparse plantings. He could use plots of land
with different degrees of fertility, some of which might otherwise
go unplanted by increasing the use of other inputs (labor, fertilizers,
water, and so on). All things considered, many authors have
preferred to use acreage as the measure of output, and not tonnage,
rather than introduce into the model (with tonnage) variations
dependent upon a number of factors outside of cultivator control.
Thus past prices, actual and expected, weighted naively or sophisti-
catedly, are postulated to affect planting decisions primarily.

However, a number of possible circumstances may cloud
conceptual distinctions. In certain cases past-planting shifts in
prices may effect a radical shift in harvesting, as opposed to
planting, decisions. Most such situations arise for long-maturing
and/or perennial crops (to be discussed later), * but images of crop
destruction in North America during the 1930s or in Europe during
the more recent transitional problems connected with the implementation of common European Economic Community agricultural policies,
or of the various distortions introduced into the behavior patterns
(again of North American cultivators) by the psychedelic patterns
of the Nixon administration's economic phases interacting with
exploding worldwide demand, demonstrate that the period between
planting and harvesting can see drastic dislocations in market
conditions facing cultivators, even when the crop in question has
a short growing season.

Output statistics, like those relating to price, have been
included in supply models in both absolute and relative terms. In
the latter situations, deflation indices have been constructed, considering the various competing crops, and in some cases elaborate

_____

*Such formulations frequently involve inclusion in the model of
prices current at harvest time, as well as those motivating planting
decisions; see Chapter 7.

weighting schemes have been devised that purport to honor changes indicated among the alternative crops.

One last point about output, whether in acreage or tonnage terms, parallels what has been said above about prices. The Nerlove model assumes that the output adjustment coefficient, γ in equation 3.9, remains constant over the time period in question. Yet obviously, as output increases, generally more and more land will be needed for production. This would usually infer that cultivators will be employing increasingly inferior land. If their ultimate aim is to increase output, it seems unlikely that the amount of additional area brought into cultivation, per unit of output, will be constant over time. In practice a farmer may respond to prices by changing acreage and/or other inputs in order to improve yield.

The distinction made above between acreage and tonnage as measures of output involves consideration of crop yield, and variations therein of both a short-term (such as those due to weather) and long-term (such as those due to improvements in technology) nature. Nerlove expressed output primarily in tonnage terms, with some practical considerations related to acreage. Later works have attempted to compromise and capture the effect of this somewhat elusive "middle-ground" concept—yield. The modifications in the basic supply model have taken different forms. Variously, one of the three equations 3.14, 3.7, or 3.9 is rephrased to include yield:

$$Q_t^D = a_o + a_1 P_t^e + a_2 Z_t + a_3 Y_t^e + u_t \tag{4.2}$$

$$P_t^e - P_{t-1}^e = \beta(P_{t-1} - P_{t-1}^e) + \delta_1 (Y_{t-1}^e - Y_{t-1}) \tag{4.3}$$

or

$$Q_t - Q_{t-1} = \gamma(Q_t^D - Q_{t-1}) + \delta_2 (Y_{t-1}^e - Y_{t-1}) \tag{4.4}$$

where Y^e is expected yield, expressed as:

$$Y_t^e - Y_{t-1} = b_1(Y_{t-1}^e - Y_{t-1}) \tag{4.5}$$

The expected yield equation used by some researchers often includes other factors, such as the ratio between desired and actual output (Q_t^D/Q_{t-1}). Expected yield terms can only account for short-run changes in yield or the effect of prices on yield if inputs such as fertilizer and pesticides are used. However, they do pick up effects of long-run shifts in yield for whatever reason, such as the use of inferior land or technical change. Putting in last year's yield can capture possible changes in response to a big yield last year either as the naive expectation that a big yield last year means

a big yield this year and times are good, or a big yield last year
means times were good so we don't need to work hard this year.

These modifications made in the model answer three criticisms
that can be made when yield is ignored. First, with the term
$(Y_{t-1}^e - Y_{t-1})$ we can account for unexpected variations in yield and
for how rapidly cultivators adjust their yield expectations. Second,
if the ratio Q_t^D/Q_{t-1} is included in equation 4.5, we pay heed to
the likelihood that cultivators' desired output or acreage will also
depend upon the quality of the land available. Third, having
reformulated the model, any objection to the assumption of a
constant output adjustment coefficient seems less important, since
in effect we have allowed for differences in land quality. The
resulting more fully specified model also allows government officials
the possibility of obtaining evidence as to the effects on output of
a range of potential policies that influence crop yield.

Nerlove specifically indicates the inclusion of a relevant
nonmarket (that is, neither price, acreage, or yield) variable, Z,
as a means of avoiding the problem of identification in the econometric process of estimating the structural parameters. Although
Z must enter the model nonsymmetrically, few subsequent authors
so inclined seemed to have trouble finding a candidate for this task.
In some cases, in fact, difficulties have arisen in choosing which
nonmarket factors to exclude.

A measurement of weather variation seems to be most commonly
encountered, with a wide variety of methods used to gauge this
concept—absolute versus relative terms; rainfall, humidity, frost
indices; annual or seasonal measurements; and so on. In many
other cases concepts essentially related to infrastructure seemed
important and measurable to the researcher, and thus are more
or less directly included in the statistical analysis of the basic
model. But in still other situations, yardsticks difficult to quantify
are represented, with varying degrees of justification, by proxy
variables.

Most frequently used as such a proxy is a simple time or trend
variable, whose presence is intended to identify such monotonic
time-related effects on overall output as advances in agrotechnology,
social advancements within the infrastructure that are supposed
to encourage the market-oriented cultivator, or secular growth in
the demand of the industrial and/or consumption sectors for the
output of the agricultural sector.

The decision to use a trend variable rather than a more direct
measure of postulated influences on supply is generally based on
difficulties in obtaining reliable time-series data for the factor in
question. However, in other cases, several such influences are
thought to be related to output, yet so interrelated among themselves

that separate inclusion might involve problems of multicollinearity
in the estimating process.

Among the various studies discussed in the following chapters,
there is one particularly notable deficiency in most: Rarely do we
see any attempt to evaluate peasant reaction to risk. In this regard
the effects of such factors as crop diversification need to be clearly
examined as regards changes in indicators of risk, such as standard
deviation of price. The relative risk involved in crops grown for
different purposes, such as subsistence or market, domestic or
export sale, and so on, also seems relevant, as does the question
as to whether any form of government control over prices is exerted.
In individual papers cited below, attempts to include certain risk-
related concepts are encountered, but generally no overall satisfactory
approach to this problem is found.

The third major type of modification made in later studies of
the basic Nerlovian models is found in analyses of nonannual crops,
both those with multiple producing seasons (perennials) and those
whose planting-to-harvesting period exceeds a single year. While
most such crops are tree crops, whose supply is complicated on
both scores, research is available for several commodities whose
production involves a number of unique considerations. While all
these situations are discussed in some detail in Chapters 7 and 8,
some general observations are pertinent now.

Since tree crops (as well as other perennials) are generally
both slow to mature and long-lived, each case seems to call for
an individualized approach to the formulation of price expectations.
While we have included a few studies of perennials that incorporate
only current prices and their relationships with harvesting decisions,
these are only tangentially influenced by the Nerlove model. More
directly descended from the latter are those works that seek to
explain planting decisions, and here current expectations of prices
to be realized several years hence are the relevant market factor
(though some authors may also include harvest-time prices in an
attempt to capture short-term effects on output actually gathered
or marketed).

Another important consideration in analyzing planting decisions
is the capital-stock effect, that is, the influence on new cultivation
of the preexisting "portfolio" of both bearing and prepubescent
plants, and several alternative forms of representing this concept
in the supply model will be seen below.

PROBLEMS OF ESTIMATION

Still further modifications to Nerlove's analytic method have
been occasioned, not so much by conceptual peculiarities of a

particular crop and/or region, but by problems arising from the statistical estimation procedures employed. As has been mentioned already, Nerlove outlined a difficulty in his own model—an inability to distinguish between the price expectation coefficient, β, and the area adjustment coefficient, γ, if either is equal to unity, when least-squares techniques are used. He suggested inclusion of a nonmarket variable, whose nonsymmetric entrance into the supply model can be justified, as a way of avoiding parameter identification problems. Several later studies* have devised methods of securing estimates of all structural coefficients, and these have often involved alterations of, assumptions about, or restrictions on the supply model. Other statistical problems have led to the adoption of alternative approaches, such as first-differences formulations, in attempts to counteract the effects of collinear independent variables.

However, from an empirical viewpoint, many of the supply models proposed below have been incorrectly estimated. For instance, in some cases the possible existence of serial correlation among residuals has been ignored; such neglect leads to, among other things, biased parameter estimates. As a result of different researchers having employed different estimating procedures, it is difficult to compare the results emerging from different models, some of which may have been correctly estimated, others less rigidly so.

In general, estimation of the reduced form of the Nerlove model can be evaluated as follows, if ordinary least-squares techniques are utilized:

1. The estimation will be inefficient to the extent the residuals in the estimating equation (that is, the reduced form of the supply model) are serially correlated, a very likely event.

2. Nerlovian output adjustment models include lagged values of the dependent variable on the right-hand side of the estimating equation, leading to inconsistent parameter estimates due to the existence of serial correlation.

3. Nerlove's parameter identification problem is inevitable, unless some conceptually reasonable and statistically significant factor, which enters the supply model nonsymmetrically, can be found.

_____

*Including those like Behrman and Nowshirvani, which used maximum-likelihood estimating techniques, or the works of DeCanio, Askari, and Cummings, which impose certain restrictions on one or another structural coefficient.

One way to approach the problem of efficiency and consistency in the parameter estimates is to employ nonlinear maximum likelihood estimating techniques. Various resolutions to problems arising from serial correlation and lagged dependent variables enjoy currency among researchers; for example, both Hildreth-Lu and Cochrane-Orcutt methods for accounting for serial correlation are now commonly available in statistical software packages. Finally, specification of one or the other adjustment coefficients (β or γ) within some range allows an alternative solution to the identification problem, even if no asymmetric variable is included in the supply model. However, many of the studies discussed below, particularly the earlier or less comprehensive efforts, have either passed over, at least in part, potential estimating problems or have been conducted under circumstances that ruled out employment of theoretically available compensating econometric techniques. The reader is thus cautioned of the existence of such limitations in the works recounted below. Clearly, if a Nerlovian model of the standard form is used, its estimation using ordinary least squares would lead to the above problems.

Specifically, the estimation procedure is outlined below, taking as a standard Nerlove model:

$$A^D_t = b_1 + b_2 P^e_t + b_3 W_t \tag{4.6}$$

$$P^e_t - P^e_{t-1} = b_4 (P_{t-1} - P^e_{t-1}) \tag{4.7}$$

$$A_t - A_{t-1} = b_5 (A^D_{t-1} - A_{t-1}) \tag{4.8}$$

where: A_t, A^D_t = actual and desired acreage in time t
   P_t, P^e_t = actual and expected price in time t
   W_t = weather index in time t.

The reduced form of the above model can be obtained as:

$$A_t = b_1 b_4 b_5 + b_2 b_4 b_5 P_{t-1} + b_3 b_5 W_t - b_3 b_5 (1 - b_4) W_{t-1}$$

$$+ [(1 - b_4) + (1 - b_5)] A_{t-1} - (1 - b_4) (1 - b_5) A_{t-2}$$

$$+ b_5 U_t - b_5 (1 - b_4) U_{t-1} \tag{4.9}$$

or:

$$\underline{A} = \underline{X} B + W \tag{4.10}$$

where: $B_1 = b_1 \, b_4 \, b_5$
$B_2 = b_2 \, b_4 \, b_5$
$B_3 = b_3 \, b_5$
$B_4 = b_3 \, b_5 \, (1 - b_4)$
$B_5 = (1 - b_4) + (1 - b_5)$
$B_6 = - \, (1 - b_4) \, (1 - b_5)$

and $\underline{W}$ is the vector of disturbances, with u_t being the original disturbance:

$$W_t = b_5 \, u_t - b_5 \, (1 - b_4) \, u_{t-1}$$

A sufficient condition that the adjustment process described converges is:

$$\left| 1 - b_4 + 1 - b_5 \right| < 1$$

If simple least-squares estimation is used on this model, some difficulties will be encountered:

- Even without the lagged value of the dependent variable, the estimator will be inefficient as the Ws are likely to be serially correlated.
- Also, the simple least-squares estimates will be inconsistent as the equation contains lagged values of the dependent variable.
- The equation is overidentified as the bs can be recovered from the Bs in more than one way.

The way to approach this problem of efficiency and consistency is to maximize the likelihood function of the observation with respect to the bs. Under the assumption that the Ws are distributed $N \, (O, \, \sigma^2, \, I)$, I being the identity matrix, the following can be written as the log of the likelihood function:

$$L \, (\underline{A} \, \underline{X}, \, b, \, \sigma^2) = - \left[\frac{I}{2} \right] \log \, (2\pi) - \left[\frac{I}{2} \right] \log \sigma^2$$

$$- \, [1/2 \, \sigma^2] \, (\underline{A} - \underline{XB})' \, (\underline{A} - \underline{XB}) \qquad (4.11)$$

The likelihood function is maximized when the sum of the square residuals is minimized. And the estimation of the bs can be obtained by solving:

$$\partial \, W'W / \partial b_i = 0$$

These estimates are consistent, asymptotically unbiased, and efficient.

Two computational techniques can be used to estimate the parameters. First, a nonlinear estimation program can be used. Second, regressing using a range of values for b_4 (as it is expected to be between 0 and 1), the correct maximized likelihood estimate of b_4 can be obtained when the sum of squared residuals is minimized. This technique is based on the fact that the model is linear in the new bs and of course yields estimates of their values as well. The actual grouping of equation 4.11 is as:

$$A_t - (1 - b_4)\,A_{t-1} = b_1 b_4 b_5 + b_2 b_4 b_5 P_{t-1} + b_3 b_5\,(W_t - (1 - b_4)\,W_{t-1})$$

$$+ (1 - b_5)\,(A_{t-1} - (1 - b_4)\,A_{t-2})$$

$$+ b_5 u_t - b_5\,(1 - b_4)\,u_{t-1} \tag{4.12}$$

In the discussion so far, independently distributed disturbances have been implicitly assumed. However, in the estimations the following structure should in general be assumed for these disturbances:

$$W_t = b_6\,W_{t-1} + E_t \tag{4.13}$$

where E_t, the disturbance, is normally distributed.

When the above nonlinear computation method is used, the significance levels and standard errors for the coefficients are not likely to be correct but are conditional on the value of the expectation coefficient finally used. More accurate asymptotic standard errors could be computed by inverting the Hessian of the log likelihood function evaluated at the maximum likelihood point. In these cases as well as in those that involve a lagged dependent variable (as is found in many of the studies surveyed in this book and summarized in Appendix B) where serial correlation has been corrected for by one of the iterative techniques, what are called "t values" in such studies are not truly distributed as "t," and the significance levels reported in the tables are not correct. Fisher and Temin, and later DeCanio have taken care of this by referring to "quasi t values" and "quasi significance," which they have defined.[3] In cases where the expectation parameter has been estimated but the correct asymptotic standard error has not been computed they refer to "conditional quasi t values" and "conditional quasi significance." The same is true for the F statistics; that is, they are not actually F distributed nor is the test correct for the reasons given above. These problems are found to some degree in most of the studies using this procedure considered in this work.

Because of the many problems in estimation, the studies reported in our work are not all of equal quality. Some do not use a nonlinear computation method, and/or they do not correct for serial correlation, and so on. Where possible, we have tried to comment on these estimation deficiencies—inefficiency and inconsistency (such comment is not always possible given the information supplied in the original study). However, a simple generalization would be that earlier and/or less-detailed studies tend to be more subject to these shortcomings.

In our efforts to summarize these many published studies we will attempt to standardize, as far as is practicable, the terms and symbols used by the various authors. Though it is hoped this will lessen obfuscation in the intercrop and regional comparisons presented herein, it is recognized that some potential for confusion is created for the reader who wishes to proceed from our work back to its several sources. For that reason we will use such generic terms as "area," "price," "yield," and so on, in most discussions of (and in tables referring to) both specific studies and collations of the results of several works, but we will also indicate any conceptual and statistical peculiarities employed by individual authors. However, for the most part the reader is directed to consult the original sources for details as to how a particular variable has been derived, for information about data sources, and so on.

NOTES

1. The estimation of elasticities has also thrown some light on the issue of the economic rationality of peasants. However, a more direct and complete testing of the profit-maximization question is presented by John Wise and Pan A. Yotopoulos, "The Empirical Content of Economic Rationality: A Test for a Less Developed Economy," Journal of Political Economy 77 (November-December 1969).

2. Franklin Fisher in chapter 2 of A Priori Information and Time Series Analysis (Amsterdam: North-Holland, 1962), pointed out this problem. He discovered the possibility of letting adjustments or weights be influenced by economic events (such as turning points) rather than assuming that there would be the same weight for the same length lag regardless of what happens.

3. Franklin Fisher and Peter Temin, "Regional Specialization and the Supply of Wheat in the U.S., 1867-1914," Review of Economics and Statistics 52 (May 1970); and Stephen DeCanio,

"Agricultural Production, Supply and Institutions in the Post-Civil War South" (Ph.D. dissertation, Massachusetts Institute of Technology, 1972).

A majority of the supply analyses that have utilized the Nerlove approach have been like the prototype in their concern for annual crops—that is, crops whose sowing-to-sowing cycle is one year or less and for which a single harvest is obtained for each seeding. These studies, as will be seen, have involved a wide variety of crops and geographical regions, as well as a cross-section of the stages of economic development. (A few studies pertain to time periods prior to the recent past, that is, the post-World War II era, but these are exceptional. The quality of time-series data from earlier periods is a serious restriction on any researcher so inclined.)

In an attempt to give some structure to our discussions we will consider first those works that have examined cereals and related basic food crops. Much of the interest in agricultural output in the past decade is centered in the developing world, and here these commodities are primarily subsistence crops. However, our range here is wider, since research is available for cereal production in several advanced economies, as well as for particular crops in developing countries that are largely cultivated for the market. With this important qualification we might consider, at least for convenience, the subject of this chapter to be food or subsistence crops. In the next chapter we will take up those edible and inedible crops that, in any country where they are grown, are primarily intended for the market and thus might be termed, if somewhat inexactly, cash crops.

Jere Behrman's work was probably one of the first major studies to use a Nerlove supply model, and with the aid of nonlinear statistical procedures he estimated structural parameters for output of several crops cultivated in Thailand.[1] Also formulated was a model based on the Olson-Krishnan version of the marketed surplus hypothesis.[2]

In the first case Behrman states a four-equation version of Nerlove's model:

$$A_t^D = a_0 + a_1 P_t^e + a_2 Y_t^e + a_3 \sigma_{P_t} + a_4 \sigma_{Y_t} + a_5 N_t + a_6 M_t + u_{1_t}$$

(5.1a)

$$A_t = b_0 + A_{t-1} + \gamma (A_t^D - A_{t-1}) + u_{2_t}$$

(5.1b)

$$P_t^e = c_0 + P_{t-1}^e + \beta (P_{t-1} + c_1 D_{t-1} - P_{t-1}^e) + u_{3_t}$$

(5.1c)

$$Y_t^e = d_0 + d_1 (R_t - \bar{R}) + d_2 t + d_3 t^2 + u_{4_t}$$

(5.1d)

where: A_t^D = desired acreage
P_t^e = expected price
Y_t^e = expected yield
σ_{P_t}, σ_{Y_t} = standard deviations in last three periods

N_t = farm population
M_t = malaria death rate
D_{t-1} = dummy for proximity to Bangkok
R_t = rainfall
t = time trend

Desired acreage and expected price are of course not observable; they can be expressed in distributed lag form as:

$$A_t = \sum_{i=0}^{\infty} (1 - \gamma)^i (b_0 + \gamma A_{t-1}^D + u_{21\ t-1})$$

(5.2a)

$$P_t^e = \sum_{i=0}^{\infty} (1 - \beta)^i (c_0 + \beta [P_{t-1-i} + c_1 D_{t-1-i}] + u_{31\ t-1})$$

(5.2b)

In discussing the values these coefficients are likely to have and the significance of these values, Behrman points out the inadequacies of the relationships expressed in equations 5.2a and 5.2b, brought on in large part by the assumption that the adjustment and expectation coefficients are assumed to be constant. Though he can suggest no alternative formulation simple enough to use in analysis, Behrman emphasizes the possibility of misspecifications due to this assumption.

To eliminate the nonobservable variables, equations 5.2a and 5.2b are substituted in the model, and manipulation of these equations yields:

$$\underline{A} = \underline{X}B + \underline{W} \tag{5.3a}$$

$$Y_t^e = d_o + d_2 t + d_3 t^2 \tag{5.3b}$$

where $\underline{X}$ is a matrix in which the tth row contains the following elements:

$$1, A_{t-1}, A_{t-2}, P_{t-1}, D_{t-1}, Y_t^e, Y_{t-1}^e, {}^\sigma P_t, {}^\sigma P_{t-1}, {}^\sigma Y_t, {}^\sigma Y_{t-1},$$

N_t, N_{t-1}, M_t, M_{t-1} and $\underline{W}$ is a vector of disturbances.

Using maximum likelihood estimation procedures, he obtains parameter values for the total supply curves of four crops, both nationally and in each of the 50 provinces where most of the expansion in production took place. (His results for kenaf, a jute-like fiber, are recounted separately in Chapter 6.)

Rice, by far Thailand's major crop, is grown both as a subsistence and as a cash crop in all sections of the country. Its production occupies 82 percent of the cultivated area, and it makes up 54 percent of the value of total agricultural production, 17 percent of national income, 43 percent of exports, and 60 percent of the caloric intake of the average Thai. In analyzing rice supply, 58 regressions were performed. If for a particular province the original regression did not indicate that one or the other or both adjustment coefficients (prices and area) were significantly different from unity at least at the 25 percent level, then that adjustment coefficient was restricted to unity in subsequent regressions. Similarly any other parameter not significantly nonzero at least at the 25 percent level was eliminated from consideration in further regressions. For five of the 50 provinces and for the nation as a whole more than one combination of variables on the right-hand side of equation 5.3a proved to be approximately equally effective in explaining the variance of the dependent variable. F tests showed that for 40 of these 58 regressions the multiple correlation coefficients were asymptotically significantly different from zero at the 10 percent level, and for all but one of the 58, at least at the 20 percent level; the values of the adjusted correlation coefficient, $\bar{R}^2$, ranged from 0.30 to 0.86, with 86 percent of the values greater than 0.50 and 67 percent greater than 0.70.

As seen in Table 5.1 the model tends to explain variance in planted rice area best in those provinces where rice is relatively

TABLE 5.1

Estimated Parameters, Thai Rice

Region and Province	Structural Coefficient of Price [a1]	Area Adjustment Coefficient [Y]	Price Adjustment Coefficient [β]	R²	Short-Run Elasticity	Long-Run Elasticity
Northeast Region						
Chayaphum	0.226c (0.08)	0.933c (0.19)	1.47c (0.19)	0.80	0.28	0.21
Nakhornratsima	1.04c (0.28)	1.59c (0.15)	0.608c (0.14)	0.56	0.55	0.57
Buriram	0.282c (0.09)	1.37c (0.19)	1.33c (0.19)	0.81	0.47	0.26
Surin	0.453b (0.18)	0.836c (0.22)	1.39c (0.23)	0.60	0.36	0.31
Srisaket	1.68c (0.49)	1.13c (0.17)	0.547c (0.11)	0.70	0.63	1.02
Ubonratthani	0.147c (0.038)	0.474c (0.13)	1.32c (0.19)	0.82	0.21	0.31
(2 formulations)	0.130c (0.044)	0.748c (0.21)	1	0.81	to 0.23	to 0.34
Nong-kai	0.496c (0.14)	0.712c (0.17)	0.502c (0.086)	0.96	0.33	0.91
Loei	—	1.302c (0.20)	1	0.36	—	—

(continued)

55

(Table 5.1 continued)

Region and Province	Structural Coefficient of Price [a]	Area Adjustment Coefficient [Y]	Price Adjustment Coefficient [β]	R²	Short-Run Elasticity	Long-Run Elasticity
Udornthani	1.87c (0.43)	1	0.354c (0.059)	0.94	0.15	0.53
(2 formulations)	0.964b (0.43)	1.575c (0.15)	0.179b (0.080)	0.94	to 0.37	to 1.04
Sakonnakhorn	0.343 (0.45)	0.686c (0.22)	0.201 (0.16)	0.96	0.03	0.25
Nakhornphanom	0.134 (0.12)	0.911c (0.23)	0.310 (0.18)	0.88	0.04	0.16
Khon-kaen	0.917 (0.61)	1.45c (0.25)	0.773b (0.18)	0.78	0.59	0.53
Mahasarakham	2.51b (1.1)	1.80c (0.13)	0.598c (0.31)	0.63	1.81	1.68
Kalasin	0.334c (0.062)	0.872c (0.098)	0.899c (0.12)	0.53	0.18	0.23
Roi-et	0.0658b (0.025)	1.26c (0.19)	1.14c (0.11)	0.44	0.39	0.28
Central Region (Bangkok plain)						
Chai-nut	0.270c (0.045)	1.03b (0.40)	0.743b (0.21)	0.94	0.19	0.25
Singh-buri	0.531 (0.50)	0.207a (0.10)	0.915c (0.17)	0.70	0.02	0.08

Province					
Lopburi	0.513[c] (0.042)	1.05 (0.92)	1.05 (0.92)	0.75		
(2 formulations)	0.510[c] (0.042)	1.05 (0.67)	1.05 (0.67)	0.75	0.50	0.46
Sara–buri	0.0824 (0.061)	1	1	0.03	0.07	0.07
Ang–thong	0.0745[b] (0.030)	0.726[c] (0.16)	0.673[c] (0.17)	0.60	0.04	0.09
Ayuthya	0.0187[c] (0.0026)	1.12[c] (0.24)	1.03[c] (0.25)	0.48	0.08	0.02
Nonthaburi	0.115[c] (0.040)	1	1	0.30	0.23	0.23
Pathum–thani	0.230[b] (0.10)	0.725[c] (0.17)	0.623[c] (0.18)	0.68	0.08	0.19
Thonburi	1.13[a] (0.58)	0.447[b] (0.21)	0.447[b] (0.21)	0.75	0.62	3.12
Phra–nakhorn (Bangkok)	0.958 (1.0)	0.667[a] (0.35)	0.437 (0.47)	0.67	0.24	0.83
Nakhornayok	0.185[b] (0.077)	0.911[c] (0.18)	0.599[c] (0.17)	0.72	0.09	0.16
Samutprakan	0.527[a] (0.29)	1.69[c] (0.095)	0.0838 (0.052)	0.94	0.11 to 0.19	0.11 to 0.95
	0.316[c] (0.047)	1	0.333[c] (0.042)	0.89		
(3 formulations)	0.0613[a] (0.031)	1	1	0.85		

(continued)

57

(Table 5.1 continued)

Region and Province	Structural Coefficient of Price [a1]	Area Adjustment Coefficient [Y]	Price Adjustment Coefficient [β]	R^2	Short-Run Elasticity	Long-Run Elasticity
Nakhornsawan	0.0682c (0.014)	0.785c (0.14)	1.13c (0.18)	0.89	0.28	0.32
Suphanburi	0.0163 (0.017)	0.348c (0.099)	1.38c (0.14)	0.65	0.03	0.07
Nakhornpathom	0.298c (0.064)	1.204c (0.21)	0.611c (0.17)	0.48	0.14	0.19
Samutsongkram	0.257b (0.095)	0.607a (0.32)	0.958b (0.37)	0.63	0.33	0.57
Samutsakhorn	0.0657c (0.023)	0.811c (0.17)	1	0.78	0.18	0.22
Central Region (southeast coast)						
Cholburi	0.0690a (0.039)	0.670c (0.12)	0.971c (0.16)	0.85	0.08 to	0.12
(2 formulations)	0.0718b (0.030)	0.937c (0.17)	0.935c (0.17)	0.83	0.11	
Rayong	0.0332 (0.027)	0.0238 (0.086)	1.56c (0.15)	0.60	0.06	0.16
Chant-buri	0.016 (0.016)	0.097 (0.11)	1	0.80	0.06	0.60
Trat	0.335c (0.071)	1.16c (0.17)	0.397c (0.10)	0.70	0.13	0.28

Central Region (marginal plains)						
Prachinburi	0.564 (0.40)	1.07[c] (0.23)	0.536[c] (0.176)	0.57	0.20	0.34
Cha-choengsao	0.240 (0.28)	0.896[c] (0.13)	1.22[c] (0.17)	0.91	0.14	0.13
Central Region (upper plain)						
Uttaradit	0.180[c] (0.043)	1.48[c] (0.15)	0.371[c] (0.082)	0.87	0.24	0.45
Sukhothai	0.127 (0.39)	1.01[b] (0.39)	1.02[b] (0.39)	0.73	0.21	0.21
Phitsnulok	0.369[c] (0.12)	1.05[c] (0.23)	0.419[b] (0.16)	0.90	0.19	0.42
Kemphaengphet	0.0171 (0.019)	1	1	0.91	0.04	0.04
Phicit	0.552[c] (0.076)	0.888[c] (0.26)	0.943[c] (0.28)	0.93	0.26 to 0.27	0.33
(2 formulations)	0.555[c] (0.069)	0.896[c] (0.23)	0.895[c] (0.23)	0.92		
Phetchabun	–	1.133[c] (0.14)	1	0.95	–	–
Uthai-thami	0.103[b] (0.045)	1.45[c] (0.15)	0.451[c] (0.14)	0.90	0.11	0.17
Central Region (western highlands)						
Tak	0.676[c] (0.14)	0.808[c] (0.18)	1.32[c] (0.19)	0.72	0.45	0.43

(continued)

(Table 5.1 continued)

Region and Province	Structural Coefficient of Price [a_1]	Area Adjustment Coefficient [γ]	Price Adjustment Coefficient [β]	R^2	Short-Run Elasticity	Long-Run Elasticity
Kanchanaburi	0.137 (0.11)	1	1	0.35	0.45	0.45
Ratburi	0.0745 (0.062)	1	1	0.38	0.07	0.07
Central Region (peninsula)						
Phetburi	0.160c (0.045)	1	1	0.71	0.29	0.29
Prachuapkhirikan	0.177 (0.15)	1	1	0.36	0.29	0.29
Kingdom of Thailand	0.121 (0.20)	1.05c (0.12)	0.922c (0.056)	0.92	0.17 to 0.18	0.19 to 0.43
(2 formulations)	0.274c (0.051)	1.60c (0.13)	0.247c (0.044)	0.89		

a10 percent significance level.
b5 percent significance level.
c1 percent significance level.

Source: Jere Behrman, Supply Response in Underdeveloped Agriculture: A Case Study of Four Major Annual Crops in Thailand, 1937–63 (Amsterdam: North–Holland, 1968).

important or where it is rapidly growing in importance, as can be
seen from the analysis across the provinces that shows that the
proportion of the variance explained by the model is positively
correlated at the 5 percent level with the percent of total land
planted in rice, with mean rice production per capita, and with
the growth rates of rice production and of production per capita.
On the other hand, no significant correlation was found at the 5 percent level between proportion of explained variance and such variables
as degree of literacy, degree of adoption of "modern" factors of
production, extent of irrigation, percentage of tenancy, or proximity
to Bangkok. The one province, Sara-buri, for which Behrman did
not obtain a nonzero multiple correlation coefficient that was
asymptotically significant at least at the 20 percent level, is
different in these respects from the other provinces, but different
in a way that cannot explain the anomolous result. Sara-buri is
relatively close to Bangkok, with good transportation links to the
capital; its peasants are relatively well educated; rice production
per capita is relatively high, thus indicating its peasants are more
likely involved in the rice market than are the average Thai peasants;
the percent of its peasants using "modern" factors of production
is not particularly low; nor are agricultural factor intensities
unusually unfavorable. In short, Behrman points out that none of
Sara-buri's characteristics seem to account for the failure of the
model to explain a significant proportion of the variance in planted
rice area. Furthermore, data, if anything, might be expected to
be more reliable in a province close to the capital than in most areas.
So no apparent explanation is indicated for this unique failure of the
model.

Behrman's calculations for the structural coefficient of price,
the area and price adjustment coefficients (and their standard
deviations), the correlation coefficient, and the short- and long-run
elasticities of area planted with respect to price are shown in
Table 5.1.

As for the other crops considered by Behrman, they have become
of increasing importance to the Thai economy in the last 20 years.
None accounted for as much as 1 percent of total value of total
agricultural production in 1951-53; the three together accounted
for 11 percent in 1963 and for 20 percent of the value of agricultural
exports.

Cassava is a root crop that is processed into tapioca flour. In
this form 75 percent of the Thai output is exported, making Thailand
one of the world's major sources of tapioca. Cassava has a long
growing season and needs an adequate and steady distribution of
rainfall. Though it may compete with other crops for labor during
the planting, the length of the growing season allows its harvesting

at otherwise slack periods. Over 87 percent of Thailand's output
is concentrated in two provinces. For one province (Cholburi)
Behrman found available data for 1950-63; for Rayong, for only
1955-63; the results he obtained are shown in Table 5.2.

TABLE 5.2

Estimated Parameters, Thai Cassava

Province	Constant	Expected Price	Expected Yield	Price Risk	Yield Risk	Area Adjustment Coefficient	Price Expectation Coefficient	R^2
Cholburi	+0.595 (1.1)	–	0.469 (0.41)	-0.380* (0.16)	-0.0590 (0.05)	+0.153 (0.19)	1	0.90
Rayong	8.66* (3.4)	–	–	-0.958 (0.79)	–	+0.625* (0.24)	1	0.23
	2.58 (8.9)	1.30 (1.1)	–	-0.874 (0.85)	–	1	1	0.14

*5 percent significance level.
 Source: Jere Behrman, Supply Response in Underdeveloped Agriculture: A Case
Study of Four Major Annual Crops in Thailand, 1937-63 (Amsterdam: North-Holland, 1968).

The model works well in explaining area variation in Cholburi
province but not in Rayong. Behrman suggests this might be due
to the expansion of tree crops in this province, alternative production
that the model does not take into consideration.

Estimated short-run and long-run elasticities of planted
cassava area with respect to the various independent variables
are shown in Table 5.3.

Maize is in small part locally consumed, but over 80 percent
is exported, making it third in value among agricultural exports.
Maize does not compete much with other crops for labor, though
if a second annual planting were made, it might conflict with rice
planting labor needs. As regards land, maize competes with
dry rice cultivation and with other upland crops, particularly kenaf
in Nakhornratsima province and various legumes in the other
provinces. Behrman's analysis shows that production of both
maize and legumes have expanded in these areas, since the latter
are frequently planted as a second crop or among the maize since
they replenish soil nitrogen and make maize cultivation more
productive. Eight provinces account for 65 percent of national
output, and Behrman examines the output of these provinces for
1949-63, obtaining the parameter estimates as shown in Table 5.4.
This model seems to explain a considerable portion of the planted

TABLE 5.3

Supply Elasticities, Thai Cassava

Province	Short-Run Elasticities of Planted Area with Respect to				Long-Run Elasticities of Planted Area with Respect to			
	Price	Yield	Price Risk	Yield Risk	Price	Yield	Price Risk	Yield Risk
Cholburi	–	0.60	-0.50	-0.09	–	3.92	-3.37	-0.39
Rayong	1.09	–	-0.44 to -0.48	–	1.09	–	-0.48 to 0.128	–

Source: Jere Behrman, Supply Response in Underdeveloped Agriculture: A Case Study of Four Major Annual Crops in Thailand, 1937-63 (Amsterdam: North-Holland, 1968).

area variation in all eight provinces, though price response coefficients were significantly nonzero in only half the provinces. Expected yield, on the other hand, proved significant in all provinces, and as can be seen in Table 5.5, supply elasticities with respect to yield are generally large in all provinces and exceed price elasticities in all but one province. Estimated short-run and long-run elasticities of planted maize area with respect to the various independent variables are seen in Table 5.5.

In attempting to estimate the price elasticity of the marketed surplus of a subsistence crop, Behrman begins with a consideration of Raj Krishna's model.[3] Marketed surplus (M) is defined as the difference between the intended quantity produced of the crop of concern (Q^I) and the demand function for on-farm consumption (C) of the crop:

$$M \equiv Q^I - C \tag{5.4a}$$

Differentiating with respect to the market price of the crop being considered (P):

$$\frac{\partial M}{\partial P} = \frac{\partial Q^I}{\partial P} - \frac{\partial C}{\partial P} - \frac{\partial C}{\partial I} \times \frac{\partial I}{\partial P} \tag{5.4b}$$

where I stands for farmer's total net income. Arguing that if a peasant only produced the crop of concern, increasing prices would boost his income in relation to the quantity produced, and that if, on the other hand, the peasant did not produce any of this

TABLE 5.4

Estimated Parameters, Thai Maize

Province	Constant	Expected Price	Expected Yield	Price Risk	Yield Risk	Malaria Death Rate	Area Adjustment Coefficient [γ]	Price Expectation Coefficient [β]	R²
Nakhornsawan	-3.64b (1.4)	—	+3.04c (0.49)	-0.257b (0.090)	—	—	1	1	0.81
	+5.498c (1.3)	—	—	-0.426c (0.15)	—	-0.217b (0.09)	1	1	0.45
	+0.374 (1.7)	+1.70 (1.1)	—	-0.445	—	—	1	1	0.20
Sara-buri	-1.57b (0.71)	—	+1.35b (0.51)	-0.0665b (0.031)	—	—	1	1	0.92
Lopburi	-8.71c (1.32)	+0.544 (1.62)	+4.05c (0.39)	-0.124c (0.044)	—	—	0.689c (0.18)	1.27c (0.19)	0.96
Nakhornratsima	-5.02 (3.2)	+0.966 (0.94)	+3.51b (1.7)	-0.705b (0.33)	—	—	0.54b (0.23)	1	0.85
Phitsnulok	+4.76c (1.3)	—	+4.36c (0.57)	-0.146 (0.11)	—	—	1	1	0.82
Phicit	+0.60 (1.7)	—	+1.89c (0.39)	-0.395 (0.25)	-0.46 (0.43)	—	1	1	0.75
	+7.42c (1.3)	—	—	-0.223 (0.30)	-0.463 (0.47)	-0.404c (0.096)	1	1	0.70
Phetchabun	-9.99a (5.2)	+6.70 (4.6)	+3.94c (1.4)	—	-0.115 (0.063)	—	0.315 (0.26)	1	0.73
Sukhothai	11.0c (1.8)	—	5.58c (0.69)	-0.279c (0.092)	—	—	1	1	0.89
	3.8c (0.73)	—	—	-0.553b (0.21)	-0.198 (0.15)	-0.173b (0.081)	1	1	0.39

a10 percent significance level.
b5 percent significance level.
c1 percent significance level.

Source: Jere Behrman, Supply Response in Underdeveloped Agriculture: A Case Study of Four Major Annual Crops in Thailand, 1937–63 (Amsterdam: North-Holland, 1968).

TABLE 5.5

Supply Elasticities, Thai Maize

| Province | Short-Run Elasticities of Planted Area with Respect to | | | | | Long-Run Elasticities of Planted Area with Respect to | | | | |
	Price	Yield	Price Risk	Yield Risk	Malaria Death Rate	Price	Yield	Price Risk	Yield Risk	Malaria Death Rate
Nakhornsawan	+1.92	+4.88	-1.19 to -2.09	–	-0.85	1.92	4.88	-1.19 to 2.09	–	-0.85
Sara-buri	–	2.24	-0.34	–	–	–	3.96	0.62	–	–
Lopburi	1.58	4.71	-0.30	–	–	1.81	6.83	-0.44	–	–
Nakhornratsima	0.27	1.36	-0.21	–	–	0.41	2.52	-0.40	–	–
Phitsmulok	–	2.44	-0.22	–	–	–	2.44	-0.22	–	–
Phichit	–	1.41	-0.16 to -0.28	-0.35	-12.27	–	1.41	-0.16 to -0.28	-0.35	-12.27
Phetchabun	4.47	3.68	–	–	–	14.17	11.68	–	–	–
Sukhothai	–	7.73	-0.36 to -0.70	-0.15 to -0.26	-0.22	–	7.73	-0.36 to -0.70	-0.15 to -0.26	-0.22

Source: Jere Behrman, Supply Response in Underdeveloped Agriculture: A Case Study of Four Major Annual Crops in Thailand, 1937–63 (Amsterdam: North-Holland, 1968).

crop but only consumed it, the income decrease due to a price increase would be in relation to the quantity consumed. But the peasant is both a producer and a consumer in the context of Krishna's consideration. He then represented the net effect on income of a price increase as simply the algebraic sum of these two opposite effects:

$$\frac{\partial I}{\partial P} = Q^I - C \equiv M \tag{5.4c}$$

Then substituting in equation 5.4b:

$$\frac{\partial M}{\partial P} = \frac{\partial Q^I}{\partial P} - \frac{\partial C}{\partial P} - M \frac{\partial C}{\partial I} \tag{5.4d}$$

Multiplying through by P/M and then manipulating the results yields an expression in elasticity terms:

$$\frac{P}{M} \times \frac{\partial M}{\partial P} = \frac{Q^I}{M} \frac{P}{Q^I} \times \frac{\partial Q^I}{\partial P} - \left[\frac{Q^I}{M} - 1 \right] \left[\frac{P}{C} \times \frac{\partial C}{\partial P} + \frac{M}{Q^I} \times \frac{PQ^I}{I} \right.$$

$$\left. \times \frac{I}{C} \times \frac{\partial C}{\partial I} \right] \tag{5.4e}$$

or $e = r\, b - (r - 1)\,(g + m\, k\, h)$ \hfill (5.4f)

where: e is the elasticity of marketed surplus with respect to price;
r is the reciprocal of m, the sale ratio of the crop which is equal to M/Q^I;
b is $\frac{P}{Q^I} \times \frac{\partial Q^I}{\partial P}$, the price elasticity of the cash crop with respect to its market price;
g is the elasticity of consumption of the cash crop on the farm with respect to its price;
k is PQ^I/I, the ratio of the total value of the production of the cash crop to the total net income of the farmer;
h is $\frac{I}{C} \times \frac{\partial C}{\partial I}$, the elasticity of consumption of the cash crop with respect to total net income.

Behrman criticizes this formulation for including only one price, that of the crop being considered, which leads to the limiting assumption that the farmer's cash income comes from one crop only, for its implicit assumption of complete adjustment, and for using P_1, defined as a relative price, occasionally as though it were an absolute price. Offering an alternative, Behrman begins with Raj Krishna:

$$M = Q^I - C \tag{5.5a}$$

But he then objects that it is not enough to allow only the absolute price of the cash crop under consideration (P_1) to change; the aggregate price for all income sources of a producer of the crop being considered other than that from this particular crop, (P_2), and the aggregate price for all commodities other than this particular crop which are consumed by a producer of this crop, (P_3), must be included for their possible effects on farmer behavior. Thus:

$$\frac{\partial M}{\partial P_1} = \frac{\partial Q^I}{\partial (P_1/P_2)} \frac{\partial (P_1/P_2)}{\partial P_1} - \frac{\partial C}{\partial (P_1/P_3)} \frac{\partial (P_1/P_3)}{\partial P_1}$$

$$- \frac{\partial C}{\partial I} \times \frac{\partial I}{\partial P_1} \tag{5.5b}$$

Approximating, inasmuch as the first partial derivative of gross income with respect to P_1 is substituted for the first partial derivative of net income with respect to P_1, and expressing his results in elasticity terms:

$$\frac{P_1}{M_1} \frac{\partial M_1}{\partial P_1} \cdot \frac{Q^I}{M_1} \doteq \left[\frac{P_1/P_2}{Q^I} \frac{\partial Q^I}{\partial (P_1/P_2)} \right] - \left[\frac{Q^I}{M_1} - 1 \right] \left[\frac{P_1/P_3}{C} \frac{\partial C}{\partial (P_1/P_3)} \right.$$

$$+ \left\{ \frac{I}{C} \frac{\partial C}{\partial I} \right\} \left\{ \frac{P_1 Q^I}{I} \right\} \left\{ 1 + \frac{P_1/P_2}{Q^I} \frac{\partial Q^I}{\partial (P_1/P_2)} \right\} \right] - \left[\frac{Q^I}{M_1} - 1 \right]$$

$$\left[\frac{I}{C} \frac{\partial C_1}{\partial I} \frac{P_1/P_2}{Q_A} \frac{\partial Q_A^I}{\partial (P_1/P_2)} \right] \left[1 - \frac{P_1 Q^I}{I} \right] \tag{5.5c}$$

or: $e \doteq rb_1 - (r - 1)[g + hk(1 + b_1)] - (r - 1)hb_2(1 - k)$ (5.5d)

where: Q^I is the intended production of all other commodities;
        b_1 is the price elasticity of the cash crop with respect to the ratio of P_1 to P_2;
        b_2 is the price elasticity of the intended quantity of goods and services (Q_A^I) other than Q^I, the cash crop produced, with respect to P_1/P_2.

Discussing the implications of the differences between Raj Krishna's and his own formulation, Behrman compares the estimates Raj Krishna made (using equations 5.4 for Punjabi wheat with those made for the same crop with equations 5.5, showing that for significant ranges of plausible parameter values, Behrman reports negative elasticities, while Raj Krishna calculates positive values, with obviously different policy implications.

Behrman applies equations 5.5 to test the supply response of the marketed surplus of Thai rice, the only crop he examined of which a significant portion is consumed by the farmers themselves. Examination was possible only on a nationwide basis, since many variables were not available on the provincial level.

To obtain price and income elasticities for on-farm consumption of rice, since time series of such consumption do not exist, Behrman considered the following demand function (equation 5.6) for per capita rice consumption for the entire population:

$$C_t = a_o + a_1 \left(\frac{P_1}{P_3}\right)_t + a_2 I_t^n + u_t \tag{5.6}$$

Since two-thirds of Thailand's total population live on rice-producing farms, this approximation seems reasonable. The equation expresses the demand for rice as a linear function of the price of rice in relation to consumption alternatives and of the expected normal income of the consumer (I_t^n). Equation 5.7 expresses a formulation for expected normal income:

$$I_t^n = b_o + I_{t-1}^n + b_1 (I_{t-1} - I_{t-1}^n) + v_t$$

$$= \sum_{i=o}^{\infty} (1 - b_1)^i (b_1 I_{t-1-i} + v_t) \tag{5.7}$$

a Nerlove-type equation that makes expected normal income a function of that of the last period and some proportion of the difference between last period's actual and expected normal income. (A stability condition in this formulation is that the adjustment coefficient b_1 be between 0 and 2.) Substituting equation 5.7 into equation 5.6 yields a reduced form:

$$C_t = a_2 b_o + a_o b_1 + (1 - b_1) C_{t-1} + a_1 \left(\frac{P_1}{P_3}\right)_t - a_1 (1 - b_1) \left(\frac{P_1}{P_3}\right)_{t-1}$$

$$+ a_2 b_1 I_{t-1} + w_t \tag{5.8}$$

Though the structural parameters are overidentified, Behrman estimated the model by making a number of assumptions about the disturbance term and by using nonlinear maximum likelihood estimating procedures.

The results obtained indicated no significant consumption responses to relative price or income changes during the period 1947 to 1962. Behrman suggests this result can be explained either as due to data inadequacies, particularly in regard to changes in rice inventories, or because aggregate rice consumption may not respond significantly to changes in relative prices or income—rather, peasant families, instead of changing total consumption, may shift to cheaper or more expensive grades of rice when faced by relative price or income changes.

Whichever explanation may more exactly represent the actual situation, the estimates obtained indicated using zero as the price and income response (g and h) in equation 5.5d. Using an estimate for the sales ratio $r = 2.375$, and two alternate formulations for nationwide supply [(A), a function of P_t^e, σ_{Y_t} and N_t; and (B) a

function of P_t^e, Y_t^e and σ_{Y_t}], computed time paths for the adjust-

ment of the price elasticity using equation 5.5 (with g and h equal to zero) of market surplus were as shown in Table 5.6.

Behrman says the results suggest three observations. First, if the second formulation better represents the actual situation than the first, then partial adjustment may be of more interest than complete adjustment since the latter may require a rather long time. Second, both sets of estimates for price elasticity of the marketed surplus are positive because total production price response estimates are positive and no counteracting income effects in consumption are observed. And finally, since no counteracting income effects were observed, the estimated price elasticity of the marketed surplus of Thai rice is greater than price elasticity of total supply.

TABLE 5.6

Thai Rice: Time Paths for
Elasticity Adjustment
(years)

Formulation	1	2	3	4	5	10	15	20
(A)	0.43	0.45	0.45	0.45	0.45	0.45	0.45	0.45
(B)	0.40	0.29	0.71	0.61	0.83	0.96	1.00	1.02

Source: Jere Behrman, Supply Response in Underdeveloped Agriculture: A Case Study of Four Major Annual Crops in Thailand, 1937-63 (Amsterdam: North-Holland, 1968).

In another study of food grains, Vahid Nowshirvani examined the planting behavior of peasants in two Indian regions, Bihar state and the eastern half of Uttar Pradesh state, which are among the poorest areas on the subcontinent in the production of rice, wheat, and barley.[4] (For example, 19 of the 40 districts considered by Nowshirvani are in the lowest decile regarding value of farm output per farm family; another 10 fall in the second lowest decile.) Uttar Pradesh generally has a larger proportion of owner-cultivated holdings—77.5 to 95.0 percent in the state's districts, with a median of 88.7 percent—than Bihar, whose districts range from 55.0 to 90.8 percent with a median of 68.3 percent. Similarly, Uttar Pradesh peasants hold somewhat larger farms—with district averages ranging from 3.7 to 13.3 acres around a median of 4.6 acres—than do those of Bihar, where district averages range from 3.4 to 6.3 acres, also with a median of 4.6 acres.

Nowshirvani used a model of modified Nerlovian type:

$$A_t^D = b_1 + b_2 P_t^e + b_3 R_t + b_4 T + u_t \tag{5.9a}$$

$$P_t^e - P_{t-1}^e = \beta \, (P_{t-1} - P_{t-1}^e) + \pi \, (Y_{t-1} - Y_{t-1}^e) \tag{5.9b}$$

$$A_t - A_{t-1} = \gamma \, (A_t^D - A_{t-1}) \tag{5.9c}$$

where: R is rainfall,
        T is a trend variable, and
        Y is crop yield.

The formulation of equation 5.9b allowed consideration that farmers recognize a correlation between harvest conditions and price changes and that, based on their experience, they tend to discount for that part of price change caused by transitory supply abnormalities in forming their price expectations. Regressing separately first differences of prices on first differences of yields indicated that this discounting might be of some significance as far as rice, the most important crop, is concerned, but not in the case of the other two crops.

As far as the problem of distinguishing between the price expectation and area adjustment coefficients (β and γ) is concerned, while the presence of another variable in addition to P^e in the desired acreage equation can overcome the identification problem, Nowshirvani questioned the validity of the assumption that short- and long-run supply response to such a variable is similar to that caused by price or income changes, or to assume that such an additional variable may even provoke both short- and long-run supply responses. To bypass this problem he proposed to identify these two coefficients by imposing restrictions on the disturbance terms, and he used both ordinary least-squares and maximum likelihood procedures to obtain parameter estimates.

Nowshirvani first considered the supply response of what are basically subsistence crops in the two Indian states considered: rice, wheat, and barley; he then contrasted farmer behavior in regard to these crops with that for two crops that are notably important as cash crops in this region: groundnuts and sugarcane. (His results for these crops are summarized in Chapters 7 and 8, respectively.)

Because of data limitations, supply estimates for the pre-World War II period in Uttar Pradesh were performed on the division, rather than the district, level. Table 5.7 lists the districts making up each division. Since postwar price series were available only for a relatively short period, Nowshirvani pooled the data from similar contiguous districts in order to improve the statistical reliability of the resulting parameter estimates. As will be seen in Tables 5.8 through 5.17, pre- and postwar geographical groupings are only in some cases identical. (Since only postwar data were available for Bihar, no similar problem arises in this case.)

As regards rice, very little supply response to price changes was apparent in the analysis of the agricultural history of Uttar Pradesh state using two different formulations in each case—only the rainfall variable proved to be consistently significant.

The long-run elasticities for the period 1909 to 1938, using each of the two supply equation formulations, are listed in Table 5.8.

TABLE 5.7

Uttar Pradesh Divisions

Division	Districts
1	Allahabad, Fatehpur, and Kanpur
2	Banda and Hamirpur
3	Hardoi, Lucknow, Kheri, Rae Bareli, Sitapur, and Unnao
4	Bahraich, Barabanki, Faizabad, Gonda, Partapgarh, and Sultanpur
5	Azamgarh, Basti, Deoria, and Gorakhpur
6	Ballia, Ghazipur, and Jaunpur

Source: Vahid Nowshirvani, "Agricultural Supply in India: Some Theoretical and Empirical Studies" (Ph.D. dissertation, Massachusetts Institute of Technology, 1962).

TABLE 5.8

Supply Elasticities, Uttar Pradesh Rice

Formulation	Division					
	1	2	3	4	5	6
(A)	-0.320	-0.238	-0.193	+0.60	-0.361	-0.35
(B)	-0.312	-0.078	-0.047	+0.50	-0.288	+0.002

Note: (A) indicates the supply model omitting yield; (B) that which includes yield.

Source: Vahid Nowshirvani, "Agricultural Supply in India: Some Theoretical and Empirical Studies" (Ph.D. dissertation, Massachusetts Institute of Technology, 1962).

During the postwar period (1953-62), price response for Uttar Pradesh rice proved similarly insignificant, as did response to rainfall—only the trend variables prove significant in any districts.

Both versions of the supply model (with and without crop yield as a variable) were tested for Bihar state rice output during the postwar period. Generally, price parameters proved to be more statistically significant than in Uttar Pradesh, though exceptions were found. Again both rainfall and yield variables seemed to contribute little to the explanation of output variation, while the trend variables were significant in many districts.

When the supply of wheat was examined in the two states the results were much the same as for rice: There was practically no evidence of any significant supply response of wheat-to-price changes in either state; in the prewar period the estimated coefficients were even negative, though not significantly nonzero (except in one division). Since other studies have indicated that wheat supply emanating from irrigated regions is more price responsive than that from nonirrigated regions, Nowshirvani tested for any notable distinction between the two types of crop land: There was at least some improvement from the price response viewpoint—three divisions showed positive coefficients, though none were significantly nonzero.

The wheat supply parameter estimates for Uttar Pradesh in the pre-World War I and II periods (1909 to 1917 and 1921 to 1938) are shown in Table 5.9, while Table 5.10 lists those calculated for the postwar era. For Bihar, Nowshirvani presented the estimates listed in Table 5.11 for wheat supply between 1952 and 1963 (with the standard errors shown in parentheses).

If we contrast the two states, little difference as far as price responsiveness is apparent. In both the rainfall and trend variables show somewhat more influence on output than do wheat prices.

In Nowshirvani's analysis of the third subsistence crop, barley, a somewhat greater likelihood of positive price responsiveness appeared in both Uttar Pradesh and Bihar. He suggested that the lower variance in barley yield, as compared to the other cereal crops, might explain this tendency; a similar lower variance was noted for wheat in irrigated regions, along with positive price parameter estimates, as indicated above. Pre- and postwar estimated supply coefficients are shown in Tables 5.12 and 5.13 for Uttar Pradesh and in Table 5.14 for postwar Bihar (along with the standard errors).

Summarizing his findings, Nowshirvani pointed out the general insignificance of estimated price coefficients in the supply analysis of subsistence crops and the significance of the same estimates for the cash crops (see Chapters 6 and 8)—the former results being in disagreement with other studies of Indian crop studies, some of

TABLE 5.9

Prewar Estimated Parameters,
Uttar Pradesh Wheat

	Division					
	1	2	3	4	5	6
Constant	394.3[c]	192.3	1,376.3[c]	1,390.8[c]	757.4[c]	115.5[c]
	(109.6)	(160.2)	(442.2)	(223.0)	(223.9)	(33.3)
Price	-16.51	-24.53	-107.16	-88.44[b]	-25.04	-3.26
	(19.57)	(26.27)	(90.03)	(40.31)	(47.54)	(6.97)
Rainfall	2.77	7.36[a]	1.47	0.16	-3.08	0.59
	(1.99)	(3.54)	(3.58)	(3.25)	(6.29)	(1.09)
Time trend	3.75[c]	7.05[c]	3.96	3.67[a]	5.72[b]	1.86[c]
	(.99)	(1.44)	(3.77)	(2.12)	(2.54)	(.36)
Price expectation coefficient	0.70	0.87[b]	0.56	0.80	0.75	0.80
	(.50)	(.37)	(.42)	(5.45)	(.87)	(1.09)
Area adjustment coefficient	1.08[b]	0.74[c]	0.93[a]	0.78	0.55	0.86
	(.47)	(.25)	(.51)	(5.37)	(.81)	(1.07)
$\bar{R}^2$	0.51	0.74	0.30	0.47	0.65	0.69
Long-run price elasticity	-0.31	-0.57	-0.53	-0.43	-0.14	-0.11

[a]10 percent significance level.
[b]5 percent significance level.
[c]1 percent significance level.
  Source: Vahid Nowshirvani, "Agricultural Supply in India: Some Theoretical and Empirical Studies" (Ph.D. dissertation, Massachusetts Institute of Technology, 1962).

TABLE 5.10

Postwar Estimated Parameters, Uttar Pradesh Wheat

	Allahabad, Fatehpur, Kanpur, Partapgarh, Rae Bareli, Sultanpur, and Unnao	Banda and Hamirpur (Division 2)	Bahraich, Barabanki, Faizabad, Gonda, Hardoi, Kheri, and Sitapur	Azamgarh, Basti, Deoria, and Gorakhpur (Division 5)	Ballia, Ghazipur, and Jaunpur (Division 6)
Constant	0.874c	0.921c	0.768c	0.183	0.117
	(.258)	(.154)	(.199)	(.955)	(.536)
Price	-0.004	-0.008	0.015	0.046	0.039
	(.013)	(.008)	(.010)	(.053)	(0.25)
Rainfall	0.089c	0.098b	-0.033	-0.005	0.090
	(.031)	(.041)	(.047)	(.086)	(.065)
Time trend First district	0.020a	0.027c	0.013a	0.038	0.025
	(.011)	(.006)	(.007)	(.032)	(.015)
Time trend Second district	0.012	0.027c	0.009	0.048	0.026
	(.010)	(.006)	(.008)	(.047)	(.015)
Time trend Third district	0.026c	—	0.019a	0.043	0.039a
	(.010)		(.010)	(.042)	(.017)
Time trend Fourth district	0.018a	—	0.010	0.031	—
	(.010)		(.007)	(.031)	
Time trend Fifth district	0.017a	—	0.010	—	—
	(.010)		(.008)		
Time trend Sixth district	0.016	—	0.014	—	—
	(.010)		(.009)		
Time trend Seventh district	0.016a	—	0.010	—	—
	(.009)		(.008)		
Price expectation coefficient	0.648b	1.178c	0.873	1.260b	0.613
	(.253)	(3.70)	(.677)	(4.59)	(.401)
Area adjustment coefficient	0.925c	1.055c	0.773	0.237	0.946b
	(.228)	(.300)	(.684)	(.316)	(.375)
$\bar{R}^2$	0.46	0.72	0.15	0.31	0.43
Long-run price elasticity	-0.077	-0.134	0.237	0.758	0.698

[a]10 percent significance level; [b]5 percent significance level; [c]1 percent significance level.

Source: Vahid Nowshirvani, "Agricultural Supply in India: Some Theoretical and Empirical Studies" (Ph.D. dissertation, Massachusetts Institute of Technology, 1962).

TABLE 5.11

Estimated Parameters, Bihar Wheat

	Bhagalpur, Gaya, Monghya, Patna, and Shahabad	Champaran, Darbhanga, Muzaffarpur, and Saran	Hazaribagh, Palamau, and Santal Parganas
Constant	0.713[c]	1.012[c]	-0.476
	(.148)	(.286)	(.560)
Price	0.003	-0.008	0.019
	(.005)	(.012)	(.020)
Rainfall	0.194[c]	0.089	0.200[c]
	(.051)	(.129)	(.067)
Time trend First district	[d]	0.010 (.009)	0.093[c] (.017)
Time trend Second district	0.005 (.008)	0.015 (.010)	0.073[c] (.016)
Time trend Third district	0.010 (.008)	[d]	0.094[c] (.020)
Time trend Fourth district	[d]	-0.004 (.010)	[d]
Time trend Fifth district	[d]	[d]	[d]
Price expectation coefficient	0.556[c] (.147)	1.341[c] (.210)	0.591[c] (.188)
Area adjustment coefficient	1.341[c] (.123)	0.438[b] (.187)	1.493[c] (.165)
$\bar{R}^2$	0.26	0.10	0.65
Long-run price elasticity	0.078	-0.158	0.408

[a]10 percent significance level.
[b]5 percent significance level.
[c]1 percent significance level.
[d]Estimate not quoted.

Source: Vahid Nowshirvani, "Agricultural Supply in India: Some Theoretical and Empirical Studies" (Ph.D. dissertation, Massachusetts Institute of Technology, 1962).

which are discussed later in this chapter. In trying to explain the complexities and contradictions in the calculations he eliminated as improbable an income effect greater than the substitution effect (which would bring about a backward-bending supply curve), or that the estimation procedures induced biases of sufficient magnitude to make the price coefficient estimates negative, or that choice of inappropriate price deflators is responsible. He suggested that the rather limited success in estimating supply response for food grains indicated that for the postwar period particularly, price changes might largely be overshadowed by other considerations, since governmental development programs and food control measures have had substantial influence over peasant behavior.

TABLE 5.12

Prewar Estimated Parameters, Uttar Pradesh Barley

Districts	Constant	Price	Rainfall	Trend	Price Expec- tation	Area Adjust- ment	Long-run Elas- ticity	R^2
Allahabad, Banda, Hamirpur, Jaunpur, and Kanpur	+0.735* (0.122)	+0.007* (0.037)	+0.359* (0.019)	-0.005* (0.001)	+0.440* (0.126)	+0.843* (0.191)	0.31	0.58

*1 percent significance level.

Source: Vahid Nowshirvani, "Agricultural Supply in India: Some Theoretical and Empirical Studies" (Ph.D. dissertation, Massachusetts Institute of Technology, 1962).

A simple model, like that of Nerlove, based on some sort of a weighted average of past prices, might well be insufficient to explain the formation of price expectations. The extent of commercialization of the crop could be the most plausible explanation of the pattern of the results*—significance of price coefficients appeared for cash crops and also for food grains in those regions where appreciable marketed surpluses have occurred historically. Nowshirvani concluded that price response is indicated in peasant behavior

---

*Nowshirvani contrasted his results with those found by Raj Krishna in his study of the Punjab in this chapter and pointed out that much larger proportions of food crops are marketed in the Punjab than in Uttar Pradesh or Bihar. He concluded that Raj Krishna's findings ought not to be taken as typical of the price responsiveness of Indian subsistence farmers.

TABLE 5.13

Postwar Estimated Parameters, Uttar Pradesh Barley

	Allahabad, Fatehpur, Kanpur, Lucknow, Partapgarh, Rae Bareli, Sultanpur, and Unnao	Bahraich, Barabanki, Faizabad, Gonda, Hardoi, Kheri, and Sitapur	Azamgarh, Basti, Deoria, and Gorakhpur	Ballia, Ghazipur, and Jaunpur
Constant	0.890c	1.091c	0.694c	0.948c
	(0.150)	(0.211)	(0.220)	(0.101)
Price	0.003	0.008	0.050a	0.002
	(0.013	(0.017)	(0.028)	(0.008)
Rainfall	0.060c	0.103	0.005	0.041b
	(0.020)	(0.169)	(0.150)	(0.016)
Trend First district	n.q.	-0.018b (0.009)	-0.029c (0.009)	0.005 (0.003)
Trend Second district	n.q.	-0.019a (0.010)	-0.038c (0.009)	-0.0001 (0.003)
Trend Third district	n.q.	-0.023b (0.011)	-0.031c (0.010)	-0.004 (0.003)
Trend Fourth district	n.q.	-0.019b (0.009)	-0.018b (0.007)	–
Trend Fifth district	n.q.	-0.021b (0.009)	–	–
Trend Sixth district	n.q.	-0.025b (0.010)	–	–
Trend Seventh district	n.q.	-0.016 (0.010)	–	–
Trend Eighth district	n.q.	–	–	–
Price expectation	0.566c	0.856	1.606c	0.984c
	(0.177)	(0.753)	(0.183)	(0.246)
Area adjustment	0.915c	0.733	0.460b	1.211c
	(0.184)	(0.740)	(0.168)	(0.240)
Long-run elasticity	0.037	0.088	0.495	0.025
R^2	0.30	0.26	0.69	0.41

[a]10 percent significance level; [b]5 percent significance level;
[c]1 percent significance level.

n.q. = Estimate not quoted.

Source: Vahid Nowshirvani, "Agricultural Supply in India: Some Theoretical and Empirical Studies" (Ph.D. dissertation, Massachusetts Institute of Technology, 1962).

TABLE 5.14

Estimated Parameters, Bihar Barley

	Bhagalpur, Gaya, Monghya, Patna, and Shahabad	Champaran, Darbhanga, Muzaffarpur, and Saran	Hazaribagh, Palaman, and Santal Parganas
Constant	0.648[c]	0.293	-0.249
	(0.135)	(0.320)	(0.423)
Price	0.011	0.024	0.025
	(0.007)	(0.015)	(0.022)
Rainfall	0.184[c]	0.704[a]	0.210
	(0.050)	(0.400)	(0.157)
Trend First district	-0.003 (0.006)	n.q.	0.067[c] (0.019)
Trend Second district	-0.002 (0.006)	n.q.	0.055[c] (0.018)
Trend Third district	-0.002 (0.007)	n.q.	0.070[c] (0.021)
Trend Fourth district	n.q.	n.q.	n.q.
Trend Fifth district	n.q.	n.q.	n.q.
Price expectation	0.635[c]	1.445[c]	0.820[a]
	(0.185)	(0.174)	(0.449)
Area adjustment	1.129[c]	0.532[c]	1.143[b]
	(0.156)	(0.162)	(0.434)
Long-run elasticity	0.170	0.323	0.395
R^2	0.30	0.12	0.40

n.q. = Estimate not quoted.

[a]10 percent significance level.

[b]5 percent significance level.

[c]1 percent significance level.

Source: Vahid Nowshirvani, "Agricultural Supply in India: Some Theoretical and Empirical Studies" (Ph.D. dissertation, Massachusetts Institute of Technology, 1962).

and that the model he used, simplified because of data limitations, is responsible for much of the inconclusiveness in his studies of food grains.

A farmer who grows both food grains for his own consumption and cash crops must decide what proportion of his land to devote to each crop. Such decisions are similar to those treated in portfolio theory. Nowshirvani constructed a risk model in an attempt to describe these allocative decisions.[5] If P_1, Y_1, P_2, and Y_2 represent, respectively, the prices and yields of the food crop and the cash crop, a, the proportion of land devoted to cultivation of the food crop, M, the amount of manufactured goods, F, the amount of food consumed by the peasant, $\sigma_{P_1}^2$, $\sigma_{Y_1}^2$, and so on, the variances of P_1, Y_1, and so on, and if P_1, P_2, Y_1, and Y_2 are random variables with probability distributions <u>known</u> to the peasant, who is assumed to be a utility maximizer whose utility function is $u = u(M, F)$ and who is subject to the budget constraint:

$$a\, P_1 Y_1 + (1 - a)\, P_2 Y_2 - P_1 F - M = 0 \qquad\qquad (5.10a)$$

then, subject to the first-order conditions

$$\frac{\partial u}{\partial F} - \lambda\, P_1 = 0 \qquad\qquad (5.10b)$$

$$\frac{\partial u}{\partial M} - \lambda = 0 \qquad\qquad (5.10c)$$

where λ is a Lagrange multiplier, a solution for the optimal values of both F and M can be obtained; from these, the optimal value of a can be found.

The solution of utility maximization problems is, of course, easy enough to describe in functional notation, while application of the technique to anything suggesting a real-life situation is something else again. In order to reach some sort of a solution to a peasant allocation decision model under conditions of risk, Nowshirvani made numerous simplifications and assumptions.

His model assumed a utility function that is quadratic in terms of income, given by:

$$u = (1 + b)I + b\, I^2 \qquad\qquad (5.11)$$

where I is total cultivator income with boundary conditions $u(0) = 0$ and $u(-1) = -1$, and restraints on b are $-1 < b < 0$ for risk averters. Assuming that prices and yields are independently distributed, he derived from

$$I = a\, P_1 Y_1 + (1 - a)\, P_2 Y_2 - P_1 \bar{F} \tag{5.12}$$

that

$$\bar{I}_c = \bar{P}_2 \bar{Y}_2 - \bar{P}_1 \bar{F} \tag{5.13}$$

$$\sigma_c^2 = \sigma_{Y_2}^2 (\sigma_{P_2}^2 + \bar{P}_2^2) + \sigma_{P_2}^2 \bar{Y}_2^2 + \sigma_{P_1}^2 \bar{F}^{-2} \tag{5.14}$$

$$\bar{I}_F = \bar{P}_1 \bar{Y}_1 - \bar{P}_1 \bar{F} \tag{5.15}$$

$$\sigma_f^2 = \sigma_{Y_1}^2 (\sigma_{P_1}^2 + \bar{P}_1^2) + \sigma_{P_1}^2 \bar{Y}_1^2 + \sigma_{P_1}^2 \bar{F}^2 - 2\bar{Y}_1 \bar{F}\, \sigma_{P_1}^2 \tag{5.16}$$

where: $\bar{F}$ is the fixed requirement of food,

$\bar{I}_c$ and $\bar{I}_f$ are the expected value of income when all land is in cash or food crops respectively,

σ_c^2 and σ_f^2 are the variances of these expected incomes,

$\bar{Y}_1$ and $\bar{Y}_2$ are the expected value of food and cash crop yields, and

$\sigma_{P_1}^2$ and $\sigma_{P_2}^2$ are the variances of the prices of food and cash crops.

Since the food crop is consumed in large part by the farmers themselves, it is inherently a less-risky venture from the price viewpoint, even when the food and cash crops have similar expected values of prices and variance.

Nowshirvani solved for the optimal value of a, assuming that all prices and yields are independently distributed, and found that:

$$a = \frac{(1+b)(\bar{Y}_2 \bar{P}_2 - \bar{Y}_1 \bar{P}_1) + 2b[(\sigma_{Y_2}^2 + \bar{Y}_2^2)(\sigma_{P_2}^2 + \bar{P}_1^2) + \bar{Y}_1 \bar{F}(\sigma_{P_1}^2 + \bar{P}_1^2) - \bar{Y}_2 \bar{P}_2 \bar{Y}_1 \bar{P}_1 - \bar{Y}_2 \bar{P}_2 \bar{P}_1 \bar{F}]}{2b[(\sigma_{P_1}^2 + \bar{P}_1^2)(\sigma_{Y_1}^2 + \bar{Y}_1^2) + (\sigma_{P_2}^2 + \bar{P}_2^2)(\sigma_{Y_2}^2 + \bar{Y}_2^2) - 2\bar{Y}_1 \bar{P}_1 \bar{Y}_2 \bar{P}_2]} \tag{5.17}$$

Inspection indicates that the denominator is negative, and since a must be positive and less than unity, the numerator must be both negative and smaller in magnitude than the denominator. With this formulation for a, he examined the influence on the proportion of land allocated by the peasant to food crop allocation of changes in expected prices and variances of the prices and yields of the alternate crops.

If, for example, government agencies are engaged in price stabilization schemes (that is, trying to reduce price variances), then the effect of changes in variance can be seen in the following:

$$\frac{da}{d\sigma_{P_1}{}^2} = \frac{2b \ D \ \bar{Y}_1\bar{F} - 2b \ N \ (\sigma_{Y_1}{}^2 + \bar{Y}_1{}^2)}{D^2} \tag{5.18}$$

$$\frac{da}{d\sigma_{P_2}{}^2} = \frac{2b \ (\sigma_{Y_2}{}^2 + \bar{Y}_2{}^2) \ (D - N)}{D^2} \tag{5.19}$$

where N and D stand, respectively, for the numerator and denominator of equation 5.17, and b is negative. In the latter case, clearly $\frac{da}{d\sigma_{P_2}{}^2}$ is positive: therefore stabilization of the price of the <u>cash</u> crops (that is, $\sigma_{P_2}{}^2$ becoming smaller) results in an increase in the portion of available land allocated to this crop—which certainly makes economic sense. In the former case the outcome is less obvious; $\frac{da}{d\sigma_{P_1}{}^2}$ is positive if $\bar{Y}_1\bar{F} > \frac{N}{D}(\sigma_{Y_1}{}^2 + \bar{Y}_1{}^2)$, an inequality more likely to be true the smaller the amount of land allocated to food $(a = \frac{N}{D})$ and the smaller the variance of the yield $(\sigma_{Y_1}{}^2)$ of the food crop. Though this behavior seems perverse, Nowshirvani offered a reasonable explanation. If a farmer has only a small proportion of his land planted in the food crop and thus purchases some of his fixed food requirements, an increase in the variance of food prices increases the variance of his income and he will then prefer to grow more of his own food; should production exceed his consumption requirement there is no difference between the food and cash crops. Thus stabilization of food prices may sometimes lead to reduction in food production—farmers, if assured of stable food prices, may switch to production of higher-return cash crops. Nowshirvani points out that this likelihood has particular ramifications in India, where the government policy of stabilization of retail food prices in rural areas might well have a detrimental effect on food production, and he suggests price stabilization schemes might better be directed at producer prices.

The effects of changes in yield variance are fairly straightforward.

$$\frac{da}{d\sigma_{Y_1}{}^2} = \frac{-2b \ N \ (\sigma_{P_1}{}^2 + \bar{P}_1{}^2)}{D^2} < 0 \tag{5.20}$$

$$\frac{da}{d\sigma_{Y_2}^2} = \frac{2b\,(D - N)\,(\sigma_{P_2}^2 + \bar{P}^2)}{D^2} > 0 \qquad\qquad (5.21)$$

Reductions in the yield variance of either crop will result in an increase in the proportion of land allocated to that crop—an economically sensible prediction.

As regards the effects on a of changes in the expected values of prices and yields, the derivatives show that conclusions are somewhat more difficult to draw, and Nowshirvani suggested that the effects of expectation changes may be easier to see using Tobin's geometrical analysis.[6]

The consequent change in the proportion of land allocated to the cash crop will depend on the relative sizes of the derivatives of income (from cash crops) and income variance with respect to cash crop price. The smaller the variance in cash crop yield, the smaller the change in the variance of income, and the more likely an increase in cash crop area. Higher expected incomes from the food crop due to higher prices for this crop go with lower expected incomes from the cash crop, but the variance of growing the food crop is also raised, and the final outcome can go either way—the lower the food crop yield variance, the more likely a is increased. Finally, increases in yield expectation of either crop lead to increases in the area planted in that crop that are greater the smaller the variability of the price of the crop under consideration.

In summary Nowshirvani argued that if risk is considered in crop supply analysis a negative area response to price may be the result, and that the magnitude of this response is a function of the natural variability of the yield of the crop in question. The lower the yield variability the more likely the area-price response will be positive. He suggested that if crop diversification seems advisable primarily to reduce risk rather than because of physical production reasons, stabilization schemes may well be better than price incentives as policy instruments in provoking crop acreage shifts.

Nowshirvani's results pointing to the fact that the Nerlove model does not, in this case, give good positive price elasticity is one of the few major exceptions to such a finding. The Nowshirvani results could be justified on the grounds that the study was for a poor region in India and thus commercial behavior could be absent. However, many researchers, on not finding positive price response, may have tinkered with the basic Nerlove model until desired results were obtained. Thus the Nowshirvani result may be less of an anomaly than it looks.

If Nowshirvani's results, with no significant positive price
response, are in fact representative of farmers' behavior, then
standard government policy is of little use. That is, increased
crop prices would do little to expand area planted. Under such
circumstances the government might make available other inputs,
such as fertilizer, increased irrigation, pesticides, and new strains
of seed, at little or no cost to the farmer. Furthermore, the
government may undertake policies that would make farmers more
market oriented. In short, policies other than price increases
must be used to increase output.

Uttar Pradesh agriculture was also the concern of R. D. Singh
and Dinkar Rao, who investigated the production of the six principal
food grains grown in the state: rice, wheat, barley, maize, jowar,
and bajra.[7] Their study covers the entire state, unlike that of
Nowshirvani's, which is limited to the poorer eastern districts.

Singh and Rao employed a Nerlovian model but they estimated
an equation framed in logarithmic terms

$$\text{Log } A_t = \log b_0 + b_1 \log P_{t-1} + b_2 \log A_{t-1} + b_3 \log T \qquad (5.22)$$

where: A is acreage;
         P represents prices (expressed in three separate formula-
             tions: (a) presowing wholesale price, (b) postharvest
             wholesale price and (c) annual average farm price); and
         T a trend variable.

An earlier version of the model tested included the price of the
major crop; the authors found little statistical significance was
indicated for the estimated coefficients of this variable and report
only the results they obtained using equation 5.22. The latter
was applied for all crops in the state as a whole, as well as for
four regions: Eastern (15 districts), Western (18 districts),
Central (9 districts), and Bundelkhand (4 districts), but even for
these, 5 percent significance level was only obtained for bajra
(in the Eastern region), jowar (in Bundelkhand), and rice (in the
Western region).

The cultivators of the Western region showed the most consistent
geographic pattern of positive supply response to price, though
most regressions on the statewide level also indicated positive
price coefficients. The strongest elasticities for wheat and barley
as well as the only positive rice response were found for the west,
the state's most important wheat-producing section. Barley, for
which Nowshirvani estimated positive price-output links even for
districts and time periods where little responsiveness was indicated
for rice and wheat, proved somewhat contrary in this study: slightly
negative elasticities for the Eastern region considered by Nowshir-

vani, as well as in the Central and Bunkelkhand regions, though
positive for the Western region and the state as a whole. The
strongest positive elasticities are seen for maize in the Central
region, and maize elasticities are both positive and fairly consistently
statistically significant for the rest of the state. Though statewide
estimates show only small responsiveness for the millets (bajra and
jowar), notably larger elasticities are indicated for some areas,
such as for both crops in Bundelkhand region.

Estimated coefficients for the trend variable were mostly
positive and statistically significant for rice, wheat, and maize,
and negative and significant for barley, bajra, and jowar—which
the authors interpreted as indicative of a gradual tendency of
cultivators to substitute for these latter crops, which are generally
considered inferior to both the other cereals and alternative cash
crops.

In another study of Indian agricultural output, Jawahar Kaul
analyzed five food crops—wheat, gram, bajra, rice, and barley—in
Punjab state, providing supply parameter estimates for both
statewide output, as well as for several districts.[8] (Also considered
were two cash crops—cotton and sugarcane—and Kaul's results for
these are seen in Chapters 6 and 8.) Unlike Uttar Pradesh and
Bihar on which Nowshirvani's study focuses, the Punjab is a very
prosperous agricultural region. Wheat, rather than rice, is the
principal cereal crop, and most of the major crops are as much
raised for the market as for subsistence purposes.

Kaul used a Nerlovian-type acreage adjustment model, including
crop yield, rainfall, and trend variables in his output equation.
Using ordinary least-squares techniques he estimated parameters
for several districts in the state, distinguishing between districts
where irrigation predominated and those where rainfall supplied
most of the moisture. The irrigated districts were Amritsar,
Ferozepur, Ludhiana, Jullundur, Sangrur, and Bhatinda; the rain-fed
districts were Hissar, Karnal, Rohtak, Hoshiarpur, Gurgaon,
Ambala, and Mohendragarh.* For each of the crops he considered

-----

*The percentage of cropped area in each district that was
irrigated is as follows:

Amritsar	88	Hissar	37
Ferozepur	66	Karnal	36
Ludhiana	62	Rohtak	32
Jullundur	62	Hoshiarpur	12
Sangrur	56	Gurgaon	12
Bhatinda	56	Ambala	10
		Mohendragarh	5

separately only those districts in which its cultivation was important.

For the state as a whole, wheat prices proved to be significant
at the 20 percent level or better, whether total or unirrigated
acreage is used as the output variable, but the district-level analysis
showed price a significant variable in only three irrigated districts
(Ludhiana, Jullundur, and Sangrur) and in the irrigated districts
taken as a group. In the rain-fed districts price was never significant, while rainfall was significant at the 5 percent level in three
of these districts plus the rain-fed districts taken as a group.
Short-run price elasticities for the districts range from 0.04 to
0.17, while long-run elasticities are slightly higher, from 0.08
to 0.37.

For gram and bajra, on the other hand, the calculated price
parameters were frequently negative, though never showing much
significance. Kaul did not present a district-by-district breakdown
for the other crops he considered (rice and barley). However, he
commented that rice, which is grown mostly in the high-rainfall
districts of Kangra, Hoshiarpur, and Ambala, had positive though
not significant price coefficients and short- and long-run elasticities
of 0.24 and 0.40, respectively, for the state as a whole. Barley
proved to have the highest elasticity values: 0.53 for the short run
and 0.60 for the long run.

In a later study Kaul, together with D. S. Sidhu, presented
adjustment coefficient and supply elasticity estimates for Punjab
state for the period 1960 to 1969, and these are seen in Table 5.15.[9]

TABLE 5.15

Estimated Parameters, Punjabi Crops

Crop	Area Adjustment Coefficient	Supply Elasticity	
		Short-Run	Long-Run
Wheat	0.14 to 0.17	0.02 to 0.08	0.15 to 0.58
Maize	0.79 to 0.85	0.11 to 0.13	0.14 to 0.16
Rice	0.26 to 0.30	0.19 to 0.24	0.64 to 0.68
Cotton (Desi)	0.53 to 0.58	0.45 to 0.68	0.79 to 1.17
Groundnuts	0.17 to 0.24	0.51 to 0.78	3.05 to 3.25

Source: J. L. Kaul and D. S. Sidhu, "Acreage Response to
Prices for Major Crops in Punjab—An Econometric Study," Indian
Journal of Agricultural Economics 26 (October-December 1971).

A large number of less geographically disaggregated studies of
food crops on the Indo-Pakistani subcontinent have been published,
among them that of Raj Krishna, who examined the price responsiveness shown by cultivators of several irrigation-dependent crops in
India's Punjab province during the inter-World War period.[10]

Using a Nerlovian area adjustment supply model in which output
was expressed in terms of planted irrigated acres and rainfall,
relative price and yield variables were included, he obtained the
parameter estimates (and standard errors) shown in Table 5.16.
Prices show fairly consistent strength in influencing output, though
negative coefficients are indicated for jowar and gram.

A more recent study of Punjabi agriculture has been offered
by C. C. Maji, D. Jha, and L. S. Venkataramanan, who concentrated
on production of the three major cereals—wheat, rice, and maize—
from 1948 to 1965.[11] In their analysis they used a variant of the
Nerlovian area adjustment model, but they take note of Behrman's
attempts to include a measure of risk in the supply function.

A risk-aversion hypothesis holds that rational farmer behavior
is to maximize expected utility by optimizing expected return for a
given level of variance in the expected return. Thus, for example,
an endeavor for which a smaller potential return is likely, but
with smaller variance, might be preferable to a larger potential
return with a larger variance. Behrman used as risk measures
the standard deviations in price and yield over the preceding three
periods; in this study that for price alone was included in some
regressions.

Other variables were harvest prices (included both in absolute
and deflated terms*), prices of alternative crops (used for rice
only), yield of the crop relative to competing crops, and a trend
variable. A measurement of total irrigated area did not prove
significant in most preliminary testing but was reported for rice.
Regressions were run using a logarithmic expression of the acreage
equation, and the resulting estimated elasticities and area adjustment
coefficients are shown in Table 5.17.

The consistently positive estimates for the price parameter
are in line with the results found in other studies of Punjabi cereals
(see Raj Krishna, Kaul, Cummings), but Maji, Jha, and Venkataramanan observed that the notable differences in estimated
coefficients, especially for wheat, depending upon whether absolute
or relative prices were used, indicated a need for more investigation

─────────

*Wheat prices were deflated by the weighted prices of three
competing rabi (spring) season crops, rice and maize by those of
six alternative kharif (summer) season crops.

TABLE 5.16

Estimated Parameters, Punjabi Cereals

Crop	Time Period	Relative Price	Relative Yield	Total Irrigated Acreage	Rainfall	Lagged Planted Irrigated Acreage	Area Adjustment Coefficient	Supply Elasticity		R^2
								Short-Run	Long-Run	
Maize	1914/5 to 1943/4	2.12d (0.51)	—	—	—	0.60d (0.13)	0.40	0.23	0.56	0.79
Rice	1914/5 to 1945/6	3.07d (0.99)	8.01c (3.16)	—	—	0.48d (0.15)	0.52	0.31	0.59	0.79
Bajra	1914/5 to 1945/6	0.03d (0.01)	—	0.17c (0.06)	-0.12c (0.05)	0.76d (0.09)	0.24	0.09	0.36	0.92
Jowar	1914/5 to 1943/4	-4.70a (2.75)	—	-0.30c (0.12)	8.80c (3.85)	—	—	0	-0.58	0.59
Wheat (irrigated)	1914/5 to 1943/4	4.74c (2.08)	—	2.61c (1.18)	—	0.41b (0.24)	0.59	0.08	0.14	0.92
Wheat (unirrigated)	1914/5 to 1943/4	8.44a (4.96)	5.36 (4.19)	—	59.16d (13.20)	—	—	0	0.22	0.71
Gram	1914/5 to 1945/6	-11.48a (7.96)	—	—	111.11d (26.77)	—	—	0	-0.33	0.66
Barley	1914/5 to 1945/6	3.02 (3.59)	—	—	20.50d (6.46)	0.23a (0.17)	0.77	0.39	0.50	0.54

[a]20 percent significance level; [b]10 percent significance level; [c]5 percent significance level; [d]1 percent significance level.

Source: Raj Krishna, "Farm Supply Response in India-Pakistan: A Case Study of the Punjab Region," Economic Journal 73 (September 1963).

TABLE 5.17

Supply Elasticities, Punjabi Cereals

		Elasticity	
Formulation	Adjustment Coefficient	Short-Run	Long-Run
Wheat			
1[a]	0.021	0.109	0.508
2[a]	0.528	0.540	1.023
3[b]	0.997	0.669	0.671
Maize			
1[a]	0.846	0.562	0.664
2[a]	0.820	0.284	0.346
3[b]	0.911	0.494	0.542
Rice			
1[a]	–	0.494	–
2[a]	0.466	0.182	0.390
3[a]	0.866	0.325	0.376
4[b]	0.223	0.150	0.672
5[b]	0.200	0.113	0.565

[a]Relative prices.
[b]Absolute prices.

Source: C. C. Maji, D. Jha, and L. S. Venkataramanan, "Dynamic Supply and Demand Models for Better Estimations and Projections: An Econometric Study for Major Foodgrains in the Punjab Region," Indian Journal of Agricultural Economics 26 (January–March 1971).

of what constitutes the best specification of price expectation. Price-risk coefficients, while showing the expected negative sign, were not very significant in this case; the authors suggested, however, that a more precise representation of risk might result in more statistical significance.

The major crops grown in the truncated southeastern part of Punjab, which has become the state of Haryana, were the subject of a paper by R. P. Singh, Parmatma Singh, and K. N. Rai.[12] They focused on the cultivation of cereals—wheat, barley, rice, maize, gram, and bajra—and two cash crops between 1950 to 1970 (desi cotton and rape and mustard seed; see Chapter 6). The simple explanatory model they used represented area in terms of harvest prices, rainfall in the presowing period, and agricultural technology. The latter was expressed as yield per acre, rather than the simple trend variable used in other studies of India.

The authors reported fairly sizable positive supply elasticities for four crops that were derived from statistically significant estimated price coefficients. Rainfall coefficients were positive and significant in four cases (wheat, barley, rice, and bajra), but in only a single case (maize) did the yield proxy for technology show significance.

In other research into Indian cereal cultivators' supply response, M. S. Rao and Jai Krishna used various models to analyze wheat production in Uttar Pradesh from 1950 to 1962.[13] Their initial effort tested a dozen different formulations of price expectations, with wheat acreage then regressed on wheat prices and a weighted index of competing crop prices (barley, gram, sugarcane, and rape and mustard). Table 5.18 lists these formulations.

Several of these models did not explain much of the annual acreage variation, and wheat prices showed little statistical significance. Using several criteria, including the R^2 values, the authors concluded Models VI and VII are the most promising in explanatory

TABLE 5.18

Expected Price Models, Indian Wheat

Model	Prices
I	Average price during preceding year
II	Three-month average of presowing prices
III	Average price during preceding three years
IV	Three year average of presowing prices
V	Modal price in previous year
VI	Modal price in all preceding years
VII	Average price during all preceding years
VIII	Predicted price from linear trend in realized price
IX	Three-month average of postharvest prices
X	Three-year average of postharvest prices
XI	Average of postharvest and presowing prices
XII	Three year average of postharvest and presowing prices

Source: M. S. Rao and Jai Krishna, "Price Expectation and Acreage Response for Wheat in Uttar Pradesh," Indian Journal of Agricultural Economics 20 (January-March 1965); and "Dynamics of Acreage Allocation for Wheat in Uttar Pradesh: A Study in Supply Response," Indian Journal of Agricultural Economics 22 (January-March 1967).

power but cautioned against putting too much reliance on calculated parameters resulting from any response model, stressing the need to explore the underlying hypotheses regarding price expectations.

In the second phase of their work the authors incorporated several of these price formulations (I, II, V, IX, and XI) into three variants of the basic Nerlovian model. Wheat acreage was expressed as a function of lagged acreage, a weather index and: (A) an index of wheat prices (deflated by those of alternate crops) and per acre wheat yield; (B) (deflated) wheat price index and wheat yield index; and (C) an index of (deflated) gross income from wheat cultivation. They also tested three non-Nerlovian models, identical to these but omitting lagged acreage and estimated supply elasticities and area adjustment coefficients resulting from regressions based on the Nerlove models.

The results using model B were marginally better than the others. Of the other variables included in the models, the weather index proved significant at the 5 percent level or better in 10 out of 15 cases, while yield (and gross-income parameters) never showed significance at even the 10 percent level.

Their results using non-Nerlovian models (not shown) demonstrated uniformly less explanatory power regarding acreage variations, with most values of R^2 falling between 0.50 and 0.57.

In still another analysis of cereals production in the Gangetic plain region of northern India, S. P. Sinha and B. N. Varma could find no significant effect of prices on output in Bihar during the period 1956 to 1968.[14] They concluded only institutional changes are likely to affect positively the supply of food grains.

As part of a major study of long-term agricultural prospects in India, the National Council of Applied Economic Research (NCAER) used a Nerlove dynamic model, among others, to analyze the supply of cereals from 1938 to 1957.[15] (Certain estimates were also reported for cotton, groundnuts, and tobacco; these are reported in Chapter 6.) During this time the boundaries of many states changed radically, and estimated price elasticities were thus reported only for a few states, as well as for a district or two in each. These are seen in Tables 5.19 and 5.20.

Two different variations of the Nerlovian area adjustment model were used by B. L. Sawhney to investigate the supply of jowar and bajra in Bombay state (the present states of Maharashta and Gujarat) during the period 1949 to 1964,[16] and they are described by equations 5.23 and 5.24:

$$A_t = b_0 + b_1 P_{t-1} + b_2 Y_{t-1} + b_3 W_t + b_4 A_{t-1} + u_t \qquad (5.23)$$

$$A_t = c_0 + c_1 (P_{t-1} Y_{t-1}) + c_2 W_t + c_3 A_{t-1} + u_t \qquad (5.24)$$

TABLE 5.19

Supply Elasticities, Indian Cereals

State	Rice	Wheat	Barley
Assam	+0.10	–	–
Bombay	–	+0.64	–
Uttar Pradesh	+0.18	+0.06	+0.16
Orissa	+0.05	–	–
West Bengal	+0.30	–	–
Madras	+0.28	–	–
All-India	+0.22	+0.16	+0.16

Source: National Council of Applied Economic Research, Long-Term Projections of Demand for and Supply of Selected Agricultural Commodities—1960/61 to 1975/76 (New Delhi, 1962).

TABLE 5.20

Supply Elasticities, Selected Indian Districts

State	District	Crop	Elasticity
Assam	Goalpara	Rice	+0.09
Andhra Pradesh	East Godavari	Rice	+0.03
	West Godavari	Rice	+0.11
Bombay	Thana	Rice	+0.07
	Ahmedabad	Wheat	+0.28
	Sholapur	Jowar	+0.50
Madhya Pradesh	Raipur	Rice	+0.04
West Bengal	Midnapore	Rice	+0.24
Madras	Thanjavur	Rice	+0.09

Source: National Council of Applied Economic Research, Long-Term Projections of Demand for and Supply of Selected Agricultural Commodities—1960/61 to 1975/76 (New Delhi, 1962).

where: A_t is crop acreage,
         P_{t-1} is lagged crop price relative to alternate (bajra/jowar,
            groundnuts, and cotton) crop prices,
         Y_{t-1} is lagged crop yield relative to alternate (bajra/jowar,
            groundnuts, and cotton) crop yields,
         $P_{t-1}Y_{t-1}$ is lagged relative gross income per acre,
         W_t is rainfall during the sowing season.
With these two models he estimated the supply parameters. While
both models performed in rather lackluster fashion with these crops,
their explanatory power was notably better with the cash crops
(cotton and groundnuts, whose results are discussed in Chapter 6)
for which it was used.

The responsiveness of acreage in pulses to prices has been
analyzed for Andhra Pradesh state by Tej Bahadur and N. Haridasan.[17] Output of three varieties of gram (red gram, green gram,
and horse gram) was examined for three regions of the state using
a simple linear model. Positive parameter estimates for the price
variable were reported for all regressions, but standard errors
were not indicated; short-run elasticities calculated from the
estimates are shown in Table 5.21 for the period 1957 to 1967.

A detailed study of the agriculture of Madras (Tamil Nadu)
state has been presented by V. Rajagopalan.[18] Madras lies on
the (relatively) rain-rich tropical southeast coast of the subcontinent.
The summer or southwest monsoon sweeps in from the Indian Ocean
from June through August, and then switches in the fall to become
the even heavier northeast monsoon off the Bay of Bengal. During
the earlier period crops are sown in the light soils, and then as
the autumn rains fill tanks and reservoirs, cultivation of the
heavier soils is begun. ("Light" and "heavy" refer to the loam
and clay content of the soil.) Irrigation using well water is also
important in several districts in the state (Coimbatore, Madurai,
Salem, and Tiruchirapalli), and Rajagopalan focuses his attention
on the irrigated crops of the state.

Madras is a heavily populated region, most of whose inhabitants
are members of rural smallholding families; in 1961 the state had
a density of more than 630 persons per square mile, almost 75
percent of whom lived in rural areas, and the average cultivated
area per rural household was only 4.6 acres. Rajagopalan set
out to delineate specific regions of the state on the basis of agro-
climatic characteristics, to estimate supply elasticities of the
food crops rice and the millets cumbu (bajra) and ragi, and of the
cash crops groundnuts, cotton, and sugarcane (which are separately
discussed in Chapters 6 and 8), and to explain any regional differences in these calculations. These crops in 1961 accounted for,
respectively, 35, 7, 5, 13, 5 and 1 percent of the total area sown

TABLE 5.21

Supply Elasticities, Andhra Pradesh Pulses

Region	Red Gram	Green Gram	Horse Gram
Andhra	+0.669	+0.179	+0.259
Rayalseema	+0.255	+0.410	+0.062
Telengana	+0.323	+0.202	+0.291

Source: Tej Bahadur and N. Haridasan, "A Note on the Price-Acreage Responses of Pulses in Andhra Pradesh," Indian Journal of Economics 52 (October 1971).

in the state. Rice, sugarcane, and cotton are the major crops grown on the smaller irrigated farms, and more prosperous peasants can also add millets and pulses in order to balance land use seasonally.

Rajagopalan began his analysis by dividing the state into three regions: (I) four northeastern coastal districts—Chingleput, North and South Arcot, and Thanjavur; (II) four interior districts—Coimbatore, Madurai, Salem, and Tiruchirapalli; and (III) two southeastern coastal districts—Ramanathapuram and Tirunelveli.

The agriculture of Region I depends mostly upon the fall or northeast monsoon. The cropping pattern for both irrigated and unirrigated cultivation is similar throughout the region, with rice, groundnuts, and sugarcane as the principal crops, and canals and tanks being the dominant forms of irrigation. Generally a considerable rice surplus (over local consumption needs) is produced and exported both to the rest of Madras and to neighboring states. Groundnuts are grown both under irrigation and rain-fed conditions, while rice and particularly sugarcane depend upon irrigation facilities.

Region II relies on both monsoons, and well irrigation predominates. Millets, cotton, and rice are the biggest crops, with most of the cotton output going into the region's highly developed textile industry. This plus a number of other industries tends to keep the problems of unemployment and underemployment less severe than in most parts of India, and it has even led to some labor shortages in agriculture and, in consequence, to relatively more mechanized forms of cultivation.

The third region depends mostly upon rain-fed tanks, filled by the northeast monsoon, for irrigation. Millets, rice, and cotton are the most important crops, with rice relatively more important when rains are timely, millets when they are not. Industrial development is not very advanced in this region, and it is the economically most backward part of Madras.

Table 5.22 summarizes some of the more relevant agricultural data of the state and the three regions.

Rajagopalan tested three variants of the basic Nerlovian supply hypothesis, as expressed (in reduced form) by equations 5.25, 5.26, and 5.27:

$$A_t = a_0 + a_1 A_{t-1} + a_2 A_{t-2} + a_3 P_{t-1}^R + a_4 T + u_t \tag{5.25}$$

$$A_t = b_0 + b_1 A_{t-1} + b_2 P_{t-1}^R + b_3 T + u_t \tag{5.26}$$

$$A_t = c_0 + c_1 A_{t-1} + c_2 Y_{t-1} + c_3 P_{t-1} + c_4 P_{t-1}^S + c_5 T + u_t \tag{5.27}$$

where: A_t is total acreage in the crop,

P_{t-1} is lagged absolute crop price,

P_{t-1}^R is lagged relative crop price (deflated by prices of substitutes),

P_{t-1}^S is lagged substitute crop price,

Y_{t-1} is lagged crop yield, and

T is time.

The principal substitutes for each crop in the three regions are shown in Table 5.23.

The hypothesis that underlies equation 5.27, that the adjustment process is of a different form, received little supporting evidence in the regressions undertaken, particularly, as might be expected, in the cases of the subsistence crops. The only exceptions in which the coefficients of A_{t-2} showed any notable statistical significance were for cash crops (to be discussed later); sugarcane, which is not an annual crop, evinced some signs of slower area adjustment. The results that Rajagopalan obtained from estimating the parameters of equations 5.26 and 5.27, which differ from one another in the use of relative versus absolute prices of the reference and substitute crops, showed generally better results (in terms of the amount of variation in acreage explained) when absolute prices equation 5.27 were used. Resulting coefficient estimates (and their standard errors) are shown in Table 5.24 for each of the three regions' food crops analyzed over the period 1939 to 1961.

Overall the results are quite mixed. Evidence for some kind of acreage adjustment process (whether over one year or longer) is present, though in about half the cases the adjustment coefficient is not significantly different from unity. The calculations indicate only occasional influence of prices (in any formulation) on the output

TABLE 5.22

Major Crops, Madras State
(in percent)

	Madras State	Region I	Region II	Region III
Total cultivated area in state	100.0	33.8	49.7	16.5
Region in rice	33.5	55.6	47.6	29.1
State's rice	100.0	58.5	27.2	14.3
Rice irrigated	23.3	25.7	18.1	30.5
Region in cumbu	7.2	3.2	8.9	11.9
State's cumbu	100.0	15.1	57.8	27.1
Cumbu irrigated	14.0	12.3	19.6	3.3
Region in ragi	5.1	4.3	6.6	4.2
State's ragi	100.0	27.7	58.6	13.3
Ragi irrigated	49.6	80.6	34.1	54.9
Region in sugarcane	0.9	1.0	0.9	0.2
State's sugarcane	100.0	42.1	53.9	4.2
Sugarcane irrigated	99.0	100.0	99.5	82.4
Region in groundnuts	11.5	18.9	9.4	3.4
State's groundnuts	100.0	45.9	49.4	4.7
Groundnuts irrigated	2.8	3.1	2.1	7.8
Region in cotton	6.1	0.1	7.0	15.0
State's cotton	100.0	0.8	54.2	45.0
Cotton irrigated	25.1	5.9	36.3	10.1
Yields per acre (lbs.)				
Rice	1,867	1,762	2,023	2,021
Cumbu	852	781	885	825
Ragi	1,264	1,377	1,277	1,015
Sugarcane	6,647	6,387	6,914	5,506
Groundnuts	1,051	1,036	1,064	1,081
Cotton (lint)	271	–	263	280
Average holding per household (acres)	3.4	2.8	3.8	4.5

Source: V. Rajagopalan, "Supply Response for Irrigated Crops in Madras State, India" (Ph.D. dissertation, University of Tennessee, 1967).

TABLE 5.23

Major Crop Substitutes, Madras State

Crop	Region I	Region II	Region III
Rice	Sugarcane and Groundnuts	Sugarcane	Sugarcane
Cumbu	Groundnuts	Groundnuts	Groundnuts and Cotton
Ragi	Groundnuts	Groundnuts	Groundnuts
Sugarcane	Rice	Rice	Rice
Groundnuts	Ragi	Ragi and Rice	Ragi and Rice
Cotton	–	Sugarcane, Groundnuts, and Rice	Sugarcane and Groundnuts

Source: V. Rajagopalan, "Supply Response for Irrigated Crops in Madras State, India" (Ph.D. dissertation, University of Tennessee, 1967).

of food crops (though he found indications of a role for prices in Madras sugar production; see Chapter 8).*

Discussing some of the more unexpected results, Rajagopalan argued that the situation in Region I where ragi seems not to be much affected by ragi prices but positively influenced by the prices of the substitute crop can be plausibly explained by the fact ragi is mainly used for domestic consumption. He speculated that if farmers grow ragi primarily for domestic consumption, rising groundnuts prices may lead to a substitution of unirrigated groundnuts acreage for unirrigated ragi acreage and an increase in irrigated ragi. Though the price data reported for both crops

————

*Due to lack of complete time series for each district, Rajagopalan used statewide average prices to project about half his price series for the districts. He justified this partly on the grounds that during World War II, district prices could not (legally) have varied much from the average statewide price, and the war years constituted about half the years for which he carried out his projections. Perhaps his assumptions about this data were not as reasonable as he believed.

TABLE 5.24

Estimated Parameters, Madras Food Crops

Region	Crop	Model	Lagged Area		Lagged Price[a]		Yield	R^2
			$t-1$	$t-2$	Crop	Substitute		
I	Rice	5.27	0.289[b] (0.215)	—	-4.266 (6.39)	9.80[e] (2.86)	14.74[e] (5.55)	0.424
	Cumbu	5.27	0.100 (0.226)	—	+0.097 (0.205)	0.137 (0.091)	-0.005 (0.112)	0.537
	Ragi	5.26	0.460[e] (0.153)[e]	—	-44.42[e] (11.45)	—	—	0.701
		5.27	0.287 (0.261)	—	-1.415 (1.19)	1.637[d] (0.568)	-0.318 (1.81)	0.722
II	Rice	5.27	-0.202 (0.233)	—	3.18[d] (1.38)	0.530 (0.697)	5.28[e] (1.28)	0.689
	Cumbu	5.25	0.806[e] (0.247)	-0.341[b] (0.255)	-26.71 (25.71)	—	—	0.490
	Ragi	5.26	0.453[d] (0.161)	—	3.36[d] (1.24)	-0.608[c] (0.247)	-1.635[c] (0.674)	0.661
		5.27	0.283[d] (0.116)	—	-0.669[c] (0.319)	-0.420[e] (.087)	-0.122 (0.321)	0.929
III	Rice	5.24	-0.297 (0.236)	—	3.169[b] (2.080)	0.482 (0.936)	1.715 (1.547)	0.219
	Cumbu	5.22	0.227 (0.200)	0.413[c] (0.221)	2.119 (3.086)	—	—	0.252
		5.24	0.310[b] (0.181)	—	0.098 (0.261)	0.305[c] (0.118)	-0.010 (0.027)	0.473
	Ragi	5.24	0.639[e] (0.115)	—	0.150 (0.396)	0.265[c] (0.133)	-2.268[e] (0.529)	0.843

[a]Relative prices for equations 5.22 and 5.23; absolute prices used with equation 5.24; [b]20 percent significance level; [c]10 percent significance level; [d]5 percent significance level; [e]1 percent significance level.

Source: V. Rajagopalan, "Supply Response for Irrigated Crops in Madras State, India" (Ph.D. dissertation, University of Tennessee, 1967).

represents an average of the prices paid for both irrigated and
unirrigated output, in fact a premium is paid for for the <u>unirrigated</u>
output of both crops, and groundnuts, of course, are far more of
a cash crop than is ragi. (For his groundnuts results, see Chapter 6.)
It should be pointed out that the perverse ragi-groundnut relationship
along with a negative ragi output-ragi price link was found only in
Region I. In Region II, where groundnuts are also a major crop,
the statistically significant parameter of groundnuts prices in the
ragi acreage model was negative, as it also was in Region III,
though groundnuts here are a considerably less important crop.

Rajogopalan also considered the effects of income on acreage
changes, in an attempt to learn whether these food crops might be
considered as normal or inferior goods and whether increasing
industrialization and the resultant shifts in demand affected supply
behavior. In Region I income was significant only in the groundnuts
equation; in Region II, only in the case of rice; and in Region III,
for both sugarcane and cotton, and these results are seen in Table
5.25. This income model also pointed to and/or strengthened the
importance of prices as determinants of acreage in these four cases,
and these plus earlier results indicated that the price parameters
show reasonable statistical significance in the cases shown in
Table 5.26.* Rajagopalan then presented elasticity and cross-
elasticity calculations for some of these crops and these are listed
in Table 5.27. He concluded that any regional differences in supply
responsiveness were due to differences in the degree of industrialization, in the source of irrigation water and in the region's dependence
on rainfall, and to government procurement policies. For example,
in the rice surplus Region I, rice prices show no significance in
affecting rice acreage. Might not, Rajagopalan asked, this be due
either to the stifling effect of price controls† on price influences
and/or a tendency for reported data to understate <u>actual</u> prices?
Farmers in the more industrialized Region II showed more price
responsiveness, though, oddly, not as far as cotton was concerned.
Region III, the economically most backward area, displayed, as
would be expected, a generally low degree of market orientation.

───────────

*Rajagopalan uses the 5 percent significance level as his minimum
standard. As a result the elasticities he calculated and which are
presented in Table 5.27 are only for some of the cases for which
we indicate significant price parameters in Table 5.24.

†The Indian government, during the 1950s particularly, has
pursued policies with the intent of assuring cheap and plentiful rice
supplies throughout the country. These have been implemented
with a mixed bag of compulsory price and procurement regulations.

TABLE 5.25

Estimated Parameters, Income Model, Madras Regions

Crop and Region	Measure of Income	Lagged Area	Lagged Price		Income	R^2
			Crop	Substitute		
Groundnuts (I)	National	0.0002	1.181[b]	-0.255	8.91[c]	0.381
		(0.204)	(0.525)	(n.q.)	(2.97)	
	Per capita	-0.038	0.948[b]	-0.324	45.31[c]	0.501
		(0.185)	(0.407)	(1.063)	(11.71)	
Rice (II)	National	0.170	2.544[a]	-0.298	9.04[b]	0.616
		(0.254)	(1.807)	(0.804)	(3.53)	
	Per capita	0.169	2.682[a]	-0.651	41.31[b]	0.597
		(0.261)	(1.844)	(0.801)	(17.58)	
Sugarcane (III)	National	-0.299	0.048[a]	-0.085	0.455[b]	0.778
		(0.245)	(0.033)	(0.085)	(0.200)	
	Per capita	-0.209	0.021	-0.063[c]	1.508[a]	0.749
		(0.252)	(0.030)	(0.008)	(0.912)	
Cotton (III)	National	0.403[b]	0.494[b]	0.251	3.24[b]	0.514
		(0.183)	(0.178)	(0.580)	(1.22)	
	Per capita	0.393[b]	0.389[b]	0.177	+15.27[b]	0.509
		(n.q.)	(n.q.)	(0.579)	(5.88)	

[a] 20 percent significance level.
[b] 5 percent significance level.
[c] 1 percent significance level.

Source: V. Rajagopalan, "Supply Response for Irrigated Crops in Madras State, India" (Ph.D. dissertation, University of Tennessee, 1967).

TABLE 5.26

Price Parameter Significance, Madras Regions

Region	Subsistence Crops			Cash Crops		
	Rice	Cumbu	Ragi	Sugar-cane	Ground-nuts	Cotton
I	no	no	yes	yes	yes	–
II	yes	yes	yes	yes	no	no
III	yes	yes	yes	yes	no	yes

Source: V. Rajagopalan, "Supply Response for Irrigated Crops in Madras State, India" (Ph.D. dissertation, University of Tennessee, 1967).

TABLE 5.27

Estimated Elasticities and Cross-Elasticities, Madras Regions

Crops and Prices		Regions		
		I	II	III
Rice:	rice price	–	0.11	*
	substitutes' price	0.17	–	–
Cumbu:	cumbu price	–	0.83	0.90
	substitutes' price	–	-0.48	–
Ragi:	ragi price	–	*	–
	substitutes' price	0.37	-0.28	*

*Elasticities not calculated by Rajagopalan, but indicated (by the price parameters) to be positive and significantly non-zero at at least the 20 percent level.

Source: V. Rajagopalan, "Supply Response for Irrigated Crops in Madras State, India" (Ph.D. dissertation, University of Tennessee, 1967).

Another multicrop study of Madras was conducted by M. C. Madhavan, who considered the supply of four food crops—rice, sorghum, ragi, and cumbu—and four cash crops (which are discussed in Chapters 6 and 8)—cotton, groundnuts, sesamum, and sugar.[19] Focusing on the postwar period, 1947 to 1965, he used a Nerlovian model expressed in logarithmic terms with crop acreage a function of lagged crop price (deflated by that of a competing crop), lagged yield and acreage of the crop and its competitor, and a rainfall index compiled for the sowing period. Madhavan included in each regression only a single alternate crop, not any kind of weighted average of several alternatives. He reasoned this to be a proper model for Madras where competing crops tend to be few, as well as for a situation where it is desirable to evaluate policies aimed at increasing acreage in one crop at the expense of another. His elasticity estimates and adjustment coefficients are shown in Table 5.28.

TABLE 5.28

Supply Elasticities, Madras Cereals

| Crop | Competing Crop | Elasticity | | Area Adjustment Coefficient |
		Short-Run	Long-Run	
Rice	Ragi	−0.05	−0.07	0.69
	Sugar	+0.03	0.04	0.80
Sorghum	Cumbu	+0.15	+0.21	0.73
	Groundnuts	+0.20	+0.28	0.72
	Cotton	+0.02	+0.03	0.70
Ragi	Rice	+0.09	+0.16	0.57
	Cumbu	+0.15	+0.31	0.48
	Sugar	+0.11	+0.16	0.67
	Groundnuts	+0.13	+0.23	0.56
Cumbu	Sorghum	+0.03	+0.15	0.20
	Ragi	−0.22	−0.73	0.30
	Cotton	−0.14	−0.31	0.45
	Groundnuts	−0.15	−2.50	0.06

Source: M. C. Madhavan, "Acreage Response of Indian Farmers: A Case Study of Tamil Nadu," Indian Journal of Agricultural Economics 27 (January-March 1972).

Price coefficient estimates show statistical significance in the supply of all cereals but rice. The author felt the rice regressions nevertheless showed cultivator responsiveness, since yield proved significant, and Madras government policies had been primarily aimed at increasing rice yields. The negative and significant price parameters indicated for cumbu also seemed logical to Madhavan. He explained that cumbu is perhaps the best dry crop grown almost entirely for subsistence and is thus the rescuer of last resort should the monsoon fail.

Though his results for both cereal and cash crops signified economic rationality in cultivator allocative decisions, he cautioned that farmers most likely are limited in their ability to respond to changes in the terms of trade by the practical realities of the region's overall situation—little possibility of expanding the supply of land exists.

A study of rice cultivation in three districts in Madras state—Madurai, Ramathapuram, and Tiranelveli—by S. R. Subramanian and others between 1937 and 1966 was carried out using a Nerlovian area adjustment model with acreage expressed in terms of lagged rice prices, gross area irrigated, the area planted to sugarcane and to bananas, and lagged rice area.[20] Regression estimates revealed negative and significant coefficients for lagged rice acreage and prices and for area in sugarcane, while the indicated signs for gross irrigated area and area in bananas were positive. The value of R^2 was 0.97.

The authors felt gross irrigated area was of particular importance regarding paddy output because in this area rice depends upon irrigation water, the supplies of which can fluctuate considerably, rather than upon more stable underground water sources. Water supply in fact would act to restrain any positive response in output (for example, to rising prices).

Another recent study of cereals production in India has been reported by A. Parikh.[21] Like his earlier study of cash crops (see Chapter 6), it focuses on the data gathered by Dharm Narain for the period 1900 to 1939,[22] which allowed Parikh to use various formulations of the basic supply model, using lagged acreage, prices (deflated by both a general price index and by prices of competitive crops), proceeds and yields per acre, and total area under all crops, plus weather and a time-trend variable. Some of the models he tested are shown in Table 5.29, and selected parameter estimates obtained from these regressions can be seen in Table 5.30.

As can be seen, price coefficients in many regressions were not significantly different from zero. The only significant price parameter, for wheat in Madhya Pradesh/Berar, was strongly

TABLE 5.29

Supply Models, Indian Cereals

Model	Variables (right-hand side)
A	P_{t-1}, I_{t-1}, W_t, A_{t-1}
B	P_{t-1}, Y_{t-1}, W_t, A_{t-1}
C	P_{t-1}, I_{t-1}, W_t, Z_{t-1}, A_{t-1}
D	P^R_{t-1}, I_{t-1}, W_t, Z_{t-1}, T
E	P_{t-1}, I_{t-1}, W_t, Z_{t-1}, T
F	P_{t-1}, I_{t-1}, W_t, T
G	P_{t-1}, I_{t-1}, A_{t-1}, A_{t-2}
H	P_{t-1}, Y_{t-1}, A_{t-1}, A_{t-2}

Notes: A indicates area, P prices deflated by a general price index, P^R crop prices relative to alternate crop prices, I deflated per acre proceeds, Y per acre yield, W rainfall at sowing time, Z total area under all crops during same season.

Source: A. Parikh, "Farm Supply Response: A Distributed Lag Analysis," Oxford Institute of Statistics Bulletin 33 (1971).

negative. Model A incorporates a measure of net proceeds per acre, and its parameter is both positive and significant, indicating farmers respond positively to economic incentives, if not to the specific impulse of price. In estimates for Bombay/Sind, however, no significance was found for either prices or net proceeds (though what response indicated is negative). Only Punjabi cultivators show positive (if not very sizable) price responsiveness. In all cases the weather variable proved the most notable influence on wheat supply.

Positive price responsiveness (this time significant) is demonstrated by rice cultivators in Bihar/Orissa, while negative significant response was found in Madras. Several models tried for Bengali supply showed little promise of explaining output variations; in particular, coefficients for lagged acreage never proved significant, indicating the area adjustment model's inappropriateness in this case.

The generally weak performance of the various models tested perhaps indicates, more than anything else, the dominance of

TABLE 5.30

Estimated Parameters, Indian Wheat and Rice

Crop/Area	Model	Elasticity		Adjustment Coefficient	R^{2a}
		Short-Run	Long-Run		
Wheat					
Madhya Pradesh/ Berar	A	negative[b]	–	0.54	–
	B	negative[b]	–	0.54	–
	G	–4.68	–8.66	0.56	–
Bombay/Sind	B	–	–	0.42	–
	H	negative[b]	–	0.20	–
Uttar Pradesh	B	–	–	0.65	0.70
	G	negative	–	0.39	–
Punjab	A	+0.06[b]	+0.10	0.63	0.66
	B	positive[b]	–	0.62	0.66
	F	positive[b]	–	–	>0.66
Rice					
Bihar/Orissa	A	+0.24	–	[b]	0.95
	C	+0.16	–	[b]	–
Bengal	E	–	–	–	0.59
Madras	C	–0.14	–0.15	0.82	0.96
	D	–	–	–	0.97

[a]Only a few R^2 values were directly quoted by Parikh.
[b]Indicates value not significantly different from zero.
Source: A Parikh, "Farm Supply Response: A Distributed Lag Analysis," Oxford Institute of Statistics Bulletin 33 (1971).

institutional factors generally unrelated to market agriculture as determinants of subsistence production. That pre-World War II Indian peasants were strongly aware of market incentives as far as cash crops were concerned can be seen in the account Parikh presented in his earlier study (see Chapter 6).

The data base provided by Dharm Narain was also used in a recent study by Sushil Krishna, which looked at the supply responsiveness of the cultivators of two cereals and two cash crops (cotton and jute; see Chapter 6).[23] A Nerlove partial adjustment model was used, and the estimating equation expressed acreage as a function of lagged prices, relative crop yield, total area planted, rainfall, and lagged acreage. Prices were deflated by an index of competing crops, whose yields were used in formulating the

relative yield measure. Both linear and logarithmic versions of
the model were estimated using ordinary least-squares techniques.

In neither case did the relative yield or rainfall variables show
any appreciable degree of statistical significance. Prices seem to
have little evidence on wheat output, but the estimate for Bengali
rice, unlike most others made for pre-Independence Indian cereals,
is statistically significant, with a short-run elasticity of about +0.06,
rising to about +0.19 in the long run.

Walter Falcon used a simplified area adjustment model to
examine wheat and cotton cultivation in West Pakistan from 1933/34
to 1958/59.[24] (His results for cotton are summarized in Chapter 6.)
The price variable included in the output equation was deflated by
a weighted average of five alternative crops (rice, bajra, jowar,
corn, and sugarcane).

Wheat is the major food grain of West Pakistan with as much
as 75 percent of a farm's output being consumed by the cultivator's
family, and to its cultivation is devoted about four times as much
area as cotton, the second most prominent crop. It is grown in
three distinct areas, one of which is rain-fed, the second irrigated,
and the third both rain-fed and irrigated, with more than two-thirds
the acreage irrigated on the average over the period analyzed.
Falcon found that lagged relative prices explained little or none of
the supply variation in rain-fed area but were significant in irrigated
areas; his short-run supply elasticity estimates were zero for
rain-fed wheat, and between 0.1 and 0.2 for irrigated wheat. This
result tallied with Falcon's original hypothesis that the likelihood
of notable price responsiveness was greater in irrigated as opposed
to rain-fed areas because of greater opportunities for crop substitution in the former areas. The rain-fed areas are subject to a
moisture constraint and only one or two substitutes exist.

As part of work more concerned with jute output (in Chapter 6),
Sayed Mushtaq Hussain used a simple linear supply model to estimate
price parameters for rice in East Pakistan (now Bangladesh), where
it accounts for an average of more than 75 percent of the cultivated
acreage in each district.[25] Three different formulations of rice
acreage were used: (A) total acreage in all rice, (B) all rice acreage
relative to all rice and jute acreage combined, and (C) aus (summer)
rice relative to aus rice and jute acreage combined. Aus rice
particularly competes with jute not only for land but also for labor
inputs during both the planting and harvesting periods. The parameter
estimates (and standard errors) he obtained for 1948 to 1963 are
seen in Table 5.31.

As part of a larger study of the factors involved in peasant
responsiveness to price incentives, one of the authors has undertaken an extensive analysis of post-World War II Indo-Pakistani

TABLE 5.31

Estimated Parameters, East Pakistani Rice

Region	Formu-lation	Constant	Price Co-efficient	Short-Run Elasticity	R^2
All East Pakistan	(A)	+1890.57	+79.49[a] (1.38)	0.043	0.18
	(B)	+0.900	+0.024[a] (0.008)	0.030	0.64
	(C)	+0.716	+0.065[a] (0.017)	0.09	0.54
Nine largest jute districts[b]	(B)	+0.855	+0.039[a] (0.011)	0.047	0.65
	(C)	+0.655	+0.083[a] (0.017)	0.12	0.60
Three largest jute districts[b]	(B)	+0.835	+0.036[a] (0.013)	0.045	0.54
	(C)	+0.602	+0.083[a] (0.020)	0.13	0.51

[a]1 percent significance level.

[b]The three largest jute districts are Dacca, Mymensingh, and Faridpur; the next six are Comilla, Rajshahi, Rangpur, Bogra, Pabna, and Jessore.

Source: Sayed Mushtaq Hussain, "A Note on Farmer Response to Price in East Pakistan," Pakistan Development Review 4 (Spring 1964).

agriculture.[26] A Nerlovian supply approach incorporating both price expectations and area adjustment elements was employed. The estimated model was essentially the same as that used by Nowshirvani (see equations 5.9a to c). However, since Nowshirvani had not found much significance for the difference between actual and expected crop yield, and inasmuch as preliminary analysis confirmed these findings, Cummings dropped the yield variable from his supply model, further commenting that available yield data was notably less reliable than that concerning other relevant factors.

Crop acreage thus was postulated as a function of lagged farm harvest-time prices, deflated by a general working-class cost-of-living index, a rainfall index indicating deviation from normal during the period just preceding and during sowing, lagged acreage, and a trend variable. Ordinary least-squares regression techniques were employed, but because of the problem of parameter identification, affecting the expectation and adjustment coefficients, consequent from the formulation of the model, the expectation coefficient was restricted to several values between zero and two. For each specified value a separate regression was run, with the best chosen by the criterion of minimal error sum of squares. Because of this procedure, no measure of statistical significance can be attached to the estimated value of the expectation coefficient. In addition the Cochrane-Orcutt technique was incorporated into the estimating procedure in anticipation of first-order autocorrelation difficulties arising from inclusion of lagged acreage in the estimating equation.

Cummings applied the supply model to acreage data for nine crops: three cereals—rice, wheat, and barley; two fibers—jute and cotton; three oilseeds—groundnuts, sesamum, and rape and mustard seed; and tobacco. The preliminary results he obtained for the cereals are discussed here, while those for the cash crops (jute, cotton, oilseeds, and tobacco) are included in Chapter 6.

Rice is cultivated throughout the subcontinent, claiming more than a fifth of total planted acreage, but its importance varies regionally. It grows best in semitropical climes where rainfall is generous—the extreme south of India, along the west coast, at the head of the Bay of Bengal in the Ganges delta. Extensive irrigation facilities can compensate for a dryer natural climate—thus, much rice is cultivated in river basins like the Sindi region of (West) Pakistan or in Punjab.

It competes only marginally with other cereals but frequently with cash crops—most notably in the context of Cummings' study, with jute in Bengal and surrounding areas. Rice is a crop of almost year-round importance across the subcontinent, with identifiable winter, summer, and autumn crops. Winter and autumn rice are the more important—the former generally in the west, the latter in Bengal, but in some states (Bengal, for example) more than one crop is significant.

This study considered all the major rice-producing regions except Bihar and Uttar Pradesh, which as for the other cereals had already been analyzed by Nowshirvani, and Madhya Pradesh and Orissa, where data problems were encountered. Estimated elasticities for selected major districts are shown in Table 5.32.

The evidence indicated somewhat more influence of prices on rice output than has been found in other studies of the subcontinent, though a majority of the estimated price parameters are negative or statistically insignificant. The most consistent pattern of positive estimates on the district level was found in Andhra Pradesh, Punjab, Tamil Nadu, and (West) Pakistan, while negative responses dominated

TABLE 5.32

Rice Supply Elasticities, Selected Districts

District	Elasticity Short-Run	Elasticity Long-Run	R^2	District	Elasticity Short-Run	Elasticity Long-Run	R^2
Andhra Pradesh				Punjab			
Chittoor	−0.26[a]	−0.30[a]	0.66	Gurdaspur	+0.37[c]	+0.26[c]	0.91
East Godavari	+0.16[b]	+0.17[b]	0.84	Tamil Nadu			
Karimnagar	−0.10	+0.08	0.83	Chingleput	+0.39	+0.42	0.81
Krishna	+0.03	+0.03	0.92	North Arcot	+0.07	+0.12	0.89
Nellore	+0.07	+0.11	0.82	Ramanathapuram	+0.22	+0.26	0.89
Nizamabad	+0.19[c]	+0.38[c]	0.95	South Arcot	+0.14	+0.16	0.86
Srikakulam	+0.09	+0.13	0.71	Thanjavar	−0.27	−0.22	0.8
Visakhapatnam	−0.15	−0.12	0.59	West Bengal			
Warangal, Khamman, and West Godavari	+0.03	+0.03	0.96	Bankura (A)	−0.03	−0.06	0.89
Assam				(W)	+0.04	+0.05	0.12
Darrang	+0.17	+0.12	0.72	Birbhum (W)	−0.015	−0.18	0.20
Garo Hills	−1.38[c]	−1.53[c]	0.48	Burdwan (W)	−0.05	−0.05	0.14
Goalpara	−0.27[b]	−0.42[b]	0.94	Cooch Bihar (A)	+0.30	+0.67	0.66
Kamrup	−0.17[c]	−0.22[c]	0.80	Howrah (W)	−0.01	−0.01	0.18
Lakhimpur	−0.14[a]	−0.12[a]	0.73	Jalpaiguri (W)	+0.07	+0.05	0.70
Cachar, Nowgong, and Sibsagar	+0.07	+0.06	0.88	Malda (A)	+0.15[a]	+0.18[a]	0.29
Gujarat				Midnapore (W)	0	0	0.56
Panch Mahals	−0.04	−0.10	0.49	Murshibad (A)	+0.31[a]	+0.41[a]	0.11
Himachal Pradesh				Nadia (A)	−0.22[c]	−0.22[c]	0.56
Mandi	−0.07[b]	−0.07[b]	0.46	24 Parganas (W)	+0.07[b]	+0.06[b]	0.80
Kerala				Purulia, Dhanbad, and Singhbum	−0.11	−0.34	0.79
Ernakulam, Kottayam, and Trichur	+0.23[c]	+0.26[c]	0.82	East Pakistan			
Trivandram and Kenya Kumari	+0.05	+0.04	0.09	Bakarganj	+0.13[c]	+0.17[c]	n.q.
Malabar and South Kanara	−0.01	−0.01	0.94	Chittagong	−0.18[a]	−0.39[a]	n.q.
Quilon and Allepey	0	0	0.38	Faridpur	−0.25[a]	−0.30[a]	n.q.
Maharashta				Jessore	+0.05	+0.05	n.q.
Bhandara	−0.04	−0.04	0.42	Khulna	+0.10	+0.12	n.q.
Chanda	−0.08[a]	−0.07[a]	0.67	Mymensingh	+0.03	+0.02	n.q.
Kolaba	−0.01	−0.01	0.91	Noakhali	−0.39[c]	−0.35[c]	n.q.
Ratnagiri	+0.02[a]	+0.02[a]	0.79	Rajshahi	−0.13	−0.16	n.q.
Thana	−0.01	−0.01	0.42	Sylhet	+0.17[c]	+0.21[c]	n.q.
Mysore				Typpera	−0.08	−0.09	n.q.
Coorg	−0.03[b]	−0.03[b]	0.96	West Pakistan			
North Kanara	+0.01	+0.91	0.88	Dadu	+0.28[c]	+0.72[c]	n.q.
Shimoga	−0.12[c]	−0.28[c]	0.97	Gujranwala	−0.36	−0.32	n.q.
				Hyderabad	+0.42[a]	+0.23[a]	n.q.
				Jakubabad	−0.06	−0.15	n.q.
				Larkana	−0.06	−0.09	n.q.
				Sheikhupura	−0.24[c]	−0.022[c]	n.q.
				Sibi	+0.13	+0.25	n.q.
				Sukkur	+0.05	+0.06	n.q.
				Thatta	+0.49[c]	+4.90[c]	n.q.

n.q. = Value not quoted.
[a] 30 percent significance level.
[b] 10 percent significance level.
[c] 5 percent significance level.

Source: John Thomas Cummings, "Supply Response in Peasant Agriculture: Price and Non-Price Factors" (Ph.D. dissertation, Tufts University, 1974).

in Assam, Maharashta, and Mysore, other regions showing mixed results.

Both rainfall and trend coefficient estimates were positive and significant in a majority of districts. The supply model performed adequately as a means of explaining acreage variation, using the value of R^2 as a criterion, except in West Bengal. The author commented that this may be due to the competition between rice and jute for inputs and indicated the need for a special formulation of the supply model for this state which would need alternative crop prices. However, such a formulation was not tested.

Wheat is the second most important cereal cultivated in the subcontinent, accounting for nearly 10 percent of planted acreage in India and 40 percent of that in West Pakistan. It is here as elsewhere in the world more a crop of the moderate climatological zones, though it can be successfully cultivated even in arid regions if adequate irrigation facilities are available. Wheat is the predominant cereal found in a wide band stretching from the Pakistani-Afghan border eastward across Punjab and along the Ganges plain into Bihar. It is somewhat secondary to rice but nevertheless important in a large number of districts in central India, particularly in interior Gujarat and Maharashta and in Madhya Pradesh, and is planted as well in those parts of Rajasthan where irrigation is adequate. Irrigated wheat in fact is found in most states—in parts of Punjab, northern Gujarat, and most of Uttar Pradesh, and, of course, throughout (West) Pakistan. Rainfed wheat predominates in interior districts of Maharashta and Mysore, the hillier districts of Punjab, and in the lower Ganges districts of Bihar.

Wheat cultivation overlaps rice in many areas but the two major cereals do not compete for inputs. Alternative crops do include barley in Uttar Pradesh, Punjab, Rajasthan, and West Pakistan; sugarcane and gram in Bihar, Gujarat, and Maharashta; and gram and peas in Punjab and Uttar Pradesh. Application of the supply model yielded the estimated elasticities shown in Table 5.33 for selected districts.

Considerably more indication of positive price responsiveness is found for wheat than for rice in India; only in Maharashta are many statistically significant negative price parameters encountered. However, in West Pakistan, while the aggregate parameter was positive, negative price-acreage links were indicated in districts and divisions that are responsible for about three-fourths of Pakistani wheat. It should be noted that few of these negative estimates are statistically significant.

Both rainfall and trend variables were strongly and positively tied to wheat acreage. The importance of rainfall was, as would be expected, particularly striking for districts in more arid regions

TABLE 5.33

Wheat Supply Elasticities, Selected Districts

District	Elasticity Short-Run	Long-Run	R^2	District	Elasticity Short-Run	Long-Run	R^2
Gujarat				Rajasthan (continued)			
Khaira	+0.50[b]	+0.41	0.39	Bundi	-0.08	-0.11	0.78
				Chittorgarh	-0.27[a]	-0.47[a]	0.87
Himachal Pradesh				Ganganagar	-0.21	-0.29	0.35
Bilaspur	+0.22[a]	+0.42[a]	0.57	Pali	+0.40[c]	+0.55[c]	0.74
Chamba	-0.03	-0.05	0.90	Sawai Madhopur	+0.03	+0.05	0.81
Mandi	-0.06[a]	-0.12[a]	0.95	Tonk	0	0	0.80
Sirmur	-0.01	-0.01	0.42	Udaipur	+0.30	+0.59	0.69
Mahasu and				Jhalawar and			
Kinnaur	-0.12[a]	-0.11[a]	0.84	Mandsaur	-0.39[a]	-0.66[a]	0.76
				Kotah and			
Maharashta				Bhilsa	-0.24[c]	-0.60[c]	0.93
Nagpur	-0.30[c]	-0.56[c]	0.95				
Nasik	-0.02	-0.02	0.34	West Pakistan			
Wardha	-0.11[a]	-0.12[a]	0.83	Attock	-0.33[c]	-0.67[c]	0.52
				Bannu	-0.05	-0.06	0.64
Mysore				D.G. Khan	-0.05	-0.04	0.55
Dharwar	+0.05[a]	+0.06[a]	0.30	D.I. Khan	-0.19	-0.12	0.55
				Gujrat	-0.13[a]	-0.20[a]	0.80
Punjab				Hazara	-0.15[c]	-0.15[c]	0.70
Amritsar	+0.02	+0.02	0.85	Jhang	-0.51[c]	-0.46[c]	0.35
Bhatinda	+0.36[a]	+0.55[a]	0.94	Jhelum	+0.05	+0.09	0.58
Ferozepore	+0.06	+0.08	0.84	Kohat	-0.19	-0.19	0.59
Gurdaspur	-0.04	-0.07	0.72	Kurram	-0.02	-0.02	0.67
Gurgaon	+0.06	+0.07	0.88	Lahore	-0.07	-0.08	0.68
Hoshiapur	-0.14	-0.20	0.35	Loralai	-0.16	-0.19	0.17
Jallundur	+0.33[c]	+0.42[c]	0.93	Lyallpur	-1.22[c]	-1.03[c]	0.69
Kangra	+0.05	+0.03	0.58	Mianwali	+0.49[a]	+0.35[a]	0.51
Kapurthala	+0.05	+0.05	0.94	Montgomery	-0.18[c]	-0.15[c]	0.83
Ludhiana	+0.21[b]	+0.21[b]	0.93	Multan	+0.01	+0.02	0.81
Rohtak	+0.02	+0.02	0.96	Muzzarfarpur	0	0	0.87
Ambala and				North Wazirstan	+0.01	+0.01	0.66
Patiala	+0.14	+0.28	0.59	Peshawar	-0.06	-0.24	0.75
Karnal and				Quetta	-0.09	-0.11	0.20
Sangrur	+0.22[c]	+0.39[c]	0.97	Rawalpindi	-0.05	-0.06	0.75
				Sanghar	+0.04	+0.05	0.61
Rajasthan				Sheikhupura	-0.07	-0.06	0.82
Bharatpur	+0.28[c]	+0.30[c]	0.95	Sialkot	-0.08	-0.07	0.30
Bhilwara	-0.01	-0.02	0.92	Sibi	+0.13[a]	+0.25[a]	0.79

[a]30 percent significance level.
[b]10 percent significance level.
[c]5 percent significance level.

Source: John Thomas Cummings, "Supply Response in Peasant Agriculture: Price and Non-Price Factors" (Ph.D. dissertation, Tufts University, 1974).

such as Rajasthan and West Pakistan. The overall performance of
the supply model in explaining variation in wheat acreage was quite
good; the F statistics (not shown) indicated that the regressions
were significant at the 5 percent level or better for more than
three fourths of the districts.

By comparison with rice and wheat, barley is a minor crop in
both India and West Pakistan. Grown over much the same area as
wheat, barley is commonly regarded as an inferior crop and frequently is grown on land less suitable for wheat. Uttar Pradesh
and Bihar produce about 70 percent of India's barley, and Nowshirvani
analyzed the output of the districts of these states. Cummings
examined the other major regions, Punjab and Rajasthan, which
together produce 20 percent of the national total, plus neighboring
Delhi and Himachal Pradesh, as well as West Pakistan.

When the supply model was applied to the barley data, the
estimated elasticities for selected major producing districts are
as shown in Table 5.34.

TABLE 5.34

Barley Supply Elasticities, Selected Districts

District	Elasticity			District	Elasticity		
	Short-Run	Long-Run	R^2		Short-Run	Long-Run	R^2
Himachal Pradesh				Rajasthan (continued)			
Chamba	-0.63[c]	-0.69[c]	0.58	Ganganagar	+0.86[b]	+0.85[b]	0.23
Mandi	-0.06	-0.06	0.26	Pali	+0.21[b]	+0.22[b]	0.25
Sirmur	+0.04[b]	+0.04[b]	0.47	Sawai Madhopur	+0.41[a]	+0.44[a]	0.53
Mahasu and				Sikar	+0.34[a]	+0.30[a]	0.64
Kennaur	-0.06	-0.10	0.65	Tonk	-0.04	-0.04	0.59
Punjab				Udaipur	+0.10	+0.12	0.65
Bhatinda	+1.20[c]	+1.15[c]	0.91	Ajmer and			
Ferozepore	+0.93[c]	+1.24[c]	0.69	Jaipur	+0.13[b]	+0.15[b]	0.64
Gurdaspur	+0.23[a]	+0.40[a]	0.33	West Pakistan			
Gurgaon	+0.77[c]	+5.92[c]	0.75	Attock	-0.06	-0.08	0.16
Kangra	+0.19	+1.00	0.83	Bannu	+0.90[a]	+0.85[a]	0.55
Mahendragarh	+1.58[c]	+3.95[c]	0.42	Hazara	+0.16[b]	+0.17[b]	0.68
Rajasthan				Kohat	+0.81[c]	+0.63[c]	0.83
Alwar	+0.56[c]	+0.85[c]	0.63	Loralai	+0.48	+0.50	0.62
Bharatpur	+0.21[b]	+0.29[b]	0.72	Mardan	-0.40[b]	-1.74[b]	0.43
Bhilwara	+0.13[a]	+0.16[a]	0.71	Muzzarfarpur	+0.01	+0.01	0.28
Bundi	+0.02	+0.04	0.86	Peshawar	+0.09	+0.24	0.72
Chittorgarh	+0.50[c]	+0.71[c]	0.79	Sialkot	+0.08	+0.06	0.49
Dungarpur	-0.34	-0.36	0.63	Thatta	-0.31[a]	-0.36[a]	0.86

[a]30 percent significance level.
[b]10 percent significance level.
[c]5 percent significance level.

Source: John Thomas Cummings, "Supply Response in Peasant Agriculture: Price and
Non-Price Factors" (Ph.D. dissertation, Tufts University, 1974).

Positive price parameters dominated on both state and district level, with the few negative statistically significant estimates confined to Himachal Pradesh state and to Hyderabad and Khairpur divisions in Pakistan, all of which are definitely minor barley areas. Nowshirvani similarly noted a tendency toward greater market responsiveness in Bihar and Uttar Pradesh for this rather inferior cereal.

Again as for the other cereals, rainfall and trend variables were linked positively to acreage, the former particularly in the drier districts of Rajasthan and Sind. In most political subdivisions, the supply model explained from half to four-fifths of the output variation.

In another article using Indian data for analysis purposes, H. Askari, and J. T. Cummings examined supply models that incorporate crop yield as an independent variable (see Chapter 4).[27] Specifically they considered the model represented by equations 4.2 to 4.4, where yield is represented in expected terms in conformance with the theoretical underpinnings of equation 4.2. Yet adding a fourth relationship to the model, like equation 4.5, in order to explain the formation of yield expectations seriously complicates the estimating problems. As a result some studies have incorporated some exogenous measure of yield, such as the average over some recent period, to the basic supply equation.

The authors held that farmer expectations in this regard depend on more than past yield, since changes in other inputs will affect current yield. Since land is not homogenous, an increase in acreage should show a negative link to yield if poorer-quality land is planted in the crop; positive changes in other inputs as well as in rainfall should generally tend to increase yield. To test this hypothesis they suggested regressing yield on the changes in acreage, nonland inputs, and rainfall, plus yield lagged one year; estimates made from such a procedure could be better than alternative formulations for yield in the supply equations.

Considering first the effects of land quality on yield, the authors encountered data limitations in that no adequate measure of nonland inputs was available. Arguing that since these inputs tended to increase secularly during the period in question, the effect this would have on yield could be erroneously attributed to similarly changing quantities of other factors of production. However, secular movements were not found in the data for rainfall, nor, in the vast majority of the cases tested, for acreage.

The authors concluded that the regression results (for each crop tested, all major states, and a large number of important districts) tended to indicate generally homogeneous land quality, on the margin, in the cultivation of rice and cotton, and declining quality for wheat, groundnuts, and tobacco. For barley and jute, positive returns to land were indicated. They argued that these results were consistent with those found elsewhere for these two crops.*

Predicted yield values then were used in the estimating equation, along with prices and a trend variable; for contrast a formulation of acreage as a function of price, actual yield, rainfall, and a trend variable was also tested (using the same estimation technique). Using various statistical criteria, such as R^2 and F statistic values and the degree of significance indicated in the regressions for the parameter estimates, the authors concluded that the supply model that included "expected" or predicted yield showed superiority over the alternative version in fairly consistent fashion for both cereal and cash crops. (Also included in the study were cotton, jute, and tobacco; for these results see Chapter 6.)

The general problem of price responsiveness was considered by a group of Indian economists meeting under the auspices of the Indian Society of Agricultural Statistics.[28] The group assumed that farmers do in fact respond positively to prices, basing their belief on the body of existing analytic evidence, while allowing for the existence of important and identifiable constraints that dampen the degree of responsiveness. The group aimed at a clarification of the circumstances surrounding the making of policy decisions regarding the use of price incentives in promoting the fulfillment of production targets, especially relative to those that rely on non-price technological factors.

Many of the papers presented reviewed critically the available literature, emphasizing the evidence regarding the importance of technically derived inputs, such as improved crop strains and the greater responsiveness of large farmers (and thus the importance of isolating price incentives aimed at the large majority of Indian cultivators who remain as nearly subsistence farmers).

-----

*Barley, considered to be inferior to its major competitor, wheat, tends to claim the poorer land, yet its cultivators show considerable positive responsiveness to price; increases in the latter call forth both more planting and better land. For jute, much Indian cultivation is in districts where the crop has grown in importance only since the partition of Bengal in 1947 left the major pre-Independence jute regions cut off from Indian factories. Again the crop over time has tended to claim the land best suited for its cultivation. The authors also tested their hypothesis for the "old" jute districts in Bangladesh; in all cases decreasing returns to land were found.

Three briefly summarized papers touched on the question of price responsiveness directly. Ms. Sud examined wheat acreage in the Punjabi district of Ludhiana, using several simple and Nerlove-type supply models that incorporated harvest prices of wheat and gram (or the relative price of wheat to gram), irrigated area, crop yield, and lagged acreage on the right-hand side of the estimating equation. Her conclusions were that lagged acreage did not add much to the overall explanatory power of the model, while its inclusion tended to lessen the significance indicated for the price and yield coefficients.

A second study by Ms. R. Thamarajakshi focused on the marketed surplus of food grains between 1951 and 1965. A simple supply model was tested using ordinary least-squares techniques, which indicated a negative responsiveness to price of the aggregated marketed outputs of rice, wheat, jowar, and grain.

Finally, V. Rajagopalan and A. Sennimalai discussed the use of three methods—a simple approach, the adaptive expectation, and lagged adjustment models—to explain cotton output variation in the Coimbatore district of Tamil Nadu between 1941 and 1966. They concluded the last method seemed most satisfactory.

Turning to other parts of Asia, M. Mangahas, A. E. Recto, and V. W. Ruttan examined the supply of rice and maize in the Philippines.[29] These two crops dominate Filipino agriculture, accounting for more than 60 percent of the total annual cultivated acreage. Because each is both a subsistence and a cash crop, the authors postulate a model based on marketable surplus, following Krishnan (see Chapter 1):

$$M_t = Q_t - C_t \tag{5.28}$$

where: M is the actual marketed surplus,
         Q is the actual output, and
         C is actual home consumption by cultivators,
and where Q_t^D, the desired output is represented as

$$Q_t^D = f(P_t^e,\ F_t^e,\ A_t^e,\ T_t^e) \tag{5.29}$$

with P_t^e being the expected harvest price of rice or maize,

F_t^e being the expected factor prices,

A_t^e being an index of expected prices of alternative crops, and

T_t^e being a measure of the expected technological response of the subsistence crop relative to alternative crops.

The authors were interested in identifying any interregional differences in price responsiveness and hypothesized initially that greater responsiveness would be found in the frontier areas (the Cagayan Valley and northern and eastern Mindanao) where settlement has been greatly expanded since World War II.

Both simple and distributed lag linear models were used, with three different formulations in each case: (A) lagged product price P_{t-1} and lagged index of all alternative crops C_{t-1} entered as separate variables; (B) using the ratio $\dfrac{P_{t-1}}{C_{t-1}}$ where C_{t-1} is the lagged price of the most important alternative crop; (C) using the same ratio but with C_{t-1} as the lagged index of all alternative crops (employed in the regression analysis of maize). Lagged wage rates for hired agricultural workers, the lagged index of the ratio of the yield of rough rice to the yield of the alternative crop or crops, and a trend variable were the other variables. The first formulation yielded poor results, probably due to the multicollinearity indicated between rice and maize prices and the alternative crop price index. For rice the second formulation gave much better results, and generally the simple models performed better than the distributed lag models when evaluated in terms of statistical significance, sign, and stability of the price coefficient. The third formulation produced better results for maize, with the simple and distributed lag models working equally well.

For the frontier regions the authors obtained no acceptable statistically significant price coefficients for either rice or maize, and acreage response was apparently dominated by technology or the trend variable. Thus they found no confirmation for their initial hypothesis concerning the likely greater price responsiveness in the newly settled areas.

Prices were significant regarding rice acreage in the other regions, with lagged factor prices significant only in eastern Visayas, technology in Ilocos, southern Tagalog, Bicol, eastern and western Visayas, and southern and western Mindanao, and the trend variable in Ilocos, southern Tagalog, western Visayas, and southern and western Mindanao. In addition to prices maize acreage was significantly influenced by factor prices in Ilocos, eastern Visayas, and southern and western Mindanao, and by the trend variable in all nine regions.

They concluded generally that the supply elasticity of rice and maize is highest in areas with access to strong commercial markets, and for rice in areas with extensive irrigation development (notably central Luzon and Bicol). Since short-run rice elasticities are generally higher than those of maize, and since the marketed portion

of the rice crop is greater (37 to 65 percent) than that of maize
(19 to 40 percent), the authors found support for the expected coincidence of greater responsiveness with greater market orientation.

The authors also computed rough estimates of the marketed
surplus elasticities, using Raj Krishna's formulation:

$$E_{M_t P_t} = E_{Q_t P_t} \left[\frac{Q_t}{M_t} \right] + E_{C_t P_t} \left[1 - \frac{Q_t}{M_t} \right] \tag{5.30}$$

where: $E_{Q_t P_t}$ and $E_{C_t P_t}$ are the price elasticities of output and

home consumption respectively, and

$\frac{Q_t}{M_t}$ is the inverse of the average marketed proportion.

A minimum value for $E_{M_t P_t}$ can be estimated by disregarding the
price elasticity of home consumption (which is assumed to be
negative anyway) and using the acreage elasticity as a lower limit
for output elasticity. These estimates are listed in Table 5.35.
With a notably smaller proportion (M_t/Q_t) of the maize crop being
marketed, its marketed surplus price elasticities are generally
higher than those of rice.

In analyzing these results the authors conceded that the price
mechanism is fairly efficient in fulfilling its resource allocation
role as far as intercrop cultivation relationships are concerned,
but since they found neither much evidence of any positive relationship between prices and total agricultural output nor any measurable
yield response to price, they were less optimistic about the role
that prices play in overall Philippine development.

The behavior of rice cultivators in neighboring Indonesia has
been analyzed by Mubyarto.[30] The Indonesian archipelago, spread
over about three-fourths the land area of the United States, is
largely volcanic, endowing the nation with generous amounts of
highly fertile soils. This considerably eases the problems a nation
of 125 million and an annual population growth rate close to 3 percent
faces merely in order to feed itself, but the highly asymmetric
geographic distribution of the population nevertheless causes
continual pressure on the available agricultural resources. Well
over three-fifths the populace is crowded into about 7 percent of
the land area, the island of Java, giving this most favorably endowed
(as regards soils) of the major islands a density of more than 1,500
people per square mile. Mubyarto focused his study on Java and
adjacent Madura.

TABLE 5.35

Marketed Surplus Elasticities, Philippine Rice and Maize

Region	Rice			Maize		
	Formu-lation*	Average Marketed Proportion	Elasticity (low estimate)	Formu-lation*	Average Marketed Proportion	Elasticity (low estimate)
Ilocos	B	0.37	0.30 to 0.62	A, B, C	0.24	0.17 to 0.33
Cagayan Valley	A, B, C	0.40	negative	B	0.36	0.47
Central Luzon	B	0.65	0.20 to 0.85	A, B, C	0.26	negative
Southern Tagalog	B	0.50	0.38 to 1.28	A, B, C	0.34	0.88 to 1.76
Bicol	B	0.49	0.78 to 0.84	A, C	0.38	0.42 to 0.76
Eastern Visayas	A, B	0.43	0.34 to 0.81	B	0.27	1.85 to 2.48
Western Visayas	B	0.51	0.18 to 0.96	A, B	0.19	2.21 to 2.58
Northern and Eastern Mindanao	B	0.54	0.39 to 0.41	A, B, C	0.40	negative
Southern and Western Mindanao	B	0.44	0.57 to 0.77	A, B	0.38	0.28 to 0.34

*Formulation indicates from which regressions the price elasticity ranges were taken.

Source: Mahar Mangahas, Aida E. Recto, and V. W. Ruttan, "Price and Market Relationships for Rice and Corn in the Philippines," Journal of Farm Economics 48 (August 1966): 685–703.

Two crops a year is the rule, with three not exceptional, throughout both islands, with rice grown extensively in the wet winter months
and in lesser amounts during the dry season where irrigation facilities are available, along with a variety of crops needing less water.
With more than 80 percent of the population engaged in agriculture,
Java-Madura is obviously a region of smallholders. In 1959, 78
percent of the farmers cultivated plots smaller than half a hectare
(about 1.2 acres), with less than .05 percent of them holding five
or more hectares. Subsistence agriculture naturally dominates,
and the marketable surplus of the major food crop, rice, is generally
small relative to total output. In recent years Indonesia has had
to import an average of more than 10 percent of her total rice
requirements annually, a proportion tending to increase as urban
concentrations grow. A chronic inability to feed her own population
threatens the nation's economic development schemes and even
raises the specter of a serious deterioration in the standard of
living.

Mubyarto was concerned with the influences of price on marketable surplus, and he examined the behavior of cultivators particularly
in those regions producing a rice surplus. Most rice in Java-Madura
(about 82 percent) is grown during the wet season, though dry rice
increases in importance as demand soars with population. Mubyarto
postulated an acreage response model for each season, as seen in
equations 5.31a and 5.31b:

Wet Season: $A_{W_t} = b_1 + b_2 P_{t-1} + b_3 R_t + b_4 \overline{A}_t + b_5 T + u_t$

$$(5.31a)$$

Dry Season: $A_{D_t} = c_1 + c_2 P_{t-1} + c_3 R_t + c_4 Q_{W_{t-1}} + c_5 T + u_t$

$$(5.31b)$$

where: A_{W_t} is the total wet season rice acreage (January through
August),

A_{D_t} is the total dry season rice acreage (September to
December),

P_{t-1} is the price of rice deflated by an index of the prices
of goods commonly used by peasants (salt, coconut
oil, dry salted fish, and three low-quality textiles),

R_t is rainfall (November to June for wet, July to October
for dry),

$\overline{A}_t$ is the standing acreage on December 31 of the previous
year,

$Q_{W_{t-1}}$ is the rice production in the previous wet season, and

T is a time-trend variable.

The parameters of these models as well as for similar output and yield formulations were estimated. Both output and yield equations were expressed in logarithmic form, with output as a function of prices, rainfall, and time trend, and yield as a function of the same variables plus standing acreage on December 31 for the wet season and on August 31 for the dry crop. The parameters (and standard errors) calculated for the Java-Madura region as a whole during 1951 to 1962 are seen in Table 5.36.

Mubyarto also examined acreage response to prices on a more disaggregated basis, computing parameters for five regencies or provinces. Since acreage data was not available in a seasonal break-

TABLE 5.36

Estimated Parameters, Java-Madura Rice

Season	Independent Variable	Lagged Price	Standing Rice Acreage[a]	Previous Wet Season Rice	R^2
Wet	Acreage	0.048	0.052[d]	—	0.732
		(0.065)	(0.015)		
Dry	Acreage	0.080	1.049[d]	-0.197	0.999
		(0.061)	(0.037)	(0.170)	
Wet	Yield	0.203[b]	-0.040	—	0.894
		(0.099)	(0.023)		
Dry	Yield	0.059[b]	0.294[c]	—	0.805
		(0.029)	(0.122)		
Wet	Output	0.326[b]	—	—	0.878
		(0.155)			
Dry	Output	-0.253	-1.162	—	0.883
		(0.516)	(1.496)		

[a]On December 31 for the wet season; on August 31 for the dry season.

[b]10 percent significance level.

[c]5 percent significance level.

[d]1 percent significance level.

Source: Mubyarto, "The Elasticity of Marketable Surplus of Rice in Indonesia: A Study of Java-Madura" (Ph.D. dissertation, Iowa State University, 1965).

down for the regencies, distinction between wet and dry crops was
not possible. Table 5.37 summarizes the results. Though the
models tested for the most part explain a considerable part of the
variation of the dependent variables, in only five cases did the
price parameter prove to be statistically significant at even the
10 percent level, and in Tjilatjap regency the significant parameter
proved to be negative.

Mubyarto calculated the price elasticity of acreage to be about
0.30 for the region as a whole; since the yield and output models
were logarithmic, the calculated parameters represent the elasticities directly. Though he did not indicate elasticities for the
individual regencies, he pointed out that the region for which the
price parameter (and also the elasticity) is the most sizable,
Wonosobo, is somewhat different from the rest of the region. For
example, maize, not rice, is the principal food crop raised in
Wonosobo, and the regency is the location of a highly successful
U.S. AID-sponsored experimental project for the improvement
of maize productivity through intensive use of fertilizers and other
means.

TABLE 5.37

Estimated Price Parameters, Rice,
Indonesian Regencies

Regency	Price Coefficient	R^2
Krawang	0.030 (0.066)	0.851
Tjianjur	−0.024 (0.145)	0.765
Tjilatjap	−0.126[a] (0.068)	0.810
Wonosobo	0.565[b] (0.187)	0.577
Djember	−0.032 (0.0019)	0.798

[a] 10 percent significance level.
[b] 1 percent significance level.

Source: Mubyarto, "The Elasticity of Marketable Surplus of
Rice in Indonesia: A Study of Java-Madura" (Ph.D. dissertation,
Iowa State University, 1965).

Since the author's prime concern was with the marketable surplus of rice, his study included attempts to estimate the price and income elasticities of demand for rice by cultivator families. He applied his results to a microeconomic survey of some 560 families in Jogjakarta and Krawang regencies. In three of the four geographic subgroups into which he divided his observations, he found an inverse relationship between the proportion of output marketed (M/Q) and the elasticity of marketable surplus, and these results are shown in Table 5.38.

Mubyarto interpreted these results as lending support to the minimum cash requirement version of the marketable surplus hypothesis, in the sense that the "less commercialized" farmer with limited cash income is more (positively) responsive to cash incentives because of his stronger need for cash income, though most interpretations of this sort of peasant behavior involve a negative responsiveness of sales to prices in order to meet a cash target. Mubyarto's evidence would seem to be more indicative of farmers who adjust their cash goals upward with price increases, while those who normally sell less of their output and thus realize less cash in a "typical" year are more eager to take advantage of higher prices, perhaps to make purchases that would be impossible, or to pay debts incurred, in less favorable years.

Thus, even Mubyarto's "less commercialized" peasants might be quite market oriented, though subsistence requirements hinder their participation therein, except when higher prices have a positive income effect on their demand for nonrice goods. The "more commercialized" farmers, on the other hand, have perhaps less need to postpone purchases until better years, and thus react less enthusiastically to price increases. Furthermore, since they normally keep only a small part of output for their own use, they are less willing or able to reduce their rice consumption in high-price years.

That "economic rationality" is not universal in Indonesia, though, is indicated by the elasticities calculated for the third subgroup in Jogjakarta. This group, incidentally, is made up of families whose average size is larger and average income lower than those of the other subgroups.

The importance of rice in Asian lives is underlined by a study by Virach Aromdee.[31] Similar concerns have impressed innumerable Asian economists in recent decades, and their analyses, like Aromdee's, have often been multifaceted, considering both demand and supply, domestic production and imports.

Malaysia is one of Asia's more economically advanced nations, and its economy is strongly dependent upon primary products, tin and rubber, that presently face a very uncertain future in world

TABLE 5.38

Elasticity of Marketable Surplus,
Indonesian Rice

| M/Q | Regency Subgroup | | | |
	Jogjakarta No. 1	Jogjakarta No. 2	Jogjakarta No. 3	Krawang
77%	0.436	0.409	0.190	0.453
48%	0.533	0.433	-1.030	0.595
12%	1.320	0.628	-9.480	1.745

Source: Mubyarto, "The Elasticity of Marketable Surplus of Rice in Indonesia: A Study of Java-Madura" (Ph.D. dissertation, Iowa State University, 1965).

export markets. Maintenance of the nation's standard of living, let alone its advance, must depend upon whether Malaysia can come to feed herself. The 1950s saw a 3.5 to 4 percent annual increase in rice production, notably ahead of population growth, and much of this advance was due to considerable improvement in yield (about 2 percent a year). Malaysia's average yield in the early 1960s—more than 2,500 kilograms per hectare—was better than 60 percent above that prevailing in her two principal import sources, Burma and Thailand.

Malaysia's self-sufficiency program has involved an emphasis on technological advances and has been continually challenged by the growth in national income and in consumption demand accompanying the general rise in living standards.

Aromdee used a Nerlovian area adjustment model along with others to estimate domestic rice supply. His results are shown in Table 5.39. These short-run supply elasticities are comparable in magnitude with those of neighboring countries.*

Aromdee also undertook a wider study of rice supply in southeast Asia, with particular emphasis on Thailand, the principal exporter in the region, and two of her most important customers, Malaysia and Japan.[32] An average of 30 percent of Thai rice has been exported annually during the postwar period, and rice has been an erratic but growing source of needed foreign exchange.

———

*See, for example, Behrman for Thailand, Mangahas et al. for the Philippines, and Mubyarto for Indonesia.

In examining Thai output from 1951 to 1965, Aromdee employed several approaches. Shown in Table 5.40 are parameters estimated using four different formulations: Nerlovian models (A, B, and C) with acreage variously defined in terms of lagged (deflated) prices, lagged acreage, population, and a trend variable, and a simple nonadjustment model (D). Though formulation C explained the highest degree of variation, Aromdee indicated that there was also quite a notable amount of multicollinearity found between the population and time variables, thus lessening the accuracy of the calculated parameters. For this reason he favored formulations A and B. In these the negative parameters for lagged areas (implying an area adjustment coefficient greater than unity) are statistically significant, allowing the assumption that the adjustment coefficient is equal to one.

In comparing his results with Behrman's, Aromdee found reasonable agreement—namely, his values of about 0.4 (short-run) and 0.3 (long-run) versus Behrman's of about 0.2 (short-run) and 0.2 to 0.4 (long-run). He suggested his own model's performance (as judged by R^2 values) might be improved if variation in rainfall could be included.[33]

Examination of Thailand's chief customers required analysis of rice supply in these countries as well. An acreage and an output model was estimated for West Malaysia from 1951 to 1965, with the results seen in Table 5.39. Though the reliability attached to the estimates of the price parameters he obtained is obviously a

TABLE 5.39

Estimated Parameters, Malaysian Rice

Model	Lagged Price Parameter	Lagged Area Parameter	Price Elasticity		R^2
			Short-Run	Long-Run	
Nerlovian area adjustment	4.68[a]	0.83[b]	0.23	1.35	0.61
Total output supply	7.22	—	0.25	—	—

[a]30 percent significance level.
[b]5 percent significance level.

Source: Virach Aromdee, "Can West Malaysia become Self-sufficient in Rice by 1975?" Malayan Economic Review 14 (October 1969).

TABLE 5.40

Estimated Parameters, Thai Rice

Formu-lation	Constant	Deflated Prices	Lagged Area	Popu-lation	Time Trend	R^2	Elasticity Short-Run	Elasticity Long-Run
A	325.6	209.0[a] (132.0)	-0.27 (0.30)	0.18[c] (0.06)	–	0.48	0.39	0.31
B	3614.5	190.4 (142.7)	-0.16 (0.30)	–	110.8[c] (44.3)	0.40	0.36	0.31
C	-18708.8	167.5[a] (104.9)	-0.56[c] (0.26)	1.23[d] (0.38)	-738.1[c] (264.7)	0.71	0.31	0.20
D	-11851.6	103.4 (119.3)	–	0.77[b] (0.38)	-460.3[a] (277.9)	0.55	0.19	–

[a]20 percent significance level.
[b]10 percent significance level.
[c]5 percent significance level.
[d]1 percent significance level.

Source: Virach Aromdee, "Economics of Rice Trade among the Countries of Southeast Asia" (Ph.D. dissertation, University of Minnesota, 1968).

limiting factor, Aromdee felt that 0.23 is a conservative low-limit estimate for short-run elasticity.

A similar supply analysis was carried out for Japan during the same time period. Little statistical evidence for a significant role for prices in influencing output was found using an acreage model (in a regression with an R^2 of 0.78), indicating both short- and long-run price elasticities of acreage little more than zero. Aromdee held this result to be reasonable, pointing out that during the decade 1955 to 1965 an increase of rice prices of about 50 percent saw an increase in acreage of barely 1 percent. Any production increases in land-scarce Japan in recent years have been almost entirely on the yield side; however, Aromdee did not test an output model for Japan as he did for Thailand and Malaysia, and so could not present any most likely interesting indications of the effect of price incentives on Japanese farmers, who, though severely restricted as regards area available for cultivation, can make use of a wide range of yield-enhancing techniques. (Aromdee did test a yield model for Japan, but he regressed yield only on a trend variable.) During the period in question rice output rose by some 3.0 percent annually, mostly because of yield increases.

That identification of the magnitude of price effects on farmer behavior would be useful in the Japanese case is indicated when it is recalled that Japan, like most industrial states, subsidizes the

agricultural sector extensively through the mechanism of government
support prices. In 1965, for example, the support price of rice was
over $300 per ton, almost two and one-half times the world average
export price. Though, undoubtedly, high price support prices
would be dictated for the future by the political reality of a Japan
ruled for now more than 25 years by a conservative political coalition
in which rural interests play a strong role, no clue is offered by
Aromdee's study as to whether these subsidies are in any way
economically justifiable.

While Malaysia and Japan are Thailand's principal Asian
customers that are themselves rice producers, other countries
are also important, as can be seen in Table 5.41. Though Aromdee
discussed the likely future demand of these countries for Thai rice,
he did not examine their domestic supply conditions to the extent
he did for Malaysia and Japan. Thailand's relative decline as a
rice exporter (from 33 to 27 percent of the world market) between
1951 and 1965 is explained in terms of the growing U.S. and Chinese
roles, but lack of data and/or relevance precluded consideration
of supply conditions in those countries.

Land reform has been a burning issue across the Middle East
for more than 20 years, and in a recent study H. Askari, J. T.
Cummings, and B. Harik proposed using Nerlove-type supply
analyses as a means of determining the effects of land reform on

TABLE 5.41

Export Sales of Thai Rice, by Destination
(in percent)

Country	1951	1958	1965
Ceylon	2.8	0.6	8.5
India	13.3	2.6	11.0
Hong Kong	12.1	14.6	10.3
South Korea	1.6	0.3	0
Philippines	6.4	4.0	6.6
West Malaysia/Singapore	28.4	32.1	20.3
Indonesia	11.1	11.3	5.5
Japan	19.4	3.8	7.4
Rest of world	4.8	30.6	31.2

Source: Virach Aromdee, "Economics of Rice Trade among
the Countries of Southeast Asia" (Ph.D. dissertation, University
of Minnesota, 1968).

peasant supply responsiveness to price incentives.[34] Five countries
(Egypt, Syria, Iraq, Jordan, and Lebanon) were involved in the study:
The first three have undergone extensive land-reform programs,
while the latter two were included for possible contrast. In an
attempt to discern patterns across this disparate group, the major
crops of each country were incorporated into the analysis. These
incorporated not only several cereals, forage crops, and pulses,
the most important produce of the region, but a number of vegetables
and other cash crops as well (see Chapter 6 for cotton, oilseeds,
and vegetables).

Output was expressed in Nerlove terms: lagged prices, available
water supply, a trend variable to represent changes over time in
the technology of other inputs, and lagged output. The dependent
variable was included in two forms: acreage and yield. The authors
felt the latter was the more relevant output variable in Egypt, where
the land constraint was severe, while in Syria, Iraq, and Jordan
the availability of ample amounts of marginal land would portend
a reverse relationship between planted acreage and crop yield for
most major crops. They anticipated that in such cases price
responsiveness would show opposite signs in the price and yield
variants of the supply model, an expectation borne out for most
relevant cases.

The authors argued that if land reform had a favorable effect
on the market responsiveness of the peasantry, supply elasticities
should indicate a shift toward greater positive (or less negative)
values after land reform. Though the relatively short time series
available for Syria and Iraq hampered their statistical analysis,
the authors felt their study indicated generally favorable results
following land reform, though general output statistics showed little
or no improvement following land reform efforts in Iraq, and to
some extent in Syria as well. Generally, price responsiveness was
slight in the nonreform states—Jordan and Lebanon.

Major cereals in the Middle East show the variety of the region's
growing conditions: Egypt produces nearly equal quantities of rice,
maize, and wheat; wheat is followed by barley in importance in the
Fertile Crescent (the bulk of which is within the modern boundaries
of Syria and Iraq), while significant amounts of rice are also
cultivated in southern Iraq. Table 5.42 shows the supply elasticities
relative to price and the coefficients of determination calculated
for the major field crops using both acreage and yield models for
the relevant time periods.

A study of food-grain supply response in a very different region
is offered by Jeannine Swift who analyzed wheat production in Chile.[35]
Pointing out that a high supply elasticity for one crop does not imply
that farmers will also respond in the same way for agricultural

TABLE 5.42
Estimated Parameters, Middle East Field Crops

Crop/Country	Time Period	Dependent Variable	Price Elasticity Short-Run	Long-Run	R^2
Wheat					
Egypt	1920-40	Area yield	+0.014	+0.020	0.368
			+0.014	+0.009	0.670
	1953-72	Area yield	-0.226[a]	-0.684	0.784
			+0.911[f]	+0.436	0.831
Syria	1947-60	Area yield	-0.018	-0.031	0.742
			+1.316[d]	+1.441	0.645
	1961-72	Area yield	+0.643[b]	+3.231	0.571
			-2.374[d]	-1.073	+0.570
Iraq	1951-60	Area yield	+0.398	-4.422	0.534
			+2.096[e]	+2.352	0.912
	1962-71	Area yield	-0.850[d]	-0.335	0.774
			+1.585[c]	+1.981	0.698
Jordan	1955-67	Area yield	+0.199	+0.233	0.664
			-0.663	-0.766	0.638
Lebanon	1951-72	Area yield	+0.266[b]	+0.393	0.484
			+0.555[c]	+0.576	0.293
Barley					
Syria	1947-60	Area yield	-0.147	-0.243	0.953
			+1.872[d]	+2.690	0.790
	1961-72	Area yield	-0.570[b]	-0.572	0.327
			+0.273	+0.399	0.499
Iraq	1951-60	Area yield	+0.159	-0.281	0.905
			+0.512	+0.350	0.743
	1962-71	Area yield	-0.053	-0.187	0.886
			+0.779[e]	+21.51	0.866
Jordan	1955-67	Area yield	-0.613[d]	-0.452	0.255
			+2.852[d]	+4.040	0.524
Lebanon	1951-72	Area yield	+0.165	+0.223	0.667
			+0.087	0.098	0.626
Maize					
Egypt	1920-40	Area yield	+0.034	+0.040	0.614
			-0.162[f]	-0.250	0.747
	1953-72	Area yield	-0.184[b]	-0.129	0.744
			+0.041	+0.085	0.890
Syria	1947-60	Area yield	+0.507[b]	+0.687	0.835
			-0.426[c]	-0.612	0.416
	1961-72	Area yield	+2.266[b]	+2.164	0.559
			-0.648[b]	-0.730	0.668
Jordan	1955-66	Area yield	-0.209	-0.248	0.913
			+6.134[b]	+6.403	0.603
Lebanon	1953-72	Area yield	+0.126	+0.286	0.927
			-0.058	-0.384	0.775
Rice					
Egypt	1920-40	Area yield	+0.534[b]	+0.500	0.616
			-0.212[d]	-0.235	0.542
	1953-72	Area yield	+0.028	+0.028	0.791
			+0.077	+0.075	0.434
Iraq	1950-60	Area yield	+2.677[d]	+2.718	0.905
			-0.433[b]	-0.611	0.659
	1961-71	Area yield	+0.664[a]	+1.566	0.389
			+1.817[d]	+2.235	0.865
Vetch					
Syria	1947-60	Area yield	-0.126	-0.218	0.467
			+1.136[c]	+0.959	0.492
	1961-72	Area yield	-0.496[b]	-0.528	0.368
			+0.815	+0.810	0.339
Jordan	1955-67	Area yield	-0.370	-0.621	0.821
			-0.497[e]	-0.394	0.565

(continued)

(Table 5.42 continued)

Crop/Country	Time Period	Dependent Variable	Price Elasticity Short–Run	Long–Run	R^2
Millet					
Syria	1947–60	Area yield	+0.942[f]	+0.541	
			+0.997[c]	+1.784	
	1961–72	Area yield	+1.205[c]	+1.596	
			+0.108	+0.144	
Iraq	1953–60	Area yield	−0.852	−0.749	0.954
			−1.384[d]	−1.454	0.917
	1961–71	Area yield	−0.841[d]	−3.300	0.316
			+0.069	+0.062	0.567
Giant Millet					
Iraq	1954–60	Area yield	−25.57[f]	−7.995	0.797
			−0.533	−0.632	0.774
	1961–70	Area yield	+0.876[d]	+1.852	0.818
			+0.211[a]	+0.298	0.777
Green Gram					
Iraq	1950–60	Area yield	−0.265[d]	−0.688	0.902
			−0.311[d]	−0.431	0.621
	1961–70	Area yield	−0.243	−0.316	0.879
			+0.247	+0.527	0.486
Broad Beans					
Egypt	1920–40	Area yield	+0.139	+0.358	0.503
			+0.010	+0.006	0.509
	1953–72	Area yield	+0.251[c]	+0.354	0.496
			+0.190	+0.143	0.667
Syria	1950–60	Area yield	−0.022	−0.038	0.951
			+1.192[d]	+0.689	0.793
	1961–72	Area yield	−0.041	−0.068	0.851
			−0.150	−0.353	0.353
Jordan	1955–67	Area yield	−0.774[e]	−1.106	0.660
			−1.331[f]	−0.873	0.600
Lebanon	1958–72	Area yield	+0.535[a]	+0.678	0.890
			−0.474[b]	−0.427	0.239
Lentils					
Syria	1947–60	Area yield	−0.436[e]	−1.188	0.757
			−0.495[b]	−0.340	0.861
	1961–72	Area yield	−0.796[e]	−0.561	0.601
			−0.498[a]	−0.433	0.641
Iraq	1950–60	Area yield	−0.186[c]	−0.182	0.622
			+0.108	+0.071	0.482
	1961–71	Area yield	+6.488[e]	+0.315	0.916
			+0.181	+0.257	0.577
Jordan	1955–67	Area yield	−0.302[b]	−0.460	0.681
			−3.282[f]	−1.893	0.786
Lebanon	1955–72	Area yield	−0.282[e]	−0.541	0.482
			−0.888[b]	−0.877	0.537
Chick-peas					
Syria	1947–60	Area yield	−1.044[d]	−1.265	0.498
			+0.709	+3.043	0.382
	1961–72	Area yield	+0.431[b]	+0.505	0.797
			+0.259	+0.187	0.569
Jordan	1955–67	Area yield	+0.102	+0.087	0.240
			−0.567[b]	−0.461	0.702
Lebanon	1955–72	Area yield	+0.678[b]	+1.704	0.299
			+0.571[a]	+0.684	0.487

Note: Significance levels indicated for estimated price coefficients from which short–run elasticities were derived: [a]30 percent; [b]20 percent; [c]10 percent; [d]5 percent; [e]1 percent; [f]0.1 percent.

Source: Hossein Askari, John T. Cummings, and Bassam Harik, "Land Reform in the Middle East," International Journal of Middle East Studies, forthcoming.

produce in general, she examined not only the responsiveness of wheat to changes in the relative price of wheat, but also that of all crops to prices of agricultural goods relative to industrial products.

A Nerlove-Behrman-type model was used, with yield and rainfall both included in the acreage equation and both area adjustment and price expectation equations in the model. To avoid identification problems in the estimating procedure, Swift assumed that β, the price expectation coefficient, lies between zero and two and then ran several regressions, choosing that for which the standard error is minimized.

She used the Hildreth-Lu technique to compensate for the serial-correlation problem likely to be present in a distributed lag model, and wheat prices were deflated by an agricultural price index. Regression analysis indicated the parameter estimates (and their standard errors) for the nation as a whole and for five major wheat-growing provinces for 1942 to 1964. For those cases where the calculated expected price coefficient proved significant, the elasticity of desired area planted with respect to expected price was calculated and these are shown in Table 5.43. Swift noted that if prices were deflated by a cost-of-living index, then only Colchagua province had a significant price coefficient, with short- and long-run elasticities of 0.24 and 2.36, respectively.

She also examined the nationwide response of total crop acreage to agricultural prices. Acreage was regressed on yield, rainfall, lagged acreage, and, in turn, on index of agricultural prices deflated by industrial prices and agricultural prices alone. Her computations showed the best value of β, +1.5, a value that indicates farmers are optimists and expect prices to be higher in the next period.

TABLE 5.43

Wheat Supply Elasticities

	Coquimbo	O'Higgins	Cautin	Chile
Short-run elasticity	+0.74	+1.3	+0.5	+0.37
Long-run elasticity	+0.92	+2.0	+1.2	+3.65

Source: Jeannine Swift, "Economic Study of the Chilean Agrarian Reform," (Ph.D. dissertation, Massachusetts Institute of Technology, 1969).

Swift noted the difficulty of interpreting these parameter calculations. In her first regression the relative prices do not seem to influence desired area; the inverse relationship between absolute prices and desired area in her second formulation suggests that profit maximization may not serve accurately as a description of farmers' goals. It is possible that an income goal is more important to wheat producers, but she cautioned that the model she used had a number of flaws, including a failure to account for input prices or for the possible interpretation by farmers of government price-fixing policies as politically rather than economically motivated, the use of industrial prices as the deflator in the relative price index, and the likely exclusion from the model of other variables that might strongly affect profitability. As a result she refused to put much stock in her results as evidence of peasant motivation dominated by income rather than profit goals.

In a study of neighboring Peru, William C. Merrill devised a model to evaluate the success of a government market-control program for rice.[36] His goal was to present graphically the information most needed by officials in setting prices so as to satisfy as far as possible four goals: high producer prices, low consumer prices, reductions in rice imports, and overall program cost minimization.

As part of this study Merrill examined post-World War II behavior of Peruvian rice cultivators, using a Nerlovian price expectation approach. His estimating equation incorporated output in tonnage terms, farm prices deflated by a cost of living index, cotton (a major alternative crop) export prices deflated by rice prices, and a time variable.

He calculated an elasticity for rice supply with respect to real farm prices of +0.50. Though this value is rather high for a cereal crop in a developing country, Merrill explained it is in keeping with the character of Peruvian rice production—the crop is mostly grown on the lands of relatively few large landowners who have a strong market orientation.

Argentine cereals production, far more than that in any country so far considered, is that of a "modern" agricultural sector. Though Remy Friere's supply analysis of wheat and maize used a very simple lagged price model, his results are of interest by way of contrast with those found for Argentina's neighbors.[37] (The results of his analysis for flax, an oilseed, are included in Chapter 6.)

Wheat is the country's most important crop, and Argentina is one of the world's major wheat exporters. Its cultivation is concentrated in the Pampas and involves a notable degree of mechanization, which should imply somewhat less flexibility as regards substitute activities. Maize has long been a major crop, and the

introduction of high-yield hybrid varieties in recent years has
intensified the crop's role. Unlike the case of wheat, mechanization
has come slowly, and maize remains a labor-intensive crop.

Estimated lagged price and rainfall parameters (and their
standard errors) for wheat were +0.693 (0.140) and +0.264 (0.078)
with a short-run elasticity of +0.57. He had less success in estimating the supply parameters for maize and hypothesized that this was
due to factors affecting maize output that are not easily quantified.
One such influence, he suggested, is the agricultural labor situation
that has been seriously marked by conflict in the postwar period,
pointing to indications that farmers have frequently abandoned or
avoided maize in favor of less-labor-intensive crops in order to
avoid labor problems.

Franklin Fisher and Peter Temin, in attempting to assess the
role of regional specialization in economic growth, confronted the
problem of analyzing changes in labor productivity in the cultivation
of wheat in pre-World War I United States.[38] The United States
was, at that time in its history, like many of today's developing
nations. In discussing earlier work in this area,[39] they argued
that previous efforts had not accounted for the ways in which costs
change with output and had thus attributed all changes in labor
productivity to shifts in, and not along, the production function.
This, they held, is equivalent to the assumption that intraregional
production functions are linearly homogeneous, that is, that the
supply curve for each region is infinitely elastic, an assumption
clearly inappropriate for agriculture carried on within given
geographic boundaries. In the period of their study, 1867 to 1914,
wheat production in Eastern and Midwestern states already took
place under conditions close to complete settlement and use of
cultivable land, and the frontier rapidly shrank during this time
even on the Great Plains.

Thus Fisher and Temin turned to the estimation of a wheat
supply function as a first step in integrating consideration of supply
elasticity into discussions of technical change and productivity.
Working with data available from the U.S. Department of Agriculture
estimates as revised by later researchers, they postulated a Nerlove-
type model, with output expressed in terms of the share of acreage
planted in wheat, rather than in direct acreage terms, and the
supply equation expressed in logarithmic form. Two equations
were tested for each of 17 wheat-producing states, with lagged
wheat prices relative to an index of alternate grain crops (oats,
corn, and tame hay), lagged acreage share, and a trend variable
in each formulation and an index of wheat yield relative to that of
the alternate crops included in one of the two. Statistical estimation
was carried out using ordinary least-squares techniques and a series

of assumed values for the acreage (in crop-share terms) adjustment coefficient. Estimated parameters from the resulting regression for which the error sum of squares was minimized are shown (with their respective t values) in Table 5.44.

Analyzing these results, Fisher and Temin concluded that while the estimates for the various states show considerable variation (as might well be expected in view of the many differences among the states) they nonetheless also display notable similarities. For example, in all but four states the estimated price coefficient (and short-run price elasticity) is significantly nonzero at the 5 percent level or better. Again, while farmers in most states seemed to be price responsive, the results suggest (in all but one case) that their response tended to be slow, with the ratio of the long-run to the short-run price elasticity ranging from 3 to 4 to as high as 30—generally this ratio is about 5, indicating that after five years farmers had made only about two-thirds of their final adjustment.

Certain geographic differences are notable—for example, long-run price elasticities are generally lowest for the Eastern states, somewhat higher in the Midwest, and highest in the Plains states—that is, reflecting the relative pattern of settlement. Similarly the authors point to the homogeneity indicated in the northern Midwestern states—high long-run elasticity, high negative time trend, and fairly high adjustment speed—attributing this to the suitability of these states (Michigan, Wisconsin, and Minnesota) for dairy production: as wheat prices fell in the late nineteenth century, farmers in these states switched from wheat to dairy production.

The practical difficulties inherent in estimating supply are illustrated in a comment of Robert Higgs on the preceding article and the rejoinder by Fisher and Temin.[40] Higgs complained that while the basic model might be fine, the variables specified in the model were not the same as those represented by the data. He pointed out that the dependent variable in the model was planted acreage, while harvested acreage data was actually used. Of even more concern to him was the price series used—the only data available on a consistent basis were the prices prevailing on December 1 of every year. While spring wheat was planted after this date, winter wheat was already in the ground two to three months and thus such prices could not be a factor in planting decisions.

Fisher and Temin acknowledged data problems but defended their choice of included data on several grounds. They rejected Higgs' assertion that the winter planting dominated the total output during the period of study, citing an indication that winter wheat was of rather minor importance at the beginning of the interval though

TABLE 5.44

Estimated Parameters, U.S. Wheat

State	Constant	Price (Short-Run Elasticity)	Trend	Relative Yield	Lagged Acreage Share	Long-Run Elasticity	R^2
East							
New York	2.896	0.121c	-0.002	—	0.848c	0.792	0.96
	(1.17)	(3.05)	(1.54)		(13.73)		
	3.071	0.125c	-0.002a	0.085b	0.848c	0.822	0.96
	(1.31)	(3.30)	(1.79)	(2.11)	(14.51)		
Pennsylvania	-0.271	0.045a	-0.0001	—	0.909c	0.498	0.91
	(0.24)	(1.97)	(0.09)		(12.38)		
	-0.028	0.037	-0.0001	-0.0414	0.8894c	0.330	0.91
	(0.20)	(1.51)	(0.19)	(1.16)	(11.78)		
Maryland	-2.154b	0.070c	0.001a	—	0.815c	0.380	0.86
	(2.15)	(2.79)	(1.82)		(9.15)		
	-2.154b	0.070c	0.001a	-0.005	0.814c	0.375	0.86
	(2.12)	(2.72)	(1.80)	(0.16)	(8.94)		
Virginia	0.789	0.071b	0.0001	—	0.784c	0.329	0.88
	(0.50)	(2.31)	(0.09)		(5.50)		
	0.404	0.064a	-0.0001	-0.0159	0.750c	0.256	0.88
	(0.21)	(1.96)	(0.10)	(0.52)	(3.96)		
Midwest							
Ohio	0.217	0.191c	-0.0007	—	0.789c	0.902	0.74
	(0.07)	(2.71)	(0.44)		(6.45)		
	-1.022	0.215c	-0.0003	0.0936	0.807c	1.115	0.75
	(0.35)	(3.19)	(0.18)	(1.63)	(7.90)		

(continued)

133

(Table 5.44 continued)

State	Constant	Price (Short-Run Elasticity)	Trend	Relative Yield	Lagged Acreage Share	Long-Run Elasticity	R^2
Michigan	9.401	0.277c	-0.006	—	0.755c	1.132	0.95
	(1.20)	(3.57)	(1.41)		(5.85)		
	9.454	0.279c	-0.006	0.009	0.754c	1.134	0.95
	(1.18)	(3.47)	(1.38)	(0.10)	(5.70)		
Indiana	24.394b	0.023	-0.014b	—	0.068	0.024	0.61
	(2.36)	(0.32)	(2.43)		(0.19)		
	27.448c	0.065	-0.016c	0.176c	-0.080	—	0.63
	(4.80)	(0.63)	(4.62)	(3.03)	(0.32)		
Illinois	6.492	0.049	-0.004	—	0.720c	0.174	0.73
	(1.04)	(0.65)	(1.14)		(4.81)		
	6.350	0.045	-0.004	-0.012	0.726c	0.163	0.73
	(0.98)	(0.55)	(1.05)	(0.12)	(4.51)		
Wisconsin	36.441b	0.284c	-0.020b	—	0.728c	1.043	0.99
	(2.56)	(3.40)	(2.67)		(7.49)		
	34.731b	0.305c	-0.019b	0.092	0.748c	1.121	0.99
	(2.36)	(3.34)	(2.49)	(0.58)	(7.14)		
Great Plains and West							
Missouri	2.806	0.028	-0.002	—	0.590c	0.068	0.68
	(0.94)	(0.87)	(1.00)		(4.42)		
	1.357	0.085	-0.001	0.075	0.686b	0.271	0.69
	(0.28)	(1.11)	(0.49)	(1.18)	(2.22)		
Iowa	6.595	0.162b	-0.004	—	0.848b	1.067	0.98
	(0.16)	(2.27)	(0.18)		(2.32)		
	-2.5400	0.287c	0.0002	0.299c	0.973c	10.764	0.99
	(0.24)	(4.42)	(0.04)	(3.31)	(10.68)		

Minnesota	10.018	0.136c	-0.006a	—	0.765c	0.579	0.98
	(1.17)	(5.10)	(1.88)		(5.51)		
	8.336b	0.150c	-0.005b	0.100c	0.812c	0.796	0.99
	(2.03)	(6.04)	(2.27)	(2.98)	(8.08)		
Kansas	-18.306b	0.249b	0.009b	—	0.746c	0.982	0.68
	(2.67)	(2.41)	(2.53)		(4.32)		
	-13.515b	0.364c	0.006b	0.247b	0.854c	2.483	0.71
	(2.70)	(3.70)	(2.26)	(2.50)	(8.08)		
Nebraska	-1.720	0.085b	-0.0007	—	0.929c	1.198	0.93
	(0.31)	(2.04)	(0.23)		(7.35)		
	1.374	0.135b	-0.0012	0.110a	0.914c	1.568	0.93
	(0.24)	(2.34)	(0.40)	(1.92)	(7.43)		
South Dakota	6.191b	0.080b	-0.004b	—	0.880c	0.669	0.93
	(2.21)	(2.09)	(2.33)		(10.92)		
	5.533a	0.090b	-0.003b	0.016	0.894c	0.849	0.93
	(1.87)	(2.10)	(2.05)	(0.41)	(11.12)		
North Dakota	8.470a	0.144b	-0.005b	—	0.650c	0.412	0.82
	(1.90)	(2.62)	(2.02)		(4.25)		
	5.615	0.136b	-0.004a	0.156b	0.616c	0.353	0.85
	(1.42)	(2.68)	(1.67)	(2.25)	(4.57)		
California	8.656b	0.089	-0.005b	—	0.933c	1.336	0.97
	(2.25)	(0.96)	(2.39)		(20.12)		
	7.340a	0.069	-0.004b	0.082	0.934c	1.045	0.97
	(1.87)	(0.70)	(2.05)	(0.73)	(20.80)		

[a]10 percent significance level; [b]5 percent significance level; [c]1 percent significance level.

Source: Franklin Fisher and Peter Temin, "Regional Specialization and the Supply of Wheat in United States, 1867–1914," Review of Economics and Statistics 52 (May 1970).

it grew rapidly after the turn of the century. More importantly, they argued December 1 prices were the best available figures to explain both winter and spring plantings falling three months or so on either side of that date. The alternative price to use for winter wheat would be that of the previous December, more than nine months before planting. Price influence is incorporated into the supply model as a declining weighted series of past market prices, with that closest to the planting decision being most important. Since planting-time prices were not available, those of two to three months later, they maintained, are far better proxies than those of nine to ten months previously.[41]

It was pointed out earlier that the length of the time period chosen (or dictated by data availability) can cause serious problems in the estimating process. If it is short, and regression methods are used, a conflict arises between the desire to include all conceptually significant variables and the possibility of reducing the degrees of freedom so much as to make the estimate of doubtful utility. If, on the other hand, the period is quite long, an assumption is made that the structure is constant throughout if estimates are drawn from the period in toto. As will be seen later, this problem is particularly relevant in evaluating studies of perennial crops where complex formulations of prices and other variables are often called for in any realistic estimating equation.

However, the problem of the potentially overlong analysis period can affect annual crop studies as well. Though, more often, data deficiencies result in short series, while bountiful statistical availability usually allow the writer considerable flexibility, certain cases impel the use of longer periods. Most prominent among these are studies where specifically identifiable historical periods are of particular interest. The Fisher-Temin study and that of Stephen DeCanio on cotton are two such works—focusing on, respectively, the Populist period in the U.S. Midwest and the post-Civil War agriculture of the defeated South.[42] Another is Askari, Cummings, and Harik's study of Middle East land reform, although only for Egypt are relatively long time series available.[43]

Ordinary least-squares regressions run on such longer time periods present coefficient estimates that might properly be thought of as averages over a period when structural shifts might well be occurring. A priori suspicion of such shifts, if they are related, for example, to some specific event, can be investigated by dividing the time period or including a dummy variable. But if the shift is gradual, or even discrete but related to less-specifically identifiable causes, then estimating problems arise. Analysts can be content with "average" values for the structural parameters or can pursue an expensive process of trying many subperiod regressions. In the

latter case their final choice for optimal specification may depend
only on some rather dubious criterion like highest R^2.

This problem was of particular concern to Thomas Cooley
and Stephen DeCanio in their interest in the post-Civil War period
in the United States.[44] This 30- to 40-year interval was buffeted
by many social, political, and economic changes, whose implications
are still a matter of vigorous debate among social scientists. Thus
they held it to be a clear example of a period too complex both to
assume the constancy of an econometric structure and to identify
satisfactorily subperiods for estimating purposes.

Cooley and DeCanio approach this problem in a very different
manner than do other authors cited in this book, basing their efforts
on a number of new developments in estimating techniques.[45] These
allow identification of parameter shifts over a period of time, without
requiring a priori an identification of when these changes occur; in
other words they present the possibility of highlighting either gradual
change or change occurring in frequent, if discrete, slices. Their
concern was with the implications of the Populist political movement
for the farmers at whom it was primarily aimed, and for what they
then produced for the market—a rather wide-ranging political-
economic-historical study; we will in this work emphasize the
economic content as it relates to our general problem of supply
response.

The model employed was Nerlovian in form; the estimating
equation represented relative acreage planted in wheat as the dependent variable, expressed as a function of prices and the dependent
variable lagged one year. (For the discussion of cotton supply,
see Chapter 6.) As with the versions of this model seen above,
both price expectation and acreage adjustment processes are relevant
to the postulated explanations of producer optimization. However,
the authors concluded that available data were suitable only for
a testing of the former. They then assumed there were no barriers
to cultivator adjustment—that is, that the acreage adjustment
coefficient was equal to unity.*

---

*The authors traced their approach to that of John Muth, "Optimal
Properties of Exponentially Weighted Forecasts," Journal of the
American Statistical Association 55 (June 1960). This method
portrays producer prices as the sum of permanent and transitory
components. The authors assume the latter to be independently and
identically distributed and the former to follow a moving average
process (with independently distributed error terms). Muth outlines
a procedure that can be used for minimizing the error variance in
the farmers' process of predicting price.

To estimate structural parameters that are subject to gradual change, Cooley and DeCanio employed the new methods referred to above, setting forth their arguments regarding the pattern that governs this change. Estimation techniques were Bayesian and traced the movements in the structural parameters over the entire period at five-year intervals. The authors presented estimates at years near the beginning (1874) and end (1914) of the analysis period for short- and long-run elasticities for wheat. These estimates are based on the data used by Fisher and Temin for the same time period (1867 to 1914).

Contrasting their results with those of Fisher and Temin for wheat (and of DeCanio for cotton), Cooley and DeCanio pointed out that structural shifts are usually accounted for by variations in the constant (the intercept term). Such procedures assume that the nonconstant elements in the estimating equation represent nonvariable relationships. Given the rather simple price and lagged acreage explanation they use for wheat supply and the 40-year estimating period analyzed, the authors hold that too much would be attributed to shifts in the constant—an explanation based on no specific causality.

The authors found considerable evidence for structural shifts during the period; for nearly all the states, price elasticities declined between 1874 and 1914. Simple correlation coefficients between the elasticities calculated at five-year intervals and a trend variable emphasized this drop: In all but two states (Kansas and Maryland) the values were negative, and in the wide majority of cases considerably below -0.6. (Only for Virginia was the correlation coefficient relatively close to zero: -0.221 and -0.194 for short- and long-run elasticity respectively.) With a single exception an opposite pattern of correlation prevailed between the trend and the lagged area coefficient. The implication according to Cooley and DeCanio is that wheat cultivators tended to pay less attention to recent prices and more to those further removed, toward the end of the period of analysis. They became less flexible in response to the market during a time while wheat farming was increasingly commercialized.

The analysis revealed inconsistencies between what seemed to be the market behavior of wheat growers and that indicated for cotton farmers, so the authors proceeded to test Muth's approach, trying to separate the permanent and transitory elements in price variation over time. Their goal was to identify the effects on output of the two types of price changes, and they concluded that the Muth hypothesis was generally valid. Wheat prices during this period underwent a number of more or less permanent shifts, with relatively long periods of low or high prices. The authors argue

that their evidence indicates wheat farmers tended to weight recent
prices highly immediately after a major fluctuation had occurred
but discounted them otherwise.

A later study of North American cereals production has been
published by Andrew Schmitz.[46] He examined wheat and barley
output (and also that of flax seed; see Chapter 6 for these results)
in Canada between 1947 and 1966, using a number of simple and
Nerlovian supply models. Variables incorporated into these formulations included prices of both the crop in question and its principal
substitutes (wheat, barley, flax, and cattle compete for inputs),
lagged acreage, wheat inventories and exports, rainfall, and a
trend variable.

Using simple models he obtained estimates for the supply
elasticity of wheat ranging from 0.49 to 0.87 and, for barley, a
value of about zero. The Nerlovian model, used only for wheat,
indicated a short-run elasticity between 0.42 and 0.75 and long-run
elasticity between 0.62 and 1.30. Coefficients of determination
associated with the wheat regression were marginally higher for
the partial adjustment model, but even the various simple models
explained about 80 percent or more of the variation in wheat acreage.

Like many developed and developing countries, Australia uses
a price-stabilization scheme for basic cereal crops, the effectiveness
of which has been explored by J. H. Duloy and A. S. Watson.[47] In
this case cereal production for export is the prime consideration.

Australian farmers, like their counterparts in New Zealand,
Canada, the United States, and the Soviet Union, face a wide if
bewildering variety of possible endeavors as far as normally
successful cereal crops thriving in temperate regions are concerned.
Farmers in the first four nations most likely make their difficult
choices on price-expectations grounds; Australian farmers in
particular must choose between wheat and sheep, as well as the
alternatives of several other grains—for example, in New South
Wales in 1959 only 3 percent of all properties larger than 100 acres
carried no sheep. Certainly a high degree of supply elasticity for
wheat should be expected in a situation where a number of possible
alternatives must be taken into consideration in any explanatory
model.

Disaggregation in such a relatively homogeneous nation as
modern Australia gave the authors considerable concern; while
the availability of data made disaggregation relatively easy, the
question remained as to exactly what regions might conceivably
be distinct in a technologically advanced and highly mobile society
where markets are essentially one. Duloy and Watson constructed
their data series on 38 shires (roughly the same as the North
American county), shires being more or less climatically similar

areas in New South Wales. The shires were further grouped regarding geographic proximity, and six such groupings were studied;
these regions also approximated regions which for historical and
other reasons seemed likely to differ.

The authors argued that while a number of studies indicate the
complexity of demand analysis, supply responsiveness seems to
be a relatively simple relationship between output (or acreage
planted) and price expectations (based on recent actual harvest
prices) which, once made, are assumed to determine what farmers
actually do. Intended acreages were considered by the authors to
follow Nerlovian lines; they used two models for the period 1947/48
to 1962/63: one static, where expected price is more or less the
wheat price (deflated by the wool price) in the previous period, and
the other dynamic, where adaptive price expectations (using relative
wheat to wool prices) are involved, along with lagged acreage.

Table 5.45 shows the estimated parameters obtained through
ordinary least-squares regressions (using the dynamic model) for
both the older (A through D) and newer (E and F) cultivating regions.

As regards the newer areas, another model with an exponential
time-trend variable was tested. These results (with coefficients
of determination of 0.79 and 0.72, respectively), the authors felt,
demand a more complex formulation of the wheat supply model for
the new areas. However, their failure to carry this recommendation
through, plus the lower values of R^2 they obtained for regions E and

TABLE 5.45

Estimated Parameters, New South Wales Wheat

Region	Constant	Area Adjustment Coefficient	Price Expectation Coefficient	R^2	Elasticity Short-Run	Elasticity Long-Run
A	0.129*	0.557*	0.443*	0.91	0.47	1.07
B	0.107*	0.577*	0.423*	0.84	0.37	0.88
C	0.026*	0.534*	0.466*	0.89	0.33	0.70
D	0.179*	0.372*	0.628*	0.82	0.42	0.66
E	0.046*	0.980*	0.020*	0.86	0.16	7.95
F	0.003*	1.206*	-0.206*	0.92	1.31	-0.13

*Significant at the 1 percent level.

Source: J. H. Duloy and A. S. Watson, "Supply Relationships
in the Australian Wheat Industry: New South Wales," Australian
Journal of Agricultural Economics 8 (June 1964).

F using their time-trend model as opposed to earlier studies, left this problem unresolved. Duloy and Watson present a reasonable case for differentiating between "new" and "old" wheat cultivating regions in New South Wales and results that bolster the case for differentiation, but no real conclusions as to what the differences are.

In a very detailed study of past and present demand and supply of the principal Australian agricultural commodities, commissioned by the U.S. Department of Agriculture, F. H. Gruen and others used a Nerlovian model along with a number of other analytic tools.[48] Wheat supply was defined in terms of lagged wheat, coarse grains, and wool prices, while coarse grains were represented only as dependent upon their own and wheat prices. They presented cereals supply elasticity estimates covering the period 1947 to 1964 (as well as for wool, dairy products, lamb, and beef and veal; see Chapter 9) and these results are summarized in Table 5.46

Wheat production in New Zealand was the subject of a study by J. W. B. Guise.[49] Though livestock constitute that nation's largest agricultural resource, the land and climate allow for the cultivation of a large variety of crops. Wheat is the principal crop, but it must compete for inputs not only with livestock but also with a number of other cereals and grasses.

Guise postulated an area adjustment model with wheat prices deflated by fat-lamb prices included in each of several formulations: alone or (A) along with an index of relative wheat and alternative feed-crop prices, (B) perennial ryegrass, (C) red clover, and (D) ryegrass and clover average.

Supply elasticities calculated from the results of their marginally better fourth formulation are indicated in Table 5.47. Total supply elasticities must consider these jointly, and Guise noted that this would indicate considerably higher values than those computed for neighboring Australia by Duloy and Watson. He felt this is under-standable in light of the larger range of options open to New Zealand farmers. (Similarly, we can compare New Zealand elasticities with those presented by Fisher and Temin for the United States, where the farmer's choice of alternatives is also quite wide): The New Zealand elasticities are still somewhat larger than those for the United States, but the difference is not as large as relative to those of Australia.

He cited the estimated area adjustment coefficient, which is close to 0.60, as further indication of the propensity of New Zealand farmers to expand or contract wheat acreage fairly rapidly.

A number of works on cereals cultivation have centered on Europe, where agricultural conditions are quite different than in either the developing regions of Southern Asia or Latin America

TABLE 5.46

Supply Parameters, Cereals, Australia

Wheat	Short-run elasticity	+0.18
	Long-run elasticity	+0.85*
	Adjustment coefficient	+0.03
	Cross-elasticity-coarse grains	−0.10
	Cross-elasticity-wool	−0.59
	R^2	0.87
Coarse Grains	Short-run elasticity	+0.22
	Long-run elasticity	+0.81*
	Adjustment coefficient	+0.14
	Cross-elasticity—wheat	−0.10
	R^2	0.84

*Five-year adjustment period.
Source: Alan A. Powell and F. H. Gruen, "The Estimation of Production Frontiers: The Australian Livestock/Cereals Complex," Australian Journal of Agricultural Economics 11 (June 1967).

or the frontier economies of North America and Australia. Chronologically, we first turn our attention to another study of a now-developed country's agriculture during a less-developed stage: Scott Eddie's analysis of Hungary during the pre-World War I period.[50]

Eddie's specific interest concerned the structure of Hungarian agriculture—dominated by large estate or latifundia—and whether it might have hindered the country's overall economic development. Hungarian landholding interests rather successfully resisted any serious attempts at land reform until after the onset of socialism following World War II, and during the period of this study the holdings of the largest landlords notably increased.* At the same time small and medium-sized holdings (less than about 285 acres) rose sharply from 8 to about 20 percent of agricultural land. Both of these changes squeezed the upper middle class landowners, who

———

*Hungary during the latter half of the nineteenth century was a much larger entity than she is today—the Kingdom of Hungary (within the Austro-Hungarian Empire) included Slovakia, the present (Yugoslav Federal Republic of) Slovenia, the northern part of Serbia, and Transylvania, an area about two and a half times as large as the modern Hungarian republic.

were particularly affected by the long decline in agricultural prices,
which began with Austria-Hungary's defeat by Prussia in 1866 and
continued into the early 1890s.

By 1914 over one-third of all agricultural land was in mortmain
holdings, either directly in the hands of the crown, the nobility,
or the church and other quasi-charitable organizations, or belonging
to municipal bodies indirectly controlled by the nobility. All in all,
by modern standards, the land distribution situation considerably
deteriorated during this period.

The nineteenth-century Hungarian economy is primarily a
story of five cereal crops—wheat, rye, barley, oats, and maize—
and of their definite, if not steady, growth; overall output of the
principal grains almost tripled from the late 1860s until the outbreak
of World War I. The considerable industrialization during the period
was strongly influenced by agriculture, notably in the rapid growth
of the milling and other food-processing industries, and in the more
than eightfold increase in railroad trackage (to better than 22,000
kilometers by 1914) as the Balkan grain fields were tied to the
empire's metropolis.

Eddie's interest in the role of agriculture in Hungary's economic
expansion led him to an analysis of output response to price incentives using a Nerlovian approach. Using initially an area adjustment
model including prices (lagged both one and two years) deflated by
those of the other cereals and expressed in logarithmic terms, he
estimated his model using ordinary least squares.

The price coefficient, which in this logarithmic formulation
also represents the elasticity of observed acreage with respect to
price, was never greater than 0.12, and in many cases it was not
even significant. Even allowing for the fact that this coefficient
was the product of the original price coefficient a_1 in the structural
equation:

TABLE 5.47

Supply Elasticities, New Zealand Wheat

Elasticity with Respect to Prices of:	Wheat/Lamb	Wheat/Feed Crop
Short-run	+0.737	+0.225
Long-run	+1.218	+0.372

Source: J. W. B. Guise, "Economic Factors Associated with
Variations in Aggregate Wheat Acreage in New Zealand 1945-1965,"
New Zealand Economic Papers 2, no. 1 (1968).

$$A_t = a_o + a_1 P_t^e + u_t \tag{5.32a}$$

(or, more properly, its logarithmic equivalent) and the price expectation coefficient β in:

$$P_t^e = P_{t-1}^e + \beta(P_{t-1} - P_{t-1}^e) \tag{5.32b}$$

[or the product of a_1 and γ if an area adjustment approach is used and equation 5.32b becomes:

$$A_t - A_{t-1} = \gamma(A_t^D - A_{t-1})] \tag{5.32c}$$

and even if we assume both β and γ are less than unity (though, reasonably, not too much less—say, around 0.5 or higher), then the elasticity actually of interest (of intended output with respect to expected price) is nevertheless still very low.

A number of alternative formulations led Eddie to similar results: frequent lack of significance for the coefficient of the price variable and low values for price elasticity whenever the price coefficient did prove to be significant. Aiming for a model that best isolates price responsiveness, he estimated the parameters of the equation:

$$\left[\frac{A}{Z}\right]_t = a + b\, P_{t-1} + cT + u_t \tag{5.33}$$

where: $\frac{A}{Z}$ is the proportion of all cultivated land planted in the crop
                      in question,
            P_{t-1} is the lagged price of this crop relative to other
                      relevant crops, and
            T is a trend variable.

Though a trend variable introduces a degree of crudity into the results, often masking more than it reveals, he held that in this case it at least absorbs all effect on output not attributable to price changes. Though his results (Table 5.48) are satisfactory for the period 1871 to 1893, the calculations for the period 1893 to 1913 yield very low R^2 values (except for the case of rye), and were not reported.

In this earlier period the elasticity of the principal cash crop, wheat, is the lowest, in contrast to other studies that have indicated higher elasticities for cash crops than for subsistence crops. Similarly for this period, the calculated values for the expectations coefficient β (or the area adjustment coefficient γ, if an adjustment model is used) cluster around 0.5, quite similar to the values

TABLE 5.48

Supply Elasticities, Hungarian Cereals

Crop	Lag	Price Elasticity	R^2
Wheat	2 years	0.086[b]	0.96
Rye {1871–93	2 years	0.159[c]	0.86
Rye {1893–1913	1 year	0.189[b]	0.77
Barley	2 years	0.140[b]	0.38
Oats	2 years	0.128[a]	0.91
Maize	2 years	negative	0.34

[a]1 percent significance level.
[b]5 percent significance level.
[c]10 percent significance level.
Source: Scott M. Eddie, "The Role of Agriculture in the Economic Development of Hungary 1867–1913" (Ph.D. dissertation, Massachusetts Institute of Technology, 1967).

reported by Nerlove for the United States (that is, 0.41, 0.52, and 0.54, respectively, for cotton, wheat, and maize).

However, during the immediate pre–World War I period the calculations yielded little in the way of significant results, as though some unaccounted variable is masking price responsiveness. Investigating this possibility, Eddie applied to each of Hungary's regions the following supply equation:

$$\left[\frac{A}{Z}\right]_t = a + bP_{t-i} + c[PIO]_{t-i} + u_t \tag{5.34}$$

where PIO is the price index for the alternate crops.

The inclusion of a price index for the alternative crops, it was hoped, would not only help to isolate price responsiveness but also give some idea of the magnitude of the cross-elasticities. His results show a pervasive and significant price response, with the price parameter generally positive and alternate crop index parameter negative. Maize is a notable exception that Eddie traced to the customary crop rotation scheme, in which a maize planting followed wheat much more frequently than did any other grain. This meant maize acreage would tend to follow wheat prices, which, due to wheat's relative importance, are weighted strongly in the alternate crop index—hence maize's positive cross-elasticities. Similarly, the traditional rotation patterns seem to explain why a two-year lag yielded better results (that is, once a winter crop, for example, was sown, no spring crop could be raised in the same plot until a year had passed).

Eddie interpreted his results to indicate that Hungarian agriculture was responsive to economic incentives, though the supply elasticities were low. The negative cross-elasticities point to a notable influence of relative prices on the allocation of land to different crops, and he speculated that a more complex model, if available data allowed its testing, would accentuate this influence.

As a further test of the possibility that prices were overshadowed by other influences not included in the model, he also tested a formulation that included total railroad trackage as a variable. His calculations showed that trackage was significant at better than the 2.5 percent level in 12 out of 15 cases, and at better than the 10 percent level in 14 out of 15 cases, * another indication of response to economic stimuli.

Eddie's final conclusions were that price responsiveness, though small, was perhaps not much less than Nerlove had found for the United States. The drop in responsiveness toward the turn of the century might be explained by the increasing protection of Hungarian agriculture within the Hapsburg Empire and the simultaneous declining importance of the export market; the significance of the railroad trackage variable points to the importance of economic incentives that might best be interpreted in terms of profit maximization rather than straightforward price responsiveness— that is, farmers, faced with inelastic demand curves and better and cheaper access to the empire's growing markets and less concerned with competition with the world grain market, soon learned that rapid changes of supply in response to prices were self-defeating in a profit-maximizing context.

Cereals output in another developed country, France, has been examined by Bernard Oury.[51] The purpose of his work was to develop a quantitative model of French wheat and feed-grain production that could be used to evaluate the various price policies followed by the government in recent years. At the time of Oury's study (the early 1960s), this was particularly important in light of the then-pending integration of farm programs by the Common Market (European Economic Community, EEC) countries. He hoped to be able to predict likely response by French farmers, who produce about half of the EEC's agricultural output, to the new supranational policies.

---

*The 15 calculations involved the five crops in each of three time periods: 1871-1913, 1871-93, and 1893-1913.

Despite the relatively high capital intensity found in French agriculture, as indicated, for example, by per acre yields frequently much larger than in North America, the sector is still very much in the process of transition to modernization. Farmers still made up about a quarter of the labor force in 1960, and their productivity rates remained considerably below their North American counterparts, despite notable gains in the postwar period. Factors frequently cited as hindrances to more rapid development are the inheritance provisions of the Code Napoleon, which have led to considerable fractionalization of landholdings, and the still-high proportion of land farmed under tenancy and crop-sharing conditions.*

Wheat accounts for more than a quarter of the value realized from the cultivation of all crops, and feed grains (mostly barley, oats, and maize) have reflected the steady growth in importance of livestock cultivation in a country of rapidly rising living standards. Wheat is grown mostly in the north and northwest, where it frequently competes with oats and particularly with barley, while maize cultivation is concentrated in the southwest. Almost all the wheat is winter wheat, while only a quarter of the feed grains are winter crops. This accentuates the wheat-barley relationship, since wheat lost due to more-than-usually severe weather conditions is more often than not replaced by barley sown in the spring.

The French government instituted a wheat board in 1936 with monopsonist powers, and in the early postwar period price controls were in effect. Various pricing policies, including attempts to account for farm costs and the announcement several years in advance of "target" prices that are then gradually approached, have been followed in the interval. Although feed grains were made subject to government control before the war, their status as intermediate products has meant in effect less rigid control.

Oury constructed various models representing supply in terms of prices, past output, weather, consumption of fertilizers, and a time trend. His tests included several different expressions for most of the independent variables, and the dependent variable in the basic hypothesis was expressed alternately in yield, acreage, and production (tonnage) terms. He hoped to identify the significant factors affecting yield and acreage, and then, if possible, to construct a satisfactory "common" model to explain overall production. Nerlovian-type price and output adjustment formulations

_____

*One institutional factor of interest here is that leases in wheat areas are traditionally couched in terms of the land's potential in terms of wheat output—thus strengthening at least some degree of immobility in overall production.

figured prominently in all his analyses, which involved the period 1946 to 1961. Included in his regressions were wheat price deflated by a general price index and weather indices measuring separately aridity and the severity of the winter. Other variants included three-year moving averages of relative wheat to feed grain and wheat to barley prices (formulations 5 and 6, respectively), consumption of nitrogen fertilizer, a trend variable, and lagged output (in tonnage). These results, judged "best" using such criteria as conformity to expected coefficient sign, coefficients and standard errors relatively invariant as regards order of magnitude over a number of alternate formulations, and "good" R^2 values, are quite typical of the rather consistent results for all formulations tested, which Oury included in appendixes. Winter weather conditions were notably important in all cases. Past production (in tonnage rather than acreage terms) had the postulated negative sign, but this coefficient never showed statistical significance.

The production model (dependent variable in tonnage terms) was also estimated in light of the factors most prominent in explaining yield and acreage variations, and the short-run elasticities of acreage and production with respect to prices are shown in Table 5.49.

Had yield, acreage, and production been completely explained by the models, yield plus acreage response would equal that of production. In the only case where the same price variable (wheat prices) is significant in both yield and acreage equations, the yield elasticity was estimated to be 0.495 and 0.686, depending upon whether the trend variable or fertilizer consumption was included.

TABLE 5.49

Supply Elasticities, Production Model, France

| | | Elasticities with Respect to: | |
	Wheat Prices	Wheat-Feed Grain Prices	Wheat-Barley Prices
Model			
Acreage	0.631	0.245	0.321
Production	{1.052[a] / 0.926[b]}	0.600	0.769

[a]With N in equation.
[b]With T in equation.
Source: Bernard Oury, A Production Model for Wheat and Feed-grains in France 1946-1961 (Amsterdam: North-Holland, 1966).

Yield plus acreage price elasticity in this case was higher than
production elasticity, but somewhat closer results were noted for
elasticities with respect to other factors, notably the various
weather indices.

Several variants of the supply model were also tested for feed
grains. Prices were included both in distributed lag and three-year
average form, each deflated by a general price index. Aridity and
winter indices were included in all formulations; other variables
incorporated included relative wheat to barley and wheat to maize
prices, fertilizer consumption, a trend variable, lagged output,
and livestock inventory.

Feed-grain prices demonstrated poor explanatory power as
determinants of acreage, an occurrence not unexpected in view of
the high degree of on-farm, nonmarket consumption. A variable
representing livestock inventories, when included, not only showed
statistical significance, but resulted in a considerable jump in the
percentage of acreage variation explained. The final acreage
regressions tested added other price variables and showed, generally,
the best overall results. The production model short-run estimates
for feed grain are seen in Table 5.50.

Oddly enough, in view of the indicated importance of the relationship between livestock inventory and feed grains output, Oury does
not seem to have considered a measure of meat prices in his grain
supply models.

A number of studies of cereals production have examined the
United Kingdom, beginning with G. T. Jones who analyzed three
such crops—wheat, barley, and oats (as well as a number of
vegetables and fruits, the results for which are summarized in
Chapter 6)—the first two of which are mainly cash crops while
oats are raised mainly for forage.[52] Jones noted that wheat and
oats compete more with barley than with each other, with barley
tending to be the second choice in both wheat and oats areas, though
oats cultivation has gradually declined in favor of barley since
World War I. Jones' supply model followed generally Nerlovian
lines, incorporating both price expectation and area adjustment
mechanisms. The supply equations also included a rainfall variable
and a dummy variable to account for the government policy of
encouraging wheat production (the Wheat Act of 1933). The calculated
elasticities are shown in Table 5.51 (along with their standard
errors). His analysis reveals rainfall is significant at the 10 percent
level or better for all three crops, the dummy variable at the 1 percent level for wheat, and the oats trend variable at the 1 percent
level for both periods.

Brian Hill has examined the price responsiveness of cereal
producers in England and Wales from 1925 to 1963.[53] This entire

TABLE 5.50

Supply Elasticities, French Feed Grains

	Elasticities with respect to:				
Model	Feed-Grain Prices Distributed Lag	Feed-Grain Prices, 3-Year Average	Relative Wheat- Barley Price	Relative Wheat- Maize Price	Relative Wheat- Feed-Grain Price
Yield	$\begin{cases} 0.698^a \\ 0.520^b \end{cases}$	$\begin{cases} 1.235^a \\ 0.447^b \end{cases}$	–	–	–
Acreage	–	0.770	-0.817	-0.292	-1.223
Production	$\begin{cases} 0.919^a \\ 0.683^b \end{cases}$	$\begin{cases} 1.542^a \\ 0.849^b \end{cases}$	-1.00	-0.618	-2.435

[a]With N in equation.
[b]With T in equation.

Source: Bernard Oury, A Production Model for Wheat and Feed-grains in France 1946-1961 (Amsterdam: North-Holland, 1966).

period saw government intervention in cereals markets in attempts to stabilize farm incomes, but Hill identified three distinct subperiods as far as farmer reactions to government moves are concerned.

The mid-1920s saw the introduction and expansion of Britain's first peacetime attempts at agricultural stabilization through price controls, but not until the depression had reached its nadir in 1931 did government intervention become pervasive. Thus Hill distinguishes the period 1925 to 1931 when farmer uncertainty was high (due to severe instability and deepening depression), yet more or less constant, from the interval 1933 to 1939, when the level of uncertainty fluctuated as farmers adjusted to, and evaluated the effectiveness of, government stabilization programs. He also singled out 1956 to 1963, after the end of all wartime and recovery measures, as indicative of the future of British farmers. These years were characterized by generally low market prices for cereals, making the minimum support prices of great importance to cultivators. Hill then focused his analysis on these three periods (all of which are very short from the point of view of obtaining reliable parameter estimates using the regression techniques he employs), using a Nerlovian acreage adjustment model incorporating grain prices (weighted by acreage) deflated by a general price index.

He lumped together the acreages of wheat, barley, and oats, which have approximately the same production functions and compete for factor inputs throughout much of England and Wales. The parameters he estimated using ordinary least-squares techniques (considering also an alternate formulation of the model from 1956 to 1963 which included a measure of expected cost of production) are seen in Table 5.52.

Statistical significance and positive influence on output for the price variable are found only in the earliest period (that is, when the influence that government stabilization programs might be assumed to have been least). For the postwar years tested, Hill indicated that the strong negative correlation ($r = -0.72$) between the cost and price variables diminished the reliability of these calculated parameters. Furthermore, price changes were relatively

TABLE 5.51

Supply Elasticities, U.K. Cereals

Crop	Period	Formulation[a]	Short-Run Elasticity	Long-Run Elasticity
Wheat	1924-39	A	0.33[c] (0.08)	0.46
		B	0.41[c] (0.07)	0.98
Barley	1924-39	A	0.63[c] (0.15)	1.75
		B	0.57[c] (0.14)	2.71
Oats	1924-39	C	0.11[b] (0.06)	0.16
	1946-58	C	0.18 (0.11)	0.24

[a]A includes wheat and barley prices, rainfall, and the dummy variable; B only wheat and barley prices; C oats and barley prices, rainfall, and a trend variable.

[b]10 percent significance level.

[c]1 percent significance level.

Source: G. T. Jones, "The Response of the Supply of Agricultural Products in the United Kingdom to Price" (Part II), Farm Economist 10 (1967): 1-28.

TABLE 5.52

Estimated Parameters, England and Wales Cereals

Period	Lagged Acreage	Price	Expected Cost	R^2	Price Elasticity Short-Run	Price Elasticity Long-Run
1925–31	0.68[c]	12.45[c]	–	0.976	0.23	0.73
1933–39	-0.08	8.41	–	0.210	–	–
	0.84[b]	-14.71	–	0.541	negative	–
1956–63	-0.27	-150.10[a]	-362.80[c]	0.886	negative	–
	–	-145.60[b]	-305.10[c]	0.873	negative	–

[a]5 percent significance level.
[b]1 percent significance level.
[c]0.1 percent significance level.
Source: Brian E. Hill, "Supply Responses in Grain Production in England and Wales 1925-1963," Journal of Agricultural Economics 16 (June 1965).

much smaller than both acreage and cost changes, leading to a strong suspicion that reactions to prices might be masked by the effects of costs.

In summary Hill said his original point that the three time periods were characterized by different degrees and stability of price responsiveness was confirmed, and he expressed his disappointment that the Nerlovian model was unable to provide better results. Though he emphasized the inability for this model to account satisfactorily for endogenous shifts, such as in technology, farmer psychology, and so on, a very likely alternative explanation for the model's lack of success in this case can perhaps be more easily found in the short time periods involved, which would make even some of his results that might at first glance seem "better" (like those for 1925 to 1931) acceptable only with caution.

In a more recently published work, Hill presented a modification of Nerlove's basic model.[54] He pointed out that the basic model that incorporated price-expectations and area adjustment yields the following reduced form equation:

$$A_t = d + eP_{t-1} + fA_{t-1} + gA_{t-2} \tag{5.35}$$

where: A is acreage,
         P is price, and
         $f = (1 - \beta) + (1 - \gamma)$ and $g = -(1 - \beta)(1 - \gamma)$ where β and γ
         are the expectations and adjustment coefficients
         respectively.

However, time is unable to account for changes in the long run and
thus implies that technology is constant. Estimating problems with
the Nerlovian model have led investigators to assume either β or γ
to be unity, making the A_{t-2} term disappear in equation 5.35, and
restricting f to the range 0 to 1. $1 - f$ is then interpreted as the
rate of adjustment toward long-run equilibrium. What, though,
if long-run supply is itself shifting? The parameter f can no longer
be a rate of adjustment between short- and long-run activity, and
long-run elasticity, which depends upon the rate of adjustment, can
no longer be calculated. Nevertheless, the value of f obviously
affects current supply and the question remains as to its economic
interpretation.

Hill suggested that f indicates unexplained shifts in the supply
curve (including, for example, those due to technological changes).
A value of zero would indicate a stationary curve; the annual
percentage change in the curve due to shifts would be

$$100f \left(\frac{\overline{A}_t - \overline{A}_{t-1}}{\overline{A}_{t-1}} \right)$$

where $\overline{A}$ is mean output. Obviously f need not be restricted to the
range 0 to 1; higher values would indicate supply was changing
(in the same direction) at an increasing rate, and negative values
could indicate the presence of alternate increases and decreases
brought on by chance or some third factor.

This hypothesis was tested by formulating a model:

$$A_t = d + eP_{t-1} + fA_{t-1} \tag{5.36}$$

identical with Nerlove's model when either β or γ is assumed to be
one, but with a different meaning for f. Regressions were run on
cereals production in England and Wales during the period 1956 to
1970. He selected this period because of a notable increase in
production in the face of a decline in both money and real prices;
rejecting the possibility of a perverse supply curve leaves only
the possibility of a supply curve shift. Estimates (and standard
errors) obtained using both price and gross returns per acre are
shown in Table 5.53.

TABLE 5.53

Estimated Parameters, England and Wales,
Modified Model

Lagged Acreage Coefficient	Lagged Price Coefficient	Lagged Return Coefficient	Short–Run Elasticity	R^2
0.75[c] (0.12)	–48.41[a] (23.11)	–	–	0.93
0.83[c] (0.08)	–	15.28[b] (5.66)	0.28	0.94

[a]10 percent significance level.
[b]5 percent significance level.
[c]1 percent significance level.
Source: Brian E. Hill, "Supply Responses in Crop and Livestock Production," Journal of Agricultural Economics 22 (September 1971).

The expected perverse price relationship for this period is indicated, but economic rationality triumphs when returns per acre is substituted as an independent variable. By Hill's original hypothesis the shifter coefficient (lagged acreage) should pick up the unaccounted affect of yield changes in the first formulation, but it does not in this case. All that Hill can conclude is that lagged acreage is statistically significant but not for unknown (in the first equation) economic reasons.

Hill also tested his hypothesis for the supply of dairy products, and an account of these results is seen in Chapter 9.

Still another British study, by D. R. Colman, considered cereals production from 1955 to 1966.[55] Like Hill, he recognized that wheat, barley, and oats share similar production functions and that the production of one cannot be divorced from the influences of the others. Colman, however, separately analyzed each grain crop, rather than lumping the outputs of all three; he even attempted to distinguish between the responsiveness shown by cultivators for winter and spring wheat. He assumed that cultivators formulate some sort of overall plan each year for plantings of each crop, considering the past prices of the three cereals (expressed in terms of a measure of weighted return per acre), weather considerations, and, of course, availability of inputs. He allowed that the difference in time as regards sowing and maturing of the different outputs (particularly winter wheat versus the warm-weather crops*) gives the farmer the chance to change the overall plan to some extent during the year.

In his preliminary analysis, winter wheat acreage was expressed as a function of a weather index and, alternatively, of a lagged measure of returns per acre or a time-trend variable. In both cases the weather variable dominated (with returns per acre being insignificant in the version in which it is used). Colman commented that this is consistent with a hypothesis that intended plantings of winter wheat are accomplished only if proper weather conditions prevail in autumn, wheat prices being important, perhaps, only to the extent that they remain above some threshold value that will encourage planting to the extent weather conditions permit.

Spring wheat and oats were regressed, respectively, on the preceding season's winter wheat acreage and a relative wheat-barley returns measure, and on the preceding year's oats acreage and measures of the relative oats-barley prices and yields. The output of barley, as a residual crop, was estimated in a first-differences formulation, with changes in barley acreage represented as a function of changes in wheat acreage (with which it more directly competes) and a measure of (weighted) grains returns per acre. Estimates using this equation having satisfied Colman that barley was in fact a residual crop, he obtained his final estimates with the model:

All grains: $A_{G_t} = a_o + a_1 A_{G_{t-1}} + a_2 I_{G_{t-1}} + a_3 W_{G_{t-1}} + u_1$ \qquad (5.37a)

Winter wheat: $A_{ww_t} = b_o + b_2 T + b_3 W_{ww_{t-1}} + u_2$ \qquad (5.37b)

Spring wheat: $A_{sw_t} = c_o + c_1 A_{ww_t} + c_2 (\frac{I_w}{I_B})_{t-1} + u_3$ \qquad (5.37c)

Oats: $A_{O_t} = d_o + d_1 A_{O_{t-1}} + d_2 (\frac{P_O}{P_B})_{t-1} + d_3 (\frac{Y_O}{Y_B})_{t-1} + u_4$ \qquad (5.37d)

---

*Among these, spring wheat, oats (and mixed corn), and barley are sown in that order. Oats and mixed corn enjoy lower yields, and thus compete less with the others except when other technical factors such as soil type are important. Barley, the last crop sown, is obviously in somewhat of a residual position.

together with an identity for barley acreage:

$$A_{B_t} = A_{G_t} - A_{ww_t} - A_{sw_t} - A_{OMC_t} \qquad (5.37e)$$

where: A, I, P, and Y are acreages, returns, price, and yields,
              respectively,
         T is trend variable, and
         W is a weather index.

His parameter estimates had relatively large standard errors
associated with the coefficients of the price and return variables.
Thus he presented only his short-run elasticity estimates, and
these are as shown in Table 5.54.

Colman argued that barley's strong responsiveness tended to
confirm his hypothesis that the expansion of barley acreage during
the period under·study can be traced to the firmness of barley
prices, to increasing yields per acre for barley, and to growing
cultivation problems for wheat due to disease, soil, and weather
conditions. These problems plus the complete lack of (significant)
positive responsiveness to price of winter wheat he felt doomed to
failure British government attempts to encourage wheat production
at the expense of barley by manipulation of relative price incentives.

In an addendum to his article, Colman refined his model,
partly on the basis of the strong negative relationship indicated
between oats acreage and barley prices and partly on the increasingly
independent role barley planting decisions may involve, despite
barley's temporally determined role as a residual crop, by
restating equations 5.37d and 5.37e as:

TABLE 5.54

Supply Elasticities, British Cereals

	Barley Acreage	Spring Wheat Acreage	Total Wheat Acreage	Oats Acreage
Barley price	0.57	−0.38	−0.16	−1.51
Wheat price	0.06	0.41	0.17	—
Oats price	−0.22	—	—	1.56

Source: D. R. Colman, "A New Study of United Kingdom Cereal
Supply," Journal of Agricultural Economics 21 (September 1970).

$$A_{OMC} = \delta_o + \delta_1 A_{OMC_{t-1}} + \delta_2 (\frac{I_B}{I_O})_{t-1} + \delta_3 A_{B_t} + u_4 \qquad (5.37f)$$

$$A_{B_t} = \delta_o + \delta_1 A_{B_{t-1}} + \delta_2 (\frac{I_B}{I_w})_{t-1} + \delta_3 I_{G_{t-1}} + \delta_4 A_{w_t}$$

$$+ \delta_5 A_{OMC_t} + u_5 \qquad (5.37g)$$

From estimates based on the revised model he derived short-run elasticities using two-stage least-squares techniques for 1959 to 1969 and these are shown in Table 5.55

TABLE 5.55

Supply Elasticities, British Cereals
(Revised Model)

	Barley Acreage	Oats/Mixed Corn Acreage
Barley prices	+0.78	−0.94
Wheat prices	−0.11	+0.02
Oat prices	−0.37	+0.78

Source: D. R. Colman, "A New Study of United Kingdom Cereal Supply," Journal of Agricultural Economics 21 (September 1970).

Though relatively large standard errors for the estimated coefficients still urged care in accepting the results, the lower oats elasticity and the negative barley-to-wheat price cross-elasticity gave Colman reason to think these results are somewhat more plausible.

NOTES

1. Jere Behrman, Supply Response in Underdeveloped Agriculture: A Case Study of Four Major Annual Crops in Thailand, 1937-63 (Amsterdam: North Holland, 1968).

2. R. O. Olson, "The Impact and Implications of Foreign
Surplus Disposal on Underdeveloped Economies," Journal of Farm
Economics 42 (December 1960); T. N. Krishnan, "The Marketed
Surplus of Foodgrains: Is It Inversely Related to Price?" Economic
Weekly 17 (annual number, February 1965).

3. Raj Krishna, "Farm Supply Response in India-Pakistan:
A Case Study of the Punjab Region," Economic Journal 73 (September
1963); and "The Marketable Surplus Function for a Subsistence
Crop: An Analysis with Indian Data," Economic Weekly 17 (annual
number, February 1965). Behrman's case may be found in "Price
Elasticity of the Marketed Surplus of a Subsistence Crop," Journal
of Farm Economics 48 (November 1966).

4. Vahid Nowshirvani, "Agricultural Supply in India: Some
Theoretical and Empirical Studies" (Ph.D. dissertation, Massachusetts Institute of Technology, 1962).

5. Also discussed in Vahid Nowshirvani, "Land Allocation
under Uncertainty in Subsistence Agriculture," Oxford Economic
Papers 23 (November 1971).

6. James Tobin, "Liquidity Preference as Behavior Towards
Risk," Review of Economic Studies, February 1958.

7. R. D. Singh and Dinkar Rao, "Regional Analysis of Supply-
Price Relationship of Major Foodgrains in Uttar Pradesh," Indian
Journal of Economics 53 (April 1973).

8. Jawahar Kaul, "A Study of Supply Responses to Price of
Punjab Crops," Indian Journal of Economics 48 (July 1967).

9. J. L. Kaul and D. S. Sidhu, "Acreage Response to Prices
for Major Crops in Punjab—An Econometric Study," Indian Journal
of Agricultural Economics 26 (October-December 1971).

10. Raj Krishna "Farm Supply Response in India-Pakistan,"
op. cit.

11. C. C. Maji, D. Jha, and L. S. Venkataramanan, "Dynamic
Supply and Demand Models for Better Estimations and Projections:
An Econometric Study for Major Foodgrains in the Punjab Region,"
Indian Journal of Agricultural Economics 26 (January-March 1971).

12. R. P. Singh, Parmatma Singh, and K. N. Rai, "Acreage
Response to Rainfall, New Farm Technology and Price in Haryana,"
Indian Journal of Agricultural Economics 54 (October 1973).

13. M. S. Rao and Jai Krishna, "Price Expectation and Acreage
Response for Wheat in Uttar Pradesh," Indian Journal of Agricul-
tural Economics 20 (January-March 1965); and "Dynamics of Acreage
Allocation for Wheat in Uttar Pradesh: A Study in Supply Response,"
Indian Journal of Agricultural Economics 22 (January-March 1967).

14. S. P. Sinha and B. N. Varma, "A Study of Trends and
Variations in the Prices of Foodgrains in Bihar with Special Reference to Prices of Cereals between 1956 and 1968," a paper read at

the 31st Annual Conference of the Indian Society of Agricultural
Economics, abstracted in the Indian Journal of Agricultural
Economics 26 (October-December 1971).

15. National Council of Applied Economic Research, Long-Term
Projections of Demand for and Supply of Selected Agricultural
Commodities—1960/61 to 1975/76 (New Delhi, 1962).

16. B. L. Sawhney, "Farm Supply Response: A Case Study of
the Bombay Region," Asian Economic Review 10 (February 1968).

17. Tej Bahadur and N. Haridasan, "A Note on the Price-
Acreage Responses of Pulses in Andhra Pradesh," Indian Journal
of Economics 52 (October 1971).

18. V. Rajagopalan, "Supply Response for Irrigated Crops in
Madras State, India" (Ph.D. dissertation, University of Tennessee,
1967).

19. M. C. Madhavan, "Acreage Response of Indian Farmers:
A Case Study of Tamil Nadu," Indian Journal of Agricultural
Economics 27 (January-March 1972).

20. S. R. Subramanian, S. Varadarajan, and K. Ramamoorthy,
"Farmers' Supply Response," a paper read at the 31st Annual
Conference of the Indian Society of Agricultural Economics,
abstracted in the Indian Journal of Agricultural Economics 26
(October-December 1971).

21. A. Parikh, "Farm Supply Response: A Distributed Lag
Analysis," Oxford Institute of Statistics Bulletin 33 (1971).

22. Dharm Narain, The Impact of Price Movements on Areas
under Selected Crops in India, 1900-1939 (Cambridge: Cambridge
University Press, 1965).

23. Sushil Krishna, "Farm Supply Response in India: A Study
of Four Major Crops," unpublished paper, Tufts University, 1975.

24. Walter Falcon, "Farmer Response to Price in a Subsistence
Economy: The Case of West Pakistan," American Economic Review
54 (Proceedings) (May 1964), pp. 580-91; and "Farmer Response
to Price in an Underdeveloped Area: A Case Study in West Pakistan"
(Ph.D. dissertation, Harvard University, 1962).

25. Sayed Mushtaq Hussain, "A Note on Farmer Response to
Price in East Pakistan," Pakistan Development Review 4 (Spring
1964).

26. John Thomas Cummings, "Supply Response in Peasant
Agriculture: Price and Non-Price Factors" (Ph.D. dissertation,
Tufts University, 1974).

27. Hossein Askari and John Thomas Cummings, "Supply
Response of Farmers with Heterogeneous Land," Indian Journal
of Agricultural Economics, forthcoming 1976.

28. M. L. Dantwala, ed., "Symposium on Farmers' Response
to Prices," Journal of the Indian Society of Agricultural Statistics 22
(June 1970).

29. Mahar Mangahas, Aida E. Recto, and V. W. Ruttan, "Price and Market Relationships for Rice and Corn in the Philippines," Journal of Farm Economics 48 (August 1966): 685-703.

30. Mubyarto, "The Elasticity of Marketable Surplus of Rice in Indonesia: A Study of Java-Madura" (Ph.D. dissertation, Iowa State University, 1965).

31. Virach Aromdee, "Can West Malaysia become Self-sufficient in Rice by 1975?" Malayan Economic Review 14 (October 1969).

32. Virach Aromdee, "Economics of Rice Trade among the Countries of Southeast Asia" (Ph.D. dissertation, University of Minnesota, 1968).

33. Aromdee also quotes the work of Mohammad Raja'a El-Mir, "Location Models for the World Rice Industry" (Ph.D. dissertation, University of California, Berkeley, 1967). El-Mir estimated the Thai supply elasticity of rice with respect to export prices as 0.58 for 1952 to 1964 and 0.29 for 1958 to 1964.

34. Hossein Askari, John T. Cummings, and Bassam Harik, "Land Reform in the Middle East," International Journal of Middle East Studies, forthcoming.

35. Jeannine Swift, "Economic Study of the Chilean Agrarian Reform" (Ph.D. dissertation, Massachusetts Institute of Technology, 1969).

36. William C. Merrill, "Setting the Price of Peruvian Rice," Journal of Farm Economics 49 (February 1967).

37. Remy Friere, "Price Incentives in Argentine Agriculture," Development Advisory Service Report, Center for International Affairs, Harvard University, 1966 (mimeographed).

38. Franklin Fisher and Peter Temin, "Regional Specialization and the Supply of Wheat in United States, 1867-1914," Review of Economics and Statistics 52 (May 1970).

39. For example, William N. Parker and Judith Klein, "Productivity Growth in Grain Production in the United States 1840-60 and 1900-10," in Output, Employment and Productivity in the United States after 1800, Studies in Income and Wealth, Vol. 30 (New York: Columbia University Press for National Bureau of Economic Research, 1966).

40. Robert Higgs, "Regional Specialization and the Supply of Wheat in the United States, 1867-1914: A Comment;" and Franklin Fisher and Peter Temin, "Regional Specialization and the Supply of Wheat in the United States, 1867-1914: A Reply," Review of Economics and Statistics 53 (February 1971).

41. In a further comment on the Fisher-Temin study, Walter P. Page, "Wheat Culture and Productivity Trends in Wheat Production in the United States, 1867-1914: A Comment," Review of Economics

and Statistics 56 (February 1974), presented evidence that winter
wheat acreage in many states was in fact greater than Fisher and
Temin believed. In this regard Page backed up Higgs' assertion
and repeated as well the latter's criticism of the use of December
prices in the acreage regressions.

42. Fisher and Temin, op. cit.; Stephen DeCanio, Agriculture
in the Post-Bellum South (Cambridge: MIT Press, 1974).

43. Askari, Cummings, and Harik, op. cit.

44. Thomas F. Cooley and Stephen J. DeCanio, "Varying
Parameter Supply Functions and the Sources of Economic Distress
in American Agriculture 1866-1914," National Bureau of Economic
Research working paper, no. 57 (September 1974).

45. For a full development of the basis for these techniques,
the reader is directed to the original sources: Thomas F. Cooley,
"Estimation in the Presence of Sequential Parameter Variation"
(Ph.D. dissertation, University of Pennsylvania, 1971); Thomas F.
Cooley and Edward Prescott: "Tests of an Adaptive Regression
Model," Review of Economics and Statistics 55 (May 1963), "An
Adaptive Regression Model," International Economic Review 14
(June 1973), and "Varying Parameter Regression: A Theory and
Some Applications," Annals of Economic and Social Measurement 2
(October 1973).

46. Andrew Schmitz, "Canadian Wheat Acreage Response,"
Canadian Journal of Agricultural Economics 16 (June 1968).

47. J. H. Duloy and A. S. Watson, "Supply Relationships in
the Australian Wheat Industry: New South Wales," Australian
Journal of Agricultural Economics 8 (June 1964).

48. F. H. Gruen et al., Long-Term Projections of Agricultural
Supply and Demand, Australia 1965 and 1980 (Clayton, Victoria:
Economics Department, Monash University, 1968); also Alan A.
Powell and F. H. Gruen, "The Estimation of Production Frontiers:
The Australian Livestock/Cereals Complex," Australian Journal
of Agricultural Economics 11 (June 1967).

49. J. W. B. Guise, "Economic Factors Associated with
Variations in Aggregate Wheat Acreage in New Zealand 1945-1965,"
New Zealand Economic Papers 2, no. 1 (1968).

50. Scott M. Eddie, "The Role of Agriculture in the Economic
Development of Hungary 1867-1913" (Ph.D. dissertation, Massachusetts Institute of Technology, 1967).

51. Bernard Oury, A Production Model for Wheat and Feed-
grains in France 1946-1961 (Amsterdam: North-Holland, 1966).

52. G. T. Jones, "The Response of the Supply of Agricultural
Products in the United Kingdom to Price" (Part II), Farm Economist
10 (1967): 1-28.

53. Brian E. Hill, "Supply Responses in Grain Production in England and Wales 1925-1963," Journal of Agricultural Economics 16 (June 1965).

54. Brian E. Hill, "Supply Responses in Crop and Livestock Production," Journal of Agricultural Economics 22 (September 1971).

55. D. R. Colman, "A New Study of United Kingdom Cereal Supply," Journal of Agricultural Economics 21 (September 1970).

6

In addition to the multitude of studies of cereal crops, a large amount of work has concerned annuals we have loosely termed cash crops. Many of those presented herein involve nonfoodstuffs—most prominently, fibers, oilseeds, and tobacco—but several vegetables have also caught the attention of researchers. As with cereals, a considerable geographic diversity is found in the published material.

Among fiber crops cotton is the widest grown, and much effort has been devoted to dynamic analysis of its output, beginning with Nerlove's original work, which examined U.S. cotton. Another study of the same country, but during a somewhat earlier period is that of Stephen DeCanio who concentrated on the years 1882 to 1914.[1] At that time most cotton was grown under leasehold arrangements (both rental payments and sharecropping) on tenant-operated farms typically between 20 and 50 acres in size. Some production, however, did take place on usually larger (100 to 500 acres) owner-operated farms.

DeCanio employed several Nerlove-type supply models but obtained his best results using a logarithmic formulation that regressed harvested acreage on producer prices of cotton relative to alternative crops (corn, wheat, oats, and tame hay), the percentage of farms operated by tenants, and lagged acreage.

Using this model he estimated parameters for each of the ten major cotton-producing states. In each state the price coefficient (which in this logarithmic formulation is also the short-run price elasticity) proved significant at the 5 percent level or better, which was also true of the coefficient of lagged area in all but two states. The coefficient of the percentage of tenant-operated farms proved significantly nonzero at the 5 percent level in only one state, though the values obtained for five other states proved significant at least at the 30 percent level. His parameter estimaters (and their t values) are shown in Table 6.1.

Thomas Cooley and Stephen DeCanio used this same data for U.S. cotton in a further application of estimating techniques allowing for identification of structural shift over time.[2] They used a basic Nerlove-type model; the estimating equation represented relative acreage planted in cotton as a function of prices and the dependent variable lagged one year. Their estimating techniques were Bayesian and were applied to obtain values at five-year intervals.

In contrast to the results they found for wheat, the cotton estimates do not show a clear unambiguous pattern of change during this period. When they computed simple correlation coefficients between the parameter estimates and a trend variable they found declining short-run elasticity over time in only five states (Arkansas, Florida, Louisiana, Mississippi, and Tennessee), with increases indicated for the other five. This they felt cast doubt on the argument that Southern farmers became increasingly committed to cotton cultivation during the post-Civil War era and less willing or able to shift to alternative crops. The generally negative correlation between time and the lagged cotton area coefficient also contrasts with the relationship found for wheat. This indication would be consistent with cotton farmers becoming increasingly sensitive to recent prices (as opposed to those of more distant years) during this period.

Trying to reconcile the seemingly contradictory changes in cultivator behavior shown for wheat and cotton, Cooley and DeCanio tested the differentiated reaction (to permanent and transitory elements in price changes) hypothesis of John Muth and concluded it to be generally valid for the case examined.[3] Cotton prices tended to fluctuate randomly during the period in question, with few if any indications of permanent shifts. They argued that cotton cultivators, unlike those of wheat, tended to discount recent large fluctuations.

Michael Brennan examined the supply performance of U.S. cotton during the period 1905 to 1932, approximately the gap between the DeCanio study mentioned above and the onset of price supports.[4] Each of the three main producing areas was analyzed separately: the Southeast, the Mississippi Delta, and the Southwest.* Supply was represented as a function of the cotton price, the prices

---

*Southeast: Alabama, Georgia, Florida, North Carolina, South Carolina; Delta: Arkansas, Louisiana, Mississippi, Missouri, Tennessee; Southwest: Arizona, California, New Mexico, Oklahoma, Texas.

TABLE 6.1

Estimated Parameters, U.S. Cotton

State	Coefficient				Long-Run Price Elasticity	R^2
	Constant	Price	Tenancy Percentage	Lagged Area		
Alabama	2.91[b] (2.31)	0.176[c] (4.48)	0.388[b] (2.36)	0.627[c] (4.38)	0.472	0.879
Arkansas	2.91[a] (1.86)	0.158[b] (2.62)	0.234 (1.55)	0.600[c] (3.15)	0.395	0.811
Florida	3.53[b] (2.43)	0.134[b] (2.34)	0.446 (1.02)	0.414[a] (1.96)	0.228	0.492
Georgia	2.11 (1.51)	0.195[c] (3.55)	0.434[a] (1.74)	0.728[c] (4.73)	0.717	0.917
Louisiana	2.75 (1.31)	0.181[c] (4.50)	0.273 (0.774)	0.593[b] (2.20)	0.445	0.804
Mississippi	4.33 (0.536)	0.171[b] (2.21)	0.281 (0.351)	0.437 (0.468)	0.304	0.804
North Carolina	2.50 (0.974)	0.342[c] (4.21)	0.336 (1.14)	0.597[a] (1.89)	0.848	0.804
South Carolina	2.86 (1.64)	0.180[c] (4.25)	0.579 (1.61)	0.621[c] (3.08)	0.475	0.890
Tennessee	1.89[a] (1.86)	0.330[c] (4.47)	0.008 (0.050)	0.613[c] (4.03)	0.852	0.657
Texas	2.13 (1.14)	0.089[b] (2.06)	0.699 (1.04)	0.803[c] (5.20)	0.451	0.984

[a]10 percent significance level.
[b]5 percent significance level.
[c]1 percent significance level.

Source: Stephen DeCanio, "Economy and the Supply of Cotton, 1882-1914," paper given at the Econometric Conference at the University of Wisconsin, Madison, Wisc., April 1971.

of the principal competing crops in each region, with a trend variable added.

Cotton price coefficients were strongly significant in all three regions and the elasticities were within the lower end of the range reported by Nerlove (0.20 to 0.67) for the United States as a whole for almost the same time period. Coefficients for alternate crop prices were negative, as expected, and significant at least at the 10 percent level in all cases tested, further emphasizing the market awareness of cotton cultivators.

In a recent comment on the original Nerlove study's analysis of U.S. wheat, maize, and cotton, William G. Tomek reanalyzed the cotton data, using alternative model specifications.[5] His purpose was to illustrate the sensitivity of the empirical results to such changes.

The results from five versions were reported: (I) Nerlove's own formulation with acreage as a function of prices deflated by an index of competing crop prices, a trend variable, and lagged acreage; (II) the same except that prices are deflated by an index of input prices; (III) acreage as a function only of price and a dummy variable differentiating the period into two subperiods, 1910-24 and 1925-33; (IV) the same adding lagged acreage; and (V), as IV with a trend variable as well.

Tomek emphasized the higher R^2 results for versions III, IV, and V and the different conclusions emerging regarding the value of the acreage adjustment coefficient. In the Nerlove formulation, as well as in II, its value is close to +0.60, but in IV and V it is not significantly different from zero. He did not indicate any clear preference for any alternative model, but restated his initial concern regarding the importance and difficulty of fitting a valid model.

Though Tomek did not estimate price elasticities for cotton, the estimated price coefficients did not vary much from one another in the five regressions reported.

Cotton production in Uganda has been analyzed by Kenneth D. Frederick.[6] Although cotton cultivation in Africa has an ancient history, its modern significance in Uganda dates to the end of the nineteenth century, when the region's new British rulers began encouraging the tribal chiefs to direct their subjects toward its cultivation. Under tribal traditions individuals were granted the rights to till and share in the produce of communal lands by the chief, who in turn received a portion of the harvest, which in precolonialist days was almost exclusively food crops.

Cotton's importance swelled rapidly; exports from Uganda rose from zero in 1900 to 2,000 tons in 1910 and to 70,000 tons by 1938. Until the mid-1920s cotton was about the only cash crop grown by

Africans; at that time the colonial regime finally allowed the near-
monopoly on coffee cultivation enjoyed by European settlers to be
broken, and since then the two crops have competed for the inputs
available to the African farmer. Since little capital is needed for
either, this competition has been keen, particularly since the lands
most suitable to cotton production, on the plains around Lake Victoria,
are also the best for coffee.

Frederick used a simple lagged price model to estimate supply
parameters for the period 1922 to 1938. Two formulations were
tested; both included a trend variable, one had lagged cotton and
coffee prices accounted for separately, the other the lagged ratio
of cotton and coffee prices, and the results are seen in Table 6.2.

Competing crop prices show statistical significance, though
whether they are entered separately or relatively seems to matter
little in the overall explanatory power of the model. (Frederick's
estimates for coffee supply, presented in the same study, are seen
in Chapter 7.)

Since raw cotton is a major Nigerian export and expansion of
the domestic textile industry is high on the nation's list of development priorities, S. A. Oni undertook an analysis of the supply
responsiveness of cotton cultivators.[7] He used both simple and
Nerlove-type adaptive expectations models. Acreage as well as
total output were represented as functions of lagged producer prices
of cotton and groundnuts, an alternative crop, of a rainfall index,

TABLE 6.2

Estimated Parameters, Ugandan Cotton

Region	Cotton Price	Coffee Price	Relative Cotton to Coffee Price	Trend	R^2	Short-Run Elasticities with Respect to:	
						Cotton Prices	Coffee Prices
Uganda	2.79[b]	-4.92[c]	—	83.91[c]	0.96	0.25	-0.31
	—	—	152.5[c]	86.20[c]	0.95	0.26	—
Buganda	3.02[c]	-3.98[c]	—	48.89[c]	0.91	0.73	-0.67
	—	—	149.5[c]	48.20[c]	0.91	0.67	—
	-0.24	-0.94[a]	—	35.01[c]	0.92	—	-0.10
Rest of country	—	—	3.0	38.10[c]	0.92	—	—

[a]25 percent significance level.
[b]5 percent significance level.
[c]1 percent significance level.
Source: Kenneth D. Frederick, "The Role of Market Forces and Planning in
Uganda's Economic Development 1900-1938," Eastern African Economic Review 1
(June 1969).

a trend variable, and lagged area or output. The results he obtained
for the period 1948 to 1967 are shown in Table 6.3; though linear,
logarithmic, and exponential versions of the estimating equation
were tested using ordinary least-squares techniques, the author
presented only the outcome of the first version, which he judged
best of the three.

In a paper concerned with the effects of a government-controlled
crop marketing board on output, S. Olajuwon Olayide examined the
six major cash crops produced by Nigerian farmers.[8] Two are
annuals—cotton and groundnuts—while the other four products are
perennial plants—cocoa, palm oil, palm kernels, and rubber.
(Groundnuts are discussed later in this chapter; for cocoa, rubber,
and palm products, see Chapter 7.) All but the last are under the
control of the Nigerian Produce Marketing Company; together they
provided a major share of Nigeria's foreign exchange earnings
during the period in question, 1948 to 1967.*

A number of supply models were considered and tried; they
generally reflected the author's primary concern with perennial
crops.† Two basic models were tested using ordinary least-squares
techniques; output in tonnage terms was represented as a function of:
(a) producer price and acreage appropriately lagged (relative to the
time between planting and maturity), an index of weather and humidity
during the production season, and first and second degree trend
variables; and (b) the same as model a, but adding current world
prices for each crop, plus a disease index for cocoa. He also
regressed domestic producer prices on lagged (one-year) world
prices and a trend variable.

For annuals both versions are quasi-Nerlovian in form, including
lagged acreage (though not lagged output); the cotton estimating
equation also included the price of groundnuts. His results showed
that lagged price is quite significant in model a, but not in b, when
current cotton prices as well are included.

The author defines elasticity in a different manner for each
model. In the first case it is the ratio of the percentage change in
output to that in (lagged) producer price (e_1), in the second, the

---

*They fell from a high of about 80 percent of all exports in the
late 1940s to less than half by 1967. Much of this relative decline
was due to the increasing importance of petroleum exports since
the early 1960s.

†He cites the model-building of Merrill Bateman, Robert Stern,
Peter Ady, and Ben French, and Jim Matthews (for all of these
see Chapter 7) in reference to formulating the equation tested in
his paper.

TABLE 6.3

Estimated Supply Parameters, Nigerian Cotton

	Acreage		Total Output	
	Simple Model	Adaptive Expectations Model	Simple Model	Adaptive Expectations Model
Cotton price	+27.112	+48.165[a]	+3.568	+4.469
	(36.717)	(30.698)	(4.772)	(4.462)
Groundnuts price	−0.318	−0.861	−0.407	−0.313
	(1.676)	(1.420)	(2.175)	(2.065)
Rainfall index	−6.931	−12.046[a]	−0.905	−1.290
	(9.493)	(7.912)	(1.234)	(1.166)
Trend	+49.925[b]	+57.931[b]	+6.092[b]	+7.054[b]
	(8.113)	(7.580)	(1.054)	(1.112)
Lagged acreage	−	−0.379[b]	−	−
		(0.128)		
Lagged output	−	−	−	−0.243[a]
				(0.133)
R^2	0.800	0.877	0.800	0.839
Price elasticity				
Short-run	+0.231	+0.383	+0.207	+0.259
Long-run	−	+0.278	−	+0.209
Cross	−0.052	−0.040	−0.014	−0.011

[a]20 percent significance level.
[b]1 percent significance level.
Source: S. A. Oni, "Econometric Analysis of Supply Response Among Nigerian Cotton Growers," Bulletin of Rural Economics and Sociology 4, no. 2 (1969).

sum of e_1 and the ratio of the percentage change in output to that in current world prices. His regressions of producer prices on world prices allow him a third method of estimating price elasticity—that relative to world prices. For cotton the elasticity values were calculated to be +0.032 and +0.040 from the two supply models, with the portion relative to world prices between +0.024 and +0.040.

In his conclusions the author, again more concerned with the perennial crops, argued for less market restriction, basing his case on the important influence on harvesting decisions that current world prices show for each crop.[9]

Several of the studies reporting cotton supply data concern the
Indo-Pakistani subcontinent. Raj Krishna applied his area adjustment
model to Punjab for 1922 to 1941, estimating parameters for the two
important varieties grown in the state.[10] His results are shown in
Table 6.4 (along with the standard errors).

In a separate work focused on the post-Independence period
(1948-61), Raj Krishna reported short- and long-run supply elasticities of 0.64 and 1.33 for nationwide Indian cotton output.[11]

Also investigating Punjabi cotton was Jawahar Kaul, again using
a Nerlovian acreage adjustment model including crop yield, rainfall,
and trend variables in the formulation.[12] Price coefficients and
elasticities are shown for the period 1951 to 1964 in Table 6.5.
Though the long-run price elasticities in particular are sizable,
the price parameters actually show little statistical significance,
unlike those calculated for prewar Punjab by Raj Krishna.

Also reporting on cotton in the Haryana remnant of erstwhile
Punjab were R. P. Singh, Parmatma Singh, and K. N. Rai.[13]
Their simplified supply model expressed acreage in terms of lagged
harvest prices, rainfall during the presowing period, and technology
represented in terms of crop yield. Acreage figures for the Desi
variety alone were used. Only the price coefficient proved significant in the regression estimates; the resulting calculations for the
short-run elasticity showed a value of +0.622.

In a very detailed recently published study, A. Parikh investigated the supply response of cultivators of cotton, jute, groundnuts,
and sugarcane, the principal Indian cash crops, during the period
1900 to 1939.[14] (The results for jute, groundnuts, and sugarcane
are recounted later in this chapter and in Chapter 8.) Parikh's
analysis, only a severely condensed version of which was published,
involved fitting 34 different variations of the supply model to output

TABLE 6.4

Estimated Parameters, Punjabi Cotton

Variety	Relative Price	Relative Yield	Total Irrigated Acreage	Lagged Acreage	Area Adjustment Coefficient	Elasticity Short-Run	Long-Run	R^2
American	+6.23[b] (1.08	—	+0.34[b] (0.09)	+0.56[b] (0.13)	+0.44	+0.72	+1.62	0.96
Desi	+6.83[b] (1.36)	+3.24[a] (1.14)	—	+0.45[b] (0.13)	+0.55	+0.59	+1.08	0.85

[a]5 percent significance level.
[b]1 percent significance level.
　Source: Raj Krishna, "Farm Supply Response in India-Pakistan: A Case Study of the
Punjab Region," Economic Journal 73 (September 1963).

TABLE 6.5

Estimated Parameters, Punjabi Cotton

Variety	Price Coefficient	Elasticity Short-Run	Long-Run	R^2
American	+7.13 (17.36)	0.34	2.84	0.73
Desi	+0.46 (1.15)	0.29	1.19	0.85

Source: Jawahar Kaul, "A Study of Supply Responses to Price of Punjab Crops," Indian Journal of Economics 48 (July 1967).

data.* These included both Nerlovian price expectations and area adjustment formulations, as well as simpler time trend functions and more complex models with two lagged variables.

Parikh reports estimated parameters for cotton from regressions on cotton acreage as a function of: (A) lagged cotton price deflated by a general price index and lagged acreage; (B) lagged deflated cotton prices, per acre yield, rainfall at sowing time, and lagged acreage; (C) lagged (one and two periods) deflated prices, rainfall (lagged one and two periods), and lagged (one and two periods) acreage; and (D) lagged deflated prices, deflated proceeds per acre, rainfall, total area under cultivation during same season, and lagged acreage. His estimates are shown in Table 6.6.

In analyzing these results (and others not shown), Parikh commented that the elasticities and adjustment coefficients for this dry-season crop in Madhya Pradesh/Berar are only half those calculated by Nerlove for the United States during approximately the same period. The greater degree of explanatory power shown by model B (which included lagged yield and a weather index as independent variables) as compared to the simple Nerlovian model (formulation A), Parikh felt, points to a likely increase in supply responsiveness in later years as technological advances and irrigation facilities became more available to cultivators after Independence.

_____

*The authors are grateful to Dr. Parikh for supplying us with a copy of the original unedited version of his paper, and much of what we quote is from this, not the published, version.

TABLE 6.6

Estimated Parameters, Cotton

Area	Formu-lation	Price Coefficient	Lagged Area Coefficient	Adjustment Coefficient	Elasticities Short-Run	Long-Run	R^2
Madhya Pradesh/	A	+ 84.49[b]	+0.832[a]	+0.17	+0.10	+0.16	0.79
Berar	B	- 38.10	+0.792[a]	+0.20	n.q.	n.q.	0.89
	C	+102.1[b]	+0.618[a]	n.q.	+0.12	+0.72	0.66
Punjab	A	+157.3[a]	+0.956[a]	+0.05	+0.43	+9.74	0.87
	D	n.q.	n.q.	+0.52	+0.23[c]	+0.44[c]	n.q.

n.q. = Not quoted in paper.
[a]10 percent significance level.
[b]5 percent significance level.
[c]Relative to proceeds per acre.
Source: A. Parikh, "Market Responsiveness of Peasant Cultivators: Some Evidence from Prewar India," Journal of Development Studies 8 (1972).

Punjabi cotton during this earlier period was already extensively grown on irrigated land, and its supply does show a greater responsiveness to price variations, though the long-run elasticity estimate (using formulation A) is obviously too high. Model D incorporated a lagged measure of proceeds per acre, the coefficient of which proves statistically significant, and the short- and long-run elasticities with respect to net proceeds are more reasonable in magnitude (0.22 and 0.44, respectively). Likewise, the adjustment coefficient (0.51) is closer to Raj Krishna's estimates for Punjabi cotton supply between 1922 and 1943 (0.42 for American and 0.55 for Desi cotton).

Another estimate for the nationwide supply elasticity of cotton in India was reported by the National Council of Applied Economic Research (NCAER), with a figure for jarilla variety cotton of 0.75.[15]

The final crop analyzed by Sushil Krishna was cotton, again using Dharm Narain's data—in this case, for Bombay province from 1904 to 1939.[16] Krishna used a partial-adjustment Nerlove formulation, with acreage expressed in terms of lagged prices (relative to those of two major competing crops—jowar and bajra), total area planted in the three crops, rainfall, and lagged cotton acreage. Both linear and logarithmic versions of the model were estimated using ordinary least-squares techniques. Rainfall showed little significance in either regression, a situation similar to that he found for the other three crops he considered. For the other explanatory variables, some degree of statistical significance (at the 20 percent level or better) was found for each model. The estimated price parameter was significant at the 20 percent level in the linear case and at better than the 5 percent level in the logarithmic form. The value of R^2 was also slightly higher in the latter regression—0.38 as opposed to 0.37 for the linear version. Short- and long-run supply elasticities relative to cotton prices were calculated to be about +0.15 and +0.25 respectively using the logarithmic equation.

In the study by B. L. Sawhney of agriculture in Bombay state between 1949 and 1964 he applied to cotton output his two variants of the Nerlovian area adjustment model: acreage expressed as a function of (A) lagged cotton prices relative to those of alternate crops (bajra, jowar, and groundnuts), lagged cotton yield relative to that of the same crops, rainfall, and lagged acreage, and (B) the product of relative prices and relative yields (that is, relative gross income), rainfall, and lagged acreage.[17]

The explanatory power of both models as regards acreage variation Sawhney felt to be rather good, with the gross income model performing marginally better, as it does also for groundnuts (see later in this chapter). Sawhney speculated that this indicates more likely success for agricultural policies aimed at improving income per acre. While he may very well be right, one can draw from his results the conclusion that price-enhancing policies alone would be as effective: The significance of the gross income parameter for groundnuts seems due to the influence of relative yield, while the role of gross income in affecting cotton and jowar can be traced to the strength of prices as a determinant of output.

V. Rajagopalan included cotton in his major study of the agriculture of Madras state between 1939 and 1961.[18] Cotton is grown to some extent in only two of the three regions into which he divided the state: About 7 percent of the four interior districts and 15 percent of the two southeastern coastal districts is devoted to cotton cultivation. Two variations of the basic Nerlovian model were used in estimating the cotton supply parameters: acreage expressed as a function of (A) relative cotton prices, deflated by a substitute crop (sugarcane, groundnuts, and rice) price index, lagged (one and two periods) acreage, and a trend variable; and (B) per acre cotton yield, lagged absolute cotton prices, lagged substitute crop prices, lagged acreage, and a trend variable.

While substitute price coefficients are negative as expected in both regions, and statistically significant as well, cotton prices are significant only in one regression for the southeastern districts. For the latter region Rajagopalan reported a supply elasticity of +1.28, and crosselasticities of −0.51 and −0.76 for the interior and southeast, respectively.

The paper of M. C. Madhavan also included a study of cotton output in Madras.[19] He expressed acreage in terms of lagged prices deflated by those of a competing crop (in turn, sorghum, cumbu, groundnuts, and sesamum prices were used), lagged yields and acreage of both cotton and the competing crop, and a rainfall index. Madhavan's supply equation was tested in logarithmic form for the period 1947 to 1965 and ordinary least-squares estimating techniques.

Price coefficient estimates showed little statistical significance except when cotton prices were deflated in terms of groundnuts, the major competitor throughout the state; short- and long-run elasticities are shown in Table 6.7. Again those calculated from the groundnuts formulation stand out.

Madhavan commented that cotton prices were quite stable during the period of his study and he argued that this stability tended to assure cultivators a fairly steady income from its cultivation. This he felt might have been enough to cause the secular growth in cotton acreage that characterized the era.

For the northwestern part of the subcontinent, two studies of West Pakistani cotton supply are available. Both used a simple supply equation expressing the percentage change in cotton acreage as a function of the ratio of cotton prices and a weighted average price of alternate crops. Walter Falcon reported a short-run supply elasticity of +0.41 for the period 1933 to 1958,[20] while Ghulam Mohammed, examining a slightly later span, 1949 to 1962, estimated the same elasticity to be +0.53.[21]

Indo-Pakistani cotton cultivation has also figured in John Cummings' study.[22] During the postwar period on which he focuses, domestic markets in the subcontinent have been marked by a rapid

TABLE 6.7

Supply Elasticities, Madras Cotton

| Competing Crop | Elasticity | | Area Adjustment Coefficient |
	Short-Run	Long-Run	
Sorghum	+0.01	+0.02	0.68
Cumbu	+0.01	+0.02	0.51
Groundnut	+0.31	+0.54	0.57
Sesamum	+0.04	+0.11	0.39

Source: M. C. Madhavan, "Acreage Response of Indian Farmers: A Case Study of Tamil Nadu," Indian Journal of Agricultural Economics 27 (January-March 1972).

expansion of the textile industries; demand increases have led to rapid changes in the importance of cotton in many new areas. Most cultivation, however, still takes place in the traditional cotton belt, running from Cape Comorin at the southern extremity of India northward along the west coast to Pakistan's broad Indus Valley. Gujarat and Maharashta alone account for about two-thirds of Indian output, with most of the rest grown in Mysore, Madhya Pradesh, and Punjab. Relatively, cotton is even more important in (West) Pakistan, claiming more than 10 percent of the cultivated acreage, with production centered in Multan, Hyderabad, Sargodha, and Hyderabad divisions.

Two distinct varieties are important in the northwestern part of the subcontinent. The native stock known as Desi and a hybrid generically called American frequently compete for inputs. The latter generally commands a higher market price and enjoys higher per acre yields but incurs its growers somewhat greater production costs. Several earlier studies have considered these two strains separately, and Cummings reports similarly for (West) Pakistan, though not for Punjab.

The Nerlove model used for estimating purposes explained cotton acreage in terms of deflated cotton prices, a rainfall index, lagged acreage, and a trend variable.

While some negative price parameters were estimated, statistical significance in such cases is mostly limited to Kerala and Tamil Nadu, two minor cotton states, plus a few districts in nearby Andhra Pradesh. Positive price responsiveness is indicated even more consistently in (West) Pakistan, and for both varieties.

The author remarks that, considering the growth in demand for cotton, the large number of estimated negative trend coefficients was surprising. No particular pattern, though, seemed discernible, with districts with both positive and negative trends in all parts of the cotton belt.

Hossein Askari and John Cummings also examined cotton supply in their paper exploring the effects of changes in land quality on crop yield.[23] They used two supply models, each incorporating different measures of crop yield as a dependent variable—one using actual yield figures, the other a predicted series resulting from separate regression estimates. Though on the whole they found the second version worked better in explaining acreage variation, not much difference was found for cotton.

In their paper seeking to define differences in cultivator price responsiveness following land reform in the Middle East, Askari, Cummings, and Harik included cotton, an important cash crop in three countries recently undergoing land reform—Egypt, Syria, and Iraq.[24] They estimated the price elasticities calculated for

the periods preceding and following land reform implementation.
They were calculated from least-squares regressions run on a
Nerlove supply model postulating output (in either area or yield
terms) as a function of lagged prices, water availability, a trend
variable standing for secular changes in inputs like technology,
and lagged output.

In Egypt overall planted acreage is a severe constraint, though
crop substitution within this limit is of course possible. The authors
claimed that crop yield was generally the more relevant supply
variable in Egypt, and noted the shift indicating greater market
responsiveness in the postrevolutionary period. Beginning in 1952
and continuing through the rest of that decade, about one-sixth of
the fertile Nile Valley and delta region were sequestered from their
former owners—members of the deposed royal family, urban bourgeois
landlords, and a menagerie of foreigners powerful under the old
regime.

In the Fertile Crescent, whose bulk is found within the modern
borders of Syria and Iraq, agriculture is very much of a marginal
operation, with large quantities of land planted or ignored depending
upon the cultivators' expectations for the upcoming season. Increases
in planting involve substandard land and decreases in yield; positive
responsiveness to price increases implies that short-run jumps in
cultivated acreage are the easiest way for market-sensitive cultivators to react. Thus the authors argued generally for positive acreage
elasticities (and negative yield elasticities) as indicative of market
responsiveness. In Syria the post-land-reform results support
the effectiveness of the procedure; the Iraqi evidence is weak, but
slightly perverse—all in all, though, little statistical backing was
evident for any hard conclusions in either country.

Some further evidence regarding Middle Eastern cotton is
offered by Robert Stern, who used a simple supply model to analyze
pre-World War II Egyptian output.[25] Output was expressed in
relative terms, with the ratio of acreage of cotton to that of competing
crops (maize, wheat, rice, and barley) expressed as a linear function
of the lagged price ratio. Stern calculated the arc elasticities for
each crop year from 1899-1900 to 1937-38, obtaining mean and
median values of +0.48 and +0.38, respectively. Because in
several of the pre-World War I years much of the crop destroyed
by pests and the enlargement of the Aswan Dam was completed
in 1912, he recalculated the elasticities for the period 1914-15
to 1937-38, reporting for this shorter interval mean and median
values of +0.78 and +0.52.

A fiber of more localized importance is jute, most of which is
grown in the region around the head of the Bay of Bengal. It has
long been the major export crop of first India, and later East Pakistan,

now Bangladesh. The significant role of jute in foreign exchange earnings has prompted a number of studies.

One of the earliest was published by Ralph Clark, who used a simple supply model, phrased in logarithmic terms, which expressed output (in both area and tonnage terms) as a function of both lagged jute and rice prices.[26] He applied it to a number of geographic regions—all Bengal, East Bengal, and India and Pakistan. He computed a short-run supply (tonnage) elasticity for East Bengal of 0.60.

L. R. Venkataramanan, in his study of jute production in undivided pre-Independence India, used a simple supply model.[27] He presented estimates of +0.46 and +0.73 for short- and long-run elasticity for the period 1911 to 1938.

Robert Stern, in a study of jute production in the former East Pakistan, presented elasticity estimates for undivided Bengal and northeast India—the combined provinces of Bengal, Bihar, and Orissa—during the half-century preceding World War II.[28] Although jute is the dominant export crop of this region, its cultivation is relatively small compared to rice, with the area in jute never exceeding 11 percent of that in rice from 1893 to 1939, nor about 9 percent of the total area in rice and the ten other significant crops of the area (wheat, sugarcane, cotton, linseed, rape and mustard, sesamum, barley, jowar, bajra, and gram).

He used a simple model, expressing (A) relative jute to rice acreage as a function of lagged relative jute to rice prices and (B) relative jute to rice and ten other major crops' acreage in terms of lagged relative jute to a weighted average of rice and ten other crop prices.

Stern then modified his basic model by adding the Nerlovian notion of area adjustment. Testing this model he obtained estimates for Bengal of +0.68 and +1.03 for short- and long-run elasticities (of relative jute to rice and ten other crop prices), respectively, with $R^2 = 0.42$.

In another study of the former East Pakistan, Sayed Mushtaq Hussain calculated postwar (1948 to 1963) jute supply elasticity, and also explored the price response of the acreage given to rice cultivation.[29] Two principal rice crops are harvested each year, and the summer rice (aus) competes closely with jute not only for land but also for labor in both the planting and harvesting periods.

He used a simple linear supply model, estimating supply parameters for East Pakistani jute with three variants of the basic model: (A) total acreage in jute, (B) jute acreage relative to total rice and jute acreage, and (C) jute acreage relative to aus rice plus jute acreage—all expressed as functions of lagged relative jute-to-rice prices. Table 6.8 shows the estimated parameters (and standard errors) thus obtained.

TABLE 6.8

Estimated Parameters, Pakistani Jute

Area	Formu-lation	Constant	Price Coefficient	Short-Run Elasti-city	R^2
East Pakistan	A	+966.9	+56.07[b] (1.475)	0.38	0.59
	B	+0.047	+0.042[b] (0.011)	0.36	0.54
Nine largest jute districts[c]	B	+0.060	+0.042[b] (0.011)	0.42	0.65
	C	+0.163	+0.087[b] (0.020)	0.35	0.54
Three largest jute districts[c]	B	+0.087	+0.036[a] (0.016)	0.29	0.43

[a]5 percent significance level.

[b]1 percent significance level.

[c]The three largest jute districts are Dacca, Mymensingh, and Faridpur; the next six are Comilla, Rajshahi, Rangpur, Bogra, Pabna, and Jessore.

Source: Sayed Mushtaq Hussain, "A Note on Farmer Response to Price in East Pakistan," Pakistan Development Review 4 (1964).

In a later work Hussain developed the basic approach of the above paper into a more sophisticated analysis of how subsistence farmers make allocative decisions between food and cash crops.[30] He hypothesized that peasants may be economically "rational," that is, market oriented, but as constraints placed on their ability to exploit an economic opportunity by subsistence considerations tighten, then their economic responsiveness deteriorates. Since East Pakistan's agricultural sector has been so dominated by rice and jute cultivation, he focused his attention there, simplifying the situation by assuming that allocative decisions are limited to these two choices and that all peasant income is derived from these two sources and is in turn spent on food (rice) and a nonfood good(s). He also assumed that for a given piece of land the relative jute-to-rice yield is constant, although this ratio may vary locationally, and that the peasant utility function can be entirely described in terms of food (either domestically produced or bought) consumed in excess of minimum survival levels and of nonfood good(s).

Under these assumptions, peasant income (I) and consumption expenditures (C) can be expressed by the equations:

$$I = P^e_{R_s} (A_R Y_R - QR_d) + P^e_J (A - A_R) Y_J \qquad (6.1)$$

$$C = P^e_{R_b} QR_b + P_N N \qquad (6.2)$$

where: $P^e_{R_s}$, $P^e_{R_b}$ and P^e_J are the expected harvest and retail prices

of rice and harvest prices of jute,

P_N is a composite price for nonfood goods,

A and A_R are the total cultivated area and the area in rice,

Y_R and Y_J are the normal yields of rice and jute per unit of land,

QR_d and QR_b are the quantities of rice domestically produced and bought on the market, and

N is the nonfood consumption good.

Constraints acting on the peasant are A, total available land, and his family's survival needs, that is, the sum of R_d and R_b must be greater than or equal to the minimum amount of rice needed to survive, R_m. Under these conditions Hussain maximizes utility in light of various production possibilities that could face a peasant: jute or rice specialization ($P^e_{R_b} Y_R < P^e_J Y_J$ or $P^e_J Y_J < P^e_{R_s} Y_R$, respectively, and termed by Hussain Categories I and II), rice production up to level R_d, then devoting remaining land to jute (if $P^e_{R_s} Y_R < P^e_J Y_J < P^e_{R_b} Y_R$ of if $P^e_J Y_J = P^e_{R_s} Y_R$ under conditions of risk, and both termed Category III), and a choice between either specialization course (if $P^e_J Y_J = P^e_{R_b} Y_R$). All jute comes from land described by Categories I and III, all rice from II and III, and given the relevant prices and yields and minimum food requirements, the amount of land in each category will be given by αA, βA, and γA.

Area under jute can be described by:

$$A_J = \alpha A + (A - \frac{Rm}{Y_{R_{III}}}) (1 - \theta) \qquad (6.3a)$$

where: $Y_{R_{III}}$ is normal yield for rice on Category III land, and

$(1 - \theta)$ is the weight assigned to the utility gained from nonfood goods.

Or $\quad A_J = \alpha A + (1 - \theta)(A - A_m)$ $\hfill$ (6.3b)

where A_m is the land needed to grow the minimum amount of food needed for survival. A_m is assumed to be linearly dependent on time (T) and both α and θ to be linearly dependent on the ratio $\dfrac{P_J^e}{P_{R_b}^e}$. Therefore equation 6.3b can be rewritten:

$$A_J = a_o + a_1 \frac{P_J^e}{P_{R_b}^e} + a_2 T \frac{P_J^e}{P_{R_b}^e} + a_3 T \qquad (6.4)$$

By a similar process he expresses area devoted to rice as:

$$A_R = b_o + b_1 \frac{P_{R_b}^e}{P_J^e} + b_2 T \frac{P_{R_b}^e}{P_J^e} + b_3 T \qquad (6.5)$$

Equation 6.4 was estimated in hope of identifying both peasant responsiveness to price (indicated by the coefficient a_1) and the effect of the constraint of subsistence farming (a_2). Some regressions included two-year as well as one-year lagged prices, but the former never showed statistical significance at the 10 percent level. His best results were obtained using a model that also incorporated a measure of risk, N, which was equal to the difference between the standard deviations of retail rice and harvest jute prices over the last three years.

All coefficients save two were statistically significant at the 5 percent level or better, and Hussain concluded that the importance of both a growing subsistence constraint and risk considerations was clearly indicated. He maintained that the presence of this constraint makes adaptation of the Nerlove adjustment model inappropriate for the East Pakistani case. Further evidence of the deterioration over time of the ability of the agricultural sector to feed itself is seen in the swelling of East Pakistan's urban area despite little expansion in employment opportunities.

In analyzing the policy implications of his study, Hussain was pessimistic regarding both the future of jute export earnings and of food output per capita unless the subsistence constraints are eased by improvements in rice (and/or jute) yields and in internal transportation and communications networks and efforts are made to reduce the risks peasants perceive in jute cultivation.

Another extensive study of jute cultivation in India and Pakistan was conducted by A. K. M. Ghulam Rabbani.[31] With rice competing with jute throughout the area for both land and labor, rice prices largely determine jute's opportunity costs and must be considered in any explanation of supply. Rabbani used two variants of the Nerlove model: a price expectations formulation with planted acreage a function of expected prices, and an acreage adjustment approach with acreage expressed in terms lagged relative jute-to-rice prices, relative jute-to-rice yields, lagged acreage, and a trend variable.

Rabbani stressed the conceptual differences between the two models—namely, the former emphasizes the way in which past experience determines present expectations about factors such as prices and yields that in turn affect levels of inputs and outputs, while the latter features technological and institutional constraints that impose limits on how rapidly actual acreage, yield, and so on, can be brought to desired levels. Though the lags found in each model are both important and neither can, a priori, be assumed to be nonexistent, serious estimation problems ruled out use of one model containing both lags.

Using ordinary least-squares techniques, regressions were run on two variations of each model for several geographic regions. In the case of the price expectation model both a restricted version in which β, the coefficient of expectation, was assumed to be equal to unity and one in which no constraint was imposed on β were tested; the results for the former indicated poor performance in explaining acreage variation, and the Durban-Watson test frequently indicated the presence of serial correlation, and for these reasons only the estimates using the second unrestricted version are reported below. The acreage adjustment model was tested both with and without a trend variable. The parameter estimates (and standard errors) Rabbani obtained are seen in Table 6.9.

In commenting on the results Rabbani pointed to the generally better results from the India-wide pre-Independence regressions that were limited to the interwar period (1921-22 to 1938-39), omitting the unstable World War I period. As regards the regional analysis, most jute production in the pre-Independence period was centered in Bengal, and in particular in those parts of East Bengal that later became the province of East Pakistan. Only after Independence did Indian government promotional policies succeed in matching and then surpassing the production levels of East Bengal. Rabbani noted from an initial cursory examination of the data using a scatter diagram that East Bengali cultivation seemed quite distinctly different in the pre- and post-Independence eras, and so separate regressions were run for the two periods (1931-32 to 1946-47 and

TABLE 6.9

Estimated Parameters, Jute

Area	Period	Model	Lagged Prices	Lagged Area	Relative Yield	Trend	Elasticity Short-Run	Long-Run	R^2
India and Pakistan	1911-12 to 1938-39	E.P.[a]	+ 7.40[d] (0.129)	+0.419[d] (0.129)	—	—	0.38	0.65	0.59
		A.A.[a]	+ 8.73[d] (0.122)	+0.393[d] (0.116)	—	—	0.45	0.73	0.68
			+ 9.26[d] (0.125)	+0.411[d] (0.115)	—	+13.10 (9.82)	0.47	0.80	0.71
	1921-22 to 1938-39	E.P.	+10.27[d] (1.89)	+0.508[d] (0.129)	—	—	0.49	1.00	0.74
		A.A.	+10.42[d] (1.74)	+0.466[d] (0.121)	+ 9.60[b] (4.85)	—	0.49	0.93	0.79
			+10.41[d] (1.80)	+0.465[d] (0.126)	+10.03 (7.76)	~ 1.51 (2.11)	0.50	0.93	0.79
Bengal	1912-13 to 1938-39	E.P.	+ 8.42[d] (1.42)	+0.430[d] (0.113)	—	—	0.78	0.84	0.69
		A.A.	+ 8.53[d] (0.11)	+0.390[d] (0.112)	+ 5.20[b] (2.91)	—	0.48	0.84	0.72
			+ 9.18[d] (0.11)	+0.419[d] (0.110)	+ 4.47[d] (0.11)	+10.90 (6.68)	0.52	0.90	0.75
East Bengal	1931-32 to 1946-47	E.P.	+23.57[d] (3.49)	+0.083 (0.104)	—	-29.66 (39.15)	1.35	1.67	0.89
	1949-50 to 1962-63	E.P.	7.38[d] (1.93)	+0.391[c] (0.185)	—	—	0.40	0.66	0.65
	1949-50 to 1962-63	A.A.	+ 6.40[d] (0.25)	+0.394[b] (0.236)	- 4.03[d] (0.38)	- 2.64 (25.07)	0.39	0.65	0.69
West Bengal	1951-52 to 1961-62	E.P.	+ 3.72[d] (0.366)	0.065 (0.135)	—	—	0.70	0.74	0.92
		A.A.	+ 3.71[d] (0.457)	+0.016 (0.190)	+ 0.509 (1.23)	+ 1.86	0.70	0.71	0.93
Assam	1951-52 to 1961-62	E.P.	+ 1.11[d] (0.26)	+0.255 (0.185)	—	—	0.43	0.57	0.68
		A.A.	+ 1.06[d] (0.31)	+0.198 (0.232)	- 0.031 (0.512)	+ 0.703[c] (2.565)	0.41	0.51	0.70
Bihar	1949-50 to 1961-62	E.P.	+ 2.66[d] (0.47)	+0.188 (0.139)	—	—	0.80	0.97	0.78
		A.A.	+ 2.61[d] (0.48)	+0.095 (0.158)	+ 0.329 (0.635)	+ 6.36[d] (4.82)	0.78	0.88	0.82
Orissa[e]	1950-52 to 1961-62	E.P.	+ 0.383	+0.013	—	—	0.75	0.77	0.75
		A.A.	+ 0.401	+0.097	+ 0.237	+ 1.11	0.79	0.88	0.82
Indian Union	1951-52 to 1961-62	E.P.	+ 8.98[d] (0.88)	+0.251[c] (0.116)	—	—	0.76	0.99	0.93
		A.A.	+ 8.79[d] (0.96)	+0.23[b] (0.13)	- 0.086 (2.68)	9.22[d] (1.13)	0.74	0.96	0.94

[a]E.P. means Expected Price; A.A., Acreage Adjustment; [b]10 percent significance level; [c]5 percent significance level; [d]1 percent significance level; [e]standard errors not quoted.

Source: A. K. M. Ghulam Rabbani, "Economic Determinants of Jute Production in India and Pakistan," Pakistan Development Review 5 (Summer 1965): 191-228

1949–50 to 1962–63). These revealed post-Independence price elasticities of less than 40 percent of those of the earlier period.* Rabbani held that this reduction was due to the growing pressure of population on the land and the consequent increase in the subsistence cultivation of rice.

On the other hand, post-Independence regressions run for areas within the Indian Union yield price elasticities nearly twice those of East Pakistan (except for those in Assam state). Rabbani attributed this to the favorable jute-to-rice price ratio in India, as opposed to the rapid increase in the relative price of rice in Pakistan following Independence.

As part of an attempt to devise a stabilization scheme for jute, Sayeedul Huq estimated supply parameters for East Pakistani output between 1948 and 1966.[32] He used both a simple linear equation expressing acreage as a function of lagged relative jute-to-rice prices† and a Nerlovian formulation that included lagged acreage. His estimated parameters (and standard errors) are shown in Table 6.10, along with elasticities calculated from his results.

Given the strong significance indicated for a positive price response by cultivators, Huq proposed government policies for influencing output through a stabilization board that would set the

---

*A complicating factor in the East Bengali acreage models was the existence of government licensing policies in effect from 1941 to 1960, supposedly to limit output. Rabbani included a dummy variable in the East Bengali supply equation and assigned it a value of unity during years in which this policy was in effect, and zero in other years. He initially hypothesized that because the enforcement of the provisions of this policy was at best weak and usually nonexistent that it had no noticeable affect on jute production. The regressions did not reveal significance at even so low a level as 40 percent for the coefficient of the dummy variable, and so he concluded this hypothesis was reasonable.

†Recently in "A Note on the Price Response Studies in Relation to Jute," Indian Journal of Agricultural Economics 27 (January–March 1972), M. A. Jabbar commented on the several studies of East Bengali jute output that have incorporated relative jute-to-rice prices into their supply models. These works, he pointed out, assumed complete substitutability between jute and rice, or at least aus (summer) rice. However, results of research conducted by Jabbar indicated that only about 75 percent of the area in the principal aus and jute areas is in fact suitable for each of the crops. He suggested further work is needed to identify more precisely the role of substitutability in jute planting decisions.

TABLE 6.10

Estimated Parameters, Pakistani Jute

Model	Constant	Lagged Relative Price	Elasticity Short-Run	Elasticity Long-Run	Lagged Acreage	R^2
Simple	+1143.4	+503.6* (113.5)	0.29	–	–	0.54
Nerlove	+ 330.3	+617.7* (162.7)	0.35	0.83	+0.427* (0.190)	0.72

*1 percent significance level.

Source: Sayeedul Huq, "Jute Price Stabilization and Resource Allocation between Jute and Rice in East Pakistan," Pakistan Economic Journal 19, no. 2 (1968/69).

next year's official price, well in advance of planting, at the level calculated to evoke the desired acreage response. A secondary but necessary tool would be the creation of a buffer stock mechanism.

By way of contrast a recently published paper analyzing West Bengali jute supply by P. C. Bansil noted little or no price responsiveness of acreage during the period 1958 to 1970.[33] A weather variable showed statistical significance and Bansil concluded that, given normal weather conditions, a core area of 420–430,000 hectares was planted in jute.

A. Parikh, in the study already referred to, also considered jute production in the prewar (1900–39) regions that remained part of India after Independence.[34] Parikh's analysis employed a number of models of varying degrees of complexity, and the three used for analyzing jute express jute acreage as a function of (A) lagged relative jute to competitive crop prices and lagged jute acreage; (B) lagged relative jute to competitive crop prices, per acre yield, rainfall at sowing time, lagged total cropped area, and a trend variable; and (C) lagged jute prices deflated by a general index, per acre yield, and lagged (one and two periods) jute acreage. The estimated parameters he reported are shown in Table 6.11.

Parikh's estimates of elasticity in Bengal are quite low—far below those presented by Stern and Rabbani (see earlier in this chapter). Though relative to those calculated by Rabbani for the post–World War II period, Parikh's figures show the same pattern of low elasticity in an old producing area (Bengal) and high elasticity in new producing areas (Bihar, Orissa). The measure of price used

(jute relative to rice) proved consistently to be highly significant
in all regressions and regions, including Assam for which the author
did not make elasticity estimates. A very strong role for a time-
trend variable was indicated in one model tested for Assam, due
apparently to the opening of considerable virgin territory to jute
cultivation during this period. Many of the new settlers were
experienced jute growers fleeing the economically oppressive
zamindari tax-collecting system prevalent in Bengal, and both
their nemesis and their migration might explain the sluggishness
of Bengali supply responsiveness.

Sushil Krishna included pre-Independence Bengali jute in his
study based on Kharm Narain's data.[35] Using a partial adjustment
model he expressed acreage in terms of lagged prices (deflated by
those of the competing crop, rice), relative crop yield, total area
in jute and rice, rainfall, and lagged jute area. Both linear and
logarithmic versions of the model were tested using ordinary least-
squares techniques. Rainfall and yield showed little significance in
either case, total area was significant at the 1 percent level in the
logarithmic model, while price and lagged jute area were significant
at this level in both models. Short- and long-run price elasticities
estimated from the two models were +0.49 and +1.16 (linear) and
+0.57 and +1.29 (logarithmic); R^2 values were 0.72 and 0.75,
respectively.

In a short paper discussing the use of the Nerlove supply model,
Shyamal Roy presented by way of example an analysis of jute produc-

TABLE 6.11

Estimated Parameters, Indian Jute

Region	Model	Relative Price Coefficient	Lagged Acreage	Elasticities Short-Run	Elasticities Long-Run	Area Adjustment Coefficient	R^2
Assam	A	0.427*	1.01*	n.q.	n.q.	negative	0.90
	B	0.381*	–	n.q.	n.q.	–	0.86
	C	0.448*	0.865*	n.q.	n.q.	0.135	0.81
Bihar/ Orissa	A	0.845*	0.350*	0.51	0.78	0.650	0.65
West Bengal	B	0.764*	0.613*	0.014	0.12	0.387	0.84

n.q. = Value not quoted.
*10 percent significance level.
Source: A. Parikh, "Market Responsiveness of Peasant Cultivators:
Some Evidence from Prewar India," Journal of Development Studies 8 (1972).

tion between 1949 and 1965 in one of West Bengal's major producing
areas, 24 Parganas district.[36] He estimated values of +0.11 and
+0.82 for the short- and long-run supply elasticity.

The most recent study of jute supply is also the most disaggregated geographically. John Cummings applied a Nerlovian model
with acreage expressed in terms of deflated jute prices, a weather
index, lagged acreage, and a trend variable not only to post-World
War II data from the leading producing states but also to that of
most of the districts in the area.[37]

With only a single exception the price coefficients were positive,
and most estimates were significantly nonzero at the 30 percent
level or better. Most of the short-run supply elasticities were
between +0.45 and +0.75, a range comparable to that found in most
of the other studies included herein. The trend coefficients showed
some significance in less than a third of the districts and almost
half of these were negative, a mixed pattern the author concluded
is indicative of the somewhat sluggish postwar jute market.

In a paper concerned with the effects of changes in land quality
on crop yield, H. Askari and J. T. Cummings analyzed the major
jute-producing regions.[38] Two supply models were tested; one
regressed acreage on prices, actual yield, rainfall, and a trend
variable, while in the other the dependent variables were price,
yield (as predicted by a separate expected yield equation), and a
trend measure. In the study as a whole the authors concluded the
second model performed better. Only for Bangladesh does the
preferred version indicate results at variance with those found in
other studies.

Jere Behrman, in his study of Thailand, included an analysis
of the supply of kenaf, a fibrous plant that is used in the production
of gunny bags, rope, and paper.[39] Though it is inferior to jute
and has had to compete in the last 20 years with the many synthetic
packaging materials, kenaf has enjoyed the fastest expansion of
the four Thai crops examined by Behrman. It is generally considered
to be the most price responsive of Thai crops.

Kenaf is grown on land that can alternatively be used for maize
production, and Behrman found that considerable substitution of
kenaf for maize production took place in response to relative price
changes once farmers became familiar with kenaf cultivation.
Some output is used domestically but more than two-thirds is
exported. Thai kenaf production is largely concentrated in eight
provinces that account for 82 percent of national output.

Behrman used the same model he employed for rice, maize,
and cassava, incorporating Nerlovian formulations of both area
adjustment and price expectations. The acreage equation was
expressed in terms of expected yield, risk in price and yield

(represented by a three-year standard deviation), and the malaria death rate. His estimates, for the period 1954 to 1963 and for short- and long-run elasticities are shown in Table 6.12.

Overall performance of the model in explaining acreage variation was quite good in all eight provinces, and the estimated positive price parameters are significantly nonzero at the 10 percent level or better in most regressions. Even more indicative of the market orientation of kenaf cultivators are the notably high price elasticities, even for the short run. Thus the general opinion that kenaf is Thailand's most price-responsive crop seems to be borne out.

The cultivation of oilseeds is important in almost all parts of the world, and when it is also remembered that they are put to a wide variety of uses as human and animal food, as well as inputs in the industrial sector, it is not surprising that several supply studies of these crops have been published in the last few years.

Again many of these endeavors have concerned India. Vahid Nowshirvani included groundnuts cultivation in his study of Uttar Pradesh, using a Nerlovian model that incorporated a formulation of both price expectations and area adjustment.[40] Considering the three districts in the state where most of the production takes place (Lucknow, Sitapur, and Hardoi), he lumped them together for the period 1953 to 1964 and obtained estimates for the long-run price elasticity of +0.89, a price expectation coefficient of +0.55, and an area adjustment coefficient of +0.73, all of which were statistically significant at the 20 percent level or better, from a regression for which the value of R^2 was 0.91.

The NCAER study also applied its price-expectations model to groundnuts.[41] While output was apparently analyzed for several areas, supply elasticities were reported for only four cases: an all-India estimate of +0.22; Bombay state, +0.21; Madras state, +0.23; and North Arcot district (Madras), +0.08. All were computed for the period 1938 to 1951.

The results of a study covering several states are reported by P. Boon-raung and others.[42] Using data from the period 1953 to 1968 they postulated a Nerlovian model with lagged prices, acreages, and price indices of competing crops, plus annual rainfall and time trend as independent variables. From their parameter estimates they calculated the supply elasticities with respect to the prices of groundnuts and of competing crops shown in Table 6.13.

While most of the elasticities, both with respect to groundnuts and other crop prices, are of the expected sign, it is notable that negative price responsiveness is indicated for two major cultivating areas, Madhya Pradesh and Mysore, which were in 1962 responsible for about 7 and 12 percent of national output, respectively.

TABLE 6.12

Supply Elasticities, Thai Kenaf

Province	Short-Run Elasticities of Planted Area with Respect to				Long-Run Elasticities of Planted Area with Respect to			
			Risk				Risk	
	Price	Yield	Price	Yield	Price	Yield	Price	Yield
Mahasarakham	1.90 to 2.89	–	-1.25	-1.20 to 1.35	1.52 to 2.89	–	-1.25	-0.91 to 1.20
Nakhonratsima	2.61	–	–	–	4.09	–	–	–
Chayaphum	0.88	–	–	–	1.19	–	–	–
Ubormratthani	3.28 to 7.71	1.74	-3.63	-0.56 to 0.75	3.28 to 42.6	1.74	-3.61	-5.59 to 0.75
Khon-kaen	1.26 to 2.08	2.23 to 5.18	-0.37	-0.79	2.08 to 11.3	2.36 to 5.18	-0.39	-0.79
Buriram	1.11 to 2.71	–	-0.38	-0.68 to 1.18	1.11 to 2.71	–	-0.38	-0.68 to 1.18
Srisaket	3.30	2.99	–	–	3.13	2.85	–	–
Roi-et	3.31	–	–	–	4.56	–	–	–

Source: Jere Behrman, Supply Response in Underdeveloped Agriculture: A Case Study of Four Major Annual Crops in Thailand, 1937–63 (Amsterdam: North-Holland, 1968).

TABLE 6.13

Supply Elasticities, Indian Groundnuts

Area	Elasticity with Respect to Prices of:	
	Groundnuts	Competing Crops
India	0.22[a]	−0.40[b]
Andhra Pradesh	0.35[c]	−0.61[b]
Madhya Pradesh	−0.23[b]	−
Maharashta-Gujarat (Bombay)	0.24	−
Mysore	−0.11[b]	−0.08[a]
Punjab	0.60[d]	−0.42[a]
Rajasthan	0.62[b]	−
Tamil Nadu (Madras)	0.15	−
Uttar Pradesh	0.31[c]	−0.11[b]

[a]20 percent significance level.
[b]10 percent significance level.
[c]5 percent significance level.
[d]1 percent significance level.
    Source: P. Boon-raung, J. S. Sharma, T. V. Moorti, and
M. M. Wagner, "Supply Response for Groundnut in India," a paper
read at the 31st Annual Conference of the Indian Society of Agricultural Economics, abstrated in the Indian Journal of Agricultural
Economics 26 (October–December 1971).

    J. Mahender Reddy concentrated on a single district—Kurnool—
in Andhra Pradesh for the period 1931 to 1943.[43] He used several
formulations of the basic Nerlovian model, with lagged prices,
acreage, and yields, plus a weather index and time trend as
independent variables, but the coefficients of weather and lagged
area proved statistically insignificant in all the regressions in
which they were included. His best estimate for short-run elasticity
was 0.76.
    B. L. Sawhney used two variations of the Nerlovian area
adjustment model to estimate supply parameters for groundnuts
in Bombay state (the present states of Gujarat and Maharashta)
over the period 1949 to 1964.[44] The formulations were: (A) a
price model with acreage expressed as a function of lagged prices
and yields of groundnuts relative to competing crops (cotton, bajra,
and jowar), rainfall during the sowing season, and lagged area; and

(B) a gross income model, with acreage a function of the product of relative prices and relative yields, rainfall, and lagged area.

Sawhney felt that the marginally better performance of the gross income model augured for greater success of agricultural policies aimed at raising incomes per cultivated acre, as has been mentioned earlier in this chapter in connection with his analysis of cotton output in the same paper. However, it may again be pointed out that the significance of gross income may flow from the stronger significance indicated for one of its components, yield.

Rajagopalan also analyzed groundnuts in his study of Madras state, where they are the most important cash crop, accounting for close to an eighth of the state's acreage.[45] Cultivation is particularly heavy in the northeastern coastal districts and a bit less in the interior. Two variations of the basic Nerlovian model were used to estimate groundnuts supply: acreage expressed in terms of (A) lagged groundnuts prices deflated by an index of substitute crop (ragi and rice) prices, lagged (one and two periods) acreage, and a trend variable; and (B) lagged absolute groundnuts prices and substitute crop prices entered separately, lagged per acre groundnuts yield, lagged acreage, and a trend variable.

Though little statistical significance was found for the role of groundnuts prices in output, except in the southeast where they are a much less important crop, the perverse price pattern was clear in the major districts and was further accentuated by the positive parameter estimated for substitute crops in the northeast and the negative yield parameters in all three regions. The only elasticity estimates presented by Rajagopalan are -0.50 with respect to groundnuts prices in the northeast region and a cross-elasticity of -0.87 in the interior region.

Madhavan included both groundnuts and sesamum in his study of Madras, using a model that expressed acreage as a function of lagged prices relative to those of a competing crop, lagged yield and acreage of the oilseed and the competing crop, and an index of rainfall.[46] Competing crops were entered singly, not as a weighted average of all so designated. For groundnuts Madhavan considered cumbu, ragi, sorghum, cotton, sesamum, and sugarcane to be competitors; only cotton and groundnuts played a similar role as regards sesamum. Price elasticities are shown in Table 6.14, along with the area adjustment coefficients. Madhavan found generally more statistical significance for the price coefficients of oilseeds than he did for the other food and cash crops he considered. The role of prices in sesamum output seems particularly notable.

Parikh's more recent study also included analysis of some of the major Indian groundnuts regions.[47] Of the several variants of the supply model he used, the results from testing four with

TABLE 6.14

Supply Elasticities, Madras Oilseeds

Crop	Competing Crop	Elasticity Short-Run	Long-Run	Area Adjustment Coefficient
Groundnuts	Cumbu	+0.22	+0.31	0.72
	Ragi	+0.34	+0.65	0.52
	Sorghum	+0.19	+0.31	0.62
	Cotton	+0.18	+0.21	0.85
	Sesamum	+0.03	+0.04	0.68
	Sugar	+0.11	+0.12	0.92
Sesamum	Cotton	+0.48	+0.32	1.53
	Groundnut	+0.42	+0.31	1.48

Source: M. C. Madhavan, "Acreage Response of Indian Farmers: A Case Study of Tamil Nadu," Indian Journal of Agricultural Economics 27 (January-March 1972).

groundnuts data were reported: acreage expressed as a function of (A) lagged groundnuts prices deflated by a general price ratio and lagged area; (B) lagged deflated prices, per acre yield, rainfall at sowing time, and lagged area; (C) lagged deflated prices, lagged deflated proceeds per acre, and lagged (one and two periods) area, and (D) lagged (one and two periods) relative groundnuts to competitive crop prices, weather, and acreage. The results of Parikh's regression analysis are shown in Table 6.15 for the period 1914 to 1939.

Positive responsiveness is indicated in all three provinces, though elasticity values are not quoted for Madhya Pradesh, where the Boon-raung study indicated negative response during a more recent time period. For Bombay, Parikh's estimates are somewhat high even for short-run elasticity when compared with other results.

Postwar cultivation of three important oilseeds in India and Pakistan were analyzed by Cummings: groundnuts—the leading such crop in India; sesamum—of secondary importance through the subcontinent; rape and mustard seed—the major oilseed in both erstwhile provinces of Pakistan.[48]

Groundnuts are most commonly found in Gujarat and Maharashta, which together supply two-thirds of the Indian total, and almost all of the remaining are produced in the southern states of Andhra Pradesh, Mysore, and Tamil Nadu. Pakistani cultivation is nil.

TABLE 6.15

Estimated Parameters, Indian Groundnuts

Region	Model	Lagged Price	Lagged Acreage	Elasticity Short-Run	Elasticity Long-Run	Adjustment Coefficient	R^2
Bombay/						
Sind	A	9.14[c]	0.979[b]	0.400	19.24	0.021	0.96
	B	n.q.	n.q.	0.499	5.96	–	n.q.
	C	11.89[c]	1.00[b]	0.513	5.27	0.097	n.q.
Madhya Pradesh/						
Berar	A	1.715[c]	0.976[b]	n.q.	n.q.	0.024	0.96
Madras	D	174.63[a,b]	0.799[b]	0.80	3.71	0.201	0.81

n.q. =Value not quoted.
[a]Relative groundnuts to competitive crop prices.
[b]10 percent significance level.
[c]5 percent significance level.
Source: A. Parikh, "Market Responsiveness of Peasant Cultivators:
Some Evidence from Prewar India," Journal of Development Studies 8 (1972).

Sesamum is grown in many groundnuts regions but is more a northern crop, with Rajasthan and Madhya Pradesh the leading states. It is also raised in both East and West Pakistan, though to a lesser extent in both than rape and mustard seed, which are customarily sown together in a wide, relatively moderately climed belt stretching along the Gangetic plain from Punjab to Assam. All three are kharif (summer) crops generally, competing with rice in many areas, but not with wheat. Cotton is also a competitive crop in several states.

The supply model used for analysis was Nerlovian, incorporating both price expectation and area adjustment formulations. Crop acreage was expressed as a function of deflated crop price, a weather index, lagged acreage, and a trend variable. Estimated elasticities for selected major producing districts are shown for each crop: Table 6.16, groundnuts; Table 6.17, sesamum; and Table 6.18, rape and mustard seed (for East and West Pakistan only).

A number of groundnuts price parameters were negative, but only for Gujarat and Rajasthan on the state level were the estimates significant. Nevertheless, the negative pattern was continued on the district level, giving the impression that cultivators were not very market oriented. The author pointed out that this judgment is

TABLE 6.16

Groundnuts Supply Elasticities, Selected Districts

District	Elasticity		R^2
	Short–Run	Long–Run	
Andhra Pradesh			
Anantapur	+0.27[a]	+1.29[a]	0.97
Chittoor	+0.43[a]	+0.60[a]	0.98
Ludhapah	−0.06	−0.08	0.46
Kurnool	+0.46[c]	+1.64[c]	0.63
Visakhapatnam	−0.29	−0.34	0.46
Gujarat			
Junagadh	+0.35[c]	+2.50[c]	0.96
Panch Mahals	−0.09	−0.10	0.39
Sabarkantha	−0.39[c]	−0.36[c]	0.69
Amreli, Bhavnagar,			
Jamnagar, and Rajkot	+0.16[a]	+0.89[a]	0.95
Surat and West Kandesh	−0.07	−0.08	0.54
Maharashta			
Akola	+0.17[b]	+0.27[b]	0.90
Amraoti	+0.34[b]	+0.64[b]	0.92
Aurangabad	+0.72[c]	−1.95[c]	0.80
Bhir	+0.23	+0.19	0.44
Buldana	−0.66[c]	−0.82[c]	0.90
East Khandesh	−0.16	−0.29	0.33
Nasik	−0.19[b]	−0.18[b]	0.42
North Satara	+0.06[a]	+0.10[a]	0.62
Parbhani	+0.24	−3.43	0.56
Poona	−0.18	−0.16	0.74
Sangli	−0.05	−0.08	0.68
Sholapur	−0.11	−0.08	0.14
Yeotmal	−0.08	+1.33	0.84
Mysore			
Bellary	−0.41[c]	−0.38[c]	0.61
Bijapur	−0.32	−0.25	0.67
Dharwar	+0.11	+0.11	0.76
Kolar	+0.11	+0.15	0.33
Belgaum and Kolhapur	−0.29[c]	−0.35[c]	0.83
Mysore and Coimbatore	−0.06	−0.06	0.76
Tamil Nadu			
Madurai	−0.53[c]	−0.37[c]	0.69
North Arcot	−0.12	−0.09	0.56
Salem	+0.15[a]	+0.13	0.43
South Arcot	+0.13[a]	+0.12	0.40
Tiruchirapalli	+0.15	+0.13	0.57

[a]30 percent significance level.

[b]10 percent significance level.

[c]5 percent significance level.

Source: John Thomas Cummings, "Supply Response in Peasant Agriculture: Price and Non–Price Factors," (Ph.D. dissertation, Tufts University, 1974).

TABLE 6.17

Sesamum Supply Elasticities, Selected Districts

District	Short-Run	Long-Run	R^2
Andhra Pradesh			
East Godavari	−0.03	−0.05	0.88
Karimnagar	+0.03	+0.03	0.65
Bihar			
Palamau	−0.71*	−1.45*	0.79
Kerala			
Allepey and			
Quilon	−0.79*	+6.58*	0.99
Maharashta			
Chanda	+0.16	+0.47	0.41
Punjab			
Gurdaspur	+0.47	+0.49	0.44
Rajasthan			
Banswara	+0.44	+0.49	0.44
Bhilwara	+0.64	+1.19	0.27
Bundi	+0.64	+1.28	0.30
Dungarpur	+0.57	+0.69	0.43
Nagour	+0.20	+0.14	0.61
Pali	−0.15	−0.16	0.93
Tonk	+0.49	+1.14	0.26
Ajmer and			
Jaipur	+0.10	+0.08	0.64
Banaskantha			
and Sirohi	+0.09	+0.12	0.65
Tamil Nadu			
Tiruchirapalli	+0.18	−0.11	0.50

*5 percent significance level.

Source: John Thomas Cummings, "Supply Response in Peasant Agriculture: Price and Non-Price Factors" (Ph.D. dissertation, Tufts University, 1974).

TABLE 6.18

Rape and Mustard Supply Elasticities,
Selected Districts

| District | Elasticity | |
	Short-Run	Long-Run
East Pakistan		
Bogra	+0.81[c]	+0.85[c]
Dinajpur	+0.37[c]	+0.70[c]
Mymensingh	+0.35[a]	+5.83[a]
Pabna	0	0
Rangpur	+0.43[a]	+0.52
West Pakistan		
Attock	-0.27	-0.64
Dadu	+0.28[c]	+0.31
D.I. Khan	-0.60[a]	-0.36[a]
Hyderabad	-0.57[c]	-2.48[c]
Khairpur	-0.06	-0.06
Larkana	+1.39[c]	+2.44[c]
Mianwali	+0.61[c]	+0.80[c]
Nawabshah	+0.71[a]	+0.74[a]
Sanghar	-0.84[b]	-4.94[b]
Sibi	+2.74[c]	+5.71[c]
Sukkur	+0.75[b]	+1.29[b]
Thatta	-0.87[a]	-0.88[a]

[a]30 percent significance level.
[b]10 percent significance level.
[c]5 percent significance level.
Source: John Thomas Cummings, "Supply Response in Peasant Agriculture: Price and Non-Price Factors" (Ph.D. dissertation, Tufts University, 1974).

somewhat mitigated when the more important groundnuts districts are examined, but nevertheless the influence of prices on acreage is hardly overwhelming.

While some negative price parameters were also estimated for sesamum, positive responsiveness is indicated for most of the major producing states and districts in India. For rape and mustard seed positive parameters are also generally indicated, and the positive elasticities are frequently larger than +0.5.

Askari and Cummings included Indian groundnuts production
in their paper on the effects on crop yield of changes in the quality
of land devoted to its cultivation.[49] They used two different supply
models; in one, yield was represented as an independent variable
by actual data, and in the other, predicted values of yield found
from a separate regression were employed. In the study as a whole,
the second model proved to be the better estimating tool. Selected
parameters are shown in Table 6.19.

Also reporting on rape and mustard seed were R. P. Singh,
Parmatma Singh, and K. N. Rai, who used a simplified supply
model to analyze acreage in Haryana between 1950 and 1970.[50]
In their model, they expressed acreage in terms of lagged harvest
prices, rainfall in the presowing period, and agricultural technology
(expressed in terms of crop yield). They found little significance
for any of the variables and an R^2 of about 0.376; the estimated
price coefficient was negative, but the relatively high standard
error led the authors to conclude there was little price responsiveness shown by the crop's cultivators.

Groundnut output in Nigeria was analyzed by Olayide in a study
largely concerned with perennial crops.[51] He used two different
supply models, which are quasi-Nerlovian in format, incorporating
lagged acreage into supply equations where current output is expressed in tonnage terms. Elasticities associated with groundnuts
prices in each case were estimated to be +0.295 and +0.725,
respectively. As was indicated earlier in this chapter, these two
versions of elasticity differ in that the second includes the elasticity
due to current world prices; from the second model the latter
elasticity was estimated to be +0.485, while that due to lagged
producer prices was set at +0.240—very close to the elasticity
derived from the first variant of the supply model that includes
only producer prices.

In their study of Middle East land reform, Askari, Cummings,
and Harik analyzed oilseed output in the region—sesamum in Syria,
Iraq, and Jordan and linseed in Iraq.[52] The supply model employed
represented output (in both acreage and yield terms) as a function
of lagged prices, water availability, farm technology and other
secularly increasing inputs in the form of a trend variable, and
lagged output. Sesamum elasticities are up, relative to yield,
in Syria after land reform, with positive shifts noted for both area
and yield in Iraq. On the other hand, linseed elasticities show a
postreform decline, though little significance for the price coefficients were noted (see Table 6.20).

A few studies of Western hemisphere oilseeds are also available,
beginning with Remy Friere's application of a simple linear supply

TABLE 6.19

Estimated Supply Parameters, Indian Groundnuts

Region and Time Period	Supply Model	Lagged Price	Yield	R^2	Price Elasticity Short-Run	Price Elasticity Long-Run
Andhra Pradesh (1953-66)	I	+92.68[c] (39.78)	-0.48 (0.84)	0.552	+0.530	+0.434
	II	-12.25 (35.01)	-5.59[c] (2.00)	0.804	-0.070	+0.228
Maharashta (1956-67)	I	-30.61[d] (4.29)	+0.19 (0.42)	0.486	-0.215	-0.197
	II	+13.82[c] (5.98)	+3.42[d] (0.56)	0.839	+0.097	+0.328
Mysore (1955-66)	I	-23.36[a] (14.07)	+0.89 (0.34)	0.849	-0.170	-0.113
	II	-23.42 (19.04)	+0.78 (0.92)	0.411	-0.170	-0.150
Punjab (1953-66)	I	+3.36[d] (0.97)	+0.25[d] (0.03)	0.967	+0.311	+0.898
	II	+1.96[b] (1.05)	+0.35[d] (0.05)	0.983	+0.182	+0.852
Rajasthan (1954-68)	I	-6.92[d] (1.95)	+0.013 (0.087)	0.979	-0.420	-0.335
	II	-5.12 (2.26)	+0.34 (0.27)	0.987	-0.310	-1.237

[a]20 percent significance level; [b]10 percent significance level; [c]5 percent significance level; [d]1 percent significance level.

Notes: Figures in parentheses are standard errors. I: Actual yield and rainfall are independent variables. II: "Expected" or predicted yield is the independent variable.

Source: Hossein Askari and John Thomas Cummings, "Supply Response of Farmers with Heterogeneous Land," Indian Journal of Agricultural Economics, forthcoming 1976.

TABLE 6.20

Estimated Parameters, Middle East Oilseeds

Crop/ Country	Time Period	Dependent Variable	Price Elasticity Short-Run	Long-Run	R^2
Sesame					
Syria	1947–60	Area	+3.266[c]	+10.47	0.586
		Yield	−1.043[b]	−0.788	0.489
	1961–72	Area	−0.430	−0.403	0.587
		Yield	+0.579[a]	+0.991	0.712
Iraq	1950–60	Area	−0.846	−1.142	0.478
		Yield	−0.800[d]	−0.995	0.850
	1961–71	Area	+1.120[e]	+1.816	0.980
		Yield	+2.298[b]	+2.762	0.857
Jordan	1955–67	Area	+0.223	+0.145	0.683
		Yield	−0.637[b]	−0.446	0.707
Linseed					
Iraq	1950–60	Area	+2.328[d]	+2.440	0.952
		Yield	+2.463[e]	+2.197	0.904
	1961–71	Area	−2.846[c]	−14.232	0.852
		Yield	−2.717[d]	−3.036	0.850

Significance levels indicated for estimated price coefficients from which short-run elasticities were derived:
[a]30 percent
[b]10 percent
[c]5 percent
[d]1 percent
[e]0.1 percent
Source: Hossein Askari, John Thomas Cummings, and Bassam Harik, "Land Reform in the Middle East," International Journal of Middle East Studies, forthcoming.

model (acreage expressed as a function of lagged prices and rainfall) to flaxseed cultivation in Argentina.[53]

His regressions indicated statistical significance for both price and rainfall parameters at the 5 percent level or better, a short-run elasticity of +1.10, and a value of R^2 equal to 0.95.

Another simple model was applied by Andrew Schmitz to Canadian flaxseed output between 1947 and 1966.[54] He presented estimates of short-run elasticity between +0.08 and +0.19.

Still a third relatively simple non-Nerlovian model for the
supply responsiveness of Canadian rapeseed cultivators has been
analyzed by Brian Paddock.[55] Rapeseed is cultivated for its
vegetable-oil content, and since World War II it has gained considerable importance among prairie-province farmers. The crop requires,
among other inputs, considerable farm management skill, like one
of its chief competitors, flax. The other principal competitor for
inputs is wheat, a much simpler crop to cultivate, which, however,
has had a marketing handicap vis-a-vis both rapeseed and flax in
the last decade or so.

Paddock tested several models for the period 1951-67 and
obtained his best results using a logarithmic supply function expressing rapeseed acreage as a function of lagged rapeseed prices, lagged
flax prices, current wheat exports, and trend variable. Since the
estimated coefficients of a logarithmic model represent elasticities,
a fairly elastic response of rapeseed cultivation was indicated with
respect to all four postulated variables. The author argued that
these elasticities might even be higher (particularly for prices)
were it not for the assigned acreage quotas that prevail. Paddock
discussed the possibility of using a Nerlovian-type lag to indicate
price expectations, as well as an area adjustment formulation,
but he did not proceed further in this regard.

Soybean production in the United States has shown phenomenal
growth in the past generation, reflecting the myriad of uses to
which this crop has been put in modern society. A high-protein
commodity in strong demand as animal feed in North America as
well as for a number of human food products and industrial purposes
worldwide, its supply has been analyzed by James P. Houck and
Abraham Subotnik.[56] Since their interest is in the most recent
period, they dealt with an agricultural sector well accustomed to
government price-support and acreage-control programs, and in
their efforts they moved in a major new direction with the basic
Nerlovian supply model.

Rapidly expanding demand for soybeans has consistently kept
the market price above the support price and no acreage controls
have ever been placed on soybeans. Nevertheless, government
programs have undoubtedly influenced soybeans indirectly through
their effects on competitive crops, and it is on the latter that
the authors particularly focused in their study, with secondary
attention given to the effects on acreage of changes in soybean
support prices. With these goals they first developed a theoretical
model to explain the "effective support prices" for soybeans by
combining the policies affecting several relevant crops. Next
they presented a distributed lag estimation model that incorporated

both actual and effective support prices. Then they applied the model
to the period 1946 to 1966 and examined implications of their results
for changes in soybean support prices.

Since American price support programs for key commodities
involve participation by cultivators in some or other acreage limitation scheme, the validity of any supply analysis depends upon the
degree to which both price and acreage factors affecting all relevant
crops are incorporated into the process. The authors suggested a
method of weighting announced support rates by the acreage restrictions imposed on participating farmers, beginning with a simple
acreage supply function:

$$A = a_o + a_1 P \qquad\qquad\qquad (6.6)$$

where A is harvested acreage and P the relevant supply-inducing
price.

If a support price P_S is announced, but restricted so that it
can be realized only if cultivators hold their acreage to A_S, we
can see then a "bonus" of $P_S - P_f$ (per unit) is thus paid them.
P_f, the market price that would induce acreage A_S, is termed by
the authors the "effective support price"—the alternative cost of
devoting A_S to this commodity—and is the variable they hold which
influences producers in their planting decisions regarding the
various alternative crops. A society wishing to subsidize the agricultural sector would set the support price above the effective
support price, thus affording cultivators an income bonus equal to
P_S A B P_f,* if they agree to acreage limitations.

In order to deflate the support price, equation 6.6 is evaluated
at both P_S and P_4 and solved for the price parameter, yielding

$$a_1 = \frac{A' - a_o}{P_s} = \frac{A_s - a_o}{P_f} \qquad\qquad (6.7)$$

which means that

_____

*This analysis is relevant for the alternative crops the authors
consider for all of which both price supports and acreage restrictions are coexistent. However, for soybeans this is not the case
since acreage allotments have not been enforced. In such a case
a support price higher than the market price would yield a bonus
larger than P_S A B P_f if the supply curve is relatively elastic,
but as has been indicated, soybean market prices have fairly
consistently led support prices.

$$P_f = \frac{A_s - a_o}{A' - a_o} P_s \qquad (6.8)$$

and if a_o is small relative to A_s and A', then equation 6.8 can be approximated by

$$P_f = \frac{A_s}{A'} P_s \qquad (6.9)$$

expressing the effective support price as a function of the announced support price and the ratio of allowable to desired acreage.

The supply model Houck and Subotnik postulated included an acreage equation of Nerlovian area adjustment type:

$$A_t = b_o + b_1 P^e_t + b_2 P^e_{c_t} + b_3 A_{t-1} + u_t \qquad (6.10)$$

with P^e indicating expected prices for the crop in question and P^e_c expected prices for a competitive crop (a measure that can be extended to include several crops).

However, expected prices of all relevant crops must be expressed in terms of both actual farm prices and effective support prices:

$$P^e_{i_t} = w_{i_1} P_{i_{t-1}} + w_{i_2} P_{f_{i_t}} \qquad (6.11)$$

where P^e_i is the expected price for crop i, P_i is its actual farm price, and P_{f_i} its effective support price—a formulation assumed to be appropriate for crops with both mandatory and voluntary acreage control programs. If equation 6.11 is substituted in equation 6.10 the result is

$$A_t = c_o + c_1 P^e_t + c_2 P_{f_t} + c_3 P^e_{c_t} + c_4 P_{f_{c_t}} + c_5 A_{t-1} + u_t \qquad (6.12)$$

where P_f is the effective support price for soybeans and P_{f_c} that for alternative crops, weighted in some or other fashion. Neither of these are directly observable, but from equation 6.9 each can be defined in terms of announced support price and the ratio of allowable to desired acreage. Using this procedure Houck and Subotnik calculated effective support prices for the relevant competitive crops—wheat, maize, oats, and cotton (but not for soybeans, since no acreage restrictions had ever been imposed on the crop).

The supply function itself was estimated, using ordinary least-squares techniques, on a regional basis, using six recognized soybean-producing regions: the Lake states, the Corn Belt, the Plains states, the Delta states, the Atlantic states, and all other soybean states.* In all but the Atlantic region the Nerlove distributed lag model was used, though in each region a somewhat different specification was tested because of the differing importance of alternative crops in each region. They reported that in each case the models including the measures of effective support prices yielded notably better results than did parallel models without such measures.

Short-run supply elasticities for the regions are shown in Table 6.21; both soybean price elasticities and cross elasticities were calculated, for both actual and effective support prices. Price parameter estimates and elasticities without exception proved to have the expected signs: positive for actual and effective support prices of soybeans, negative for all competitive crop prices. Market price elasticities were generally higher than those calculated for support prices, which the authors feel is reasonable, indicating a more intensive reaction to the immediate market impulses than to the perhaps somewhat more plodding changes in bureaucratic policies.

The authors also examined the effect (in 1969) of a price-support decrease, considering the growth in importance of soybean inventories. This effect, they explained, is actually spread over several years, and they calculated a distributed lag effect over the following five years of acreage decreases in the approximate ratio 0.15:0.35:0.22:0.16:0.12.[57]

Tobacco is also a crop cultivated in many parts of the world, and its obvious cash-crop nature makes it of particular interest in supply analyses of close to subsistence agricultural economies. Four works concerning tobacco have been published in recent years—two are set in Africa, two in India-Pakistan.

A. A. Adesimi considered the market response of tobacco farmers in a study of post-World War II Nigeria.[58] The crop,

---

*The Lake states: Minnesota, Wisconsin, and Michigan; the Corn Belt: Illinois, Iowa, Indiana, Ohio, and Missouri; the Plains states: Kansas, Nebraska, North Dakota, and South Dakota; the Delta states: Arkansas, Mississippi, and Louisiana; the Atlantic states: North Carolina, South Carolina, Virginia, Maryland, and Delaware; all other soybean states: New York, New Jersey, Pennsylvania, West Virginia, Georgia, Florida, Kentucky, Tennessee, Alabama, Oklahoma, and Texas.

TABLE 6.21

Supply Elasticities, U.S. Soybeans

| | Elasticities with Respect to | | | | | | | | |
| | Actual Prices | | | Effective Support Prices | | | | | |
Region	Soybeans	Corn	Oats	Soybeans	Corn	Wheat	Oats	Cotton
Lake states	+0.91	-0.49	—	+0.87	-0.44	-0.35	—	—
Corn belt	+0.50	-0.50	—	+0.17	-0.13	—	—	—
Plains states	+2.10	-1.70	—	+1.20	-0.27	—	-0.69	—
Delta states	+0.75	—	-0.81	+0.64	—	—	-0.31	-0.38
Atlantic states	+1.70	—	-1.70	+2.40	—	—	-1.30	-1.14
Other states	+3.30	-3.00	—	+1.10	-0.28	—	-1.28	—
United States	+0.69	-0.41	—	+0.62	-0.10	—	-0.75	—
	+0.84	-0.65	-0.09	+0.43	-0.17	-0.04	-0.19	-0.04

Source: James P. Houck and Abraham Subotnik, "The U.S. Supply of Soybeans: Regional Acreage Functions," Agricultural Economics Research 21, no. 4 (October 1969).

which is marketed after it is air-cured, needs little capital input, and is thus a very popular cash crop in Nigeria's western provinces. It competes for land and labor inputs with yams, cassava, and maize.

Adesimi used an area adjustment model and initially included consideration for a likely effect on tobacco output of the lagged prices of these three alternative crops and for a time-trend variable. However, only yam prices showed a significant effect on tobacco acreage in all tests; for this case all parameters were statistically significant at the 5 percent level or better.

From the first formulation Adesimi presented an area adjustment coefficient of +0.73, short- and long-run elasticities of +0.60 and 0.82 with respect to tobacco prices and of -0.96 and -1.32 with respect to yam prices.

The author concentrated on these results from the first formulation: acreage expressed in terms of tobacco prices alone, along with lagged area and the trend variable. Although the alternate crop price parameter estimates in other formulations do not in all cases enjoy the significance of tobacco prices, they seem to warrant somewhat more explanation than the author gave them; for example, does the positive sign of the yam price parameter in the second and fourth formulation possibly indicate a relationship between tobacco and yams that is not really competitive for inputs? Adesimi did not consider such a hypothesis, and the reader unfamiliar with the pecularities of Nigerian agriculture is left in the dark.

Another study of African tobacco production is presented by Edwin R. Dean for Malawi.[59] His principal interest was determining whether the tobacco growers' labor supply curve (and hence that for tobacco itself) is backward-bending. In Malawi, as elsewhere in the developing world in general and Africa in particular, it has frequently been alleged that peasants have income goals only and therefore react perversely to prices. More sophisticated arguments have succeeded those originally put forth by colonial officers of a generation or more ago whose opinions in this matter were at least suspect of Kiplingesque racism. For example, a good case is made that the African peasant finds a high degree of economic and social comfort, security, and stability in a traditional agricultural structure where (in most parts of the continent) population pressures have yet to challenge the fertility of the available land.[60] Venturing outside the tribal economy in pursuit of cash may be unavoidable (for example, to pay taxes) or even occasionally desirable (to purchase "modern" goods like bicycles and radios, or traditional ones like wives), but usually the cash goal is specific. Furthermore, such contacts with the cash economy are frequently unpleasant (for example, contract labor in white-dominated areas) or potentially troublesome (such as selling cash crops in markets

that are often under government control; and whether the government
is black or white, the likelihood of red tape, petty extortion by
minor officials, and so on, remains high).

Obviously the possibility of a backward-bending supply curve
must be considered by policy makers in a country like Malawi
where cash crops supply the major share of foreign exchange earnings.
Tobacco has been grown commercially in Malawi since the turn of
the century. Though originally introduced onto European-owned
farms, it underwent rapid growth in the 1920s, and since 1927 the
majority of output has been from African-owned lands. However,
even into the 1960s about 40 percent of Malawi's tobacco continued
to be grown on European-owned farms, usually by African tenants.

Agriculture as a whole dominates the Malawi economy, accounting
for about 45 percent of gross domestic product. Though only 4 percent of the nation's land belongs to Europeans, almost a quarter of
the value of agricultural output and 40 percent of all exports is
traceable to this sector. Tea production in the tropical southern
lowlands accounts for most of this, with tobacco in second place.
Tang oil and livestock compete for inputs on European lands; on
African farms tobacco is the most important cash crop, with cotton,
groundnuts, and livestock (cash crops), and maize, millets, manioc,
and pulses (subsistence crops) as the chief competitors. However,
Malawi's most important export by far is purely African—labor.
Migrant workers in Rhodesia, South Africa, and Mozambique,
according to crude estimates, earn almost twice as much annually
as all commodity exports, and perhaps an eighth of their earnings
are directly remitted home.

Demand elasticity for Malawi's exports ranges from quite high
(for tea and probably groundnuts and cotton) for those products for
which Malawi supplies a very small part of the eventual market's
demand, to fairly low (for the principal exports, labor and tobacco—
both of which are concentrated in markets, white southern Africa
and the United Kingdom, respectively, where the Malawi source
is rather large relative to the whole market—furthermore, the
overall elasticity of demand for tobacco in the United Kingdom seems
to be quite small).

All of this indicates the need for Malawi to be cautious in
adopting price policies that may affect her relatively sparse sources
for foreign exchange. Dean pointed out that the male population
in Malawi's central uplands, where most of the tobacco is grown,
show notably less tendency to join the migrant work force, the chief
alternate means of earning cash, which he logically took to indicate
a preference by farmers to earn their cash at home. The question
remained as to the best way to translate this preference into higher
export earnings.

Dean postulated two alternate supply models, both phrased in first-differences terms, as seen in equations 6.13 and 6.14

$$\Delta'S = a_o + a_1\Delta'P^T_{t-1} + a_2\Delta'P^T_{t-2} + a_3\Delta'P^I_{t-1} + a_4\Delta'\overline{W}_{t-1} + a_5\Delta'R_t$$

(6.13)

and
$$\Delta'S = b_o + b_1\Delta'\left[\frac{P^T}{P^I}\right]_{t-1} + b_2\Delta'\left[\frac{\overline{W}}{P^I}\right]_{t-1} + b_3\Delta'R_t$$
(6.14)

where: Δ' indicates percentage change,
S is output sold per capita and per grower in different
   formulations,
P^T is tobacco price,
P^I is a price index for cash goods,
$\overline{W}$ is a weighted wage (obtainable abroad) index, and
R is a weather index.

His positive (and generally significant) price coefficients and the negative (if insignificant) wage coefficients offer contrary evidence against the presence of a backward-bending supply curve. Though Malawi farmers may have specific income goals in the short run, their economic behavior is "rational" in the European-American sense. A short-run price elasticity of about 0.48 was calculated, which is comparable with that calculated by Adesimi for Nigerian tobacco. The models tested did not succeed in explaining even half the output variation, which indicates the presence of other important but unaccounted-for influences.

Dean also conducted several field tests to determine if prices were affected by certain institutional factors: namely, age, sex, and tribal difference. In two rural markets in Malawi and one city market in Congo-Brazzaville he surveyed to see if sellers charged lower prices when dealing with fellow tribesmen or if young rather than old women traders were more generous with young male buyers. Though admitting the need for further testing along these lines, Dean found his results indicated no discernible and consistent patterns, and he could only conclude that adoption of the null hypothesis (that social group was not a determinant of price) was the most logical course.

The NCAER study of Indian agriculture applied a price expectations supply model to nationwide tobacco output and includes an estimate of short-run elasticity equal to +0.71 for virginia tobacco.[61]

The last cash crop considered by Cummings in his study of India and Pakistan was tobacco.[62] Though it is definitely a minor commodity throughout the subcontinent, never accounting for more than .05 percent of the acreage in India or either former wing of

Pakistan, its high market price makes it quite important to some
cultivators. Production is scattered throughout the region reflecting
the rather specific soil conditions and other inputs needed for its
cultivation. Half of Indian tobacco originates in Andhra Pradesh
and neighboring parts of Mysore and Tamil Nadu, while another 20
percent comes from Gujarat. In the present Bangladesh nearly
half is grown in Rangpur district, and West Pakistani cultivation
is concentrated in northern districts.

Cummings applied a Nerlovian model incorporating deflated
tobacco prices, a rainfall index, lagged area, and a trend variable
to output data from roughly 1950 to 1965, the period varying slightly
regionally. Estimated elasticities are quoted for selected districts
in Table 6.22. The supply analysis indicated notably more statistical significance for the estimated price parameters in West Pakistan
than elsewhere. In India positive parameters of some significance
are found for both major producing states, but not much significance
is found on the district level. Similarly, not much evidence for
supply response to price was found in East Pakistan, particularly
for the major producing area, Rangpur.

The author argued that the increased importance since Independence of the domestic and export markets for tobacco could be seen
in the generally positive and significant trend coefficients. This
market growth, coupled with tobacco's overall advantage regarding
per acre value of output vis-a-vis alternative cash crops, could
explain a strong positive trend in acreage planted despite indifferent
indications of price responsiveness. He also noted the generally
smaller degree of explanatory power exerted by the model, as
measured by R^2 value, for tobacco as compared to the other crops
he analyzed, and hypothesized this might be accounted for by the
very minor nature of tobacco cultivation in most regions, since
generally higher values are found for the regressions carried out
for the more important tobacco districts.

Tobacco production in India, Pakistan, and Bangladesh was
also considered in the study of Askari and Cummings.[63] Their
principal concern was the effect on crop yield of changes in land
quality, and they tested two different supply models that incorporated
measures of yield as independent variables. In the first, actual
yield figures were used, and in the second, a series predicted by
a separate regression; on the whole they concluded the second
version performed better.

R. D. Singh and P. R. Rao concentrated their efforts on four
districts along India's southeastern coast—Guntur, Krishna, West
Godavari, and East Godavari.[64] The first-named accounts for
up to 80 percent of the national output of virginia; the four districts
together grow as much as 95 percent of India's virginia in a typical

TABLE 6.22

Supply Elasticities, Tobacco,
Selected Districts

| District | Elasticity | | R^2 |
	Short-Run	Long-Run	
Andhra Pradesh			
East Godavari	-0.30	-0.38	0.55
Guntur	-0.07	-0.06	0.37
Krishna	+0.08	+0.07	0.28
Khammam,			
Warangal, and			
West Godavari	+0.08[a]	+0.11[a]	0.67
Bihar			
Muzzarfarpur	+0.12[c]	+0.33[c]	0.52
Gujarat			
Baroda	+0.02	+0.11	0.72
Kaira	+0.07	+0.16	0.65
Maharashta			
Sangli	-0.12	-0.20	0.51
Mysore			
Kolar	+0.32[c]	1.33	0.99
Belgaum and			
Kolhapur	-0.05[a]	-0.11	0.75
Mysore and			
Coimbatore	-0.02	-0.04	0.29
East Pakistan			
Faridpur	+0.14[b]	+0.19	0.62
Rangpur	0	0	0.86
West Pakistan			
Attock	+0.16	+0.21	0.29
Lahore	-0.26	-0.27	0.47
Mardan	+0.46	+0.46	0.57
Peshawar	+1.29[a]	+2.30	0.50

[a]30 percent significance level.
[b]10 percent significance level.
[c]5 percent significance level.

Source: John Thomas Cummings, "Supply Response in Peasant Agriculture: Price and Non-Price Factors" (Ph.D. dissertation, Tufts University, 1974).

year. Cultivation of this variety has grown rapidly in importance
in recent years—from about 41,000 hectares in 1940 to nearly
115,000 hectares in the late 1960s.

The authors were particularly concerned that this rapid growth
in cultivation had drawn increasingly less suitable soils to the crop
and concentrated their efforts in an attempt to determine farmer
motivations that might have impelled such a planting expansion.
They used a Nerlove-type model including both price expectations
and area adjustment formulations (for 1940 to 1967). The reduced
form used for estimating purposes represented tobacco acreage
as a function of lagged prices (deflated by an index of the price
of the principal competing prices), preplanting rainfall, a measure
of price risk in terms of the standard deviation of price in the three
preceding years, tobacco yield relative to that of the main competitor
crops, lagged production costs, a dummy variable representing
the presence (or nonpresence) of severe disease and pest problems,
a trend variable, and finally, lagged tobacco acreage. Both linear
and logarithmic representations were employed, but the authors
found the latter to be preferable and only these results were reported.

Singh and Rao ran a number of regressions on each of the four
districts and on the region as a whole, and they generally concluded
that only four variables on the right-hand side of the estimating
equation showed much significance: lagged relative tobacco prices,
lagged acreage, the trend variable, and rainfall. Their elasticity
estimates ranged from 0.35 to 1.34 with the average for their four
districts being 0.42. The authors concluded that while yield-
enhancing technical change was important to increase the tobacco
crop, its cultivators clearly demonstrate a favorable response to
market incentives.

In his extensive study of British agriculture G. T. Jones focused
on the production of several vegetables and soft fruits (berries).[65]
Many of these crops are highly competitive, not only one with another
but with a number of alternative cereal and livestock enterprises.
The supply model used by Jones was Nerlovian in form, incorporating
both price expectation and area adjustment hypotheses, and also
included a measure of rainfall. His estimated elasticities (and
standard errors) are shown in Table 6.23.

Each crop analysis bore out the expected positive price–acreage
relationship, though many of the short-run elasticities are rather
small. Jones also noted that vegetables in general demonstrated
pronounced negative relationships (not shown) between acreage
cultivated and the price index of other farm products and between
acreage and the amount of spring rainfall, indicating strong evidence
of farmers' substitution of the profitable but more unreliable vegetable crops for other crops. The inclusion of vegetable prices in

TABLE 6.23

Supply Elasticities, British Vegetables and Berries

Crop	Period	Short-Run Elasticity	Long-Run Elasticity
Beans[a]	1938-58	0.39[b,f] (0.14)	0.53[b]
Peas[a]	1938-58	0.65[g] (0.12)	3.10
Potatoes	1924-39	0.11 (0.07)	0.33
Potatoes[a]	1884-1914	0.11 (0.09)	0.31
Vegetables (combined)	1924-58	0.32[g] (0.06)	1.45
	1946-57	0.30[g] (0.06)	0.94
Celery	1928-58	0.10 (0.07)	0.71
Carrots	1928-58	0.39[g] (0.07)	1.77
Cabbage	1928-58	0.30[g] (0.06)	0.83
Brussels sprouts	1928-58	0.20[g] (0.06)	0.59
Onions	1928-58	0.59[g] (0.09)	1.64
Cauliflower	1928-58	0.05 (0.12)	0.42
Green Peas	1936-58	0.15 (0.09)	0.45
Broad and runner beans	1936-58	0.16[e] (0.08)	0.47
Tomatoes	1936-58	0.17[f] (0.06)	1.05
Open-air vegetables	1924-58	0.28[g] (0.07)	0.78
Glasshouse vegetables	1936-58	0.10 (0.06)	0.56
Soft-fruit[c] (combined)	1924-39 and 1946-58	0.18[g] (0.05)	0.58
	1946-58	0.30[f] (0.13)	1.00
Strawberries[d]	1924-39 and 1946-58	0.20[f] (0.08)	0.60
	1946-58	0.30[f] (0.13)	1.03
Raspberries[d]	1946-58	0.21[f] (0.10)	1.40
Blackcurrants[d]	1946-58	0.29[g] (0.07)	1.16
Gooseberries[d]	1946-58	0.10[f] (0.04)	0.91

[a]Includes Scotland, others England and Wales only. [b]Relative to the ratio of beans price to wheat price. [c]The first soft-fruits formulation includes fruit and vegetable prices, lagged yield, and a trend variable; the second only fruit prices. [d]The first strawberry formulation includes strawberry prices, lagged yield, and a trend variable, the second only prices; for raspberries, blackcurrants, and gooseberries, prices only. [e]10 percent significance level. [f]5 percent significance level. [g]1 percent significance level.

Source: G. T. Jones, "The Response of the Supply of Agricultural Products in the United Kingdom to Price" (Part II), Farm Economist 10 (1967).

the regressions run on soft fruits uncovered a negative relationship
significant at the 10 percent level, pointing to some substitution
between vegetables and soft fruits.

The supply responsiveness of South Australian potato farmers
has been analyzed by T. J. Mules and F. G. Jarrett.[66] They
presented a look at a cash crop that is only of minor importance
in the agriculture of the region,* one that is mostly sold locally—
only about 15 to 25 percent of the crop is transported across state
lines. All intrastate sales must theoretically be made through
the South Australian Potato Board, which sets harvest, wholesale,
and retail prices; these, however, are strongly influenced by the
prevailing prices in other states, to which producers are free to
transport their output.

The two principal producing areas are the truck-farming belt
around the state capital, Adelaide, and the southeastern section
of the state. Both areas are similar climatologically, and weather
extremes are moderated in any case by extensive irrigation. Three
crops a year are possible in both areas: an early (planted from
April to August) and a midseason (September to October) crop,
both relatively minor, and a late-season (November to March) crop
that accounts for more than 75 percent of South Australia's potato
production.

Mules and Jarrett first examined, for the period 1952-53 to
1963-64, the explanatory power of a simple cobweb model based
on the hypothesis that potato price instability is due to a combination
of lagged price responsiveness on the supply side and a very low
price elasticity of demand. They used both one- and two-year lag
versions of this model, but in both cases the correlation coefficients
proved low (0.22 and 0.36 respectively). They then tested a
Nerlovian distributed lag model,† incorporating a longer time

---

*Average annual gross value of the South Australian potato crop
was about $2 million during the period 1953 to 1963, and the number
of growers registered with the Potato Board never exceeded 2,000.

†The authors begin with a supply equation of the form:

$$A_t = a + \sum_{i=0}^{\infty} b_i P_{t-1} \tag{6.15}$$

and assume that after a certain point, for example, $i = k$, the
series of coefficients b_i ($i = 0, 1, 2, \ldots$) can be approximated by
a convergent geometric series.

period for the formation of farmers' price expectations, and estimated
an equation with acreage expressed as a function of lagged potato
prices (deflated) and lagged acreage. Short- and long-run elasticities of +0.36 and +1.09 for the state as a whole were estimated
using this model in a regression that explained 83 percent of acreage
variation.

Although the Nerlovian model seemed to fit the data rather well,
the authors proposed that a possibly important difference between
the two potato regions needed further exploration. The Adelaide
area accounts for 70 percent of South Australia's potato output and
generally supports a truck-farming agriculture for the metropolis,
whereas the southeast area is primarily a fat-lamb and dairy-
producing region, where potatoes are grown primarily for their
value as short-run return endeavors for farm improvement rather
than as part of any long-term optimum product mix. To test their
"cash-return" hypothesis they tested a model of the form:

$$A_{i_t} = a + b_1 P_{i_t} + b_2 Y_{i_{y-1}} \tag{6.16}$$

where: A_{i_t} = the number of acres planted in potatoes by registered
             growers in each area in season i and year t;

        P_{i_t} = deflated price in each area at planting time for
             season i in year t; and

        $Y_{i_{t-1}}$ = yield in tons per acre in each area for season i
             in the previous year.

Differentiated seasonal yield was not available, so annual data was
substituted, and price data included for each seasonal equation was
that of the most immediate prices prevailing at the time each crop
was planted.

The authors held that the low correlation coefficients obtained
for the regressions run on the early-season and especially the
important late-season output in the Adelaide area indicated the
"cash-returns" hypothesis does not seem to operate in this truck-
farming region (as expected). But for the southeast region the
results suggested strong support (also as expected) for this hypothesis. They argued that the negative coefficients for price and yield
(both of which were significant at the 1 percent level for the late-
season crop) signal that potatoes are seen by their cultivators more
as a "means to an end" (that is, some defined cash requirement)
rather than as an end in themselves. Though the authors did not
pretend to suggest any far-reaching policies, they strongly rejected
the adequacy of any simple cobweb approach, justifiably pointing
to the likely existence of a rather complicated response pattern,
differentiated along regional (and motivational—truck-farming versus
constant cash returns) lines.

TABLE 6.24

Estimated Parameters, Middle East Vegetables

Crop	Country	Time Period	Dependent Variable	Price Elasticity		R^2
				Short-Run	Long-Run	
Onions	Egypt	1920–40	Area	+0.500	−55.55	0.523
			Yield	+0.052[a]	+0.061	0.472
		1953–72	Area	−0.114[a]	−0.090	0.308
			Yield	+0.164[b]	+0.128	0.389
	Syria	1950–60	Area	−0.204[c]	−0.183	0.943
			Yield	+0.619[d]	+0.668	0.651
		1961–72	Area	+0.090[a]	+0.135	0.710
			Yield	−0.178[c]	−0.413	0.754
	Lebanon	1953–72	Area	+0.416[b]	+0.459	0.237
			Yield	−0.094	−0.080	0.201
Tomatoes	Jordan	1955–67	Area	−0.010	+0.010	0.651
			Yield	+0.010	−0.205	0.844
Eggplant	Jordan	1955–66	Area	−0.670[e]	−4.467	0.944
			Yield	−0.580[d]	−0.457	0.874
Potatoes	Syria	1950–60	Area	+0.651[d]	+1.297	0.874
			Yield	+0.341[d]	+0.348	0.829
		1961–72	Area	−1.759[b]	−2.851	0.909
			Yield	−0.348[a]	−0.352	0.336
	Jordan	1955–67	Area	−0.672	+1.377	0.251
			Yield	+0.374	+0.562	0.412
	Lebanon	1953–72	Area	−0.396[d]	−0.502	0.783
			Yield	+0.543[b]	+0.582	0.731

Significance levels indicated for estimated price parameters from which short-run elasticities were derived:

[a] 30 percent; [b] 20 percent; [c] 10 percent; [d] 5 percent; [e] 1 percent.

Source: Hossein Askari, John Thomas Cummings, and Bassam Harik, "Land Reform in the Middle East," International Journal of Middle East Studies, forthcoming.

As part of their attempt to examine the effects of land reform on cultivator responsiveness in the Middle East, Askari, Cummings, and Harik considered the output of several vegetables of varying degrees of importance.[67] Their supply model related output (in either acreage or yield terms) to lagged prices, water availability, a trend variable as a proxy for changes in other inputs like technology, and lagged output.

In Table 6.24 are shown the price elasticities and coefficients of determination for the regressions they carried out on both acreage and yield models. The authors postulated that certain behavior patterns would be indicative of greater responsiveness in the post-reform periods, but for the crops grouped herein these distinctions were less relevant. Egyptian onions showed the greater postreform price responsiveness (relative to yield) that was expected, and in Syria an area criterion yielded the same improvement. Tomatoes and eggplants were considered only in Jordan (which does not have land reform programs)—for neither crop was much market responsiveness noted. Potatoes are a minor crop in all three countries considered (Syria, Jordan, and Lebanon) from the viewpoint of area, but they are a major income-producing item for its cultivators throughout the area.

NOTES

1. Stephen DeCanio, "Tenancy and the Supply of Southern Cotton 1882-1914," a paper given at the Econometrics Conference in Madison, University of Wisconsin (April 1971), and "Agricultural Production, Supply, and Institutions in the Post-Civil War South" (Ph.D. dissertation, Massachusetts Institute of Technology, 1972).

2. Thomas Cooley and Stephen DeCanio, "Varying Parameter Supply Functions and the Sources of Economic Distress in American Agriculture 1866-1914," National Bureau of Economic Research working paper, 1974.

3. John Muth, "Optimal Properties of Exponentially Weighted Forecasts," Journal of the American Statistical Association 55 (June 1960).

4. Michael J. Brennan, "Changes in Cotton Acreage in the Southeast: Implications for Supply Functions," Journal of Farm Economics 40 (November 1958): 835-44.

5. William G. Tomek, "Distributed Lag Models of Cotton Acreage Response: A Further Result," American Journal of Agricultural Economics 54 (February 1972).

6. Kenneth D. Frederick, "The Role of Market Forces and Planning in Uganda's Economic Development 1900-1938," Eastern African Economic Review 1 (June 1969).

7. S. A. Oni, "Econometric Analysis of Supply Response Among Nigerian Cotton Growers," Bulletin of Rural Economics and Sociology 4, no. 2 (1969).

8. S. Olajuwon Olayide, "Some Estimates of Supply Elasticities for Nigeria's Cash Crops," Journal of Agricultural Economics 23 (September 1972).

9. In a rejoinder, David Blandford (in "Some Estimates of Supply Elasticities for Nigeria's Cash Crops: A Comment," Journal of Agricultural Economics 24 [September 1973]) took considerable issue with Olayide's methodology and argument.

His first criticism is that supply-demand interaction was represented by a single equation. In all fairness, Olayide recognized this limitation—it is undoubtedly a serious problem relative to the vast majority of supply-oriented studies included herein. Most authors, explicitly or otherwise, who are sensitive to this problem, refer to the difficulty in the specification and estimation of a model framed in terms of both sides of the market.

Secondly, and of particular concern here, Blandford argues with both the methodology followed in deriving elasticity estimates and the presenting of such estimates that come from price coefficients that frequently show little statistical significance. He points out that the value of such elasticities is not high enough to serve as convincing evidence for the policy recommendations made by Olayide.

10. Raj Krishna, "Farm Supply Response in India-Pakistan: A Case Study of the Punjab Region," Economic Journal 73 (September 1963).

11. Raj Krishna, "Cotton Production and Price Policy since Independence," University of Delhi, Institute of Economic Growth, 1964.

12. Jawahar Kaul, "A Study of Supply Responses to Price of Punjab Crops," Indian Journal of Economics 48 (July 1967).

13. R. P. Singh, Parmatma Singh and K. N. Rai, "Acreage Response to Rainfall, New Farm Technology and Price in Haryana," Indian Journal of Agricultural Economics 54 (October 1973).

14. A. Parikh, "Market Responsiveness of Peasant Cultivators: Some Evidence from Prewar India," Journal of Development Studies 8 (1972). As with Parikh's earlier article quoted in Chapter 5 (see note 21 on p. 159) the data source is Dharm Narain, The Impact of Price Movements on Areas under Selected Crops in India 1900-1939 (Cambridge: Cambridge University Press, 1965).

15. National Council of Applied Economic Research (NCAER), Long Term Projections of Demand for and Supply of Selected Agricultural Commodities—1960/61 to 1975/76 (New Delhi, 1963).

16. Sushil Krishna, "Farm Supply Response in India: A Study of Four Major Crops" (unpublished paper, Tufts University, 1975).

17. B. L. Sawhney, "Farm Supply Response: A Case Study of the Bombay Region," Asian Economic Review 10 (February 1968); see Chapter 5 for his results for jowar and bajra.

18. V. Rajagopalan, "Supply Response for Irrigated Crops in Madras State, India" (Ph.D. dissertation, University of Tennessee, 1967).

19. M. C. Madhavan, "Acreage Response of Indian Farmers: A Case Study of Tamil Nadu," Indian Journal of Agricultural Economics 27 (January-March 1972).

20. Walter Falcon, "Farmer Response to Price in an Under-developed Area: A Case Study of West Pakistan" (Ph.D. dissertation, Harvard University, 1962).

21. Ghulam Mohammed, "Some Physical and Economic Determinants of Cotton Production," Pakistan Development Review 3 (Winter 1963).

22. John Thomas Cummings, "Supply Response in Peasant Agriculture: Price and Non-Price Factors" (Ph.D. dissertation, Tufts University, 1974).

23. Hossein Askari and John Thomas Cummings, "Supply Response of Farmers with Heterogeneous Land," Indian Journal of Agricultural Economics, forthcoming 1976.

24. Hossein Askari, John Thomas Cummings, and Bassam Harik, "Land Reform in the Middle East," International Journal of Middle East Studies, forthcoming.

25. Robert Stern, "Price Responsiveness of Egyptian Cotton," Kyklos 12 (1959).

26. Ralph Clark, "The Economic Determinants of Jute Production," FAO Monthly Bulletin of Agricultural Economics and Statistics 3 (September 1957): 1-10.

27. L. R. Venkataramanan, "A Statistical Study of Indian Jute Production and Marketing with Special Reference to Foreign Demand" (Ph.D. dissertation, University of Chicago, 1958).

28. Robert Stern, "The Price Responsiveness of Primary Producers," Review of Economics and Statistics 44 (May 1962): 202-07.

29. Sayed Mushtaq Hussain, "A Note on Farmer Response to Price in East Pakistan," Pakistan Development Review 4 (1964).

30. Sayed Mushtaq Hussain, "Economic Development of the Agricultural Sector of an Underdeveloped Country with Special Reference to Pakistan," (Ph.D. dissertation, University of California, Berkeley, 1968), and "The Effect of the Growing Constraint of Subsistence Farming on Farmer Response to Price: A Case Study of Jute in Pakistan," Pakistan Development Review 9 (Autumn 1969).

31. A. K. M. Ghulam Rabbani, "Economic Determinants of Jute Production in India and Pakistan," Pakistan Development Review 5 (Summer 1965): 191-228.

32. Sayeedul Huq, "Jute Price Stabilization and Resource Allocation between Jute and Rice in East Pakistan," Pakistan Economic Journal 19, no. 2 (1968/69).

33. P. C. Bansil, "Farmer Response to Jute and Paddy Prices," a paper read at the 31st Annual Conference of the Indian Society of Agricultural Economics, abstracted in the Indian Journal of Agricultural Economics 26 (October-December 1971).

34. Parikh, op. cit.

35. Sushil Krishna, op. cit.

36. Shyamal Roy, "Farmers' Response to Price in Allocating Acreage to Jute in West Bengal," Journal of the Indian Society of Agricultural Statistics 24 (June 1972).

37. Cummings, op. cit.

38. Askari and Cummings, op. cit.

39. Jere Behrman, Supply Response in Underdeveloped Agriculture: A Case Study of Four Major Annual Crops in Thailand, 1937-63 (Amsterdam: North-Holland, 1968).

40. Vahid Nowshirvani, "Agricultural Supply in India: Some Theoretical and Empirical Studies" (Ph.D. dissertation, Massachusetts Institute of Technology, 1962).

41. NCAER, op. cit.

42. P. Boon-raung, J. S. Sharma, T. V. Moorti, and M. M. Wagner, "Supply Response for Groundnut in India," a paper read at the 31st Annual Conference of the Indian Society of Agricultural Economics, abstracted in the Indian Journal of Agricultural Economics 26 (October-December 1971).

43. J. Mahender Reddy, "Estimation of Farmers' Supply Response—A Case Study of Groundnut," Indian Journal of Agricultural Economics 25 (October-December 1970).

44. Sawhney, op. cit.

45. Rajagopalan, op. cit.

46. Madhavan, op. cit.

47. Parikh, op. cit.

48. Cummings, op. cit.

49. Askari and Cummings, op. cit.

50. Singh, Singh, and Rai, op. cit.

51. Olayide, op. cit; see earlier in this chapter for cotton, and in Chapter 7 for cocoa, rubber, and palm products.

52. Askari, Cummings, and Harik, op. cit.

53. Remy Friere, "Price Incentives in Argentine Agriculture," Development Advisory Service Report, Center for International Affairs, Harvard University, 1966 (mimeographed).

54. Andrew Schmitz, "Canadian Wheat Acreage Response," Canadian Journal of Agricultural Economics 16 (June 1968).

55. Brian W. Paddock, "Supply Analysis of Rapeseed Acreage," Canadian Journal of Agricultural Economics 19 (July 1971).

56. James P. Houck and Abraham Subotnik, "The U.S. Supply of Soybeans: Regional Acreage Functions," Agricultural Economics Research 21, no. 4 (October 1969).

57. In a later article, "Supply Analysis for Corn in the United States: The Impact of Changing Government Programs," American Journal of Agricultural Economics 54, no. 2 (May 1972), Houck and M. E. Ryan developed the concept of a weighted support price somewhat further in an attempt to gauge the effect of various market control programs on corn output. Support prices are disaggregated and a supply model including both direct supports and acreage diversion payments was used. Additional applications of this model have been reported by Ryan and M. E. Abel in "Corn Acreage Response and the Set-Aside Program," "Supply Response of U.S. Sorghum Acreage to Government Programs," and "Oats and Barley Acreage Response to Government Programs," Agricultural Economics Research 24 (October 1972) and 25 (April and October 1973).

58. A. A. Adesimi, "An Econometric Study of Air-Cured Tobacco Supply in Western Nigeria 1945-1964," Nigerian Journal of Economics and Social Studies 12 (November 1970).

59. Edwin R. Dean, "Economic Analysis and African Responses to Price," Journal of Farm Economics 47 (October 1962), and Supply Response of African Farmers (Amsterdam: North-Holland, 1966).

60. Dean quotes a number of recent works by anthropologists, sociologists, and economists to this effect; for example, Melville J. Herskovits, The Human Factor in Changing Africa (New York: Knopf, 1962); and Elliot J. Berg, "Backward-Sloping Labor Supply Functions in Dual Economies—The Africa Case," Quarterly Journal of Economics 75 (1961).

61. NCAER, op. cit.

62. Cummings, op. cit.

63. Askari and Cummings, op. cit.

64. R. D. Singh and P. R. Rao, "Determinants of Supply Behavior: The Case of Virginia Tobacco in India," Artha Vijnuna 16 (September 1974).

65. G. T. Jones, "The Response of the Supply of Agricultural Products in the United Kingdom to Price" (Part II), Farm Economist 10 (1967).

66. T. J. Mules and F. G. Jarrett, "Supply Responses in the South Australian Potato Industry," Australian Journal of Agricultural Economics 10 (June 1966).

67. Askari, Cummings, and Harik, op. cit.

From the viewpoint of supply models and their endogenous and exogenous components, perennial crops may require special treatment on almost every level of quantitative analysis. The basic reason for these departures from the methods employed in the studies outlined in the previous two chapters is, of course, the longer time horizon that must be considered by the cultivators of perennials. However, as several authors mentioned in the present chapter indicate, this time element may affect the representation within the supply model of factors such as output, price, and yield expectations, weather and technological inputs, each in a different way. Thus the adaptation of the Nerlove approach to annual crops to perennials is not merely a matter of applying uniformly a longer time lag, then proceeding with ordinary least-squares or maximum-likelihood estimating procedures. The planting of a perennial is very much like the acquisition of a piece of capital; that is, both last for more than the current time period. Clearly this analogy is even stronger when the product of concern is derived from livestock. Thus the response for perennials and livestock cannot merely be modeled into the usual Nerlove form; rather, such analyses must also face many standard issues raised in capital theory.

For example, such perennials as tree crops generally have a multistaged profile as regards annual yields—several years pass after planting before any output is realized, followed perhaps by a period of semimaturity during which yields continue to advance, then peak output may be realized for a few or many years, concluding with a gradual decline to levels where it is no longer profitable to maintain the plant. Clearly price expectations, which have to be formulated well ahead of planting, affect this output profile. If a tree takes j years before any fruit is borne, then prices in period

t – j which affected the original planting decisions, for now newly
bearing trees, are obviously of major importance regarding planting
in the present period t. Moreover, if another k years must pass
before a tree reaches full maturity, so must prices in period t – j – k
influence present planting, and so on.

The age profile of the existing stock of trees will certainly
affect per acre yields and thus total output in any given period.
This profile is determined not only by new planting, but also by
decisions to eliminate older trees. A proper conceptualization
of income, if not price, expectations must weigh losses during the
next j years, as measured by expected prices during that period,
as a result of uprooting older bearing plants and replacing them
with seedlings, against gains that will begin to be realized after
the new plants begin to bear and then surpass the annual yields
that would have been gained from the older trees had they not been
replaced.

Not only may complex weighting patterns attached to prices of
many seasons past affect present output, but so may present prices.
If cultivator decisions regarding planting and replacement affect
output in any given period, so too will their harvesting decisions.
Most studies of annuals, by using prices lagged one period, implicitly
assume planted and harvested acreage to be approximately, if not
exactly, the same; in effect, in the absence of evidence to the
contrary, the period between sowing and reaping is held to be too
short for any change in prices to occur that is drastic enough to
invalidate the use of planted acreage as a measure of crop output.

However, several researchers have indicated the inapplicability
of this reasoning to perennial crops. Output is harvested from a
stock of plants of varying ages whose existence reflects past prices,
but present profitability must balance recent prices against current
costs. These considerations can lead to a wide variety of cultivator
reactions, depending upon, for example, competing economic activities at critical times during and immediately surrounding the harvest
period, the need for and cost of inputs such as hired labor not
available from within the cultivator family, and so on. Low current
or recent prices should negatively influence harvested output, while
high prices might lead to exertion of every possible effort to maximize output.*

---

*A number of simple non-Nerlovian supply models that incorporate
only recent prices have been employed by authors primarily interested
in identifying short-term effects of prices on crop output. The
results of some of these researchers (see Frederick for coffee,
Chen for rubber) have been included herein to provide comparative

This flexibility regarding harvesting behavior also affects the methods employed to represent output in the supply model. In studies of annual crops many researchers have used planted acreage as their dependent variable, either because all output measures (including tonnage and harvested acreage) are believed to behave similarly over time, or because in some countries (like India) or for certain crops (such as subsistence cereals) planted acreage is the most reliable available statistical series. However, for perennials any reliable gauging of the influence of prices on output requires the latter be phrased more reliably than in acreage, terms that in effect indicate only potential output. Thus most authors discussed in this chapter use some measure of output, either harvested or marketed, expressed in tonnage terms.

Just as the long plant lifetimes require special conceptualization of price expectations, so too must climatological influences be incorporated in supply models on an ad hoc basis. For example, not only would rainfall in period t affect output in period t, but perhaps as importantly, a notable departure from normal such as a drought or an excessively moist year might significantly influence output for many coming years, because of the long-range effects of the weather abnormality on all existing plants. Such events have been handled variously by different authors, with some including dummy variables that merely inject a binomial "before and after" representation of a weather disaster, while others have sought to recognize the declining importance of such occurrences as time advances.

In addition to the need for specific consideration of possible peculiarities regarding almost any other variable introduced into the supply model for a perennial crop, the studies outlined in this chapter also encountered statistical problems regarding data availability that were much more limiting than for annual crops. Particularly in developing countries (though by no means only in such cases), reliable data series needed for supply analysis may have been published for only a relatively short recent period. Estimating procedures allow at least the possibility of reasonable validity being attached to estimates obtained for annual crops from time

----

results relative to those of more complex studies of the crops in question. Other more complex studies deriving non-Nerlovian models are not reported herein for reasons of economy of space; for example, Ben French and Raymond Bressler's paper on California lemon production ("The Lemon Cycle," Journal of Farm Economics 44 [November 1962]), which added new plantings and removals formulations to a cobweb-type model.

series as brief as 12 to 15 years, a period for which relevant data
is obviously available for a great variety of annual crops in many
countries, as Chapters 5 and 6 testify.

However, two specific problems arise for perennial crops.
First, if output is to be studied over a period of n years, information
regarding such variables as prices and climate must be available
for several years before the beginning of time when output is actually
analyzed. In fact since many perennials are export crops, relevant
price data at least can often be found for a sufficiently long period
to conduct a reasonably valid statistical analysis, even in countries
where researchers might still be hampered by lack of data in
conducting similar analysis of, for example, basically subsistence
annual crops.

A second problem might occasionally be more difficult to overcome. Time series analysis is limited on both ends regarding the
number of observations that are to be included: The time series
must be sufficiently long to allow enough degrees of freedom to the
estimating procedure if it is to have any resulting significance when
all economically relevant variables have been included. While on
the other hand, the longer the period under study, the more likely
basic changes in infrastructure, and so on, will result in shifts in
the underlying supply situation.

The longer time horizon for perennial crops introduces into
the estimating equation, in most cases, a larger number of variables
than in the case of annual crops: for example, prices from several
past periods, rather than a single price lagged by a period or two,
dummies accounting for notable past climatological or other occurrences. While in many cases variables initially hypothesized as
economically relevant may in fact show no statistical significance
and might therefore be eliminated from the estimating processes,
initial testing of the hypothesis requires their inclusion and, thus,
demands that the available time series be long enough to evaluate
reliably their relevance.

On the other hand, if the data available for analytical consideration allows lengthy time series, the possibility of structural shifts
must be considered and if found potentially notable, representation
thereof must be added to the model. Some such likely shifts should
be easy to identify—for example, the initiation of government market-
control boards, land reform programs, and so on—and their inclusion,
in dummy or other format, would not much constrict the degrees
of freedom available for eventual estimating when available data
series are lengthy. The problems in this regard are the structural
changes that are not so easily anticipated or discovered, and thus
we encounter an argument for not unduly prolonging a period to
be analyzed—say, for example, setting a provisional upper limit
of 25 or 30 years.

In fact a careful approach to any consideration of structural shift, coupled with relatively long data series available, might lead the researcher to a desire to distinguish between the supply structures existing before and after some such major event as the initiation of government control over marketing of the crop in question, not by the approximate and inexact tool of a dummy variable, but by subdividing the time period and separately estimating the supply parameters before and after the change of interest. The resulting shortening of the data series available for regression analysis may of course confront the researcher with the problems just discussed above that are relevant to less lengthy perennial time-series analysis.

Thus the horns of the analytic dilemma may be both clear and sharp, though no exact delimitation of precisely what time period is too short or too long can be made. A Nerlovian approach to the supply of perennials is empirically possible and, given the over-simplified static short-run alternative of formulating output in terms of current or very recent factors, highly desirable. However, the economist embarking a research in this area must move in essentially uncharted waters and remain ultrasensitive to the peculiarities of his chosen concern, even though he begins at essentially the same starting point as his colleague interested in annual crops—the basic price expectations, area adjustment supply model—and has available to him the results of other studies of perennial crops.

One of the earliest major studies of a perennial crop using a dynamic Nerlovian supply model was published by Merrill Bateman for cocoa, a crop that dominates the export trade of Ghana.[1] Cocoa grows on trees, and it is of course a perennial, which means that decisions to plant it are based not on the expected price the crop will bring at the conclusion of a single growing season but on expectations of income streams spread over the life of the tree. However, balanced against this expected income are the maintenance costs of a perennial plant, that is, of cultivation during the pre-maturity period when little or no yield occurs and of continuance during later years of the tree's lifetime when costs may begin to rival expected yields.

For cocoa the yield is zero during the first five to eight years following planting. The only direct cost of maintaining the plants during this period is a required annual weeding; the indirect costs of income foregone due to the planting of a long-maturing rather than an annual crop are somewhat mitigated by the fact that during the first four years after a field is planted in cocoa it can also be used in part for the cultivation of other crops. Maize and cassava, grown in alternate rows with cocoa plants, provide the necessary lateral shade for the young plants, as well as some produce for the farmer. Since food crops can be planted and harvested throughout the year in accordance with the farmer's consumption needs, cocoa, once it reaches maturity, does not compete with these crops for labor inputs.

In constructing his model Bateman focused first on the forces that motivate farmers to plant new trees and then on the relationship between acres planted and output harvested.

Since any planting decision about a perennial crop affects output over a period of several years, Bateman assumed that when cocoa planters made these decisions they were motivated by a desire to maximize the present discounted value of future streams of net returns. The present discounted value of future streams of net returns is equal to the difference between the discounted gross revenue stream (R_t) and the stream of discounted costs (C_t). R_t is represented by

$$R_t = \sum_{i=o}^{n} \frac{P_{t+i}}{(1+r)^i} \times Y^e_{t+i} \times A_t, \tag{7.1}$$

where: P^e_{t+i} is the expected real producer price of cocoa in period
          $t + i$,
          r is the peasants' subjective rate of discount,
          Y^e_{t+i} is the expected yield per acre of cocoa in period
              $t + i$, with yield expressed as a function of
          A_t, the number of acres planted in period t, and
          n is the expected age when the trees cease to bear.
Discounted costs, C_t, are then represented by

$$C_t = \sum_{i=o}^{n} \frac{C^e_{t+i}}{(1+r)^i} \tag{7.2}$$

where: C^e_{t+i} is the expected value of real costs incurred in period
$t + i$ that is due to cocoa <u>planted</u> in period t (with these costs
expressed as a function of A_t). The farmer wishes to maximize
the difference between these two streams with respect to acreage
planted in period t, so a solution can be obtained by differentiating
with respect to A_t setting the result equal to zero, and solving for A_t

$$\frac{d}{dA_t}(R_t - C_t) = \sum_{i=o}^{n} \left[\frac{P^e_{t+i}}{(1+r)^i} \times Y^{e\,'}_{t+i} \times A_t \frac{P^e_{t+i}}{(1+r)^i} Y^e_{t+i} \right]$$

$$-\sum_{i=o}^{n} \frac{C^{e\,'}_{t+i}}{(1+r)^i} = 0 \tag{7.3}$$

Equation 7.3 says that the acreage planted in cocoa in any period is a function of the following streams: expected real prices discounted over time, expected marginal yields per acre, expected total yields per acre, and expected marginal costs discounted over time. Bateman contended that the first stream—expected discounted prices—dominates the planting decision-making process, with the other three either being relatively stable or changing slowly and in response to price changes. Following World War II the introduction of coffee cultivation into Ghana required the peasant to consider still another stream, that of potential income for an alternate perennial crop. Bateman argued that the most important variable affecting coffee income expectations is producer prices and that the yield and cost characteristics of coffee are similar to those of cocoa.

Thus Bateman postulated that cocoa and coffee price expectations are the major determinants in cocoa planting decisions and that the cocoa supply function in terms of acres planted annually then can be represented as:

$$A_t = a_o + a_1 \overline{P}_t + a_2 \overline{PC}_t + u_t \tag{7.4}$$

where: P_t is the mean value of discounted expected future prices of cocoa, and

$\overline{PC}_t$ is the mean value of discounted expected future coffee prices.

These mean values are of the form:

$$P_t = \frac{\sum\limits_{i=o}^{n} [P^e_{t+i}/(1+r)^i]}{n+1} \tag{7.5a}$$

$$\overline{PC}_t = \frac{\sum\limits_{i=o}^{n} [PC^e_{t+i}/(1+r)^i]}{n+1} \tag{7.5b}$$

Price expectations are formed in a Nerlovian pattern:

$$P^e_t - P^e_{t-1} = \beta_1(P_t - P^e_{t-1}) \tag{7.6a}$$

$$PC^e_t - PC^e_{t-1} = \beta_2(PC_t - PC^e_{t-1}) \tag{7.6b}$$

then with the simplifying, if not necessarily justifiable, assumption that $\beta_1 = \beta_2 = \beta$, equations 7.6a and 7.6b are substituted in 7.4 to yield

$$A_t = a_o\beta + a_1\beta \overline{P}_t + a_2\beta \overline{PC}_t + (1 - \beta) A_{t-1} + u_t \tag{7.7}$$

However, data on newly planted acreage are not available for Ghana. Output data can be found, and Bateman reformulated his model in these terms. Output is a function of cumulative planting, which in the case of cocoa is subject to the following considerations: the first five to eight years following planting have yields of zero; prior to peak productions, two distinct periods of growth per acre and per tree occur; the amount of rainfall during certain crucial periods in each growing season affects annual output; and finally, as with other perennial crops, prices at harvesting time may have noticeable effect on the amount harvested.

Amelonado, the original type of cocoa tree introduced into Ghana in the nineteenth century, still accounts for 90 percent of the cocoa grown. Its life cycle is as follows: up to 7 years after planting—seedling cocoa and young cocoa not yet in bearing; 8 to 15 years—young bearing trees; 16 to 30 years—cocoa in full bearing; and over 30 years—older mature plants. The trees in the latter category will show gradually declining annual yields, depending upon soil and growing conditions. While trees in good soil may live and produce good yields for more than a century, the typical tree survives no more than 40 to 50 years and is thus in peak productivity no more than 30 or 40 years.

When trees first begin to bear (about seven years after planting), yields per tree and per acre at first remain stable for three or four seasons, then display a rapid increase to a much higher level, after which output per tree grows only gradually.

To represent this Bateman presents the equation (expressed in output [Q] terms):

$$Q_t = b_1 \sum_{t=k}^{s-1} A_{t-i} + b_2 \sum_{t=s}^{\infty} A_{t-i} + b_3 R_{t-1} + b_4 P_t \tag{7.8}$$

Output in period t (Q_t) thus depends on cumulative planting (trees planted less than k years ago [6 or 7 years] yield nothing and are thus ignored; trees planted more than k but less than s years ago [10 or 11 years] yield notably less than those more than s years old, and thus the model distinguishes between the two age groups), on rainfall (R_{t-1}) during crucial parts of the period preceding the harvest in question, and finally, on current prices (P_t), which may motivate decisions regarding actual harvesting inputs.

Bateman then expressed the output equation in first difference terms

$$Q_t = b_1 A_{t-k} + (b_2 - b_1) A_{t-s} + b_3 R_{t-1} + b_4 P_t \qquad (7.9)$$

and combined this with the planting equation 7.4 to obtain his final estimating equation:

$$\Delta Q_t = a_o b_2 \beta + a_1 b_1 \beta \, P_{t-k} + a_1 (b_2 - b_1) \beta \, P_{t-s} + a_2 b_1 \beta \, PC_{t-k}$$

$$+ A_2 (b_2 - b_1) \beta \, PC_{t-s} + b_3 \Delta R_{t-1} + b_4 \Delta P_t$$

$$+ (1 - \beta) [Q_{t-1} - b_3 \Delta R_{t-2} - b_4 \, P_{t-1}] + w_t$$

$$= c_o + c_1 P_{t-k} + c_2 P_{t-s} + c_3 PC_{t-k} + c_4 PC_{t-s} + c_5 \Delta R_{t-1}$$

$$+ c_6 Q_{t-1} + c_7 \Delta R_{t-2} + c_8 \Delta P_{t-1} + w_t \qquad (7.10)$$

Bateman tested both additive and multiplicative forms of the model, examining both aggregative and regional supply responses. On an aggregative basis he tried various combinations of regions looking for evidence of homogeneity, but found only three regions—Volta, Central, and Ashanti (Sunyani), and possibly a fourth, Western—that showed any indication of interregional homogeneity. The best results were obtained using an additive formulation.

When Volta, Central, and Sunyani regions are pooled, and the constant is suppressed, all the indicated coefficients are highly significant, as they are also when Volta and the Western regions are pooled. F-statistic values are generally low, but there is at least an indication of the likelihood of a cross-regional homogeneity. Three of the four regions displaying this tendency are characterized by similar soil types—so-called Class III soils, the lowest grade suitable for cocoa cultivation, predominate in the Western, Volta, and Sunyani regions. The age profiles of the tree stocks in all four regions also show some homogeneity, since they are the most recent areas brought under cocoa cultivation.

In contrast pooling together the data of older and newer regions, or even of the older planted regions by themselves, exhibits no homogeneity. In all such cases the coefficients for lagged output, rainfall, and recent prices (ΔP_t and ΔP_{t-1}) were statistically insignificant and close to zero. Coffee prices in the year of planting (PC_{t-s}) of the cocoa trees presently (in period t) undergoing rapid expansion of output (after three or four seasons of initially lower yields) were omitted from the estimating equation since this variable did not prove significant in the individual supply calculations of three of the four regions. The results also suggest strongly that recent producer prices have little effect on harvesting decisions. A humidity variable, included in initial testing to give some measure of the extent to which humidity-promoted fungus diseases affect yields, did not prove to be significant when tested in the aggregate supply equation, but did prove significant in many of the regions.

Examining supply response on a regional basis, Bateman used a formulation similar to equation 7.10 and another in which prices were expressed in terms of cocoa to coffee ratios, rather than separate inclusion of both price series. Both included humidity and both were tested as both additive and multiplicative models but for all regions the best results were obtained when the additive approach was employed and prices of the two competing perennials were separately considered.

In commenting on the statistical significance of the different variables in the separate regional supply equations, Bateman emphasized that coffee prices lagged eight years, that is, those of the period in which were planted the cocoa trees now (in period t) first bearing fruit are significant in all the type III soil regions where coffee is an alternate crop (coffee is not grown in the Central region), while coffee prices lagged 12 (or in two regions, 13) years, that is, coffee prices in the year in which the cocoa trees now (in period t) undergoing their second spurt in output were planted, are significant in only one of these regions. On the other hand, the earlier (12- or 13-year lag) coffee prices prove significant in both of the regions having better grade (I and II) cocoa soils and in which coffee is an alternate crop—Ashanti (Old Ashanti) and Eastern regions.

The regions in which only type III soils are found are, as mentioned above, the areas that have most recently been devoted to cocoa. Bateman indicated that the importance of lagged coffee prices is reflected in the period during which the increase in the rate of bearing is most strongly concentrated. While the second spurt in yield is significant in prime cocoa regions, trees planted in marginal soils do not show such a marked increase in output 12 or 13 years after planting. Furthermore, Bateman pointed out that the magnitude of the supply response to cocoa prices is also clearly related to soil type. Marginal cocoa soils, the last to be planted, dominate in the regions where response to price changes is greatest. Regional supply elasticities, calculated at the sample means, are shown in Table 7.1.

Bateman concluded that response to both cocoa and coffee prices varies inversely with the length of time that a region has been planted in cocoa, the smallest elasticities (0.32 and -0.37) being found in the Eastern region, where the Ghanaian cocoa industry began, and the largest (0.47 and -0.53) in the Sunyani region, where cocoa was only recently introduced. He explained

TABLE 7.1

Supply Elasticities, Ghanaian Cocoa

Region	Cocoa Prices (t - k)	Cocoa Prices (t - s)	Coffee Prices (t - k)	Coffee Prices (t - s)	Rainfall	Humidity
Central	0.19	0.25	—	—	0.29	—
Western	0.35	0.36	-0.54	—	0.16	—
Volta	0.32	0.29	-0.64	—	0.13	-0.08
Eastern	—	0.32	—	-0.37	0.15	-0.04
Old Ashanti	0.12	0.30	—	-0.52	0.15	-0.09
Sunyani	0.47	0.40	-0.53	-1.00	0.82	-0.30

Source: Merrill Bateman, Cocoa in the Ghanaian Economy: An Econometric Model (Amsterdam: North-Holland, 1968).

this variation in terms of soil conditions: the cocoa industry began in those areas where the soil was most suitable for cocoa (type I soils); as the industry expanded, cultivation spread to other areas of the country where cocoa soils of less suitable types were found— the best (and rarest) cocoa soils are so planted as long as the crop is commercially marketable, though harvesting decisions are to some degree price-sensitive; both planting and harvesting decisions in the poorer soil region would be expected to be sensitive to price variation.

Examining the activities of the national Cocoa Marketing Board, which was founded after the outbreak of World War II, Bateman claimed that it was fortuitous that it kept producer prices low in the 1950s—otherwise the combination of high price elasticities of supply and the low demand elasticities found in the world market would have led to a severe glut in the 1960s (though the London-directed board, unaware of this disparity in elasticities, did not anticipate the possibility of any glut and kept producer prices low mostly to accumulate hard currency reserves with which to finance national development schemes and/or to help support sterling in world financial markets).

In a revised version of this study Bateman also tested a supply model that portrayed the existing stock of cocoa trees as a function of crop prices:[2]

$$S_t^D = c_o + c_1 P_t^e + c_2 PA_t^e + u_t \qquad (7.11)$$

where: S^D is the desired stock of cocoa trees,

   P^e is expected real producer prices for cocoa,

   PA^e is expected real producer prices for alternative crops.
Adjustment in the stock of trees is cast in Nerlovian terms—that is,
it is in proportion to the difference between actual and desired tree
stock

$$S_t - S_{t-1} = \gamma (S^D_t - S_{t-1}) \qquad\qquad (7.12)$$

where γ is the stock adjustment coefficient. Paralleling the Nerlove
approach, Bateman combined equation 7.12 with a price expectations
equation that includes recognition of the complex pattern of varying
cocoa yields and the stock equation 7.11. The model allows for the
obvious constraint placed on the cultivator in his attempts to adjust
his stock of trees.

   Estimating price elasticities for the period 1949-62 using this
model, he obtained the values for both short-run elasticities (which,
with the exception of the Western region, are similar to those he
calculated earlier) and long-run elasticities, which are shown in
Table 7.2.

   As part of a study into the likely effects of a world marketing
agreement, Jere Behrman examined the price responsiveness of
cocoa producers in several countries.[3] Though he based his model
to some extent on Bateman's work, he criticized the latter's assumption that the actual area planted in cocoa trees is a function of the
expected prices projected by the cultivators over the bearing period
of the trees. Behrman argued that a better starting point would be

TABLE 7.2

Supply Elasticities, Ghanaian Cocoa
Stock Adjustment Model

Region	Short-Run	Long-Run
Central	0.51*	1.28*
Eastern	0.39*	0.77*
Volta	0.53*	1.06*
Western	0.31	0.68

*10 percent significance level.

Source: Merrill J. Bateman, Cocoa in the Ghanaian Economy:
An Econometric Model (Amsterdam: North-Holland, 1968).

that <u>desired</u> area in cocoa is a function of the expected prices of both cocoa and the principal alternate crop, coffee.

$$A_t^D = a_o + a_1 P_t^e + PC_t^e + u_t \tag{7.13}$$

where: A_t^D is the desired area in cocoa,

P_t^e is the expected price of cocoa, and

PC_t^e is the expected price of coffee.

A Nerlovian area adjustment formulation was included in Behrman's initial model, but a lack of data regarding area planted in cocoa caused Behrman to recast his hypothesis in output terms.

$$Q_t = b_o + \sum_{i=0}^{\infty} Y_i A_{t-i} + b_2 P_t + b_3 P_{t-1} + v_t \tag{7.14}$$

where: Q_t is cocoa output in tons,

Y_i is the average yield per unit area i years after planting, and

P_t is actual cocoa price.

Past annual plantings in cocoa (ΔA_{t-i}) were thus weighted by average yields in the <u>present</u> period of such plantings; recent prices are included in an attempt to discern any short-run harvest response. A first-difference formulation eliminates the infinite series in equation 7.14, and algebraic manipulation yields Behrman's estimating equation (including coffee prices):

$$Q_t = c_o + c_1 \Delta Q_{t-1} + c_2 \Delta Q_{t-2} + c_3 \Delta P_t + c_4 \Delta P_{t-1}$$

$$+ c_5 \Delta P_{t-2} + c_6 \Delta P_{t-3} + c_7 \Delta P_{t-n_1} + c_8 \Delta P_{t-n_2}$$

$$+ c_9 \Delta PC_{t-n_1} + c_{10} \Delta PC_{t-n_2} + w_t \tag{7.15}$$

where: n_1 is the age at which trees first bear fruit, and

n_2 is the age at which the second substantial increase in yield occurs.

Table 7.3 shows the importance of cocoa in the economies of each of these producing nations, the role each plays in the world cocoa market, and the short- and long-run supply elasticities with respect to cocoa prices.

In considering the implications of the results for a possible international marketing agreement, Behrman argued that though little or no short-run price responsiveness is present in six of the

TABLE 7.3

Supply Elasticities, Cocoa

Country	Cocoa as Percent of All Exports	Percentage of World Cocoa Supply	Elasticity Short-Run	Elasticity Long-Run
Ghana	66.0	36.5	–	0.71
Nigeria	19.3	17.3	–	0.45
Ivory Coast	21.4	8.3	–	0.80
Cameroon	28.0	6.4	0.68	1.81
Brazil	4.7	9.3	0.53	0.95
Ecuador	12.6	3.2	–	0.28
Dominican Republic	6.7	3.1	0.03	0.15
Venezuela	3.5	1.6	0.12	0.38

Source: Jere R. Behrman, "Monopolistic Cocoa Pricing," American Journal of Agricultural Economics 50 (August 1968).

eight countries, any attempt to bolster high prices by restrictions on supply would have to be accompanied by stockpiling. The substantial values of long-run elasticity for all but the oldest producing areas (the Dominican Republic, Ecuador, and Venezuela) demonstrate the need to take care lest high and stable prices lead to a cocoa glut. Behrman suggested that either producers would have to be isolated from world prices or strong planting restrictions would have to be strictly enforced. The future success of all the policies needed to promote the success of a world cocoa agreement is favored by the long experience of the individual countries with their individual marketing boards.[4]

Robert Stern has also published a study of the cocoa market.[5] Like Bateman and Behrman, he stressed the influence of prices on new plantings, but he also encountered data limitations in this regard. Only for Nigeria during the period 1919-20 to 1944-45 was such information available. Using this data he formulated a planting model, with new plantings expressed as a linear function of real cocoa prices (both planting acreage and cocoa prices were included in terms of moving five-year averages). Ordinary least-squares regression techniques revealed a highly significant price parameter estimate, a value of $R^2 = 0.86$ and a short-run elasticity of planting with respect to prices of +1.26.

For other nations no such comparable planting data was available, so Stern used a first-differences supply model phrased in output terms, as shown in equation 7.16

$$\Delta Q_t = a_o + a_1 \Delta P_t + a_2 P_{t-8} \qquad (7.16)$$

including thus both current prices and those current at the planting of newly bearing trees.

Stern applied this output model to cocoa data from five other producing nations: Ghana, Ivory Coast, Cameroon, Brazil, and Ecuador. However, only in Ghana did his regressions show current prices (ΔP_t) to be significant, while lagged prices showed no notable effect in any case. The two interwar periods he tested (1919/20-1938/39 and 1919/20-1945/46) yielded values of the correlation coefficient between 0.26 and 0.31, while even lower values were found for these regressions based on postwar production and on the entire period 1919/20-1963/64. For the interwar periods he calculated supply elasticities with respect to current prices of 0.17 and 0.15 respectively.

Cocoa output in Nigeria was considered in a study of several of that country's cash crops conducted by S. Olajuwon Olayide.[6] His two supply models were planting models allowing for a seven-year maturity period for new trees.

Olayide used ordinary least squares to estimate the parameters. The author traced his techniques to those used by Bateman, Stern, Ady, and French and Matthews,* though he stressed that Ady's model involved difficulties with multicollinearity, leading him to drop output lagged one year as an explanatory variable, and that the French-Matthews model contained several independent variables not quantifiable given Nigerian data sources.

Producer prices at the time of planting showed little influence on changes in cocoa output, using the degree of statistical significance indicated for price coefficient estimates as a criterion. But he found more importance for current prices. The author incorporated these circumstances into his concluding argument for a less rigid form of control on the part of the commodity marketing boards.

Supply elasticities derived from the two models were estimated to be +0.197 and +0.596, respectively. A comparison of the three elasticity estimating processes indicated values relative to lagged producer prices (the first model) between +0.15 and +0.20, but

---

*See notes 1 and 5 in this chapter for Bateman and Stern; see notes 20 and 32 later in this chapter for Ady and French and Matthews.

relative to world prices the value was identified only within a broad range, +0.04 to +0.44.

Another extensively studied tree crop has been coffee, and again a considerable variety of approaches have been followed by researchers. Planting, output, and capital stock models have been formulated and tested, with estimated values of both short- and long-run price responsiveness presented. As with the published cocoa studies, coffee researchers have been sensitive to earlier works—criticizing, building upon, modifying the models used by their predecessors, and thus a certain continuity can be seen in the same half dozen works discussed below.

Kenneth Frederick was first to apply a Nerlovian supply model to coffee in his study of Uganda.[7] Though this crop is native to the region, systematic cultivation dates only to about 1900, when British colonial authorities, encouraged by coffee's success in neighboring Kenya, introduced seedlings of the arabica species. During the next 20 years production expanded rapidly with more than 27,000 acres planted in 1920, mostly in plantations. However, after 1920, acreage declined as rapidly as it had grown, due primarily to various diseases that attacked plants below an altitude of about 4,500 feet.

Attention then turned to robusta coffee, the species native to Uganda. Robusta, less flavorful and desirable than arabica, commands a lower price in the world market, but because of its use as a filler in blended coffees and particularly in soluble (instant) coffees (which are as much as 50 percent robusta), its cultivation has benefitted from the rising consumer demand for coffee in the twentieth century. Being native to the region, robusta fares much better under local conditions and can be profitably grown in Uganda at elevations around 4,000 feet. More importantly, due to low initial capital inputs, it can easily be grown by small farmers and thus can serve as an important cash crop in what is primarily a subsistence agriculture economy. In the 1960s more than 90 percent of Ugandan coffee was grown on African-owned holdings no larger than three acres. The rapid expansion of cultivation since World War II, which has made Uganda the world's fifth largest coffee producer, can be traced largely to the crop's popularity with small farmers. This is due not only to its low capital inputs but also to the relatively low labor inputs after the initial stages of cultivation, to the fact that coffee harvesting in Uganda can be spread over several months (thus minimizing any competition with other crops for available labor), to the robusta tree's long profitable lifetime (30 years or more), and to the higher per-acre yields and revenues coffee enjoys relative to cotton, the main alternative crop.

The rapid growth of coffee in Uganda's export trade has occurred despite the fact that her robusta is of less-than-average quality by world standards. This deficiency is brought on in large part by conditions connected with smallholder cultivation—such as uneven harvesting techniques (both ripe and unripe berries being picked together), poor handling between tree and market, inconsistent grading of beans for quality, and so on.

Frederick's model was somewhat less sophisticated than either those used by later coffee researchers or by Bateman. His approach was actually a planting, not a supply, function, linking the annual change in coffee acreage (new planting) to lagged prices (alternatively, coffee export and relative cotton to coffee prices), lagged coffee acreage, and a trend variable.

He applied this model to the post-World War II period, a time marked by rapidly expanding coffee acreage (about 10 percent a year), using several different formulations including various combinations of the above enumerated independent variables. New planting in Uganda as a whole and in some of the major coffee-producing subdivisions was analyzed, but in none of Frederick's regressions did the estimated coefficient for lagged coffee acreage prove to be statistically significant. Calculated parameters (and the corresponding standard errors) are shown in Table 7.4.

In analyzing these results Frederick recalled that the Ugandan government's policy after World War II was to discourage farmers from switching from cotton to coffee cultivation. However, little use of price incentives was made in pursuing this policy, and an International Bank for Reconstruction and Development (IBRD) study in the early 1960s concluded that the structure of export duties and government-maintained price stabilization funds actually encouraged coffee cultivation at the expense of cotton. The above trend parameter estimates for Uganda as a whole and for Buganda province (which has over 85 percent of the nation's coffee acreage) testify to the failure of the government's efforts, but the continued growth of coffee acreage in the face of declining prices in the 1950s and early 1960s, coupled with the small value of R^2 in the regressions containing only a price variable, would seem to indicate that the price mechanism alone would not serve as a panacea to curb coffee's growth—coffee (or cotton-coffee) prices explain so little of acreage variation that other unconsidered factors must be present. Frederick suggested, for example, that farmers may need alternative crops more attractive than cotton to attract potential coffee acres.

For the districts of Buganda province where most of the coffee is grown, Mengo and Masaka (which have about 75 and 20 percent of Buganda acreage, respectively), the regressions indicate parameters

TABLE 7.4

Estimated Parameters, Ugandan Coffee

Region	Constant	Coffee Prices	Relative Cotton-to-Coffee Prices	Trend	R^2
Uganda	+ 3.10	+0.49c	—	—	0.20
(1947–62)	(10.21)	(0.20)			
	- 3.62	+0.31a	—	+1.77b	0.31
	(10.16)	(0.21)		(0.98)	
	+66.28c	—	-43.11a	—	0.32
	(13.64)		(13.99)		
	+42.30a	—	-29.75a	+1.36	0.35
	(29.96)		(17.19)	(1.06)	
Buganda	+ 2.83	+0.47c	—	—	0.21
province	(9.68)	(0.19)			
(1947–62)	- 4.05	+0.29a	—	+1.81b	0.35
	(9.43)	(0.19)		(0.91)	
	+63.23c	—	-41.13c	—	0.32
	(12.97)		(13.30)		
	+37.47a	—	-26.78a	+1.46a	0.37
	(21.44)		(16.05)	(0.99)	
Mengo	+ 2.37	+0.37a	—	—	n.q.
district	(16.33)	(0.27)			
(1951–61)	- 1.86	+0.35	—	+0.50	n.q.
	(22.95)	(0.29)		(1.78)	
	+48.81c	—	-31.95a	—	0.02
	(17.96)		(21.36)		
	+60.74a	—	-37.44a	-0.75	n.q.
	(39.95)		(27.08)	(2.07)	
Masaka	+17.61c	-0.16	—	—	0.03
district	(6.41)	(0.11)			
(1951–61)	+ 6.48	-0.20a	—	+1.31c	0.38
	(6.81)	(0.09)		(0.53)	
	+ 4.26	—	+ 5.18	—	n.q.
	(7.92)		(9.42)		
	-26.55c	—	+19.34c	+1.94c	0.41
	(11.27)		(8.04)	(0.62)	

n.q. = Value not quoted.

[a]20 percent significance level; [b]10 percent significance level; [c]5 percent significance level.

Source: Kenneth D. Frederick, "Coffee Production in Uganda: An Economic Analysis of Past and Potential Growth" (Ph.D. dissertation, Massachusetts Institute of Technology, 1965).

of the same sign for Mengo as for Uganda and Buganda but a perverse
price-to-acreage response in Masaka.

During the 1950s coffee acreage grew in both districts, though
at different rates—about 8.5 percent a year in Masaka but by more
than 12 percent in Mengo. However, Frederick presents graphical
evidence to illustrate that the rate of growth of acreage in Mengo
was high in the early 1950s and much lower after 1957, whereas in
Masaka acreage growth was sluggish until 1958 and thereafter very
rapid. Nationally, coffee prices rose steadily to a peak in 1954,
dropped to a plateau through 1958, and then fell sharply. He
suggested Mengo's slower rate of growth in the late 1950s may
reflect the effect of falling prices (hence the positive coefficient
for price). In addition most of the government's anticoffee policies
were directed at Mengo, the principal area of cultivation, and the
availability of unused potential coffee land in the district was becoming
increasingly tight.

In Masaka, with more untapped land suitable for coffee cultivation, acreage rose rapidly, despite falling prices, reflecting, as
Frederick hypothesized, those nonprice influences on acreage not
included in the planting equation. He felt the importance of the
latter were indicated by the low percentage of acreage variation
explained by the price variable (values of R^2 between only 0.20 and
0.32 in Uganda and Buganda). Thus, he concluded, whatever non-
price influences are present in the Ugandan coffee industry as a
whole are concentrated in Masaka, where available land and less
government attention combine to override the expected positive
price-to-acreage relationship.

In a later study Frederick examined pre-World War II coffee
production in Uganda, again relative to cotton cultivation.[8] His
supply model for this period was much simpler than that cited for
postwar coffee planting variation. Output was represented as a
linear function of coffee prices lagged one period and a trend
variable. This short-run harvesting decision formulation resulted
in the estimated coefficients and elasticities shown in Table 7.5.

A more complex approach to representing the relationship
between coffee prices and output was undertaken by Marcelle Arak.[9]
She portrayed price responsiveness in Brazil in terms of changes
both in the number of coffee trees and in the yield per tree.

Changes in the number of trees depends upon new planting,
abandonment, and elimination decisions of farmers. Again as
with cocoa, the perennial nature of coffee requires consideration
of a number of special factors—planting decisions motivated by the
expectation of income streams continuing over several years and
by the differing yields of the trees over their life spans (ranging
from zero through the first four years, rapid growth until optimal

TABLE 7.5

Estimated Coefficients, Prewar Ugandan Coffee

Region	Lagged Coffee Prices	Trend	R^2	Short-Run Elasticity
Uganda	0.28[c]	5.67[c]	0.98	0.63
Buganda province	0.12[a]	3.22[c]	0.97	0.42
Rest of country	0.16[b]	2.45[c]	0.91	1.04

[a]20 percent significance level.
[b]10 percent significance level.
[c]5 percent significance level.
Source: Kenneth D. Frederick, "The Role of Market Forces and Planning in Uganda's Economic Development 1900-1938," Eastern African Economic Review 1 (June 1969).

yield is realized at tree age about 9 or 10, then a noticeable decline until about age 25, with a slower decline thereafter—many bearing trees are known to be more than 80 years old).

In the case of coffee, price expectations are formulated in a complex atmosphere. Future income must be weighed against planting costs; maintenance costs during the first four years, when no yields are forthcoming and during which time no offsetting crops can be planted on the same land (unlike the situation which prevails for cocoa); and finally against the maintenance and harvesting costs of older trees, which affect abandonment and elimination decisions (followed either by coffee seedling or alternate crop planting), and the costs of planting new (that is, replacement) trees and cultivating them during the early nonproductive years.

In addition, Brazilian coffee producers must consider the myriad of government directives regulating the marketing of coffee that are aimed at promoting higher and more stable world prices. Beginning in 1933 an elaborate quota system was decreed, which designated certain portions of each crop for specific ends (though these portions were secularly variable). One fraction would be destroyed by the government, another was to be held in bonded warehouses, the third could be sold on the world market. The stockpiled portion might also eventually be sold, depending on world prices and the crops of succeeding years. However, producers were allowed to borrow from the government against these stockpiled portions. Other government regulations included taxes in kind, as well as absolute restrictions on the planting of new trees, any violation of which incurred high penalties.

Arak examined supply responsiveness in four states whose histories as coffee growers are quite varied: Sao Paulo, Parana, Espirito Santo, and Minas Gerais.

For Sao Paulo, the most important producing region from the late nineteenth century until 1959, Arak first considered a simple stock adjustment model, with new planting of coffee trees (in period t) represented as a function of expected coffee prices, cumulative planting up to time t, and the existing stock of trees in 1920. An alternative formulation employed she termed a demonstration effect model, with the dependent variable being the ratio of new planting to total existing stock of coffee trees.

The desired stock of trees in period t Arak held to be a linear function of expected coffee prices, but she felt this representation to be too simple to result in useful supply parameter estimates. Needed is a consideration of the effect of the age distribution of existing trees on new planting. Age-induced planting of seedlings was represented as a function of the percentage of existing trees ten years of age or older, for lack of a better measure, and of the "optimal" age distribution for coffee trees, which in turn Arak portrayed as a function of price expectations. In equation terms:

$$\Delta A_t^A = f(T_t) = \lambda(T_t - T_t^*) \tag{7.17}$$

where: ΔA_t^A is age-induced planting in period t;

T_t is the proportion of existing trees older than ten years;

λ is a linear function of expected coffee prices;

T_t^* is the "optimal" tree age distribution;

the adjustment coefficient λ is > 0; and $\dfrac{\delta \Delta A_t^A}{\delta T_t} > 0$.

In generating the expected price series Arak used New York market prices and the Brazilian exchange rate to calculate coffee earnings. Cultivators' expectations could be expressed in various ways. First, acting on the assumption that the government quotas applicable to the previous coffee crop are indicative of future quotas, farmers may believe that only that portion of the crop presently permitted to be sold immediately was likely to be sold in succeeding periods, making the effective price per unit $P^e = M \times P_m$, where P^e is expected price, P_m market price, and M the marketed quota fraction. Alternatively, they may expect that only the "sacrifice" portion (the part of the crop to be destroyed, as determined by the marketing control agency) was completely precluded from sale, making the effective price equal to $(1 - S_a)$ times the market price, where S_a is the "sacrifice" quota fraction.

Still another set of economic incentives is based on assumptions about the continuance of various taxes in kind—the farmer makes some guess of the future market price of coffee based on past market prices of coffee and some guess as to the continuation and magnitude of sacrifice and retained quotas—expected price can thus be expressed as a function of market price and the expected quota, which is based on an average of past quotas. Arak also postulated a price series that she called "unadjusted," based on farmers' consideration of market prices and money taxes only, which seems appropriate only if farmers are assumed to be either supreme optimists (with regard to the future removal of government regulations) or inexperienced amateurs.

The supply equations, expressed in planting and demonstration effect terms, can then be shown as:

$$\Delta A_t^A = \mu_1 ([a_o + a_1 P_t^e] - T_{1920} - \sum_{i=1921}^{t-1} \Delta A_i)$$

$$+ \lambda_1 (T_t - [b_o + b_1 P_t^e]) \tag{7.18}$$

$$\frac{\Delta A_t^A}{S_t} = \mu_2 ([a_o + a_1 P_t^e] - T_{1920} - \sum_{i=1921}^{t-1} \Delta A_i)$$

$$+ \lambda_2 (T_t - [b_o + b_1 P_t^e]) \tag{7.19}$$

where: P_t^e is expected coffee price in period t,
T_{1920} is coffee tree stock in 1920,
ΔA_i is planting of trees in period i,
T_t is proportion of existing trees older than ten years, and
S_t is the total stock of trees in period t.

Equations 7.18 and 7.19, somewhat manipulated algebraically, yield reduced forms that Arak used for estimating Sao Paulo coffee supply for the period 1930 to 1955, with the results shown in Table 7.6 (along with the standard errors). She presented an estimate of +2.02 for the short-run elasticity of annual planting with respect to expected price.

Arak then considered the hypothesis that tree stock age distribution may influence the difference between desired and actual stock. She formulated this as a linear relationship, that is, that

TABLE 7.6

Estimated Parameters, Sao Paulo Coffee

Equation	Constant	Expected Price	Lagged Cumulative Planting	Ten-Year Old Trees	R^2
7.18	-82.89*	+0.266*	-0.040*	+102.1*	0.83
	(28.76)	(0.040)	(0.017)	(37.6)	
7.19	- 0.072*	+0.00022*	-0.000014*	+ 0.084*	0.85
	(0.023)	(0.00003)	(0.000001)	(0.030)	

*1 percent significance level.

Source: Marcelle Arak, "The Supply of Brazilian Coffee" (Ph.D. dissertation, Massachusetts Institute of Technology, 1967).

μ_1 and μ_2 can be expressed linearly in terms of the proportion of trees older than ten years (T_t). If in each such linear equation the intercepts are assumed to be zero, equations 7.18 and 7.19 can be manipulated to yield the estimating equations:

$$\Delta A_t^A = \mu_1^* \, T_t(a_o + a_1 P_t^e - T_{1920} - \sum_{i=1921}^{t-1} \Delta A_i)$$

$$+ \lambda_1(T_t - [b_o + b_1 P_t^e]) \tag{7.18a}$$

$$\frac{\Delta A_t^A}{S_t} = \mu_2^* \, T_t(a_o + a_1 P_t^e - T_{1920} - \sum_{i=1921}^{t-1} \Delta A_i)$$

$$+ \lambda_2(T_t - [b_o + b_1 P_t^e]) \tag{7.19a}$$

Ordinary least-squares regression techniques yielded the parameter estimates seen in Table 7.7 (along with the associated standard errors). The short-run elasticity of planting with respect to expected coffee price was then estimated to be +2.28.

In considering coffee cultivation in Parana state, which produced no coffee as late as 1920 and has since risen rapidly to take first place among the states by 1959, Arak found that the data on new trees in Parana was not suitable for the type of model used in Sao Paulo and that an agricultural expansion model was more

TABLE 7.7

Estimated Parameters, Sao Paulo Coffee
(Age-Distribution Model)

Equation	Constant (a$_0$)	Expected Price (a$_1$)	R^2
7.18a	93.32* (37.29)	+0.37* (0.05)	0.84
7.19a	+0.075* (0.031)	+0.00031* (0.00004)	0.86

*1 percent significance level.
Source: Marcelle Arak, "The Supply of Brazilian Coffee"
(Ph.D. dissertation, Massachusetts Institute of Technology, 1967).

useful. She argued that farmers try to maximize profits by determining the optimal proportion (K) of their land to be devoted to
coffee cultivation—although she allowed that it might not seem very
realistic to represent K as a function of either expected prices or
their inverse, she nevertheless used the latter formulation, and
estimated the coefficients of:

$$\frac{\Delta A_t^A}{L_{t-1}} = a_o + a_1 \left[\frac{1}{P_t^e}\right] + a_2 \left[\frac{R_t}{L_{t-1}}\right] + u_t \qquad (7.20)$$

where: L_{t-1} is all cultivated agricultural land in period t - 1; and
         R_t is a measure of the replacement of frost-damaged trees
              in period t.

For the period 1945 to 1962, ordinary least-squares regression
techniques yielded estimates of $a_o = +0.120$, $a_1 = -3.76$, and
$a_2 = -0.172$, all significant at the 5 percent level or better, and
a value of the coefficient of determination equal to 0.50. The price
elasticity of tree stock was estimated to be +0.96.

The measure R_t is designed to account for the effect of frost,
serious cases of which occurred in 1942, 1943, 1953, and 1955,
each affecting the entire stock of existent coffee trees, and it is
based on the assumption that some percent of the trees under age
four in the year of the frost are permanently injured and are
replaced in approximately equal quantities in the two years following

the frost. It would be expected that the relation between R_t and planting would be positive.

Arak suggested that the fact that the estimated coefficient of R_t proved to be negative and significant likely indicates that some phenomenon other than replanting is exerting an influence here. Perhaps the onset of a frost causes a period of discouragement lasting some time, during which planters, having become more sensitive to the risks of coffee cultivation, do not fully respond to price changes, or else need greater price changes to induce planting increases similar in size to those in periods that have experienced no recent frosts. Perhaps replacement of all the damaged trees is not recorded when these replacements reach maturity, while simultaneously in any years in which extensive replacement takes place such tasks place heavy demand on labor and other factors involved in the planting operation, thereby restricting availability of these factors for the planting of new trees, which planting would be prompted by price expectations.

In Minas Gerais and Espirito Santo, coffee output neither experienced the rapid expansion it did in Parana, nor is data on abandonments and removals available as in Sao Paulo. As a result Arak analyzed output with a simplified planting model, expressed in Nerlovian stock-adjustment terms

$$\Delta M_t = (a_o + a_1 P^e_{t-4} - M_{t-1}) \tag{7.21}$$

where ΔM_t is the change (in period t) in the number of mature coffee trees. As formulated, this model has no place for abandonments and eliminations, though Arak found that in many years ΔM_t was negative. Ordinary least-squares techniques gave the estimated parameters shown in Table 7.8.

TABLE 7.8

Estimated Parameters, Minas Gerais and
Espirito Santo Coffee

State	Constant	Expected Price	Existing Trees
Minas Gerais	123.1	+0.27	−0.24
Espirito Santo	140.2	+0.18	−0.67

Source: Marcelle Arak, "The Supply of Brazilian Coffee" (Ph.D. dissertation, Massachusetts Institute of Technology, 1967).

Assuming that abandonment and elimination decisions are based
on more recent prices than are changes in the stock of trees, Arak
reformulated her model as:

$$M_t = \delta_1 D_1 [a_o + a_1 P^e_{t-4} - M_{t-1}] + \delta_2 D_2 [b_o + b_1 P^e_{t-4}$$

$$-M_{t-1}] + \delta_3 M_{t-1} \tag{7.22}$$

where: $D_1 = 1$, if desired stock is greater than actual stock in
          t-4, and
        = 0, otherwise
        $D_2 = 1$, if actual stock is greater than desired stock given
          expected prices in t, and
        = 0, otherwise.

The first term in this model accounts for new planting in t - 4; the
second for elimination and abandonment decisions made for stock
adjustment purposes; the third for elimination and abandonment
decisions made due to various natural causes that occurred during
t - 1. For the period 1927 to 1959 Arak estimated the parameters
shown in Table 7.9 (along with their standard errors).

Obviously the coefficient of upward adjustment (δ_1) shows
more significance in these estimates than does the downward adjustment coefficient (δ_2). Arak asserted this model performs well only
in estimating variation due to new planting. Short- and long-run
elasticity estimates obtained from these regressions are seen in
Table 7.10.

TABLE 7.9

Estimated Parameters, Minas Gerais
and Espirito Santo Coffee
(Elimination/Abandonment)

State	δ_1	a_1	δ_2	b_1
Minas Gerais	+0.150[a]	+1.94	+1.94	+1.94
	(0.080)	(1.51)	(1.51)	(1.51)
Espirito Santo	+0.728[b]	+0.39[b]	+0.670	+0.390
	(0.26)	(0.10)	(0.72)	(0.10)

[a]10 percent significance level.
[b]1 percent significance level.
  Source: Marcelle Arak, "The Supply of Brazilian Coffee"
(Ph.D. dissertation, Massachusetts Institute of Technology, 1967).

TABLE 7.10

Supply Elasticities, Minas Gerais and Espirito Santo Coffee

State	Short-Run Elasticity	Long-Run Elasticity
Minas Gerais	+0.08	+0.54
Espirito Santo	+0.20	+0.28

Source: Marcelle Arak, "The Supply of Brazilian Coffee" (Ph.D. dissertation, Massachusetts Institute of Technology, 1967).

For these two states Arak also used a very simple stock adjustment model of the form:

$$\Delta S_t = \alpha(a_o + a_1 P_{t-4} - S_{t-1})$$ (7.23)

though she recognized its inadequacies, such as lack of any provision for tree removals. Nevertheless, regression results indicated estimates not very different than those shown in Table 7.9: long-run elasticities of +0.44 for Minas Gerais and +0.20 for Espirito Santo.

In summary Arak concluded that Sao Paulo coffee farmers are price responsive to changes in price expectations, that a 1 percent change in coffee prices would result in a 6.5 million tree change in desired tree stock, which represents an elasticity of planting with respect to price of +2.28. In the other producing states, data limitations resulted in less detailed conclusions. Growers in Parana state also respond to prices positively, but with a lower elasticity, increasing desired planted area by approximately 1 percent in response to a similar increase in prices. Elasticities were still lower in Minas Gerais and Espirito Santo. As regards governmental policies, an examination of the evidence seems to indicate that regulations restricting the planting of new trees have been for the most part ineffective, since farmers' behavior during the 11-year ban (1932-42) seems quite similar to other periods. However, the high export taxes and taxes in kind do seem to have had considerable effect on price expectations.

The Brazilian coffee sector has also been analyzed by Edmar L. Bacha.[10] Interested primarily in constructing a policy-oriented econometric model, he considered Brazil's price-setting policies to be the only significant departure from a perfectly competitive market structure. His model postulated that Brazil first sets her prices, which then act as exogenous influences to determine the

world coffee price structure. Once this structure is set, the
quantity of coffee Brazil exports is residually specified by demand.
The final linkage occurs when price behavior signalled by demand
acts as an input in planting decisions.

In examining coffee supply he accepted much of Arak's earlier
analysis—both her basic reasoning and some of the specific results
of her study. Commenting on her estimates for Parana state he
maintained that she discusses what might be termed a "frontier
thesis" but does not present statistical analysis in consequence.
This thesis would embody a Nerlovian adjustment model coupled
with consideration of a demonstration effect, with the adjustment
rate γ itself a function of the adult tree stock.

The model ignores abandonments and removals and seems
adequate for a "new" coffee area. Parana was on the coffee frontier
during the period of Bacha's study (1945 to 1962), and in such a
case, he holds, it can be reasonably argued that risk is inversely
proportional to the degree to which the frontier has been settled—
that is, the more settled, the less the risk and the factor that
cultivators make adjustments (by moving to and opening still more
new lands). Supply parameters estimated using ordinary least-
squares techniques are shown in Table 7.11 (along with the standard
errors).

For Sao Paulo, Arak's results were somewhat questionable—
very high values for elasticity, and elasticity estimates that were
with respect to new planting, not desired tree stock. Bacha attempted
his own estimates for Sao Paulo, formulating an output model.

Coffee output in Sao Paulo has had a very noticeable two-year
production cycle, so Bacha expressed the relationship between output
and planted area as

$$Q_t = \alpha A_t \text{ if t is even, and} \qquad\qquad (7.24a)$$

$$Q_t = \beta A_t \text{ if t is odd} \qquad\qquad (7.24b)$$

where α is the output to area ratio in off-years, and β is the ratio
value in peak years. This resulted in separate supply equations,
each formulated in terms of expected prices and lagged output.
Assuming a very slow change in price expectations, the two supply
equations were expressed as one:

$$Q_t = a_o + a_1 D_t + a_2 P_{t-4} + a_3 D_t P_{t-4} + a_4 Q_{t-2} \qquad\qquad (7.25)$$

where D_t is a dummy variable and equal to zero if t is even, and
one if t is odd. Using export data from 1925 to 1933 and 1951 to
1961, Bacha estimated the parameters of this model. The large

TABLE 7.11

Supply Parameters, Parana Coffee

Constant	Lagged Price (t - 4)	Lagged Tree Stock	Stock Adjustment Coefficient	Long-Run Elasticity	R^2
+0.061	+0.0008	+0.00007	+0.04	+0.71	0.77
(0.083)	(0.0005)	(0.00006)			

Source: Edmar L. Bacha, "An Econometric Model for the World Coffee Market: The Impact of Brazilian Price Policy" (Ph.D. dissertation, Yale University, 1968).

standard errors indicated for $\hat{a}_0$ and $\hat{a}_1$ led him to reestimate the model with these two coefficients set equal to zero. Short- and long-run supply elasticities were evaluated as +0.23 and +1.00, respectively. Empirical estimates also indicated the peak year output to area ratio ran about 40 percent higher than that for off years during the pre-World War II period, with a somewhat larger difference noted for postwar production.

Using an output model without inclusion of the Sao Paulo production cycle, Bacha also analyzed coffee supply in Colombia and aggregate supply for the rest of Latin America and for Africa, obtaining the parameter estimates (and standard errors) shown in Table 7.12.

The most recent treatment of Brazilian coffee supply has been offered by R. Gerald Saylor; his approach compares several alternative formulations relative to their explanatory power for output in the leading producing region, Sao Paulo state.[11]

Four different specifications were employed, and each was tested in two or more variations for the period 1947 to 1970: Saylor first put forward a simplified Nerlove supply function (A), with planted area expressed as a function of deflated producer prices (averaged over the three years preceding harvesting with declining weights), a price index representing 20 major Sao Paulo agricultural products lagged one year, a trend variable, and coffee acreage lagged one year. Though coffee prices on a multiseason basis were included, this representation is essentially a harvesting, as opposed to a planting, model (Saylor allows for a maturation period of three to four years for newly planted coffee; thus his weighting system nearly spans the planting-to-first-crop interval);

TABLE 7.12

Supply Parameters, Other Coffee Producers

Region	Price t - 4	Lagged Output	Trend	R^2	Elasticity Short-Run	Elasticity Long-Run
Colombia	6.27	0.846[b]	—	0.996	0.070	0.453
(1939–64)	(4.34)	(0.114)				
Latin America	49.72[a]	0.467	—	0.992	0.276	0.518
(1943–60)	(25.84)	(0.271)				
Africa	44.09[a]	0.362	182.1[a]	0.992	0.140	0.595
(1943–60)	(27.58)	(0.274)	(96.5)			
	48.95[a]	0.765[b]	—	0.932	0.239	0.374
	(29.71)	(0.186)				

[a]10 percent significance level.
[b]1 percent significance level.

Note: Dependent variable is total output for Colombia and coffee exports for Latin America and Africa. The indicated importance of a trend variable in explaining coffee supply variation in Africa, and not elsewhere, Bacha hypothesizes was due to coffee's continued "infant-industry" status in Africa. Though perhaps this appellation might have been more appropriate before World War II when, between 1920 and 1940, African output grew from 2 to 12 percent of world supply in a growing market, the long producing lifetime of coffee trees probably indicates a longer-than-average infancy for the sector.

Source: Edmar L. Bacha, "An Econometric Model for the World Coffee Market: The Impact of Brazilian Price Policy" (Ph.D. dissertation, Yale University, 1968).

both linear and logarithmic functions were tested using ordinary least-squares techniques.

The second basic variation (B) added a dummy variable in order to account for rapid changes in supply during a six-year (1962 to 1967) government program aimed at reducing output as a means of bolstering export revenues; during this time the area devoted to coffee in Sao Paulo fell by nearly 40 percent. The method employed is designed to isolate variations in both intercept and slope,[12] and it was applied separately to the periods preceding and following the initiation of the uprooting program.

The third alternative (C) incorporates a means for differentiating between structural shifts that affect either intercept or slope while the fourth (D) distinguished between rising and falling coffee prices in order to identify a possible irreversible or ratchet effect of prices on planted acreage.[13] Estimating difficulties encountered in the last case resulted in the exclusion of the period 1963 to 1970, and for comparison purposes the simplified Nerlove model was separately estimated for the shortened interval.

Selected regression results are listed in Table 7.13 for the first three models discussed above and also for the last-named variation and the comparative Nerlove-type calculations. In comparing the results the author points out the fairly consistent elasticity estimates that result from the estimates based on the first three alternative supply models. From model B comes evidence of a strong negative influence on coffee area of the government effort to reduce the number of producing trees. He also concluded that, in contrast with Tomek's hypothesis, lagged crop area remains a significant variable even when a measure of supply shift (the intercept) is introduced.

When model D was tested in an attempt to identify differentiated cultivator reactions to rising and falling prices, Saylor encountered problems of both multicollinearity* and serial correlation using data from the entire period, but these problems disappeared when he focused on the preuprooting data—1948 to 1962. The formulation omitting lagged coffee area indicated the response to rising prices to be nearly 2.8 times that relative to price declines. When lagged area was included, the model's overall explanatory power was moderately improved, though the significance of the estimated price coefficients dropped somewhat. Nevertheless, the responsiveness of cultivators to rising prices remained notably larger than that indicated for falling prices.

In a recent paper M. R. Wickens and J. N. Greenfield have criticized use of the Nerlove model for estimating perennial crop supply.[14] They argue that the ad hoc nature of the relationships contained in the basic supply equation relating desired output to expected price, and in the partial adjustment and adaptive expectations formulations, blurs the important distinction between investment and harvesting decisions. They suggested a three-equation model made up of an investment function, a harvesting equation, and a vintage production function. Investment was represented in terms of the anticipated difference between prices and harvesting costs over the productive lifetime of the tree, average yield, and the discount rate. The harvesting function related actual production to maximum potential production and a weighted average of recent prices, and the vintage production function represented potential production in terms of the sum of the products of past plantings and the average yield of trees of appropriate age. Several of the

---

*Saylor suggests that this problem may be unavoidable in a case like that which he tested where prices rise and fall, alternately, nearly every year and that Wolffram's basic model might show better results when the price cycle is of longer duration.

TABLE 7.13

Estimated Supply Parameters, Sao Paulo Coffee

Supply Model	Lagged Coffee Price	Lagged Alternative Crop Price	Dummy Variable		Lagged Coffee Area	R^2	Price Elasticity	
							Short-Run	Long-Run
1948-70								
A (Linear)	+0.085[b] (2.076)	-5.504[c] (2.653)	-		+0.813[d] (11.396)	0.961	+0.117	+0.625
A (Logarithmic)	+0.101[b] (2.048)	-0.532[d] (3.358)	-		+0.841[d] (13.363)	0.971	+0.101	+0.635
B	+0.116[d] (2.884)	+0.251 (0.076)	-130.89[c,e] (2.128)		+0.745[d] (10.278)	0.969	+0.160	+0.627
B	+0.262[d] (5.313)	-	-586.62[d,f] (7.87)		-	0.920	-	+0.362
C	+0.105[b] (2.053)	-4.687[b] (1.928)	-85.61[f] (0.669)		+0.715[d] (4.356)	0.962	+0.144	+0.505
C	+0.132[c] (2.140)	-3.254[a] (1.073)	-11.253[f] (0.064)	-0.086[g] (0.806)	+0.672[d] (3.862)	0.964	{+0.182[h] , +0.063[i] }	{+0.554[h] , +0.192[i] }
1948-62								
A (Linear)	+0.148[a] (1.660)	+3.429 (0.654)			+0.511[a] (1.451)	0.851	+0.196	+0.401
A (Logarithmic)	+0.149[b] (2.192)	+0.198 (0.608)			+0.709[d] (5.421)	0.867	+0.149	+0.512
D	+0.376[d,j] (6.251) -0.170[c,k] (3.168)	-	-		-	0.785	{+0.591[j] , +0.212[k] }	{- , -}
D	+0.157[j] (1.007) -0.116[b,k] (1.872)	+3.337 (0.612)			+0.600[a] (1.644)	0.852	{+0.247[j] , +0.145[k] }	{+0.617[j] , +0.362[k] }

Figures in parentheses are t values.

[a]30 percent significance level; [b]10 percent significance level; [c]5 percent significance level; [d]1 percent significance level; [e]Dummy variable indicating years when uprooting program in effect, 1962-67; [f]Dummy variable to account for change in intercept between the periods 1948-62 and 1963-70; [g]Dummy variable to account for change in slope beginning in 1963; [h]1948 to 1962; [i]1963 to 1970; [j]Rising prices; [k]Falling prices.

Source: R. Gerald Saylor, "Alternative Measures of Supply Elasticities: The Case of Sao Paulo Coffee," American Journal of Agricultural Economics 56 (February 1974).

variables postulated to have a role in the model proved to be unobservable and the authors then turned to a number of proxies.
Following this procedure they estimated the investment function
separately for Brazil and concluded that investment could be
expressed in terms of lagged investment and present prices:

$$I_t = a_o + a_1 I_{t-1} + a_2 P_t \tag{7.26}$$

$$Q_t = b_o + b_1 Q_t^P + \sum_{i=o}^{m} b_{i+z} {}^2 P_{t-1} + b_{m+1} Q_{t-1} \tag{7.27}$$

$$Q_t^P = \sum_{i=o}^{m} \delta_i I_{t-1} \tag{7.28}$$

where: I is investment,
        P is wholesale coffee price,
        Q_p is actual coffee output,
        Q is potential coffee output, and
        δ_i is average yield for a tree of age i.
Equations 7.27 and 7.28 represent the harvesting and vintage production respectively; the last term in the former is included to
catch the biennial bearing cycle noted by other researchers for
Brazilian output. For the period 1932-69 the reduced form of
equations 7.26 to 7.28 was estimated using an Almon lag to represent
the coefficients of past prices. The authors interpret their results
as consistent with the underlying structure—a pattern indicated
positive response to current prices (the harvesting component of
the model), negative or little influence of prices of the past three
or so years (during which young trees bear no fruit), with price
responsiveness peaking at about six years.

In constructing a multiequation econometric model of the
Brazilian economy Jere Behrman and L. R. Klein represented
coffee acreage and yield in separate equations, combining the
predicted value of each to get total output.[15]

Acreage was represented as a function of the ratio of the
domestic coffee price to a gross domestic product deflator, lagged
two years, and lagged (one-year) coffee acreage; yield was explained
in terms of domestic coffee prices and rainfall, both lagged one
year. Ordinary least-squares regressions were run using data
from 1948 to 1964; for all four independent variables the estimated
coefficients were found to be statistically significant at the 1 percent
level or better. The acreage equation explained more variation
than did that for yield, with R^2 values indicated to be 0.95 and 0.51,
respectively.

The authors calculated a short-run supply (acreage) elasticity relative to price of +0.10; using the estimated acreage adjustment coefficient, the corresponding long-run elasticity would be about +0.11. The short-run elasticity of yield with respect to price was calculated to be +0.15.

Merrill Bateman also examined coffee supply in Colombia, using a stock adjustment model similar to the one he used in his revised study of Ghanaian cocoa (see note 2 in this chapter).[16] Using time periods and price series slightly different from Bacha's he obtained estimates for the elasticity of new acreage planted, ranging from 0.47 for the period 1947 to 1965 to 0.84 for 1952 to 1965.

A study of coffee supply in a country where it is a relatively minor crop was presented by R. L. Williams for Jamaica.[17] The mountainous interior regions of the island soon recommended their suitability for coffee cultivation to early British colonists. Introduced in 1728, the crop rapidly spread until peak output was reached in 1814, when some 34 million pounds were exported. After the abolition of slavery most plantations were abandoned, and coffee cultivation passed into the hands of smallholders. A sharp initial decline in output was followed by a return to importance until coffee accounted for 20 percent of total exports by the end of the nineteenth century. However, production declined sharply during the Great Depression and World War II. In recent years the government has undertaken several steps to increase output, hoping to bring output back to close to 10 million pounds from the 3 million level that has prevailed since the end of the war.

Since cultivation remains in the hands of small farmers,* any policies aiming at replanting and restoring coffee acreage, Williams reasoned, need the results of basic supply analysis to identify the degree of market responsiveness among present and potential growers. He felt this need to be all the more pressing, since price stabilization policies since 1953 have apparently had the twin effects of suppressing new planting when prices have been high without notably preventing a deterioration of the supply situation when prices have fallen. Particularly deleterious, according to the author, has been the influence of prices on efforts to improve coffee yields. Growers have apparently had little incentive to

---

*The number of registered coffee growers totalled about 54,000 in 1966. Most of the smallholders are organized into producer cooperatives. Few, however, depend upon the crop as their principal income source; Williams quotes a 1953 survey that indicated that less than 6 percent of the cultivators are principally dependent upon the crop.

care properly for new high-yield seedlings distributed by government agents.

Williams' interest is primarily in short-run influences on output, rather than in an analysis of planting decisions. To this end he postulated a supply model representing output as a function of lagged coffee, cocoa, and banana prices; lagged coffee output; and agricultural wages. Cocoa is often complementary to coffee cultivation, providing needed shade to young coffee plants, while bananas compete for inputs throughout much of the country. Parameters of the supply equation, framed in logarithmic terms, were estimated using both Cochrane-Orcutt and Hildreth-Lu iterative techniques to reduce the effects of serial correlation, and the results are shown in Table 7.14 for the period 1953 to 1968.

The supply equation having been expressed in logarithmic terms, the estimated parameters are of course short-run elasticities. Though satisfied with his results regarding price and wage coefficients, Williams felt that the negative lagged output estimates might indicate the logarithmic specification to be inappropriate.

Joseph K. Maitha took a somewhat different approach to the price responsiveness of coffee growers in Kenya.[18] While acreage changes may be the way price effects are demonstrated for annual crops, he argued that this is far less clearly so in the case of long-lived perennials. In coffee-producing areas, for example, all the suitable land may have long since been devoted to the crop, and the only "new" plantings may in effect be merely replacements. Maitha suggested examining instead the influence of price changes on productivity, pointing out the particular suitability of this approach

TABLE 7.14

Estimated Parameters, Jamaican Coffee

Estimating Technique	Coffee Prices	Cocoa Prices	Banana Prices	Wages	Lagged Output	R^2
Cochrane-Orcutt	+0.82[b]	+0.62[b]	-2.70[c]	-0.23	-0.85[b]	0.61
Hildreth-Lu	+0.70[b]	+0.51[a]	-2.42[c]	-0.23	-0.62[a]	0.64

[a]10 percent significance level.
[b]5 percent significance level.
[c]1 percent significance level.
    Source: R. L. Williams, "Jamaican Coffee Supply, 1953-1968, An Exploratory Study," Social and Economic Studies 21 (March 1972).

in Kenya where government attempts at controlling coffee output are implemented largely through a planting-license scheme. With acreage more or less fixed by physical and/or institutional limitations, the cultivators are nevertheless free to vary their inputs and thus both the quantity and quality of output. As has been mentioned in the earlier discussions of coffee, considerable quality (and price) differences exist for different varieties of the commodity.

Maitha's supply model embodied a constant elasticity of substitution production function and assumed constant returns to scale, and he estimated the parameters of the equation

$$\text{Log} \left[\frac{Q}{A} \right] = a_o + a_1 \log \left[\frac{R}{P} \right] \tag{7.29}$$

where: $\frac{Q}{A}$ is the coffee acreage productivity index,

   R is land rent,
   P is coffee producer price, and
   a_o includes the elasticity of substitution, a weather index,
        an index of technological progress, and distribution
        and substitution parameters.

He expressed the land rent-coffee price ratio in terms of past producer prices using an Irving Fisher distributed lag form (the weights of lagged coefficients decline arithmetically) and his estimated productivity elasticities are shown in Table 7.15.

He compared these with acreage and yield elasticities he had presented in an earlier study, where mature coffee acreage was expressed as a function of past prices, lagged output, a dummy variable to represent a shift in government policy, and a trend variable (elasticities are in Table 7.16).[19]

The considerably higher productivity elasticities,* Maitha argued, show the important role price changes play in coffee output despite the seeming low values for price responsiveness.†

———————

*When the model was expressed with yield as the dependent variable, Maitha found somewhat higher elasticities—for example, long-run estimates were +1.09, 1.27, and 1.01 for all Kenya, estates, and smallholdings respectively—values more like those for productivity elasticities.

†In a note, "Long-Run Price Elasticities in the Supply of Kenyan Coffee: A Methodological Note," Eastern African Economic Review 3 (June 1971), prompted by Maitha's first article, Derek J. Ford argued that Maitha's computations of long-run acreage and yield elasticities were erroneous. He offered alternate values that differ only slightly from Maitha's regarding acreage, but considerably in the case of yields.

TABLE 7.15

Productivity Elasticities, Kenyan Coffee

	Short-Run	Long-Run
All Kenya	0.64	0.96
Estates	0.66	0.99
Smallholdings	0.64	0.97

Source: Joseph K. Maitha, "Productivity Response to Price: A Case Study of Kenyan Coffee," Eastern African Economic Review 2 (December 1970).

Another study of tree crops was carried out by Peter Ady, who examined the production of both cocoa and coffee and evaluated the performances of several alternative supply models.[20] Ady first considered a planting model similar to that constructed by Bateman (see equation 7.7), and compares this with a stock adjustment model like Behrman's equation 7.13, but with desired stock of trees rather than desired acreage as the dependent variable. However, she reiterated earlier authors' difficulties in locating new planting and acreage data. Following their example, she recast her own model in output terms, estimating the parameters of a capital stock equation of the form:

$$\Delta Q_t = a_o + a_1 P_{t-k-1} + a_2 P^W_{t-k-1} + a_3 Q_{t-1} + a_4 \Delta W_{t-1}$$

$$+ a_5 W_{t-2} + a_6 \Delta E_t + a_7 E_{t-1} \tag{7.30}$$

where: Q is output,
P is producer price,
P^W is world price,
k is the number of years between planting and first bearing season,
W is an index of agronomic factors, and
E is an index of economic factors.

Ady included both producer and world prices under her hypothesis that the latter affect farmer expectations despite the prevalence of lower prices imposed by government marketing boards. She tested this as well as Bateman's planting model by estimating supply parameters (and standard errors), for Ugandan coffee during 1950

TABLE 7.16

Acreage Elasticities, Kenyan Coffee

	Short-Run	Long-Run
All Kenya	0.152	0.379
Estates	0.159	0.397
Smallholdings	0.204	0.511

Source: Joseph K. Maitha, "A Supply Function of Kenyan Coffee," Eastern African Economic Review 1 (June 1969).

to 1964. Both models were also applied to cocoa supply in Ghana and Nigeria, but she obtained notably better results when her capital stock model was used.

Because many Ghanaian cocoa producers were able to evade the requirement to sell to the marketing board and smuggled their produce into neighboring countries where world prices prevailed, Ady used regional data from the Old Ashanti section to compare results obtained employing the Bateman and Behrman models with her own (which contained both world and producer prices). Old Ashanti, being in the center of the country, is much less affected by smuggling and, according to Bateman's argument, is the most homogeneous region with regard to the numerous factors affecting the lag structure.

Using the same period and variables the Ady capital stock model yields a better fit than either Bateman's or Behrman's results. Estimating with the capital stock and all variables including world prices improves the fit even more. Thus the estimates obtained for the Old Ashanti cocoa supply confirm the results shown above for coffee in Uganda. The capital stock adjustment model considerably increases the explanatory power of the lagged price model. Ady also concluded that neither the Bateman nor Behrman models (using producer prices alone) do much to further a Nerlovian price expectations hypothesis in the presence of a monopsonistic marketing board. More evidence for the importance of world prices can be seen in her parameter estimates for cocoa supply in Ghana as a whole and in Nigeria.

Ady emphasized the evidence in all three countries for the market-mindedness of peasant cultivators, with positive (and usually significant) relationships indicated between planting and prices. However, the short-run situation is not so clear. Positive coefficients result for the current prices of Ugandan coffee and Nigerian cocoa, but not for Ghanaian cocoa. She suggests that considering both Ghana's dominant role in world cocoa production and her increasing output due to growth both in productivity and acreage, a more logical course may be that the larger harvests are responsible for the decline in world prices since the late 1950s, rather than resort to a perverse lower price leading to larger output explanation.

Another popular beverage, tea, is the product of a perennial plant—an evergreen shrub that in its natural state can grow to tree-like heights of 25 or more feet but under cultivation is kept to 3 to 5 feet. In India, which produces more than a third of world supply, tea is generally grown on plantations. Tea plants are grown from seed in nurseries, then are transplanted when about eight inches in height. After about two years they are pruned of most of their initial growth, and after another 12 to 18 months commercial plucking of the tea leaves begins. Plant yields continue to increase until peak maturity at about age 10, and the typical bush will produce another 20 to 40 years.

Grown only in tropical or semitropical climes, tea can be cultivated at altitudes ranging from sea level to 6,000 feet, with the most valued varieties grown at the higher elevations. In India the most suitable regions are found on the lower Himalayan slopes of the Brahmaputra Valley in Assam and adjoining districts of West Bengal, in the foothills of Kerala overlooking the Malabar coast, and to a minor extent in Kangra district in Punjab. Tea is one of India's most valuable exports, with both production and exports up sharply since the war. Her most important customers are the United Kingdom and Ireland, the Middle East, North America, and the Soviet Union.

Tea cultivation and harvesting are year-round occupations in more tropical regions such as Kerala, but in Assam harvesting must be confined to a set period of the year, and some competition for labor inputs is present. Supply analysis using a Nerlovian response model was carried out by V. Rajagopalan and others[21] who proceeded from an earlier work in which the authors were unable to identify any significant price response[22] and asked whether the correct price specification (a six-year lag) was made in this earlier study. Alternatively, they suggested inclusion of recent prices, an adaptive expectations hypothesis, and a lagged expected price (based on prices in the years preceding planting).

Six different acreage and production models were tested. Acreage was expressed as a function of: (in version A), lagged (six years) prices, maximum past area in tea cultivation, and a time trend; (B), lagged (six years) prices, maximum price in the year prior to picking, and a time trend; and (C) last year's price, the ratio of last year's price to maximum previous price, and a

time trend. The production models were formulated in terms of:
(D), last year's price and the direction of last year's change in
price; (E), last year's price and a time trend; and (F), last year's
price, the ratio of last year's price to maximum previous price,
and the product of output in year t, and the time-trend variable.
The elasticities and coefficients of determination calculated for each
model are seen in Table 7.17. All price parameters were statistically significant at the 5 percent level or better.

Though the authors presented no results for estimating models
containing more than a single price variable nor attempted any
distinction between short- and long-run elasticities, Table 7.17
demonstrates the particularly sizable effect of more recent prices
on output, while planting elasticities are notably smaller.

Another perennial crop whose supply has attracted the attention
of a number of economists has been rubber. Rubber trees produce
no usable sap in the first seven years after planting, then annual
production increases sharply to a peak yield at about age 13, holding
these levels until they are about 21 years old, and thereafter yields
decline steadily. In major producing countries the trees are grown
both on estates and smallholdings, and although the distinction is
arbitrary (Chan, for example, sets the dividing line at 100 acres),
estate production is thoroughly commercially organized, while
significant numbers of smallholders cultivate rubber on a "part-time"
basis, with other crops and economic pursuits competing for inputs.

Francis Chan Kwong Wah examined rubber output in one of the
more important producing nations, Malaya.[23] He indicated that
the advocation (in the early 1960s) of a price stabilization scheme
needed some analysis of exactly how cultivators react to price
changes. Rubber acreage, like that of other tree crops slow to
come to maturity, depends upon price expectations formed several
years before production begins, but actual output with a given stock
of trees can vary considerably depending upon labor inputs, the
intensity of tapping per tree, and the extent to which chemical
stimulants are used. Chan thus examines both the effect of current
prices (harvesting decisions) and lagged prices (planting decisions).

He used a simple non-Nerlovian supply model with rubber
output expressed as a function of price, using several different
measures of price: current prices, to examine the short-run
harvesting effect, and from the planting decision aspect, four
different formulations of lagged prices—a simple seven-year lag,
and an arbitrarily chosen three-year average prior to the time
of planting, the price net of export duty at planting, and a three-year
average price net of duty.

The low value of R^2 in the short-run model Chan interpreted
to indicate that there is little impact of current prices on harvesting

TABLE 7.17

Supply Elasticities, Indian Tea

Dependent Variable	Model	Elasticity	R^2
Acreage	A	0.088[a]	0.64
	B	0.085[a]	0.54
	B	0.157[b]	0.45
	C	0.061[b]	0.83
	C	0.024[c]	0.83
Output	D	0.264[d]	0.98
	E	0.212[d]	0.96
	F	0.351[d]	0.99
	F	0.142[c]	0.99

[a]Prices lagged six years.
[b]Maximum price in the year prior to picking.
[c]Ratio of last year's price to previous maximum.
[d]Last year's price.

Source: V. Rajagopalan and V. Meenakshisundaram, "Travails of the Tea Industry—An Economic Appraisal," Indian Journal of Agricultural Economics 24 (October–December 1969).

decisions (although the significance of this parameter estimate at the 10 percent level suggests current prices might have been profitably included in one of the long-run formulations). For this short-run model Chan estimated supply elasticities (actually, very short-run elasticities, that is, harvesting responses to present prices) for estates to be close to zero, and for smallholders, between 0.12 and 0.34. Whatever significance might be attached to these results could be used to argue that fixed cultivation and other costs isolate the harvesting decisions of estate owners from present prices, while smallholders, perhaps being less burdened by fixed costs, can react to short-term fluctuations by varying their own inputs, particularly of labor, in the tapping and collection process.

Despite the high proportion of output variation explained by the regressions using lagged three–year average price and the significance of the price parameters at the 0.1 percent level, Chan cautioned that extraneous factors not included in the model might well exaggerate the reliability of his estimates for the particular time period being considered. He explained that low prices in the immediate postwar period were in fact followed in the early and mid-1950s by low output, but that a better <u>nonprice</u> explanation for this circumstance is readily available. During the Great Depression new plantings declined drastically and did not return to more "normal" levels until after World War II. Thus the stock of peak-yield trees (10 to 20 years old) was very low in the 1950s and did not begin to increase until the trees planted after the war came to maturity. This upswing in production can be seen after 1956. Coincidentally, the very high prices of the Korean War period preceded this upswing by about seven years but were quite unrelated to the fact that the trees planted in the late 1940s were coming into their peak years.

This suggests the need for a more complex model, including, for example, consideration for the different levels of yield associated with the age distribution of the stock of trees, but Chan indicated that data limitations at the time of his study (1962) precluded this. He does show the limitations of his estimates by including provisional data for 1960 and 1961 in expanded regressions, which have considerable adverse effect on both parameter significance levels and the value of R^2.

In the longer time period the simple model used relates production (which is rapidly increasing) in 1960 and 1961 with declining post-Korean War prices, when in fact production in these years reflected much more the onset of post-World War II trees into the peak producing period. Thus he concluded the success of his simple model in explaining output variation during 1948 to 1959 must be considered a likely "fluke" until a longer time series is available.

In a paper discussing Malayan government policies toward the rubber industry, Clifton Wharton used a preliminary version of Chan's study with a bit more detail than the final version.[24] Wharton quotes negative elasticities ranging from -0.10 to -0.02 for estate production and positive values from +0.05 to +0.12 for smallholders, using different estimating equations. The best results were obtained from the most complex version including price, a measure of the age composition of the stock of trees, the acreage in mature trees, and a trend value, with R^2 values of 0.98 and 0.58 for estates and smallholders, respectively and price elasticities of -0.02 and +0.12.

Regression results using monthly rather than annual data are also reported; this analysis was undertaken in an attempt to identify differentiated reactions during periods of rising and falling prices. The indicated elasticities are shown in Table 7.18. The lack of significance attributed to price in the estate regressions indicated little short-run responsiveness to the market among these producers. But for smallholders the elasticities are both sizable and derived

TABLE 7.18

Supply Elasticities, Malayan Rubber

	Estates		Smallholders	
	Model	Elasticity	Model	Elasticity
Rising Prices				
June 1949				
to February 1951	I	-0.04^b	I	$+0.13^b$
February 1954				
to September 1955	I	$+0.04$	I	$+0.37^b$
	II	$+0.04$		
June 1958				
to May 1960	I	$+0.07$	I	$+0.20^a$
	II	$+0.10$		
Falling Prices				
March 1951				
to January 1954	I	-0.02	I	$+0.23^b$
October 1955				
to May 1958	I	-0.02	I	$+0.22^b$
	II	$+0.12$		

[a] 10 percent significance level.
[b] 1 percent significance level.

Notes: Model I includes prices only; Model II includes price, age composition, mature acreage, and trend variables.

Sources: Clifton R. Wharton, Jr., "Rubber Supply Conditions: Some Policy Implications," in The Political Economy of Independent Malaya, ed. T. H. Silcock and E. K. Fisk (Canberra: The Australian National University, 1963); and Robert M. Stern, "Malayan Rubber Production, Inventory Holdings and the Elasticity of Export Supplies," Southern Economic Journal 31 (April 1965).

from significant price coefficient estimates; furthermore, response to both rising and falling prices seems to be about the same.

Another study of Malayan rubber output during this time period by Robert M. Stern confirms Chan's general conclusions about price responsiveness, though the caution Chan expressed about the problems of this time period still stands.[25] Stern used several models and quarterly data for the period 1953 to 1960. In estimating estate responsiveness he regressed output on rubber prices deflated by agricultural workers' wages, the ratio of inventory at the beginning of the quarter to the previous quarter's sales, and a trend variable;

for smallholders he considered output as a function of deflated
current rubber and rice prices and a time-trend variable. The
trend variable was highly significant in both equations. Current
prices showed little significance for estates but were significant
at the 1 percent level for smallholders, indicating a short-run
elasticity of about 0.20.

As part of a much more detailed study of the world rubber
market,* Jere Behrman published pertinent estimates regarding
rubber supply in Malaysia and other producing countries.[26] World
sources of rubber are actually threefold—natural, synthetic, and
reclaimed or recycled rubber—and Behrman's aim was to incorporate
interactions particularly between the first two sources into his
consideration of the total market.

He estimated both short- and long-run supply behavior, allowing
for planting, removal, and abandonment decisions in his model in
the latter case. Short-run supply was considered to be a function
of the (deflated) current price of natural rubber, the area planted
in rubber, expected yields per unit area (or a trend variable), and
rainfall. Behrman postulated that expected yield (in both short-
and long-run supply equations) was a function of both rainfall and
a trend variable.

Combining the two equations into an explanatory model and
using ordinary least-squares techniques he obtained the parameter
estimates for short-run supply that are shown in Table 7.19.
Behrman emphasized that these results show that the implied price
responses are significant and relatively important only for smallholders, and are insignificant for estates, which tends to confirm
the earlier work of both Chan and Stern.

Behrman went beyond these earlier works by attempting to
obtain estimates for long-run responsiveness. As has been the
case in the other studies of tree crops we have cited, data unfortunately was not available to allow a clear distinction to be made
regarding removal, abandonment, and replacement decisions.
Thus Behrman, as have the other authors, used an indirect approach,
formulating a first-differences estimating equation with changes in
acreage in tappable trees expressed in terms of expected prices
and yields, as well as a rainfall index. Price expectations were
expressed in distributed lag terms of all past prices.

---

*The relative importance of each of the producing countries
can be seen from the following figures: West Malaysia: 37 percent
of world natural rubber supply (21 percent from estates, 16 percent
from smallholders); Indonesia: 30 percent (10 percent from estates,
20 percent from smallholders); Thailand: 9 percent; rest of world:
25 percent.

TABLE 7.19

Estimated Short-Run Parameters, Rubber

Country	Period	Price Coefficient	Short-Run Price Elasticity	R^2
Indonesia	1951-60	3.12[b]	0.47	0.86
Smallholders		3.90[b]	0.33	0.90
Estates		0.36	0.05	0.93
West Malaysia	1949-63	10.20[b]	0.14	0.88
Smallholders		6.66[b]	0.23	0.82
Estates		-3.66[b]	-0.09	0.91
Thailand	1947-63	0.57[a]	0.41	0.97
Rest of the world	1951-64	1.02[b]	0.08	0.97

[a]10 percent significance level.
[b]5 percent significance level.
Source: Jere Behrman, "Econometric Model Simulations of the World Rubber Market 1950-1980," in Essays in Industrial Econometrics, Vol. III, ed. Lawrence R. Klein (Philadelphia: Economics Research Unit, Wharton School of Finance and Commerce, 1969).

Behrman recalled the problems of obtaining satisfactory data for the period immediately preceding the period in which he is interested—that is, postwar supply is partly dependent on planting during the Japanese occupation of most of Southeast Asia during World War II. This data limitation, like those encountered by Chan, must be considered in any examination of recent rubber production in this region.

Behrman used maximum likelihood procedures to estimate the parameters of his supply model and some of his results are seen in Table 7.20. He expressed his dissatisfaction with the results, particularly for the areas other than Malaysia. The low values of the coefficients of determination that appear for Indonesia arise, he felt, from the severe data inadequacies for this country. The maximum likelihood estimates even clouded what seemed previously to be a clear distinction between the short-run responsiveness of smallholders and estates. As Behrman proceeded with the rest of his study of the world rubber market, he suggested the advisability of abandoning the above approach as far as rubber is concerned in favor perhaps of a trend—extrapolation method for any

TABLE 7.20

Estimated Parameters, Rubber

| Country | Period | Price Coefficient | Elasticity | | Number of Years for Adjustment to be 95 percent Complete | R² |
			Short-Run (1 year)	Long-Run		
Indonesia	1951–65					
Smallholders	1949–65	−0.016	−0.001	0.012	12	0.14
Estates		−0.026*	−0.023	0.026	15	0.39
West Malaysia	1949–63	–	0	0.4	16	0.52
Smallholders		10.35*	0.141	0.173	2	0.93
Estates		5.34*	0.177	0.207	6	0.91
Thailand	1947–65	3.67*	0.088	0.151	5	0.91
Rest of the World	1948–65	0.43	0.037	0.189	7	0.38
		–	0.023	0.097	7	0.38

*5 percent significance level.
Source: Jere Behrman, "Econometric Model Simulations of the World Rubber Market 1950–1980," in Essays in Industrial Econometrics, Vol. III, ed. Lawrence R. Klein (Philadelphia: Economics Research Unit, Wharton School of Finance and Commerce, 1969).

necessary forecasting—quite probably a reasonable decision considering the problems he, Chan, and Stern encountered with the still-relatively-limited rubber data from the post-World War II period.

Nigerian rubber production was included in the analyses made by Olayide of the cash crops of that nation;[27] among the six crops he considered, rubber was the only one whose marketing was not controlled by a government marketing board. The latter were the author's prime concern; he was interested in the effects of such boards on producer responsiveness.

Two supply models were tested by the author for rubber. Both concerned planting decisions and incorporated appropriately lagged producer prices and acreage (allowing for a seven-year period between planting and maturity). Prices at the time of planting showed significant influence on rubber output, but current prices were also important in the second supply model. The author presented estimates for price elasticity of +0.170 and +0.941 originating from the two models tested; in the second case, values of +0.235 and +0.206 were attributed to the influence of planting and harvesting prices, respectively.

Liberian rubber supply was recently examined by Animesh Ghoshal.[28] He employed several different models: (1) output represented in terms of current prices, mature acreage, and a trend variable; (2) a formulation similar to Bateman's for cocoa; (3) another like that used by Ady; (4) a Nerlove model; and (5) a naive model with output explained only by current prices and a trend variable. Applying all five versions to data available for the period 1950 to 1972 he found only the last two equations to be statistically significant at the 10 percent level or better using the F test. From the Nerlove model he calculated a short-run elasticity of +0.22; from the naive model he found a value of +0.12.

Ghoshal pointed out that the low elasticity values were consistent with other studies of rubber supply and suggested two explanations for such a low level of responsiveness: Either producers cannot for technical reasons vary output much in the short run, or they are not maximizers in the sense postulated by orthodox economic theory.

To explore the latter possibility he offered a test that might be more indicative of short-run responsiveness. Liberian rubber output is not homogeneous; its producers have the choice of bringing it to market in several grades, depending upon the use of other inputs, including labor. Latex brings the highest price, but the degree of premium it enjoys varies considerably from month to month.

The relative quantity of latex brought to market was expressed as the ratio of latex to all rubber sold, which was then regressed

TABLE 7.21

Supply Elasticities, Liberian Rubber

Model		Price	
Grade Ratio	Price Measure	Elasticity	R^2
Latex/all rubber	Current	+0.91	0.66
		(4.66)	
	Lagged	+1.16	0.77
		(5.82)	
Latex/coagulum	Current	+1.33	0.71
		(5.24)	
	Lagged	+1.71	0.80
		(6.23)	

Note: Figures in parentheses are t values.
Source: Animesh Ghoshal, "The Price Responsiveness of
Primary Producers: A Relative Supply Approach," American
Journal of Agricultural Economics 57 (February 1975).

on the ratio of the latex price to an average price for all grades.
An alternative formulation related the ratio of marketed quantities
of latex and of another grade, coagulum, to the ratio of their
respective prices. The equations were expressed in logarithmic
form and regressed on quarterly data from January 1969 to March
1972; prices were expressed both in current terms and lagged one
quarter. The results are shown in Table 7.21.

The relative price elasticities of supply are obviously quite a
bit higher than those obtained using the other models, though the
time periods are not identical. Ghoshal argued that the choice
cultivators face of varying in the short run the grade of rubber they
market is more meaningful than one between rubber and other crops
or between producing or not producing rubber. In these terms he
held that they are maximizers in the accepted sense of the term and
show a considerable degree of price responsiveness.

A simple supply response model for another tree crop was
explored by S. A. Oni for the case of palm products (oil and kernels)
in Nigeria.[29] He concentrated solely on the short-run effects of
current prices on harvesting decisions and formulated a supply
equation that expressed output in terms of recent producer prices,
an index of world prices, a weather index, acreage in the crop, and
a trend variable.

Parameters of the supply model were estimated using both linear and logarithmic formulations, and short-run supply elasticities for both Nigeria as a whole and the province of Eastern Nigeria, the principal producing region, are seen in Table 7.22.

Olayide's study of Nigerian agriculture also considered these two palm products for approximately the same time period—1948 to 1967.[30] Two explanatory models were tested; both were planting models including lagged prices, but the second also included prices at harvest time.

Supply elasticities relative to price for palm oil were estimated to be +0.220, and +0.502 from the two models; for palm kernels, the values were +0.048 and +0.095. When distinctions were made between the effects of domestic prices (lagged seven years) and current world prices, the author estimated elasticity values between +0.22 and +0.26, and between +0.048 and +0.050 for oil and kernels relative to domestic prices, with elasticities of about +0.244 and +0.045 for oil and kernels relative to current world prices.

Olayide argued that the strong responsiveness of Nigerian cultivators to current world prices called for a serious revision of the country's export marketing policies. This sensitivity to the world market, he felt, indicated considerable potential gain, in terms of foreign exchange, for the Nigerian economy if cultivators were exposed more directly, and beneficially, to world prices.

TABLE 7.22

Supply Elasticities, Nigerian Palm Oil
and Kernels

| | | | Elasticities | | |
| | | | Producer | World | |
Product	Region	Model	Prices	Prices	R^2
Palm oil	Nigeria	linear	0.346	−0.029	0.82
		log	0.202	−0.004	0.81
	Eastern	linear	0.697	−0.152	0.83
	Nigeria	log	0.407	−0.011	0.79
Palm kernels	Nigeria	linear	0.221	−0.009	0.62
		log	0.282	−0.002	0.66
	Eastern	linear	0.283	−0.045	0.78
	Nigeria	log	0.394	−0.114	0.70

Source: S. A. Oni, "Production Response in Nigerian Agriculture: A Case Study of Palm Produce 1949-1966," Nigerian Journal of Economics and Social Studies 11 (March 1969).

G. D. Gwyer analyzed the supply responsiveness of sisal in Tanzania, where it has dominated the export economy for many years.[31] He pointed out that the sisal industry has a number of characteristics that make it almost ideal from the viewpoint of supply analysis: a long series of price and other data that show considerable variation is available; little in the way of technological change has occurred during the period in question; and finally, Tanzanian sisal is grown under monoculture, so few complications resulting from the presence of alternate crops are present.

Sisal is a fiber crop, used for many the same purposes as jute and kenaf, which have already been mentioned. However, unlike these crops, sisal is a perennial, with a productive lifetime of from 7 to 12 years, varying with altitude and harvesting practices. The gestation period between planting and the first harvest is three years, and it is primarily grown on an estate scale.

In choosing a model for his analysis Gwyer rejected the stock adjustment model, which he holds is more suitable to perennials whose producers are unable to adjust the area under the crop to the desired level within one time period. Tanzania has no shortage of land suitable for sisal cultivation, and new plantings can be (and are) made at any time during the year. He also ruled out a liquidity-type model as appropriate primarily for cases where the financing of crop planting is a restraint, and where high planting years thus tend to follow years of good export earnings, since on the face of available data this simply does not seem to be so in Tanzania.

He chose instead a Nerlovian adaptive expectations model with new planting a function of projected expected prices over a plant's lifetime, a measure of the age composition of the sisal stock, a proxy for the expectation of increasing costs, and a dummy variable representing Tanzanian independence in 1961 (and, following that event, the likely rising anticipation by estate owners of eventual higher taxes, expropriation, or other limitations placed on a largely foreign-owned industry). In formulating price expectations Gwyer used several models: (A) a simple specification based only on current prices at the time of planting, (B) a declining weights specification, (C) an Irving Fisher lag scheme (lagged coefficients decrease arithmetically) and (D) an unweighted average price specification. The price coefficients and elasticity estimates that he obtained for the "best" regressions from a statistical viewpoint involve formulations that omit the age-composition and independence variables and are shown in Table 7.23.

In analyzing the results from the several formulations Gwyer concluded that all the evidence points to planters being influenced almost exclusively by prices in the year of planting and the two

TABLE 7.23

Estimated Parameters, Tanzanian Sisal

Model	Price Coefficient	Price Expectation Coefficient	Elasticity Short-Run	Elasticity Long-Run	R^2
A	+0.063[b]	—	0.42	0.42	0.815
B (ordinary least squares)	+0.039[a]	0.59[a]	0.44	0.26	0.878
B (two-state least squares)	+0.042[a]	0.58[a]	0.50	0.29	0.884
C	+0.078[b]	—	0.51	0.26	0.881
D	+0.072[b]	—	0.48	0.24	0.873

[a]5 percent significance level.
[b]0.1 percent significance level.
Source: G. D. Gwyer, "Long- and Short-Run Elasticities of Sisal Supply," Eastern African Economic Review 3 (December 1971).

previous years—for example, if β, the expectation coefficient, is about 0.6, then 60 percent of the weight is applied to current prices, 84 percent to current plus the previous year's prices, 93.6 percent to current plus the previous two years' prices, and so on (the sum of the weights over n periods is equal to $1 - (1 - \beta)^n$).

The author also examined the effect of current prices on harvesting decisions. Sisal is used in the form of a fiber produced from the leaves, and regular harvesting not only increases the number of leaves produced but also increases the yield by increasing the number of leaves suitable for harvesting. The relatively high costs that are incurred in the harvesting procedure impose some limitations on the frequency of harvesting. A severe cutting at each harvesting lengthens the life cycle but also increases production costs, since workers are paid on a per leaf basis and since heavy cutting means a long wait before enough new leaves have matured to make harvesting from the plant again worthwhile. Gwyer indicates that heavy cutting is thus actually a more expensive way of increasing annual output than is more frequent harvesting, and that since any variation in current prices is likely to have an effect on harvesting practices he tried to determine how much short-term price response is due to increased intensity of cutting and how much to increased frequency of harvesting.

Gwyer postulated a simultaneous equation model

$$\left[\frac{C}{M}\right]_t = a_o + a_1 P_t + a_2 T \tag{7.31}$$

$$\left[\frac{Y}{C}\right]_t = b_o + b_1 \left[\frac{C}{M}\right]_t + b_2 P_t \tag{7.32}$$

where: $\frac{C}{M}$ is the proportion of mature sisal acreage harvested,

$\frac{Y}{C}$ is the sisal yield per hectare of mature area harvested,

P is current sisal price, and

T is a trend variable.

Estimating the model parameters Gwyer found b_2 to be close to zero, indicating that the degree of harvesting is independent of prices, and that the elasticity of the proportion of mature area harvested $\left[\frac{C}{M}\right]$ to price is close to +0.09. The latter value is nearly to that of the short-term elasticity of output per hectare of mature area $\left[\frac{Y}{M}\right]$, which he had estimated independently, from an equation representing $\left[\frac{Y}{M}\right]$ as a function of sisal prices and a trend variable, to be approximately +0.06. This, he concluded, indicated that producers feel heavy harvesting and overcutting leads to increased costs, reacting to any current price stimuli by varying the frequency of harvesting.

Unsatisfied with earlier treatments of perennial crops, Ben French and Jim Matthews recently proposed a different formulation of the supply model.[32] They constructed a framework within which new plantings and acreage adjustments could be determined. It has a more general specification that they felt might be more appropriate for most U.S. perennial crops. They contrasted their work with that of Bateman, who paid little attention to the problem of plant removals and thus worked in effect with infinite crop lifetimes, and that of Arak, who considered removals but had to deal with the peculiarities of Brazilian coffee, which limited any wider application of her work.

The French-Matthews model has five parts. In the first are two functions that explain respectively the quantity of produce and the amount of desired bearing acreage. Second, there is an equation for new planting, defined in terms of an adjustment mechanism by which acreage is shifted toward the desired level, and third, a plant removals equation. Next the relationships between observable and unobservable variables are defined. Finally, there is an equation to explain variation in average yield. The authors then used a simplified version of their model to examine the supply of asparagus in the United States.

If we consider the parts of the model in turn, desired production was assumed to be based on profit expectations that are formed when producers bring together in some fashion or other expected prices, yields, and costs, plus the projected level of bearing acreage. They are then assumed to maximize long-run profitability through adjustment of production. Desired output (Q_t^D) was expressed in the following equation:

$$Q_t^D = Q_{t-1}^e + a_1(\pi_t^e - \pi_t^*) + a_2(\pi_{A_t}^e - \pi_{A_t}^*) + u_t \qquad (7.33)$$

where: Q^e is expected average output, and is equal to Y^e, normal yield,

π_t^e and $\pi_{A_t}^e$ are expected long-run profits for the crop and its alternate,

π_t^* and $\pi_{A_t}^*$ are normal long-run profits for the crop, and its alternate.

Since: $Q_t^D = Y_t^e A_t^D$ and $Q_{t-1}^e = Y_{t-1}^e A_{t-1}$ (where A is acreage) then:

$$A_t^D = \frac{Y_{t-1}^e}{Y_t^e} A_{t-1} + b_1 \frac{1}{Y_t^e}(\pi_t^e - \pi_t^*) + b_2 \frac{1}{Y_t^e}(\pi_{A_t}^e - \pi_{A_t}^*) + v_t$$
$$(7.34)$$

Since they found this formulation very difficult to estimate, they expressed normal yield (Y_t^e) as a function of an observable variable, and approximated equation 7.34 with:

$$A_t^D = A_{t-1} + c_1(\pi_t^e - \pi_t^*) + c_2(\pi_{A_t}^e - \pi_{A_t}^*) + c_3 \Delta Y_t^e + w_t \qquad (7.35)$$

where $\Delta Y_t^e = Y_t - Y_{t-1}$ which they felt was an adequate formulation for small changes in expected normal yield.

Next they emphasized that new plantings are undertaken to bring actual acreage to desired levels, a goal not immediately achievable not only since k years must pass before the young plants reach the bearing stage, but also because we must take account of replacements needed for old, diseased, or damaged plants. Thus:

$$N_t^D = A_{t+k}^D - A_{t-1} + R_{k_t}^e - N_{k_{t-1}} \tag{7.36}$$

where: N_t^D is desired new planting acreage in period t,

A_{t+k}^D is desired acreage when new planted acreage in period t matures in period t + k,

$R_{k_t}^e$ is expected (in period t) total amount of removals in the following k years, and

$N_{k_{t-1}}$ is the nonbearing acreage in period t - 1, which is equal to $\sum_{i=1}^{k} N_{t-1}$, the sum of new planting in the last k years.

Expected removals are expressed as:

$$R_{k_t}^e = a_1 A_{t-1}^o + a_2 N_{k_{t-1}} + a_3 A_{t-1} + u_t \tag{7.37}$$

where A_{t-1}^o represents acreage of already old plants, and $0 < a_i < 1$ i = 1, 2, and 3. That is, removals are equal to a proportion of the already old plants plus those fractions of both immature (N) and mature (A) plants that are damaged or diseased.

French and Matthews pointed out that a Nerlovian adjustment model could be used to explain new plantings:

$$N_t = \beta(N_t^D - \in N_{t-1}) + \in N_{t-1} \tag{7.38}$$

where: β is the adjustment coefficient, and
$\in$ is a dampening factor, which accounts for past unachievable results if equal to unity, reducing the adjustment equation to the Nerlovian equation; should $\in$ equal zero, then past failures to achieve desired planting levels have no effect on the future.

They argued that if planting decisions are implemented quite soon after they are made, and if the necessary inputs are available at that time, then $\in$ can be considered to be quite small, and this they believe to be the case for most U.S. perennials. The final form of the new planting equation then is:

$$N_t = d_1(\pi_t^e - \pi_t^*) + d_2(\pi_{A_t}^e - \pi_{A_t}^*) + d_3 \Delta Y_t^e + d_4 A_{t-1}^o + d_5 N_{k_{t-1}}$$
$$+ d_6 A_{t-1} + v_t \tag{7.39}$$

As for removals, these depend upon institutional and physical factors, short-run profit expectations (that is, if such are high, removals might be postponed a harvest or two; if low, removal might be speeded up a bit), and on random factors associated with deviations between producer plans and actions. Thus removals were expressed as:

$$R_t = e_1 + e_2 A_t^o + e_3 A_t^o (\pi_t^s - \pi_t^*) + e_4 A_t^o (\pi_{A_t}^s - \pi_{A_t}^*) + e_5 Z_t$$

$$+ e_6 N_{k_t} + u_t \qquad (7.40)$$

where: π^s and π_A^s are short-run profit expectations for the crop and its alternate, and

Z_t is a variable to account for any likely important physical or institutional factors.

Substituting the new planting and removal equations into the acreage equation 7.35 yields:

$$A_t - A_{t-1} = f_o + f_1 (\pi_{t-k}^e - \pi_{t-k}^*) + f_2 (\pi_{A_{t-k}}^e - \pi_{t-k}^*) + f_3 \Delta Y_{t-k}^e$$

$$+ f_4 A_{t-k-1}^o + f_5 A_{t-1}^o + f_6 A_{t-1}^o (\pi_{t-1}^s - \pi_{t-1}^*) + f_7 A_{t-1}^o$$

$$(\pi_{t-1}^s - \pi_{t-1}^*) + f_8 Z_{t-1} + f_9 N_{k_{t-k-1}} + f_{10} A_{t-k-1}$$

$$+ f_{11} A_{t-1} + v_t \qquad (7.41)$$

a relationship that states that changes in bearing acreages today depend upon profit and yield expectations k years ago, upon the stock of old plants last year and k years ago, upon the short-run profit expectations one year ago, on institutional factors, on the amount of nonbearing acreage k plus one year ago, and on the total acreage last year and k plus one year ago. The authors expect the coefficients f_1, f_4, f_6, and f_{10} to be positive, f_2, f_3, f_4, f_5, f_7, f_9, and f_{11} to be negative, and the sign of f_8 to depend upon whatever Z represents.

Before any estimation of the parameters of equation 7.41 can take place, the nonobservable variables—expected yield and expected and normal profit—must be redefined. French and Matthews believe yield expectations are likely to conform to a long-term trend with occasional discrete jumps, and so they represent changes in expectations as:

$$\Delta Y^e_t = f(Y_{m_{t-1}}, Y_{m_{t-2}}, \ldots) \tag{7.42}$$

where Y_m is the yield of mature plants. Expected profits, both short- and long-run, from both the crop and its alternate, are similarly specified to depend upon past actual profits, which in turn depend upon price and cost considerations.

$$\pi^e_t = g(\pi_{t-1}, \pi_{t-2}, \ldots, h_t) \tag{7.43a}$$

$$\pi^e_{A_t} = g_A(\pi_{A_{t-1}}, \pi_{A_{t-2}}, \ldots, h_t) \tag{7.43b}$$

where h_t allows inclusion of any relatively unusual occurrences like changes in legislation.

Finally the yield relationship is primarily a function of the bearing stock of plants.

$$Y_t = \sum_{i=k}^{H} w_i A_{t-i} + a_1 T + u_t \tag{7.44}$$

where: H is the average maximum bearing age, and
            T is a trend variable.

While theoretically the weights (w_i) attached to past plantings now mature could all have distinct and different values, the authors do not expect this to be true for most perennials. More likely, two or three separate bearing stages can be identified. If no data regarding the age distribution of the stock of plants is available, then little can be done but to project yields as a function of time, taking care that variations due to age cycles are not explained by a trend variable.

The final estimating equation was obtained by substituting equations 7.42, 7.43, and 7.44 into equation 7.41 and specifying a relationship between short-run profit expectations and an observable variable, such as $\pi^s_t = \pi_t$. Ordinary least-squares techniques can then be used to estimate these parameters, though the authors cautioned that the complexity of the disturbance terms requires that the initial specification in each case be made with great care.

French and Matthews applied their model to the supply of asparagus in the United States. Asparagus is a perennial with a lifetime of 10 to 15 years and an initial gestation period of two to three years. It is grown mostly in California, the Midwestern and Eastern states, and in the Pacific northwest, and the supply parameters for each of these regions were separately estimated.

Planting and removal data was not readily available, so the acreage adjustment equation 7.41 was used, omitting any consideration of alternate crops, since a very large number of such crops are available to the cultivators in these regions, and no way to represent this diversity in a noncomplicating manner could be found.

Profits in all time periods were defined in terms of grower prices deflated by an index of agricultural wages. Also unavailable was data concerning old plants, so they assumed A_t^o to be approximated by a proportion of the average harvested acreage during the previous five years. The principal institutional change of interest during the period under consideration (1947 to 1969) was the abolition of the Mexican Farm Labor program (the Bracero program) in 1964. This had a sharp but temporary effect on profit expectations and led to considerable removals in 1965. The authors represented this change with a dummy variable set equal to zero until 1965, to unity in 1965, 0.5 in 1966, 0.25 in 1967, 0.125 in 1968, and to zero again in 1969 and thereafter.

Ordinary least-squares techniques were then used to estimate the parameters of:

$$A_t - A_{t-1} = \alpha_o + \alpha_1 P_{t-1}^R \overline{A}_{t-1} + \alpha_2 \overline{P}_{t-k-1} + \alpha_3 \overline{A}_{t-1}$$

$$+ \alpha_4 \overline{A}_{t-k-1} + \alpha_5 D \tag{7.45}$$

where: P_{t-1}^R is the price to wage ratio, $\dfrac{P_{t-1}}{w_{t-1}}$,

$\overline{A}$ is the proportion of the average harvested acreage during the past five years assumed to stand for the number of old plants,

$\overline{P}_{t-k-1} = \dfrac{1}{2}(P_{t-k-1} + P_{t-k-2})$, and

D is a dummy variable.

Estimated parameters (and their associated standard errors) are shown in Table 7.24

Another attempt to devise a supply model appropriate for the analysis of U.S. perennial crops was published recently by John Baritelle and David Price.[33] Their specific interest concerned apple production in Washington; for this crop the four years following planting represent considerable cost to the cultivator with no return. Apple production begins in the fifth year, and yields rise to a peak by about the twelfth year; proper care and maintenance should then allow for 30 to 40 years of profitable harvesting.

TABLE 7.24

Supply Parameters, U.S. Asparagus

Region	α_0	α_1	α_2	α_3	α_4	α_5	R^2
California	-78.75	+0.0228[d] (0.0057)	+3.1376[d] (0.5358)	-0.5103[d] (0.1647)	+0.7678[d] (0.2526)	-8.1596[d] (1.7807)	0.856
Midwest and East	-18.24	+0.0033 (0.0052)	+1.2206[d] (0.2597)	-0.3569[d] (0.1046)	+0.3633[d] (0.1295)	-1.8357[b] (0.8477)	0.875
Pacific Northwest	-2.54	—	+0.2758[c] (0.1035)	-0.1537 (0.1192)	+0.1417 (0.1191)	+1.4438[a,d] (0.3133)	0.715

[a]The dummy in the Northwest represented an unusual shift in asparagus acreage in 1957 and 1958.
[b]10 percent significance level.
[c]5 percent significance level.
[d]1 percent significance level.
Source: Ben C. French and Jim L. Matthews, "A Supply Response Model for Perennial Crops," American Journal of Agricultural Economics 53 (August 1971).

Production was represented by the identity:

$$Q_t = \sum_i y_{i,t} \, A_{i,t} \qquad\qquad (7.46)$$

where: Q_t is total production in year t,
         $y_{i,t}$ is yield per tree for trees of age i in year t, and
         $A_{i,t}$ is the number of trees of age i in year t.
Yield was then represented as a function of past weather conditions:

$$y_{i,t} = F(W_t, \, W_{t-1}, \, \ldots, \, W_{t-n}). \qquad\qquad (7.47)$$

where W represents a measure of weather. The total number of trees in all age groups was expressed as last year's stock adjusted to account for the net change in trees due to economic causes and the losses as a result of frosts:

$$\sum_i A_{i,t} = \sum_i A_{i,t-1} + N_t - \sum_i L_{i,t-1} \qquad\qquad (7.48)$$

where: N_t is the net change in trees due to economic reasons, and
         $L_{i,t-1}$ is the number of trees of age i killed by frost.
Since trees adversely affected by frost do not die immediately, $L_{i,t}$ was expressed in lagged response terms, based on probabilities estimated from past observations.
     Economically induced changes in tree stock were expressed as the difference between new plantings and removals, with each of latter dependent upon expectations of future profitability:

$$N_t = PL_t - R_t \tag{7.49a}$$

$$PL_t = f\,[E\,(P)] \tag{7.49b}$$

$$R_t = g\,[E\,(P)] \tag{7.49c}$$

where: PL_t were new plantings in year t,
         R_t were removals in year t, and
         E (P) was expected profit.

The authors encountered data limitations in their attempts to estimate apple supply using the model. The lack of critical annual statistical series allowed only a testing of their hypothesis explaining net change. Using a modified version of the Almon lag method they represented net change in tree stock in terms of past prices and tested for the period 1953 to 1971 formulations using lags of from three to ten years. They found the highest degree of explanatory power when the total lag length was eight.

In explaining the greater influence on planting decisions of prices lagged one to six years than that of current prices, the authors pointed to input availability problems as having some effect. Seedlings must be planted one to two years before replanting in the orchard. Baritelle and Price also felt that cultivators are probably hesitant to rely only or primarily on presently prevailing returns, but prefer to base their plans on several recent years' experience.

NOTES

1. Merrill Bateman, Cocoa in the Ghanaian Economy: An Econometric Model (Amsterdam: North-Holland, 1968).

2. Ibid.

3. Jere R. Behrman, "Monopolistic Cocoa Pricing," American Journal of Agricultural Economics 50 (August 1968).

4. A recent study of Nigerian cocoa farmers suggests they may display considerable asymmetry in their price responsiveness. J. K. Olayemi and S. K. Oni report in "Asymmetry in Price Response: A Case Study of Western Nigerian Cocoa Farmers," Nigerian Journal of Economic and Social Studies 14 (November 1972), that planting elasticities relative to price increases may be about double those provoked by decreases. Their work is not based on actual planting data, but rather on an extensive survey of cocoa cultivators who were asked how much cocoa they would plant for various hypothetical producer prices, assuming factor input costs and alternative crop prices were constant. Though the

authors admit actual cultivator behavior might be different, they emphasize the danger of formulating agricultural policies that assume symmetric responsiveness.

5. Robert M. Stern, "The Determinants of Cocoa Supply in West Africa," in African Primary Products and International Trade, eds. I. G. Stewart and H. W. Ord (Edinburgh: Edinburgh University Press, 1965).

6. S. Olajuwon Olayide, "Some Estimates of Supply Elasticities for Nigeria's Cash Crops," Journal of Agricultural Economics 23 (September 1972).

7. Kenneth D. Frederick, "Coffee Production in Uganda: An Economic Analysis of Past and Potential Growth" (Ph.D. dissertation, Massachusetts Institute of Technology, 1965).

8. Kenneth D. Frederick, "The Role of Market Forces and Planning in Uganda's Economic Development 1900-1938," Eastern African Economic Review 1 (June 1969).

9. Marcelle Arak, "The Supply of Brazilian Coffee" (Ph.D. thesis, Massachusetts Institute of Technology, 1967), and "The Price Responsiveness of Sao Paulo Coffee Growers," Food Research Institute Studies 8, no. 3 (1968).

10. Edmar L. Bacha, "An Econometric Model for the World Coffee Market: The Impact of Brazilian Price Policy" (Ph.D. dissertation, Yale University, 1968).

11. R. Gerald Saylor, "Alternative Measures of Supply Elasticities: The Case of Sao Paulo Coffee," American Journal of Agricultural Economics 56 (February 1974).

12. In the manner of William G. Tomek, "Distributed Lag Models of Cotton Acreage Response: A Further Result," American Journal of Agricultural Economics 54 (February 1972). Tomek observed for U.S. cotton that alternative deflators suggest a supply shift in the data used by Nerlove, and then reestimating the supply function using a dummy variable. He found quite different implications regarding lagged acreage response.

13. Following the method outlined by R. Wolffram, who responded to a paper by Luther G. Tweeten and C. Leroy Quance, "Positivistic Measures of Aggregate Supply Elasticities: Some New Approaches," American Journal of Agricultural Economics 51 (May 1969). The latter estimated an equation including different price series depending upon whether prices had risen or fallen between t - 2 and t - 1. Wolffram's formulation of prices, in American Journal of Agricultural Economics 53 (May 1971), depends upon the accumulated sum of first differences in prices.

14. M. R. Wickens and J. N. Greenfield, "The Econometrics of Agricultural Supply: An Application to the World Coffee Market," Review of Economics and Statistics 55 (November 1973).

15. Jere Behrman and L. R. Klein, "Econometric Growth Models for the Developing Economy," in Induction, Growth and Trade: Essays in Honour of Sir Ray Harrod, ed. W. A. Eltis et al. (Oxford: Clarendon, 1970).

16. Merrill J. Bateman, "A Supply Function for Colombian Coffee 1947-1965," a RAND Memorandum, Summer 1968.

17. R. L. Williams, "Jamaican Coffee Supply, 1953-1968, An Exploratory Study," Social and Economic Studies 21 (March 1972).

18. Joseph K. Maitha, "Productivity Response to Price: A Case Study of Kenyan Coffee," Eastern African Economic Review 2 (December 1970).

19. Joseph K. Maitha, "A Supply Function of Kenyan Coffee," Eastern African Economic Review 1 (June 1969).

20. Peter Ady, "Supply Functions in Tropical Agriculture," Oxford Institute of Statistics Bulletin 30 (1968).

21. V. Rajagopalan, A. Sennimalai, S. A. Radhakrishnan, and A. Kandaswamy, "Price Elasticities—Methodological Issues with reference to Perennial Crops," a paper read at the 31st Annual Conference of the Indian Society of Agricultural Economics, abstracted in Indian Journal of Agricultural Economics 26 (October-December 1971).

22. V. Rajagopalan and V. Meenakshisundaram, "Travails of the Tea Industry—An Economic Appraisal," Indian Journal of Agricultural Economics 24 (October-December 1969).

23. Francis Chan Kwong Wah, "A Preliminary Study of the Supply Response of Malayan Rubber Estates between 1948 and 1959," Malayan Economic Review 7 (October 1962).

24. Clifton R. Wharton, Jr., "Rubber Supply Conditions: Some Policy Implications," in The Political Economy of Independent Malaya, ed. T. H. Silcock and E. K. Fisk (Canberra: The Australian National University, 1963).

25. Robert M. Stern, "Malayan Rubber Production, Inventory Holdings and the Elasticity of Export Supplies," Southern Economic Journal 31 (April 1965).

26. Jere Behrman, "Econometric Model Simulations of the World Rubber Market 1950-1980," in Essays in Industrial Econometrics, Vol. III, ed. Lawrence R. Klein (Philadelphia: Economics Research Unit, Wharton School of Finance and Commerce, 1969).

27. Olayide, op. cit.

28. Animesh Ghoshal, "The Price Responsiveness of Primary Producers: A Relative Supply Approach," American Journal of Agricultural Economics 57 (February 1975).

29. S. A. Oni, "Production Response in Nigerian Agriculture: A Case Study of Palm Produce 1949-1966," Nigerian Journal of Economics and Social Studies 11 (March 1969).

30. Olayide, op. cit.

31. G. D. Gwyer, "Long- and Short-Run Elasticities of Sisal Supply," Eastern African Economic Review 3 (December 1971).

32. Ben C. French and Jim L. Matthews, "A Supply Response Model for Perennial Crops," American Journal of Agricultural Economics 53 (August 1971).

33. John L. Baritelle and David W. Price, "Supply Response and Marketing Strategies for Deciduous Crops," American Journal of Agricultural Economics 56 (May 1974).

A number of agricultural commodities whose supply has been
analyzed with Nerlovian tools do not fit neatly into the annual and
perennial categories discussed in Chapters 5, 6, and 7. Most of
the products discussed in this and the next chapter are superficially
similar to perennials, but all show important differences. For
example, sugar, our first concern, has attributes of both perennial
and annual crops.

Its first crop can be harvested 18 to 24 months after sowing
and thereafter at 10- to 12-month intervals, and thus, strictly
speaking, it is a perennial; these succeeding crops are called
ratoons and grow from the original roots after the cane has been
cut. Though in areas with virgin soils ratoons are large in yield
and indefinite in number, in most regions yield falls rapidly after
the first crop. Many cultivators treat sugar as a one-harvest
commodity—for example, along the U.S. Gulf Coast plants are
customarily uprooted after the first cutting. Elsewhere, three or
four cuttings of cane are the rule before roots are plowed up.

Obviously, some properties of tree crops are common to sugar.
There is a relatively long period (compared to annual crops) between
planting and the first harvest, though in the case of sugar this
incomeless period is considerably shorter than it is for coffee or
cocoa or even asparagus. The longer period before maturity affects
any formulation of price expectations, which must be based in this
case on prices no more recent than 18 months prior to the first
harvest (though more current prices might affect harvesting
decisions). As with tree crops, sugar planting decisions are usually
affected by expectations of future returns from more than one harvest. However, since sugar yields drop off rapidly after the first
harvest, unlike any tree crops considered above where yields either

initially rose or "plateaued" after the first crop, and fell off only
much later, considerations of factors affecting elimination (and
replanting) decisions are potentially of more importance in the case
of sugar. Another distinction arises from the much shorter lifetime
of sugar, which simplifies the calculation of expected income
streams influencing initial planting decisions.

Many of the studies of sugar supply concern India, with some
of the available data being part of multicrop analysis already referred
to above. Vahid Nowshirvani, anxious to provide some basis for
comparison with the supply behavior of cereal crop cultivators in
Bihar and eastern Uttar Pradesh, turned his attention to sugar,
the most important cash crop in both states.[1] (It is general practice
in these states to reap two sugar crops from each planting.)

He first applied an acreage-adjustment, price expectations
model representing total sugar acreage as a function of expected
prices lagged both one and two years, lagged acreage, and a trend
variable to Uttar Pradesh for the period 1909 to 1942. Using the
Dhrymes method for parameter estimation he obtained the price
parameter estimates shown in Table 8.1 (along with their associated
standard errors). (For the geographic composition of the divisions,
see Table 5.7 above.) The calculations indicate that the price
coefficient is significant at the 10 percent level or better in four
of the six divisions tested, but since price expectation coefficient
estimates (not shown) were close to unity, Nowshirvani used the
Zellner method (with the price coefficient set equal to one) for
efficient estimating of a seemingly unrelated regression, and the
linear model:

$$A_t = a_1 + a_2 (P_{t-1} + P_{t-2}) + a_3 T + a_4 A_{t-1} \qquad (8.1)$$

with the results shown below in Table 8.2 for 1909 to 1942 (with
t statistics in parentheses).

As can be seen, notably more significance is indicated for the
price parameter estimates. Nowshirvani also noted an inverse
relationship between the magnitude of the price elasticity and the
portion of land in sugarcane, reflecting increasingly poorer land
used as this portion increases (see Table 8.3).

For the postwar period Dhrymes' method gave satisfactory
results only for two groups of Uttar Pradesh districts and the
sugar region of Bihar and these estimates (and their standard
errors) are seen in Table 8.4.

Nowshirvani also estimated postwar sugar supply using a
linear form of the equation, making the assumption that the price
expectation coefficients were equal to unity for each group of

TABLE 8.1

Supply Parameters, Uttar Pradesh Sugar,
1909-42

Region	Price	Long-Run Elasticity	R^2
Division 1	33.06[b] (13.11)	1.57	0.64
Division 2	4.59[c] (1.59)	2.55	0.65
Division 3	90.83[a] (52.62)	0.89	0.63
Division 4	51.75 (36.97)	0.54	0.56
Division 5	64.16 (56.58)	0.29	0.62
Division 6	24.75[b] (11.75)	0.32	0.84

[a]10 percent significance level.
[b]5 percent significance level.
[c]1 percent significance level.
Source: Vahid Nowshirvani, "Agricultural Supply in India: Some Theoretical and Empirical Studies" (Ph.D. dissertation, Massachusetts Institute of Technology, 1962).

districts in Uttar Pradesh, and the estimated parameters (and standard errors) are indicated in Table 8.5. For those groups of districts with significant price parameters the postwar long-run elasticities are generally higher than for the prewar period, an increase in market orientation Nowshirvani had also noted for the other crops (rice, wheat, and barley) during the later period.

A more recent examination of Uttar Pradesh sugar supply has been presented by K. L. Rathod, who focused on the generally more prosperous western part of the state.[2] His interest was in the effect on output of risk-reducing government policies, particularly minimum price guarantees. Hypothesizing that risk reduction would spur output, he formulated alternate supply models that included in one case lagged deflated gur (a semiprocessed form of sugar) prices, and, in the other case, the difference between lagged deflated gur and lagged minimum guaranteed cane prices. Should

TABLE 8.2

Uttar Pradesh Sugar, Zellner Method

	1	2	3	4	5	6
First Stage						
Constant	-166.6^b	-43.3^c	-597.5	-46.6	537.4	411.7^b
	(2.142)	(3.348)	(1.344)	(.147)	(.956)	(2.274)
Price	16.73^c	2.99^c	59.53^b	39.45^b	42.22	21.13^c
$(P_t + P_{t-1})$	(3.968)	(3.552)	(2.349)	(2.469)	(1.321)	(2.748)
Time trend	4.11^c	0.84^c	36.19^c	14.89^c	34.95^c	9.57^c
	(2.798)	(2.904)	(3.401)	(2.720)	(2.965)	(3.442)
Lagged area	0.484^c	0.346^b	0.356^b	0.418^c	0.377^b	0.179
(A_{t-1})	(3.475)	(2.454)	(2.190)	(2.674)	(2.289)	(1.091)
R^2	0.69	0.68	0.72	0.58	0.66	0.54
Durbin-Watson statistic	1.646	1.796	1.850	1.723	1.919	1.936
Second Stage						
Constant	-134.6^b	-38.3^c	-283.0	187.1	823.8^a	352.9^b
	(2.086)	(3.327)	(0.758)	(.749)	(1.812)	(2.444)
Price	15.07^c	2.64^c	45.36^b	34.25^c	43.43	20.34^c
$(P_t + P_{t-1})$	(4.209)	(3.486)	(2.124)	(2.581)	(1.622)	(3.049)
Time trend	4.30^c	0.78^c	45.47^c	18.03^c	44.37^c	8.60^c
	(3.423)	(2.930)	(5.487)	(3.867)	(4.701)	(3.557)
Lagged area	0.449^c	0.403^c	0.172^d	0.261^c	0.195^a	0.261^b
(A_{t-1})	(5.043)	(3.625)	(1.712)	(2.793)	(1.850)	(2.267)
Short-run price elasticity	0.72	1.47	0.44	0.36	0.19	0.26
Long-run price elasticity	1.43	2.46	0.53	0.48	0.24	0.35

[a]10 percent significance level.
[b]5 percent significance level.
[c]1 percent significance level.
Source: Vahid Nowshirvani, "Agricultural Supply in India: Some Theoretical and Empirical Studies" (Ph.D. dissertation, Massachusetts Institute of Technology, 1962).

cultivators be risk averters, he expected supply response to be more closely and significantly related to the second price formulation than to the first.

The Nerlovian supply models also expressed acreage in terms of lagged acreage, relative sugar-to-wheat yield, rainfall during the sowing period, and a measure of cane acreage infested with pests and plant disease. Ordinary least-squares regressions were run on logarithmic forms of both models for the period 1950 to 1967 and parameter estimates were obtained for the region as a whole,

TABLE 8.3

Uttar Pradesh, Supply Elasticity and Crop Importance, Sugar

	Division					
	2	1	3	4	6	5
Average percent of land in sugar	0.2	1.2	3.5	2.4	5.1	5.2
Long-run price elasticity	2.46	1.43	0.54	0.48	0.26	0.24

Source: Vahid Nowshirvani, "Agricultural Supply in India: Some Theoretical and Empirical Studies" (Ph.D. dissertation, Massachusetts Institute of Technology, 1962).

TABLE 8.4

Estimated Parameters, Uttar Pradesh and Bihar Sugar, Post-World War II

Region	Price Coefficient	Long-Run Elasticity	R^2
Uttar Pradesh			
Hardoi, Kheri, and Sitapur	+0.037[b] (0.011)	1.34	0.69
Bahraich, Barabanki, Faizabad, Gonda, Pratapgarh, and Sultanpur	+0.020 (0.013)	0.78	0.27
Bihar			
Champaran and Saran	+0.036[a] (0.015)	1.38	0.34

[a]5 percent significance level.
[b]1 percent significance level.
Source: Vahid Nowshirvani, "Agricultural Supply in India: Some Theoretical and Empirical Studies" (Ph.D. dissertation, Massachusetts Institute of Technology, 1962).

TABLE 8.5

Estimated Parameters, Uttar Pradesh Sugar,
1953-64

Region	Price Coefficient	Short-Run Elasticity	Long-Run Elasticity	Lagged Area Coefficient	R^2
Allahabad, Fatehpur, and Kanpur	0.012[a] (0.006)	0.44	0.77	0.426[c] (0.131)	0.35
Ballia, Ghazipur, and Juanpur	-0.003 (0.003)	-0.12	-0.29	0.605[c] (0.126)	0.50
Azamgarh, Basti, Deoria, and Gorakhpur	-0.001 (0.002)	-0.04	-0.11	0.674[c] (0.295)	0.58
Lucknow, Rae Bareli, and Unnao	0.011[b] (0.005)	0.42	0.92	0.542[c] (0.118)	0.46
Hardoi, Kheri, and Sitapur	0.018[c] (0.005)	0.63	1.19	0.475[c] (0.108)	0.59
Bahraich, Barabanki, Faizabad, Gonda, Pratapgarh, and Sultanpur	0.008[b] (0.003)	0.31	0.49	0.383[c] (0.108)	0.25

[a] 10 percent significance level.
[b] 5 percent significance level.
[c] 1 percent significance level.
  Source: Vahid Nowshirvani, "Agricultural Supply in India: Some Theoretical and Empirical Studies" (Ph.D. dissertation, Massachusetts Institute of Technology 1962).

groups of districts, and individual districts. Parameter estimates (which are elasticities, since the estimating equation was in logarithmic form) are shown for the larger subdivisions in Table 8.6, while price elasticities for individual districts are listed in Table 8.7.

In commenting upon his results Rathod pointed out the lack of much notable difference between the two price formulations in explaining cultivator response. Though no evidence is thus indicated for the premise that sugar producers are risk averters, the author cautioned against rejecting a significant role in the formulation of price expectations for minimum guaranteed price. During the period under study, average market price exceeded minimum price in 14 out of 18 years. This persistent supply gap, he believes, merely leads to stronger short-run reaction to market prices than to guaranteed levels. His model is unable to capture the effect of the latter on producer decisions involving the adoption of new cultivation techniques that incur both added cost and risk.

Sugar acreage response in the Tirkut division (Saran, Champaran, Muzaffarpur, and Darbhanga districts) of Bihar state has been examined by Dayanatha Jha.[3] During the period he considered (1912 to 1964), two notable changes affecting the statistics that he employed occurred: (1) sugarcane prices paid by the region's

TABLE 8.6

Estimated Parameters, Uttar Pradesh Sugar

Region[a]	Gur Price	Gur Price Minus Cane Price	Relative Yield	Lagged Area	Rainfall	Diseased Area	R^2
A	+0.301[c] (0.111)	–	+0.417[c] (0.153)	+0.604[c] (0.203)	+0.013 (0.026)	-0.033[c] (0.015)	0.84
	–	+0.264[c] (0.109)	+0.458[c] (0.154)	+0.599[c] (0.216)	+0.015 (0.027)	-0.039[c] (0.016)	0.83
B	+0.556[e] (0.119)	–	+0.364[c] (0.135)	+0.749[e] (0.147)	+0.072 (0.066)	-0.033[b] (0.016)	0.89
	–	+0.502[e] (0.108)	+0.359 (0.135)	+0.770[e] (0.149)	+0.065 (0.066)	-0.040 (0.016)	0.89
C	+0.473[c] (0.132)	–	+0.179 (0.226)	+0.734[d] (0.208)	-0.031 (0.066)	-0.063[c] (0.016)	0.83
	–	+0.408[d] (0.124)	+0.227 (0.101)	+0.728[d] (0.219)	-0.020 (0.068)	-0.064[c] (0.022)	0.82
D	+0.358[c] (0.153)	–	+0.629[b] (0.340)	+0.712[c] (0.024)	+0.097 (0.066)	+0.012 (0.062)	0.73
	–	+0.283[b] (0.143)	+0.692[b] (0.318)	+0.673[c] (0.228)	+0.107 (0.066)	+0.012 (0.063)	0.72
Whole region	+0.254[c] (0.112)	–	+0.727[c] (0.303)	+0.587[b] (0.328)	+0.124[b] (0.068)	-0.016[b] (0.008)	0.85
	–	+0.225[b] (0.118)	+0.749[c] (0.300)	+0.588[b] (0.304)	+0.128[b] (0.068)	-0.020[b] (0.010)	0.84

[a]The author did not identify which districts made up the groups.

[b]10 percent significance level.

[c]5 percent significance level.

[d]1 percent significance level.

[e]0.1 percent significance level.

Source: K. L. Rathod, "Farmers' Aversion to Risk—A Case of Sugarcane in Western Uttar Pradesh," Indian Journal of Economics 53 (April 1973).

TABLE 8.7

Price Elasticities, Uttar Pradesh Districts, Sugar

District	Gur Price	R^2	Gur Price Minus Cane Price	R^2
Meerut	+0.123[a] (0.076)	0.86	+0.118[a] (0.059)	0.86
Mazaffarnagar	+0.358[b] (0.153)	0.66	+0.324[b] (0.142)	0.65
Bulandshahar	+0.331[a] (0.197)	0.57	+0.303[a] (0.157)	0.53
Saharanpur	+0.579[d] (0.096)	0.92	+0.523[d] (0.087)	0.92
Bijnor	+0.395[d] (0.085)	0.90	+0.348[c] (0.082)	0.89
Moradabad	+0.318[a] (0.166)	0.55	+0.286[a] (0.154)	0.54
Bareilly	+0.599[d] (0.136)	0.77	+0.544[c] (0.136)	0.74
Etah	+0.852[a] (0.454)	0.50	+0.809[a] (0.437)	0.50
Shahjahanpur	+0.649[a] (0.336)	0.53	+0.548[a] (0.301)	0.51
Kheri	+0.515[b] (0.179)	0.90	+0.445[b] (0.169)	0.89
Hardoi	+0.471[a] (0.243)	0.67	+0.403[a] (0.215)	0.66

[a]10 percent significance level.
[b]5 percent significance level
[c]1 percent significance level.
[d]0.1 percent significance level.
Source: K. L. Rathod, "Farmers' Aversion to Risk—A Case of Sugarcane in Western Uttar Pradesh," Indian Journal of Economics 53 (April 1973).

factories are available only since 1931, with gur prices alone available for the earlier period, and (2) a complete enumeration (as opposed to sampling of production) began only in 1949. For these reasons, and in an attempt to identify other institutional factors affecting possible changes in peasant responsiveness, Jha separately analyzed the periods 1912 to 1964, 1933 to 1964, 1950 to 1964, 1912 to 1932, and 1933 to 1949.

Parameter estimates were obtained using a Nerlovian model with acreage expressed as a function of relative prices (thus ignoring the distinction between newly planted and rattooned sugar acreage), acreages and yields, acreage in the competing crop (wheat), a weather index, a time-trend variable, and a dummy variable to account for the change in the acreage estimation method in 1949. Regressions were run using both sugarcane and gur prices (relative to wheat).

In each regression relative prices were significant at the 10 percent level or better with the notable exception of the earliest subperiod, 1912 to 1932. Jha suggested that the significance of both gur and sugarcane prices since 1932 could be explained in terms of a two-price phenomenon, with farmers reacting both to the floor provided by the announced minimum prices paid by the factories for cane and to the free market prices for gur.* When expected prices for the latter are higher than the former, sugar acreage is expanded, though undoubtedly not beyond a margin of safety regarding overall marketing potentialities. The calculations reveal acreage adjustment coefficients significantly different from unity in most cases, and a notable influence of weather on acreage, but the effects of wheat acreages and lagged sugar yields seem significant only in the earliest (1912 to 1932) and latest (1950 to 1964) periods, respectively. Selected calculated parameters are shown in Table 8.8.

An obvious tendency toward greater responsiveness to price incentives and a more rapid period of adjustment to price changes can be seen in more recent years, while Jha pointed out that an apparent "leveling-out" of long-run supply elasticity as less than unity† offered the hope that farmer responsiveness to prices will not lead to glut problems.

In a later paper Jha together with C. C. Maji analyzed the same northern Bihar sugar data with a view to determining whether the sugar market displays stable or unstable equilibrium conditions.[4] To this end they postulated a simple cobweb model with linear supply and demand equations and also a dynamic model with a Nerlovian area adjustment-type supply equation. Ordinary least-squares

---

*Comparable to Rathod's hypothesis above, though Jha likewise did not test a model containing both market and minimum prices as separate variables.

†This is in contrast to Nowshirvani's calculations for long-run elasticity during approximately the same period—a value of about 1.4; see above in this chapter.

TABLE 8.8

Estimated Parameters, Tirkut (Bihar) Sugar

Period	Model	Relative Prices	Elasticity		Adjustment Coefficient	R^2
			Short-Run	Long-Run		
1912-64	Gur Prices	50.77[b]	0.23	0.55	0.14[b]	0.89
1933-64	Gur Prices	81.72[b]	0.27	0.40	0.68[b]	0.66
	Cane Prices	1066.4[b]	0.35	0.44	0.79[b]	0.71
1950-64	Gur Prices	209.5[a]	0.64	18.6	0.02	0.73
	Cane Prices	2180.6[b]	0.65	0.79	0.83[b]	0.84
1912-32	Gur Prices	-1.93	neg.	−	0.99[b]	0.71
1933-49	Gur Prices	74.48[b]	0.26	−	0.93[b]	0.72
	Cane Prices	768.1[a]	0.28	−	0.91[b]	0.66

[a]5 percent significance level.
[b]1 percent significance level.
Source: Dayanatha Jha, "Acreage Response of Sugarcane in Factory Areas of North Bihar," Indian Journal of Agricultural Economics 25 (January-March 1970).

regression techniques were applied to estimate the parameters of both versions. Combining these with their estimated demand parameters, the authors found evidence for convergence, given relatively stable demand. The evidence came not only from the cobweb formulation, but also from the area adjustment coefficient (0.731), which indicates a nearly complete cultivator adjustment in less than two and a half years.

Two studies already seen provide supply estimates for Punjabi sugar. Raj Krishna expressed sugar acreage in terms of one- and two-year lagged relative prices and lagged acreage, regressing on data from 1915 to 1943.[5] His parameter estimates (and standard errors) are seen in Table 8.9.

To output data from post-World War II Punjab and Madhya Pradesh Jawahar Kaul applied a Nerlovian model obtaining the estimates shown in Table 8.10.[6] Kaul's formation included two-year lagged wholesale prices of sugar deflated by an index of agricultural commodity prices, lagged yield and acreage, and a trend variable.

For a south Indian state, Andhra Pradesh, K. Subbarao has analyzed sugar production during the period 1952 to 1965.[7] Andhra ranks fourth among Indian states as regards sugar output, and over 90 percent of her production is concentrated in 8 districts (Srikakulam, Visakhapatnam, East and West Godavari, Krishna, Chittoor, Nizamabad, and Medak), which also account for about 60 percent of the state's rice acreage.

Subbarao used a number of models, some Nerlovian, some not; all were framed in relative terms, weighing sugar versus rice

TABLE 8.9

Estimated Parameters, Punjabi Sugar

| | | Coefficients | Elasticity | |
			Short-Run	Long-Run
Prices	t-1	$+0.72^a$	$+0.17$	$+0.30$
		(0.49)		
	t-2	$+1.45^c$	$+0.34$	$+0.60$
		(0.38)		
Lagged Area		$+0.44^b$	–	–
		(0.20)		
R^2		0.79		

[a] 20 percent significance level.
[b] 5 percent significance level.
[c] 1 percent significance level.
Source: Raj Krishna, "Farm Supply Response in India–Pakistan: A Case Study of the Punjab Region," Economic Journal 73 (September 1963).

TABLE 8.10

Estimated Parameters, Punjab and Madhya Pradesh Sugar, 1951-64

| | Price Coefficient | Elasticity | | Area Adjustment Coefficient | R^2 |
		Short-Run	Long-Run		
Punjab	$+ 2.79$	0.09	$+0.73$	0.13	0.80
	(7.62)				
Madhya Pradesh	$+36.21^*$	0.84	0.88	0.95	0.83
	(11.52)				

[*] 1 percent significance level.
Source: Jawahar Kaul, "A Study of Supply Response to Price of Punjab Crops," Indian Journal of Economics 48 (July 1967).

cultivation. Relative production, expressed as acreage, tonnage, and yield is variously regressed on lagged (one- and two-year relative prices—separate figures for newly planted and rattooned sugar acreages were not available), lagged relative acreages, yields, and gross income per acre of sugarcane. The "best fit" was indicated for two relative acreage formulations.

Subbarao referred to Michael Lipton's suggestion that farmers responding favorably to positive changes in last year's prices (and vice-versa) may not be reacting "rationally."[8] If it is observed that last year's price does not efficiently predict this year's direction of the change in price, then even if farmer acreage response to lagged price is in the same direction, it cannot be assumed such response is economically rational. Subbarao attempted to test for rationality by regressing current relative prices on lagged one- and two-year relative prices. Significant positive (for one-year lagged price) and negative (for two-year lagged price) coefficients were indicated, and he offered this as evidence of rational farmer response to last year's price.

Though no specific elasticity estimates were offered, Subbarao indicated the value of short-run supply elasticity to be at least 0.50.

V. Rajagopalan's study of agriculture in Madras (Tamil Nadu) state included an analysis of sugar, a relatively minor crop that accounts for only about 1 percent of the state's cultivated area.[9] Sugar is found in all three regions of the state: the northeastern coast, the interior districts, and the southeastern coast.

Three variations of the basic Nerlovian model were used to estimate supply parameters for sugar output between 1939 and 1961—acreage expressed as a function of: (A) lagged sugar prices deflated by those of the principal substitute crop (rice), lagged (one- and two-year) acreage, and a trend variable; (B) lagged deflated prices, lagged (one-year) acreage, and a trend variable; and (C) lagged sugar prices, lagged substitute crop prices, lagged (one-year) area, lagged yield, and a trend variable.

Rajagopalan's analysis found stronger and more consistent evidence for a significant role of prices in influencing sugar output than it did for any of the other crops he considered. Only in the southeast, the least important sugar region of the state, is little statistical significance indicated for the price parameter estimates. Short-run elasticity estimates he presented were +0.68 and +0.74 for the northeast and interior regions, respectively, while cross-elasticities (with respect to rice prices) in the two regions were −1.06 and −0.99.

Another multicrop study, that of M. C. Madhavan, also included an analysis of Madras sugar output.[10] His model expressed acreage as a function of lagged sugar prices deflated by the price of a major

competing crop, the lagged yields of both sugar and the competing
crop, the lagged acreage in sugar and the competing crop, and a
rainfall index. The competing crops were included one at a time,
not in any weighted fashion; thus, separate regressions were run
for three alternate crop formulations: sugar relative to rice, ragi,
and groundnuts. Price elasticities and sugar area adjustment
coefficients are listed in Table 8.11.

    Like Rajagopalan, Madhavan remarked on the apparently greater
price responsiveness of sugar acreage than that of other crops in
Madras. Madhavan attributed the high elasticities and rapid area
adjustment to the behavior of more prosperous landowners who
produce mainly for the market, since much of the sugar crop is
produced on largeholdings.

    A third Indian study of several crops to present parameter
estimates for sugar was that of A. Parikh.[11] He used four different
supply models in examining the period 1900 to 1939; sugar acreage
was expressed variously as a function of: (A) lagged sugar prices
deflated by those of alternate crops and lagged sugar acreage; (B)
lagged deflated prices, lagged sugar yield, and lagged acreage
(one- and two-periods); (C) lagged deflated prices, yield, and
acreage; and (D) lagged deflated prices, yield, and acreage, and
rainfall at sowing time. To account for sugar's longer maturing
period, both one- and two-year lagged prices were incorporated
into the models, though only the latter showed any statistical
significance in Punjab and Uttar Pradesh, as can be seen from the
parameters in Table 8.12. Only last year's prices were significant
in Madras, however.

TABLE 8.11

Supply Elasticities, Madras Sugar

| Competing | Elasticity | | Area Adjustment |
Crops	Short-Run	Long-Run	Coefficient
Rice	+0.62	+0.66	0.94
Ragi	+0.52	+1.21	0.43
Groundnuts	+0.63	+0.76	0.83

Source: M. C. Madhavan, "Acreage Response of Indian Farmers:
A Case Study of Tamil Nadu," Indian Journal of Agricultural
Economics 27 (January-March 1972).

TABLE 8.12

Estimated Parameters, Indian Sugar

State	Model	Price Coefficient		Elasticities		Lagged Acreage		Adjustment	R^2
		t - 1	t - 2	Short-Run	Long-Run	t - 1	t - 2	Coefficient	
Madras	A	+4.90[a]	–	+0.30[c]	+1.51	+0.81[a]	–	+0.20	0.86
	B	+6.54[a]	–	+0.39[c]	+1.08	+1.20[a]	-0.57[a]	+0.37	0.81
Punjab	C	–	+3.04[b]	+0.57[c]	+1.36	+0.62[a]	–	0.38	0.34
Uttar	A	-18.29	+154.5[a]	+6.50[c]	+7.19	+0.94[a]	–	0.06	0.75
Pradesh	B	-34.66	+121.3[a]	n.q.	n.q.	+0.56[a]	–	0.44	0.83
	D	-43.02	+122.3[a]	+0.40[c]	+0.91	+0.56[a]	–	0.44	0.83

n.q. = Value not quoted.
[a]10 percent significance level.
[b]5 percent significance level.
[c]Two-year lag.

Source: A. Parikh, "Farm Supply Response: A Distributed Lag Analysis," Oxford Institute of Statistics Bulletin 33 (1971).

Parikh explained the discrepancy in the price parameters between Madras and the other states in terms of the data used. Harvest-time prices paid to producers were available for the Punjab and for Uttar Pradesh, while average producer prices for the previous calendar year were used in Madras—that is, for Madras, one-year lagged prices were actually more like "one-and-one-half-year" lagged prices, and thus were a realistic measure of price influence on a crop that takes about one year to mature.

Still one more study to provide some supply parameter estimates for sugar supply in several Indian states was published by Y. Satyanarayana, who was interested in determining the influence on output of several institutional and market factors.[12] He tested several linear formulations expressing sugar acreage as a function of the refining capacity of sugar factories, current cane prices deflated by the lagged price of the major competing crop, lagged gur price deflated by competing crop price, and relative sugar to competing crop yield. The competing crop included was cotton for Maharashtra, wheat for Punjab and Uttar Pradesh, and rice for Madras, Mysore, Bihar, Andhra Pradesh, and India as a whole. Regressions were run for the period 1950 to 1962.

He found that only the refining capacity parameter showed consistent statistical significance; in Bihar alone did prices seem to exert much influence on output. The price responsiveness of sugar cultivators, if generally positive, appears to be quite small.

Hossein Askari undertook a study of sugar output in a country, the Philippines, that is unique among the major producing nations because of the republic's long history as a political dependency of the United States.[13] Early Filipino sugar production was geared to the metropolitan power's needs long before the 1953 international

marketing agreement between sugar producers and consumers. The
Philippines early secured a quota in U.S. sugar purchases, and
independence in 1946 brought an agreement to continue for Filipino
sugar certain preferences in the U.S. market through 1973 (though
no impartial observer would suggest that U.S. concessions in this
matter involved generosity—the Philippines in return granted U.S.
industry overwhelming advantages in their domestic market).

Askari began with Swerling's suggestion that sugar is not very
price responsive, at least insofar as decreases in price are concerned.[14] Swerling argued that this tendency was likely to be true
because of the high degree of regional specialization in sugar which
implies a local lack of alternative income sources, and any changes
in this regard are likely to be very slow. He also cited the high
fixed costs in both the cultivating and milling operations, with the
highly flexible variable costs, particularly that of labor, being
generally pegged to sugar prices. His arguments, Askari contended,
strongly advised an empirical study to determine actual supply
response.

Askari suggested that certain features are desirable in any
model purporting to represent Filipino sugar production. First,
a test for any asymmetry in supply response alternatively to positive
and negative price changes would help evaluate Swerling's arguments.
Second, since yield fluctuates both with respect to area planted and
to output, it seems desirable to use output rather than acreage
as a dependent variable, though such a formulation is quite likely
to result in a high coefficient for the yield variable. To bypass
this problem he used a model omitting yield and another including
it as an independent variable. Third, the quota for the U.S. market
allocated to Filipino sugar producers was considered in the model
as an independent variable. Fourth, crude storage figures could
be used to test the response of both output and storage to price
changes. Fifth, since cane cuttings can vary from a period of one
to two years, price expectations should be phrased in terms of both
one and two periods. Sixth, since it is possible that changes in
the sizes of production units may effect output, either a time-trend
variable should be included or else the period to be examined should
be subdivided and possible change in parameter values checked.
Seventh, an independent look at the practice of rattooning might be
gained from a test exploring the possibility of autocorrelation in the
residuals. Finally, Askari suggested a complex model appropriate
for a consideration of rattooning though data limitations prohibited
using the model to obtain parameter estimates.

The basic model he put forward was a modified Nerlovian type:

$$A_t^D = a_o + D_1 a_1 P_t^e + D_2 a_2 P_t^e + a_3 Y_t + a_4 W_t + U_t \qquad (8.2a)$$

$$P^e_t - P^e_{t-1} = \beta(P_{t-1} - P^e_{t-1})$$
(8.2b)

$$A_t - A_{t-1} = \gamma (A^D_t - A_{t-1})$$
(8.2c)

where: P_t is actual relative price,

P^e_t is expected relative price,

Y_t is actual yield per acre,
W_t is weather index,

$$D_1 = \begin{cases} 0 \text{ if } P_{t-1} - P_{t-2} > 0 \\ 1 \text{ if } P_{t-1} - P_{t-2} < 0 \text{ and} \end{cases}$$

$$D_2 = \begin{cases} 0 \text{ if } P_{t-1} - P_{t-2} < 0 \\ 1 \text{ if } P_{t-1} - P_{t-2} > 0 \end{cases}$$

The estimating equation, a reduced form of this model, represented sugar acreage as a function of lagged (one- and two-period) relative (to rice) prices and acreage, and current and lagged (one-period) yield and weather index.

An alternative supply model recognized the long maturing period of sugar, replacing the one-year lags in price and acreage in equations 8.2b and 8.2c with two-year lags, with corresponding modifications in the values of D_1 and D_2.

Askari termed both of these models inexact, but held that a more meaningful model could not be estimated due to a lack of data, inasmuch as no disaggregated data on total new plantings and on area already planted in cane (rattooned acreage) was available. The only data that are available enumerate sugar output and total acreage under cane. Thus he had a measure of cane acreages aggregated over different ages; and this he felt was clearly not the proper measure of the farmer response. The model did not recognize the fact that cane of different ages has different yields; rather it assumed an invariant average yield per acre.

Essentially the market response of cultivators takes two forms. First, the farmer responds to price changes by adjusting total area under cane. And second, the farmer responds to price changes by changing (at the margin) the age composition of the cane. In the above models the first type of adjustment is taken into account, but the second type is not incorporated into the model. As a result the model underestimates the actual price response of farmers.

Askari utilized nonlinear estimating methods to obtain the supply parameters of the above models (and several variations thereof). His conclusions included a judgment that the normal

Nerlovian price expectation equation did not yield satisfactory results and that an equation of the form:

$$P^e = P_{t-1} + \beta(P_{t-1} - P_{t-2}) \qquad\qquad (8.2d)$$

performed much better. He also found that farmers <u>did</u> respond to price incentives in one or both of two ways—changing area devoted to cane and/or changing cane yield per acre, with indications that the former type of response is the greater.

Furthermore, cultivator price responsiveness seemed to involve comparison between sugar and rice returns. Government policy confirmed this behavior pattern: Rice prices have been artificially kept low precisely to promote sugar production.

Askari also interpreted his results to indicate that many notable structural changes have occurred in the production of sugar in the Philippines—the main cause of which seems to be the numerous shifts in legislation. The supply response has increased in the last 20 years, with short-run elasticities jumping from 0.078 to 0.127 and long-run elasticities from 0.127 to 0.163.

Finally, Askari indicated that changes in the age profile of cane plants were quite small during the period of his study; as a rule, farmers continued to plow up and replant cane after three or four harvests. This lack of change was one of the reasons that he felt yield showed little price responsiveness.

NOTES

1. Vahid Nowshirvani, "Agricultural Supply in India: Some Theoretical and Empirical Studies" (Ph.D. dissertation, Massachusetts Institute of Technology, 1962).

2. K. L. Rathod, "Farmers' Aversion to Risk—A Case of Sugarcane in Western Uttar Pradesh," Indian Journal of Economics 53 (April 1973).

3. Dayanatha Jha, "Acreage Response of Sugarcane in Factory Areas of North Bihar," Indian Journal of Agricultural Economics 25 (January-March 1970). See also Dayanatha Jha and C. C. Maji, "Cobweb Phenomenon and Fluctuations in Sugarcane Acreage in North Bihar," a paper read at the 31st Annual Conference of the Indian Society of Agricultural Economics and abstracted in the Indian Journal of Agricultural Economics 26 (October-December 1971).

4. Jha and Maji, op. cit.

5. Raj Krishna, "Farm Supply Response in India-Pakistan: A Case Study of the Punjab Region," Economic Journal 73 (September 1963).

6. Jawahar Kaul, "A Study of Supply Response to Price of Punjab Crops," Indian Journal of Economics 48 (July 1967).

7. K. Subbarao, "Farm Supply Response—A Case Study of Sugarcane in Andhra Pradesh," Indian Journal of Agricultural Economics 24 (January-March 1969).

8. Michael J. Lipton, "Should Reasonable Farmers Respond to Price Changes?" Modern Asian Studies 1, part I (January 1967). Lipton reviews The Impact of Price Movements on Areas under Selected Crops in India, 1900-1939 by Dharm Narain (Cambridge: Cambridge University Press, 1965) and stresses that Narain, like many economic theorists, provides evidence that peasants respond positively to positive price changes, but ignores the fact that cultivators do not seem to learn the lesson that positive price changes are poor indicators (Lipton maintains) of future price movements. He uses Narain's data to prove his point: in 19 out of 34 years cotton price changes in t - 1 were in the opposite direction to changes in t. Economic rationality, Lipton holds, is a matter of profit maximization, and knee-jerk reactions to price changes are a poor road to improved profits. However, the Nerlove adaptive expectation model should take care of Lipton's hypothesis.

9. V. Rajagopalan, "Supply Response for Irrigated Crops in Madras State" (Ph.D. dissertation, University of Tennessee, 1967).

10. M. C. Madhavan, "Acreage Response of Indian Farmers: A Case Study of Tamil Nadu," Indian Journal of Agricultural Economics 27 (January-March 1972).

11. A. Parikh, "Farm Supply Response: A Distributed Lag Analysis," Oxford Institute of Statistics Bulletin 33 (1971).

12. V. Satyanarayana, "Factors Affecting Acreage under Sugarcane in India," Indian Journal of Agricultural Economics 22 (April-June 1967).

13. Hossein Askari, "Two Empirical Papers in Economic Development and International Trade" (Ph.D. dissertation, Massachusetts Institute of Technology, 1970).

14. B. C. Swerling, International Control of Sugar (Stanford, Calif.: Stanford University Press, 1949).

Far more complex than sugar are livestock and related products, and their analyzers have employed a wide variety of tools to help in identifying the determinants of supply. The most common approach has been to employ some form of capital stock model embodying a Nerlove adjustment mechanism. Most have also incorporated a price expectations formulation into their supply models, with expectations often incorporating recent prices as well as those of some past period (or several periods) determined by lag between adjustment decisions and the first output from stock resulting from those decisions. Some livestock products like wool, milk, and other dairy products are similar to perennials with their multiple bearing seasons, while others, like meat, have only a single "harvest." Even the self-perpetuating nature of the livestock is not unique—this replacement process is controlled by agriculturists—who, as in the case of perennials, can decide to plant or not plant the seeds or cuttings which they produce.

The first of several livestock-related agricultural commodities whose supply has been analyzed through adaptation of the dynamic Nerlove model to be considered here is milk. It shares a number of similarities with perennial crops: a relatively long maturing period, several years of production per unit, capital stock considerations on the part of cultivators, and so on. Of course a number of obvious differences between livestock products and crops are also relevant in any consideration of supply. The numerous methods used by researchers to incorporate livestock-related factors into the basic supply model can be seen in this and the following sections.

In a work published just prior to Nerlove's original paper, Harlow W. Halvorson reported on the U.S. milk industry and presented a short-run supply analysis using a simple model, which in

later work he amplified by inclusion of a Nerlove approach as well.[1]
Halvorson began by recounting a number of reasons for anticipating
that the supply responsiveness of U.S. dairy farmers would not be
too strong, at least in the short run. In much of the area where
milk is produced not only are there heavy fixed capital requirements,
but the availability of alternative agricultural opportunities, particularly for the labor supply, is often quite limited. The institutional
and economic framework in which production takes place puts a
premium on stability of output; such factors as health requirements
and pricing and marketing arrangements tend to penalize the variable
producer in the marketplace. Beyond the economics of the dairy
industry the physiology of the cows themselves impose a certain
pattern on output. After a cow's first calving, lactation follows a
fairly regular profile of temporary increase leading to a gradual
decrease.

While recalling a number of reasons that explain mostly the
slow, if steady, long-run growth (about 2 percent a year) during
the period of concern, Halvorson restricted his analysis to short-
term fluctuations in output, defining the short term as an interval
less than is necessary to alter substantially the herd size. In this
framework several means for producers to alter output in response
to price incentives are possible, but again Halvorson felt a consideration of the basic facts of the dairy industry portended responses of
small magnitude.

For example, the most immediate possible response to price
change would be alteration of the marketed proportion of milk output.
But he argued that the unmarketed share is primarily dependent on
deeply ingrained agricultural circumstances (such as the number
of calves) unlikely to be affected by transient price changes. Another
alternative would be to change the quality and/or quantity of the feed
given to the herd, but variations in output are likely to be rather
small within the range of likely shifts in feed. Short-run changes
in milk production are also possible as a result of alterations in
the breeding and culling patterns.

Halvorson's analysis involved regressions designed to trace
the effects of prices on feeding rates and of feed changes on output,
as well as those of prices on output per cow. The results of the
latter are shown in Table 9.1 for the period 1931 to 1954 (along
with the standard errors). These parameter estimates were derived
from a logarithmic formulation of a supply equation expressing output
per cow as a function of the milk-to-feed price ratio in the three-
month period preceding the season in question, hay production in
the preceding summer, and the size of the dairy herd. Obviously,
winter output elasticities are both larger and more statistically
significant than their summer counterparts, a difference Halvorson

TABLE 9.1

Short-Run Supply Elasticities, U.S. Milk

Region	Summer Season		Winter Season	
	Price Elasticity	R^2	Price Elasticity	R^2
United States	+0.029 (0.036)	0.56	+0.135[c] (0.045)	0.64
North Atlantic	+0.086 (0.057)	0.25	+0.212[c] (0.051)	0.73
East North Central	+0.032 (0.033)	0.42	+0.097[a] (0.051)	0.37
West North Central	+0.053[a] (0.028)	0.60	+0.109[b] (0.043)	0.60
South Atlantic	-0.006 (0.049)	0.34	+0.220[c] (0.054)	0.64
South Central	+0.059 (0.040)	0.73	+0.193[c] (0.055)	0.70
West	+0.029 (0.040)	0.26	+0.182[c] (0.066)	0.41

[a]10 percent significance level.
[b]5 percent significance level.
[c]1 percent significance level.
Source: Harlow W. Halvorson, "The Supply Elasticity of Milk in the Short-Run," Journal of Farm Economics 37 (December 1955).

theorized might be due to shifts in the average level of feeding between the two seasons.

Halvorson also attempted to discover whether producers were more responsive to price increases than to decreases by regressing grain fed to cows per pound of milk on the milk-to-feed price ratio, using price series made up separately of years when price increased or declined. The elasticity estimates are shown in Table 9.2 for the data of the combined East and West North Central regions only and confirm a tendency toward greater responsiveness to price increases.

In a later paper Halvorson applied a number of Nerlovian-type formulations to aggregate U.S. milk output.[2] Total milk output was expressed as a function of lagged milk prices (deflated by an index of prices received by farmers), a trend variable, and, successively, lagged milk output, the supply of hay and feed concentrates, and

TABLE 9.2

Feed Elasticities to Price for Milk

Price	Summer Season		Winter Season	
Change	Elasticity	R^2	Elasticity	R^2
Increase	+0.411	0.73	+0.611*	0.87
	(0.947)		(0.088)	
Decrease	+0.023	0.04	+0.468*	0.89
	(0.340)		(0.068)	

*1 percent significance level.
Source: Harlow W. Halvorson, "The Supply Elasticity of Milk in the Short-Run," Journal of Farm Economics 37 (December 1955).

beef and hog prices (both deflated) in the same manner as milk. Regressions were run separately for the periods 1927 to 1957 and 1941 to 1957 in an attempt to identify any effects on the milk industry of New Deal agricultural stabilization programs. The resulting estimated coefficients are shown in Table 9.3 (along with the t statistics).

For both periods the Nerlove formulations explain more of output variation than the static models. Though the period from 1927 to 1940 was too short to permit meaningful statistical analysis, particularly in view of the preponderance of Depression data, a notable difference in price elasticities and output adjustment coefficient is apparent for the later time period. Producers, Halvorson argued, became more price responsive and quicker at adjusting output as the stabilization programs of the 1930s took root. Beef prices also seemed to have gained in importance.

Using the aggregate U.S. data and the Nerlove formulation, Halvorson tested further his earlier hypothesis about differentiated producer reactions to rising and falling milk prices. Three of the above Nerlove formulations were tested—output as a function of (1) lagged prices and output and a trend variable, then adding cumulatively; (2) hay supply; (3) concentrates supply; and (4) beef prices. Output elasticities estimated with respect to rising and falling prices are shown in Table 9.4. As can be seen, the earlier evidence found for greater responsiveness to rising prices was not confirmed when the more sophisticated Nerlove models were used. Though the differences in short-run elasticities for the two subperiods were not statistically significant, the indications are in fact contrary to the earlier results—somewhat larger elasticities when prices are

TABLE 9.3

Supply Parameters, U.S. Milk

Period	Lagged Milk Prices	Time Trend	Lagged Output	Current Hay Supply	Supply of Concentrates	Beef Prices	Hog Prices	Price Elasticity Short-Run	Price Elasticity Long-Run	R^2
1927 to 1957	0.045b (4.62)	10.051b (202.4)	—	—	—	—	—	0.185	—	0.89
	0.031b (4.76)	3.162b (6.58)	0.708b (36.54)	—	—	—	—	0.128	0.438	0.95
	0.040b (10.4)	2.289b (4.34)	0.624b (35.6)	0.118b (10.2)	—	—	—	0.165	0.439	0.97
	0.038b (8.78)	2.172b (3.74)	0.606b (31.13)	0.104b (5.92)	0.017 (0.46)	—	—	0.157	0.398	0.97
	0.038b (8.42)	2.130b (2.92)	0.610b (25.83)	0.105b (5.65)	0.016 (0.34)	0.001 (0.007)	—	0.157	0.403	0.97
	0.038b (6.45)	2.130b (2.80)	0.610b (24.69)	0.105b (5.41)	0.016 (0.33)	0.001 (0.006)	-0.0004 (0.001)	0.157	0.403	0.97
1941 to 1957	0.081b (8.91)	5.417b (17.25)	—	—	—	—	—	0.304	—	0.63
	0.083b (26.42)	2.311b (5.49)	0.648b (26.31)	—	—	—	—	0.312	0.886	0.88
	0.077b (26.55)	1.561a (2.65)	0.466b (10.43)	0.175b (4.13)	—	—	—	0.289	0.541	0.91
	0.076b (24.18)	1.263 (1.26)	0.456b (9.26)	0.152a (2.41)	0.021 (0.31)	—	—	0.286	0.526	0.91
	0.049b (9.53)	2.870b (6.42)	-0.185 (0.47)	0.241b (7.99)	0.059b (3.10)	-0.060b (7.07)	—	0.184	0.155	0.95
	0.048b (7.77)	2.905b (6.42)	-0.166 (0.33)	0.230b (5.48)	0.058a (2.72)	-0.060b (6.43)	-0.004 (0.08)	0.180	0.154	0.95

a5 percent significance level; b1 percent significance level.

Source: Harlow W. Halvorson, "The Response of Milk Production to Price," Journal of Farm Economics 40 (December 1958).

falling. Halvorson concluded that the kinked supply response hypothesis, while not disproven by these results, was somewhat shaken and that further analysis in this regard was required. However it should be recalled that in his earlier paper Halvorson used feed per pound of milk as the dependent variable, while milk output served this purpose in his Nerlove analysis.

A more recent study of American milk supply was carried out by Chen, Courtney, and Schmitz.[3] They were particularly interested in identifying the pattern of past price effects on current output. They hoped to formulate a lag distribution for prices that would show greater flexibility than a Nerlove partial adjustment formulation.

They postulated that (quarterly) milk output was a function of the lagged ratio of the producer's price for milk to the average price of protein-enhanced dairy feed, technology, and a dummy

TABLE 9.4

Differentiated Response Parameters, U.S. Milk

	Formulation	Milk Prices	Lagged Output	Elasticity Short-Run	Elasticity Long-Run	R^2
Rising prices	1	0.063^b (18.3)	–	0.268	–	0.98
	2	0.031^a (2.56)	0.572^b (5.10)	0.132	0.308	0.98
	3	0.031^a (2.54)	0.580^b (5.15)	0.132	0.314	0.98
	4	0.032^a (2.45)	0.525^b (3.06)	0.136	0.286	0.98
Falling prices	1	0.049 (0.94)	–	0.197	–	0.64
	2	0.048^b (2.99)	0.894^b (26.65)	0.193	1.821	0.90
	3	0.048^b (4.81)	0.597^b (11.12)	0.193	0.479	0.94
	4	0.044^b (2.86)	0.530^b (4.73)	0.177	0.377	0.95

[a] 5 percent significance level.
[b] 1 percent significance level.
Source: Harlow W. Halvorson, "The Response of Milk Production to Price," Journal of Farm Economics 40 (December 1958).

TABLE 9.5

Supply Parameters, Californian Milk

Constant	-39.21* (4.81)	Short-run elasticity	0.38
Lagged relative prices	46.56* (4.87)	Long-run elasticity	2.54
Lagged output	0.85* (30.7)	Adjustment coefficient	0.15
Seasonal dummy	7.64* (6.59)	R^2	0.93

*1 percent significance level.
Source: Dean Chen, Richard Courtney, and Andrew Schmitz, "A Polynomial Lag Formulation of Milk Production Response," American Journal of Agricultural Economics 54 (February 1972).

variable standing for the particular quarter and compared this with a Nerlove model that omitted technology and included lagged output. Technology was represented alternatively in terms of a trend variable and an index of farm labor productivity; the seasonal dummy was set equal to zero for the first and fourth quarters and equal to unity in the second and third quarters. Regressions were run on quarterly output data for California between 1953 and 1968 and the estimated parameters for the Nerlove model are listed in Table 9.5 (along with the t statistics).

The authors determined upon a second-order polynomial to represent prices in their distributed lag formulation. The lagged weights attached to prices over the range t = 0 to t = k then were represented as:

$$\beta_t = \alpha_0 + \alpha_1 t + \alpha_2 t^2 \tag{9.1}$$

with the restriction that for t = k, $\beta_k = 0$, thus:

$$\alpha_0 + \alpha_1 k + \alpha_2 k^2 = 0 \tag{9.2}$$

Solving for α_0 and substituting in equation 9.1

$$\beta_t = -\alpha_1 k - \alpha_2 k^2 + \alpha_1 t + \alpha_2 t^2$$

$$= \alpha_1(t - k) + \alpha_2(t^2 - k^2) \tag{9.3}$$

From what was said above, we can represent output as:

$$Q_t = a + b \sum_{t=0}^{k} (\alpha_0 + \alpha_1 t + \alpha_2 t^2) P_{T-t} + cZ + dS \qquad (9.4)$$

where: Q is quarterly output,
         Z is the technology variable, and
         S is the seasonal dummy,
or, from equation 9.3

$$Q_t = a + b_1 \sum_{t=0}^{k} (t - k) P_{T-t} + b_2 \sum_{t=0}^{k} (t_2 - k^2) P_{T-t} + cZ + dS \qquad (9.5)$$

The authors presented parameter estimates for lags from five to
nine periods long and for formulations alternatively including each
of the two suggested technology variables, as well as omitting
technology considerations altogether. The seasonal dummy parameter was consistently significant at the 5 percent level or better,
and each technology measure was similarly significant in all
regressions conducted. However price coefficient estimates showed
significance only in the formulation that omitted technology. Although
the coefficients of determination were marginally higher when technology was included, the authors felt there was no strong basis to
prefer one specification over another.

To compare the Nerlove results with those using the distributed
lag analysis they chose the estimates from the regression run for
k = 8 with technology omitted; the computed price coefficients for
all the periods together with the corresponding elasticities (and
t values) are shown in Table 9.6. As can be seen, maximum price
effect is reached after three periods. The cumulative elasticity
for all eight periods is 2.53, almost identical to the long-run
elasticity calculated from the Nerlove formulation.

Despite the coincidence of total or long-run supply response
using the two models, the authors maintained that the distributed
lag representation gives a more accurate picture of the immediate
and medium-term price effects than does the geometrically declining
lag profile coming from the Nerlove model—that is, weights of 0.38
for prices in period t, 0.38 × 0.85 (the lagged output coefficient)
for period t - 1, 0.38 × (0.85)^2 for period t - 2, and so on. The
value of the distributed lag approach is enhanced, they argued,
when a quarterly supply analysis is desired.

A recent paper by Anthony Prato presented an analysis of
U.S. milk supply using a multiequation model of the dairy sector

TABLE 9.6

Distributed Lag Price Coefficients, U.S. Milk

Period	Price Coefficient	Price Elasticity
t	18.75 (0.83)	0.16
t − 1	34.03* (3.14)	0.29
t − 2	44.27* (15.3)	0.38
t − 3	49.48* (8.06)	0.42
t − 4	49.65* (4.80)	0.42
t − 5	44.79* (3.94)	0.38
t − 6	34.89* (3.52)	0.30
t − 7	19.96* (3.12)	0.17

*1 percent significance level.

Source: Dean Chen, Richard Courtney, and Andrew Schmitz, A Polynomial Lag Formulation of Milk Production Response," American Journal of Agricultural Economics 54 (February 1972).

and two-stage least-squares estimating techniques.[4] Though his approach is far more complex than either the Nerlove or distributed lag formulations, Prato's price response results are mentioned here for comparison purposes only.

Equations with size of the milk herd and yield per cow as the dependent variable and including deflated prices received by producers for processed milk resulted in very small elasticities not significantly different from zero for the period 1958 to 1968.

A number of milk-supply studies have concerned Great Britain, beginning with T. W. Gardner's analysis of output in England and Wales between 1947 and 1958.[5] Dairy cattle compete only with other grazing livestock in much of the west of Britain, but elsewhere the relationship between alternative activities is more complex. Cattle may, for example, directly compete with cereal, root, and

other crops, or they may fill a complementary role for the farmer
by consuming arable residues (though other livestock might also
serve as such complements). Gardner thus used relative prices—
milk deflated by a weighted measure for cereals, roots, fat cattle,
lambs, and pigs—with allowance for regional differences—in a
Nerlove partial adjustment model including, besides prices, only
lagged milk output. Both ordinary least-squares and maximum
likelihood estimating techniques were applied to the model. The
former method yielded mostly negative price coefficient estimates,
few of which showed any statistical significance, while the maximum
likelihood estimates are generally positive, with smaller adjustment
coefficients. Short- and long-run price elasticities derived from
the maximum likelihood estimates are listed in Table 9.7.

Gardner commented that no clear pattern emerged from his
analysis and this together with the sparse statistical significance
for his calculated parameters made him reluctant to make any
elaborate conclusions. He suggested that future investigations into
producer responsiveness might be able to make a more sophisticated
specification of the supply relationship as the passage of time eased
the data problems he encountered. Later analyses, he felt, should
be made on a county basis.

Until such more extensive data would be available, Gardner
suggested an inspection of available county figures for signs of any
relevant tendencies, and to this end he differentiated the milk-
producing counties as to the role the dairy industry plays in each.
Nineteen mostly western counties have more than two-thirds of
their areas in permanent grasslands, while 15 eastern counties have
less than half. Generally, in the former areas more than half the
farmers are registered milk producers who produce 90 gallons or
more of milk per acre of grassland, and in the latter less than
30 percent, producing less than 50 gallons per acre. As a rough
measure of price responsiveness he noted that between 1955 and
1958, when relative milk prices were falling, the number of
registered milk producers fell by 7 percent in the western counties,
but by 14 percent in the eastern ones, while in both regions the
average size of the remaining herds had risen, as had (slightly)
the overall size of the national herd.

Gardner interpreted this to indicate greater (positive) responsiveness on the part of the (eastern) farmers to whom dairy interests
were only marginal or who have more alternative activities to
attract them, while larger dairy producers (in the West) have low
(or even negative) supply elasticities. This he concluded implied
that if price incentives are to be used to deter milk production,
the reduction in relative price must needs be sufficiently sharp to
cause a drop in the number of producers large enough to offset

TABLE 9.7

Milk Supply Elasticities

| | Elasticity | |
Region	Short-Run	Long-Run
England and Wales	0.13	1.42
North	0.09	0.72
North West	-0.13	-0.33
East	0.31	2.95
East Midland	0.33	11.78
West Midland	0.01	0.03
North Wales	0.26	–
South Wales	-0.68	-1.11
Far West	0.92	–
Mid West	-0.05	-0.53
South	0.09	1.14
South East	0.17	2.34

Source: T. W. Gardner, "The Farm Price and Supply of Milk,"
Journal of Agricultural Economics 15 (May 1962).

the tendency among the remaining producers to increase herd size
and milk yield per cow.

In a recent paper Gardner together with Rosemary Walker
presented estimates of supply parameters for the period 1957 to
1969.[6] They considered that the supply of milk and other dairy
products depended not solely on milk prices but also on those of
the joint product, beef. Since the animals can be processed as
meat in the form of veal, prime beef, or cull cows, the milk-supply
response to changes in the prices of any of these would be subject
to a different time lag. Thus the size of the herd was represented
as a function of a lagged weighted average price index for calves,
fat cattle, cows and milk, deflated by an index of other farm prices,
and lagged herd size. Supply parameters estimated using ordinary
least-squares techniques are listed in Table 9.8 for both linear
and logarithmic formulations.

G. T. Jones, in a discussion attached to Gardner's first
paper, argued for a model in which yield is determined in a
separate equation and which includes both consideration of feed
prices as an explanatory variable and an attempt to distinguish
between milk and beef cattle (though the British statistics do not

TABLE 9.8

Supply Parameters, U.K. Milk

Formulation	Constant	Lagged Price	Lagged Herd	Elasticity Short-Run	Long-Run	R^2
Linear	499.09	8.54[a] (2.27)	0.67[b] (4.47)	0.22	0.66	0.87
Logarithmic	1.82	0.23[a] (2.29)	0.66[b] (4.40)	0.23	0.66	0.87

[a]5 percent significance level.
[b]1 percent significance level.
[c]Figures in parentheses are t statistics.
Source: T. W. Gardner and Rosemary Walker, "Interactions of Quantity, Price and Policy: Milk and Dairy Products," Journal of Agricultural Economics 23 (May 1972).

allow such an exact differentiation). In two studies of the United Kingdom that Jones has published, these points are considered.

In Jones' first study the total number of cows was used to represent the production of milk, while the number of calves reared to maturity stood for the beef supply, though Jones admitted the almost impossibility of drawing a firm line between dairy and beef cattle.[7] (About 80 percent of British cattle are in the dairy herd, while the rest are primarily beef cattle. For Jones' estimates of the supply of beef, mutton, pork, and poultry, see later in this chapter. He also examined the wool and egg markets, also see later in this chapter.) For the period 1924 to 1958 (omitting the war years 1940-45), he applied a supply equation that represented milk production (size of dairy herd) in terms of deflated milk, beef and feed prices, and lagged herd size. In Table 9.9 the price elasticities derived from regression analysis of this supply function are listed; all estimates were significant at the 5 percent level or better. The estimated value of the herd adjustment coefficient was 0.12. Jones remarked that the difficulty in distinguishing between the dairy and beef motives of farmers is fairly obvious. The joint-product nature of milk and beef is emphasized by the significance of both price coefficients. That the influence of beef prices is somewhat more important was buttressed by regressions run using the proportion of calves reared as the dependent variable. As can be seen from Table 9.10, while milk prices have a small

TABLE 9.9

Supply Elasticities, U.K. Milk, 1924-58

Elasticity with Respect to	Short-Run	Long-Run
Milk price	0.06	0.46
Feed price	-0.07	-0.57
Cattle price	0.10	0.88

Source: G. T. Jones, "The Response of the Supply of Agricultural Products in the United Kingdom to Price and Other Factors: Including a Consideration of Distributed Lags," (Part I) Farm Economist 9 (1961).

negative effect on calf rearing, beef prices have a larger positive effect, and the short-run effects of recent calf-rearing subsidies seem to overcome the negative effects of milk prices. All coefficients save milk prices were significant at the 5 percent level or better and the adjustment coefficient was 0.31.

Jones' second study focused on the period 1955 to 1964 and most of the same agricultural commodities as his earlier work.[8] Again using a Nerlove partial adjustment model, he experimented with several different formulations and lag lengths in attempts to cope with, among other problems, the effects on producers of the

TABLE 9.10

Price Elasticities, U.K. Calf Rearing

Elasticity with Respect to	Short-Run	Long-Run
Milk prices	-0.08	-0.12
Feed prices	-0.10	-0.41
Beef prices	0.38	0.55
Calf subsidy	0.07	—

Source: G. T. Jones, "The Response of the Supply of Agricultural Products in the United Kingdom to Price and Other Factors: Including a Consideration of Distributed Lags," (Part I) Farm Economist 9 (1961).

rapid technological change, considerable inflation, and the various
market support mechanisms. Milk production was represented in
terms of herd size and both 6- and 12-month lags were used for
both prices and herd size, and the coefficient estimates are shown
in Table 9.11. Perhaps the most notable departure from Jones'
earlier results is the apparent lack of significance of cattle price
in milk supply and the shift in sign for the calculated values of this
parameter. Jones felt the most plausible result he obtained is
the last listed in Table 9.11, making this judgment in the basis
of the estimated adjustment coefficient.

Brian Hill also examined milk supply in Britain in an article
that explored the economic significance of the Nerlove adjustment
coefficient.[9] He ignored mortality as negligible, representing the
size of the herd in period t as equal to the size in the previous
period plus the replacements and minus the culls during the last
period.

Culls might be entirely dependent on cow prices (or some
relationship between these and replacement costs), or culling might
take place at the end of an animal's productive lifetime, regardless
of prices, or finally, culling might be a function of both prices and
animal age. Hill indicated that unpublished research he had conducted indicated little if any effect of prices on culling in Britain.

Replacements he represented as a function of recent culling
and a measure of product (milk and cattle) prices, and thus herd
size can be expressed in terms of lagged prices and herd size and
lagged heifers in calf for dairying, the last being his measure for
cull-induced replacements. He used three measures of price:
a milk price index, the ratio of the milk price index to that for
cattle feed, and the ratio of the milk price index to that for cattle;
and two measures of the dependent variable: the number of heifers
in calf for dairy in December, and the number of cows and heifers
in milk in June. He applied his supply model to a very short time
period (six years), which resulted in inherent limitations on the
reliability of the estimated coefficients.

The regressions on heifers in calf clearly indicated the superiority of the milk-to-fat cattle price ratio in explaining variation, and
so this price was used in all the regressions run for the total dairy
herd. Despite the small data base, as can be seen, a number of
estimated coefficients displayed some statistical significance—in
particular, the lagged herd-size coefficient, but the results for
this regression are no better than those using only a time-trend
variable. Hill estimated a short-run elasticity for dairy herd size
of about 0.1

As with Hill's analysis of cereals production outlined previously,
his attempts to find backing for a new interpretation of the adjust-

TABLE 9.11

Supply Parameter, U.K. Milk, 1955-64

Adjustment Coefficient	Short-Run Elasticities			Long-Run Elasticities		
	Milk Price	Feed Price	Cattle Price	Milk Price	Feed Price	Cattle Price
1.24[a,d] -0.60[b,d]	0.17[b]	Positive[b]	-0.04[b]	0.47	—	-0.22
0.34[a,d]	0.18[b]	-0.18[b,c]	-0.03[b]	0.27	-0.27	-0.10
1.00[b,e]	0.23[b]	-0.16[b]	-0.24[b]	—	—	—
1.00[a,e]	0.21[b]	-0.01[b]	-0.12[b]	—	—	—
0.78[a,d]	0.23[a,c]	-0.09[a]	+0.09[a]	1.05	-0.41	0.18

[a] 6-month lag.
[b] 12-month lag.
[c] 10 percent significance level.
[d] 1 percent significance level.
[e] Value fixed at unity.
Source: G. T. Jones, "The Influence of Price on Livestock Population over the Last Decade," Journal of Agricultural Economics 16 (December 1965).

ment coefficient were somewhat inconclusive, though a longer time series available in the future might yet provide the missing evidence.

Another recent study of milk supply has been presented by D. J. Buttimer and J. G. MacAirt, who studied the responsiveness of Irish farmers between 1951 and 1968.[10] A Nerlove supply model relating size of the creamery herd to lagged herd size and to milk and alternate commodity prices, as well as trend and a dummy variable representing a government subsidy scheme in effect after 1964, was tested in several variations.

Multicollinearity proved a problem, and in attempts to reduce it the time interval was cut to 1951 to 1963 so that one of the variables, the dummy, could legitimately be eliminated. (The dummy variable had proven highly significant in the original calculations involving the longer time period.) A first-differences formulation for the 1951 to 1968 was also tested.

The authors felt that the results of neither approach to the multicollinearity problem were entirely satisfactory. The degree of its presence was lessened when the linear model was applied to the shorter time period (1951 to 1963) and it was effectively eliminated

as a serious concern in the first-differences model.* But as
determinants of herd size, price coefficients did not show much
significance in either case, and only the dummy variable proved
to be highly significant consistently in the estimates based on the
first-differences model. The multicollinearity seemed largely due
to the high correlation between lagged prices (which rose fairly
steadily throughout the period) and the time trend, but the hypothesis
originally formed was strongly based on the explanatory power of
<u>both</u> variables (the trend variable standing for technological changes,
the upgrading of management practices, the desire by rural popula-
tions for a share in rising national standard of living, among other
factors, all of which were deemed likely to affect the size of the
creamery herd). Omission of one of these variables would obviously
damage the underlying economic theory.

A number of other regressions performed (not shown) indicated,
however, that if the trend variable is eliminated the price coefficient
becomes significant, and vice-versa. Inspection of the results of
these regressions indicated that in those not subject to severe
multicollinearity the estimates of both the price and trend coefficients
were consistently between +8.0 and +10.0. Even in those regressions
where multicollinearity distorted both estimates, neither varied very
far from this range. Therefore, in the belief that it was important
to distinguish between the separate effects of the two variables in
the not-unlikely event that the collinearity between them be broken
by, for example, the then-pending entry of Ireland into the Common
Market, they presented the results of three first-difference formulation regressions that seemed best to explain herd size variation and
most free of multicollinearity distortions.

In almost all the calculations the value of the time-trend coefficient proved close to 9.0, and this stability led the authors to the
conclusion that an annual increase in the size of the herd of about
9,000 cows occurs independently of prices. Price responsiveness,
they calculated, would be on the average, close to a 9,000 increase
in the herd size per one pence increase in the price of milk. The
government heifer subsidy program, on the other hand, apparently

---

*The statistic $|R|$ shown in their results was the determinant
of the matrix of correlation coefficients for the independent variables.
The closer $|R|$ is to zero, the stronger the multicollinearity. The
significance level indicated for $|R|$ refers to its assumed χ^2 distribu-
tion if the matrix of independent variables is multivariate normal
(see M. S. Bartlett, <u>British Journal of Psychological Statistics</u>,
Section 3, Vol. 83 [1950]).

has had a far stronger influence—an increase of 35,000 cows a year since the program's inception in 1964.

If price responsiveness is expressed in elasticity terms (which the authors do not do), then, using the data presented with the article, it seems to be between 0.25 and 0.30 in the short run.

Buttimer has published another paper that takes advantage of more recently available data to include in its analysis the 1960s, a period of rapid growth of the Irish cattle herd.[11] About two-thirds of the herd is kept primarily for dairy purposes, the rest being raised for beef. (For his analysis of beef supply, see later in this chapter.)

For milk supply analysis Buttimer expressed the size of the dairy herd as a function of lagged producer prices for milk and a trend variable, with lagged prices of alternative crops and commodities inserted into variants of the basic supply model. Because of a government calf subsidy paid during the period 1964 to 1968, a slope shifter variable was included in all equations tested, and another shifter was used in an attempt to identify the effects of a beef incentive system on the dairy herd. Multicollinearity was a problem, though apparently not to the same extent as in the earlier paper.

In comparing his results with those of the earlier study the author noted that while similar herd-size responses were found in both the calf subsidy, cattle price, and trend variables, the differences for the milk price coefficient left the exact magnitude of the effect of this variable in doubt.

Buttimer did not calculate elasticities, but from the data presented with his article a short-run elasticity for milk of about 0.37 is indicated for his "best" regression; using any of the other three sets of results a value of close to 0.45 is found.

In their work on the interaction in Australia between cereals and livestock, F. H. Gruen and Alan A. Powell have examined the supply of dairy products.[12] The cereal-livestock complex accounts for nearly three-fourths of the value of Australian agricultural output and the authors approached the problem of statistical analysis with the essential interdependence of the commodities of interest as a principle consideration. The production functions used for each item were of the constant elasticity of transformation (CET) type, and in most cases a Koyck-Nerlove form of price expectations was incorporated into the model. However, they attempted to make allowance for situations where prices rise too fast for farmers to believe such increases will continue in the future by incorporating a distinction between permanent and transient elements, using Friedman's terminology, in price increases, which allows for discounting of rapid changes.

Elasticity for dairy product supply was estimated with dairy
size herd expressed as a function of lagged dairy (short run 0.19
and long run 0.42), beef (-0.13), and lamb prices (-0.19), and
lagged herd size for 1947 to 1964 ($R^2 = 0.83$).

The Nerlove supply model was used by J. Taplin and P. Smallhorn to analyze a unique "crop"—honey (clearly not a "normal"
livestock product).[13] In this case supply obviously depends upon
the number of producing hives, which in any given year depends
upon the number of hives in the previous year. Honey thus has some
of the attributes of a perennial crop, but the arrival at maturity
of the basic unit of production, the hive, takes a much shorter
period of time (only one cultivating season) than for most perennials.
The honey industry is also distinguished by its long history of price
stabilization efforts, due to the ability of producers to store their
output while awaiting expected higher prices.

Though honey is a minor commodity in Australian agriculture
(only $5.5 million in 1967), the country ranks seventh in world
production and fourth in exports. About one-third of the national
total is produced in New South Wales, and about one-fifth in each
of the states of Victoria, South Australia, and Western Australia.
The similarity of bee-keeping to perennial crops is enhanced in
Australia by the ability of her apiarists to keep the bees from year
to year. By contrast, in Canada, most of the bee stock is destroyed
at the end of the producing season; since the severe winters make
it too expensive to maintain the hives, young bees must be bred
at the start of each new season.

The modern Australian honey industry is increasingly marked
by hive mobility, following the honey flow from place to place
throughout most of the year. Honey production is dominated by
relatively few apiarists (the less than 5 percent who own more than
400 hives apiece and who together produce more than half the
national output) who may move their hives eight or ten times a year.
This concentration of production and increased mobility have contributed to a more than doubling of yield (to about 120 pounds of
honey per hive) since World War II.

Supply analysis involved three separate stages. The first
postulated that the number of productive hives could be expressed
with a Nerlovian-type lagged relationship involving the past season's
number of hives and prices along with a seasonal index as independent
variables. This model was estimated for the period 1952 to 1967
for the two states, Western Australia and New South Wales, where
adequate data was available. The results are shown in Table 9.12;
in the latter state prices did not prove significant and the authors
did not report the values of their parameter estimates.

TABLE 9.12

Supply Parameters, Australian Honey

State	Lagged Price	Lagged Hive Number	Seasonal Index	Short-Run Elasticity	R^2
Western Australia	0.539[a] (0.258)	0.997 (0.084)	1.32[b] (0.15)	0.13	0.94
New South Wales	–	positive	positive	–	–

[a]5 percent significance level.
[b]1 percent significance level.
Source: J. Taplin and P. Smallhorn, "The Supply of Honey in Australia," Quarterly Review of Agricultural Economics 23 (April 1970).

They next estimated honey supply as a function of hive number, the seasonal index, and a trend variable. Most of the resulting coefficients showed some statistical significance. Finally, they considered the role inventories play in overall honey supply and regressed total sales on honey stocks, price, and a trend variable. All three parameter estimates were positive and significant at the 5 percent level or better. The coefficient for honey stocks was 0.557, indicating that on average at any time only about half the available honey had actually been sold. From the price parameter the authors calculated a supply elasticity of about 0.35. This value represents sales from stock and is almost three times the supply elasticity at the production stage indicated above for Western Australia. Most supply responsiveness, thus, originates in the always large producer-held honey inventories.

Another rather distinct type of crop whose supply has been analyzed with a Nerlove model is eggs. Jones considered British egg production in two of his papers.[14] For the period 1927 to 1939 he represented egg output (in terms of hen population) as a function of egg prices lagged six months and lagged population, as well as other variable such as feed and pork prices—hog raising being an important alternate activity. Jones also applied his model to egg output in the United States from 1927 to 1957, and the estimated parameters are shown in Table 9.13 (along with the standard errors). As can be seen, inclusion of hog prices improved the significance

TABLE 9.13

Supply Parameters, U.K. and U.S. Eggs

		United Kingdom		United States
Adjustment		0.24	0.42[a]	0.31[c]
coefficient		(0.22)	(0.21)	(0.10)
Short-run	Egg prices	0.28	0.57	0.42[c]
elasticities		(0.38)	(0.36)	(0.08)
	Feed prices	-0.26	-0.44[b]	-0.31[c]
		(0.20)	(0.20)	(0.09)
	Hog prices	–	-0.32	–
			(0.19)	
Long-run	Egg prices	1.17	1.36	1.35
elasticities	Feed prices	-1.08	-1.05	-1.35
	Hog prices	–	-0.76	–

[a]10 percent significance level.
[b]5 percent significance level.
[c]1 percent significance level.

Source: G. T. Jones, "The Response of the Supply of Agricultural Products in the United Kingdom to Price and Other Factors: Including Consideration of Distributed Lags" (Parts I and II), Farm Economist 9 and 10 (1961, 1962); and "The Influence of Price on Livestock Population over the Last Decade," Journal of Agricultural Economics 16 (December 1965).

of the British supply parameters, although egg prices are still not quite significant at the 10 percent level.

In the second paper Jones turned to postwar British output. Running fowl population over six months old on egg and feed prices, he obtained short- and long-run elasticities of 0.55 and 1.66 for egg prices, -0.14 and -0.42 for feed prices, and an adjustment coefficient of 0.33. The egg price coefficient proves somewhat more significant than in the prewar period, while feed prices are considerably less significant.

A more recent study of the British egg market was carried out by C. A. Robertson, who focused on production during a period (1954-66) when government price stabilization programs should have reduced the uncertainty producers face.[15] Eggs more resemble honey than cocoa or coffee, but all are in a definite sense perennials with capital stock considerations important in all cases. However, adjustments in the cases of both eggs and honey can obviously be

quite rapid. Robertson concentrated on the reactions of producers
to the annually announced support prices as they then adjust flock
size. He used both a simple linear model with fowl population a
function of announced price, feed price, and average yield per hen
and a flock adjustment model that added lagged flock size. Since
he used announced prices he expected to calculate a larger responsiveness than did Jones, and his regression estimates (and standard
errors) are shown in Table 9.14.

As he expected, his short-run elasticities are higher than those
calculated by Jones for the prewar (and preguaranteed price) period.
Robertson argued that these high elasticity values indicate the
wisdom of the cuts in guaranteed prices announced during the period
in question by the Ministry of Agriculture. However, the effects
of price cuts were undoubtedly counterbalanced by the continuous
technologically induced growth in egg yields.

In an investigation of price cycles in the American egg market,
David Hartman used several alternative supply models.[16] He began
by expressing dissatisfaction with the naivete of cobweb formulations
that take short-run supply curves as fixed over extended periods
and proposed that a Nerlove-type supply explanation seemed more
attractive.

Allowing for the eight or nine months it takes a chick to become
an efficiently producing layer, output was expressed in terms of egg
and feed prices lagged three quarters, a trend variable, and an
output lagged one quarter. Ordinary least-squares techniques were
applied to measure this equation (model 2), as well as a simpler
cobweb (model 1), and a more complex adaptive expectations version
(model 3). The latter involved use of a Koyck lag structure to

TABLE 9.14

Supply Parameters, U.K. Eggs

Model	Lagged Flock Size	Egg Prices	Feed Prices	Yield	R^2	Elasticity Short-Run	Elasticity Long-Run
Linear	—	2334[a] (891.0)	-194.2[a] (68.5)	829.5[b] (207.7)	0.85	1.66	—
Flock adjustment	0.37 (0.26)	2142[a] (851.5)	-181.2[a] (65.3)	623.3[a] (244.4)	0.87	1.52	2.42

[a]5 percent significance level.
[b]1 percent significance level.
Source: C. A. Robertson, "Supply Response to Price under Certainty, with
reference to the United Kingdom Egg Market, 1954 to 1966," Journal of Agricultural Economics 22 (May 1971).

express egg and feed prices. Hartman argued that the second and
third models are superior to the cobweb model in explanatory power.

He also considered the possibility of asymmetric price response,
formulating a supply equation like the second model above but
replacing the single egg price variable with two. Only one of the
latter was nonzero in a given quarter depending upon whether egg
prices had risen or declined between the fourth and third quarters
prior to that in question. His results indicated a notably greater
degree of response to increases, with the estimated parameter for
increasing prices four times that for decreasing prices.

Another commodity with certain resemblances to perennial
crops is wool, and D. L. Dahlberg has analyzed its supply in South
Australia.[17] This state's sheep-raising regions are commonly
classified as the wheat-sheep, high rainfall, and pastoral zones.
Dahlberg used a Nerlovian adjustment model to estimate supply
parameters from 1949 to 1961 in each zone but his results were
insignificant.

While he estimated a short-run elasticity for the wheat-sheep
zone of about +0.1, he argued that no long-run value could be
derived without a priori assumptions about the lag distribution,
and long-run elasticities would be far more useful to policy makers.

He also tested a number of simple models, regressing wool
supply in the wheat-sheep zone on relative wool-to-wheat and wool-
to-lamb prices, lagged one, two, and three years, on wool-to-barley
prices lagged one year, and on improved pasture acreage. But
only pasturage and one-year lagged wool-wheat and wool-lamb
prices show much consistent significance. Using model 3, a
short-run supply elasticity of +0.42 was calculated for the wool-
wheat price ratio and of -0.47 and 0.13 for one- and two-year
lagged relative wool to lamb price, implying that if wheat and lamb
prices and acreage are unchanged, the total elasticity with regard
to wool price is -0.05 over the first year and +0.08 over the first
two years.

For the high-rainfall zone wool supply was regressed on one-,
two-, and three-year lagged wool prices deflated by an index of
all competing crops and on improved pasture acreage. Only the
latter showed any statistical significance, and prices (wool alone)
showed a similar lack of effect on wool output in the pastoral zone
where only a trend variable proved important.

The rather low values of the coefficient of determination he
calculated for the pastoral zone regressions Dahlberg attributed
to his exclusion of a weather variable, originally postulated as
important, because of lack of data.

Powell and Gruen included wool in their study of the Australian
cereals-livestock sector from 1947 to 1964.[18] They found that an

initial application of the Koyck-Nerlove concept of price proved
unsatisfactory for wool, which led to their formulation of a discounting mechanism for prices that rise rapidly, as mentioned above in
this chapter. With this incorporated into an output adjustment model
with the number of adult sheep shorn represented as a function of
lagged wool prices and shorn sheep, an index of sheep mortality
due to drought, and lagged lamb and wheat prices. Estimated
coefficients are listed in Table 9.15. As can be seen, parameters
were of the expected sign, though elasticities were somewhat smaller
than anticipated.

William Witherell also used Nerlovian techniques to examine
wool supply:[19] He concentrated his attention on the five largest
producers—Australia, New Zealand, South Africa, Argentina, and
Uruguay—who together account for 60 percent of world output, and
the largest consumer, the United States, which also produced about
one-third of its own consumption during the period 1949 to 1965.

Sheep have normal lifetimes of a bit over five years; they can
be shorn annually after a first shearing within a year of birth.
Short-run changes in the amount of wool produced may result from
unfavorable weather conditions or health problems in the flocks
and from changes in the prices of the joint products, lamb and
mutton. Long-run supply involves farmer evaluations of expectations
regarding not only wool (and lamb/mutton) prices, but also those
of alternative outputs (most frequently, cattle and cereals). In
recent years technological factors such as pasture improvement
(through fertilization, and so on) and disease control have allowed
notable increases in the wool yield, both per acre and per sheep.

Witherell used an output adjustment model with a simple
expression of expected wool price in terms of two-year lagged wool
prices. Output was defined as a function of lagged wool-lamb and

TABLE 9.15

Supply Parameters, Australian Wool

Short-run elasticity	0.07	Cross-elasticity—lamb	-0.02
Long-run elasticity	0.33*	Cross-elasticity—wheat	-0.05
Adjustment coefficient	0.02	R^2	0.98

*After 5-year adjustment.

Source: Alan A. Powell and F. H. Gruen, "The Estimation of
Production Frontiers: The Australian Livestock Cereals Complex,"
Australian Journal of Agricultural Economics 11 (June 1967).

wheat prices, rainfall, and lagged wool output, and the estimated elasticities and adjustment coefficients are shown in Table 9.16.

In assessing his results Witherell pointed out that the elasticities indicated for Australia (in which regressions a variable accounting for the quantity of phosphate fertilizer used also proved reasonably significant) are close to those calculated by Powell and Gruen, who also considered aggregate Australian output, but below those seen already that were calculated by Dahlberg. Since the latter concentrated on the wheat-sheep zone of South Australia where greater substitution between wheat and wool is possible than in the country as a whole, Witherell found his own results reasonable.

The New Zealand wool supply parameters were estimated for two different price formulations: (A) world prices (deflated) lagged two years and (B) the guaranteed floor price announced by the New Zealand government annually. Only the latter proved statistically significant (and of the right sign), but the coefficients of lamb prices were strongly positive and significant (at the 20 percent level or better) in both regressions. Wool production in New Zealand is a secondary consideration to many producers, with sheep bred primarily for meat, and whose wool is generally coarser than that of Australian animals. The indicated importance of the floor price for wool and the lamb price bear out this subsidiary role for wool production.

In South Africa sheep are raised only for their wool and on land frequently too dry for any profitable alternative use, though wheat prices lagged two years were included in the analysis as an independent variable. Here, unlike in New Zealand, the explanatory power of the two-year lagged world (A) as opposed to the local floor (B) price for wool is greater, and this Witherell attributed to the smaller size of South Africa's price stabilization fund and the invariability of the guaranteed price (in money, though not in real, terms) during the entire period.

The author noted data limitations faced in the analysis of both Argentinian and Uruguayan wool supply. In both cases two-year lagged prices proved unsatisfactory in explanatory power, and the estimates based on one-year lagged prices have the lowest R^2 values of all the countries examined. The effect of prices on wool supply seems particularly slight in Argentina. The unexpected positive signs indicated for the beef price parameters in both countries could indicate a complementarity between sheep and cattle raising (a surprise to fans of movie westerns), but Witherell felt a more likely explanation would be found in data inadequacies and model misspecification.

Of the six countries analyzed, only in the United States is wool production minor relative both to the economy as a whole and to

TABLE 9.16

Supply Elasticities, Wool

	Wool Price		Lamb Price		Wheat Price		Adjustment Coefficient
	Short-Run	Long-Run	Short-Run	Long-Run	Short-Run	Long-Run	
Australia	0.066	0.125	0.185	0.357	-0.046	-0.087	0.527
	0.084	0.276	-	-	-0.046	-0.150	0.305
New Zealand	0.028[b]	0.718[b]	0.044	1.133	-	-	0.039
South Africa	0.076[a]	0.764[a]	-	-	-0.050	-0.497	0.100
Argentina	0.042	0.202	-	-	-0.078	-0.372	0.209
Uruguay	0.212	0.481	-	-	-	-	0.439
United States	0.145	0.321	-	-	-0.387	-0.856	0.452
	0.136	0.346	0.048	0.121	⎰ -0.367	-0.932 ⎱	0.394
					⎱ -0.100[c]	-0.221[c] ⎰	

[a]World prices.
[b]Support prices.
[c]Beef prices.
Source: Alan A. Powell and F. H. Gruen, "The Estimation of Production Frontiers: The Australian Livestock Cereals Complex," Australian Journal of Agricultural Economics 11 (June 1967).

323

agricultural sector. During part of the period in question (1955 to 1965), U.S. wool producers were paid an incentive price greater than the market price by the government. The wool price variable used in the regressions is the market price through 1954 and the support price thereafter, both lagged two years. In the United States, as in New Zealand, wool is frequently a joint product secondary to lamb, and wheat and beef are often competitors for inputs. The calculated cross-elasticities indicate wheat is a particularly attractive alternative, beef less so.

Wool supply responsiveness was included by G. T. Jones in his work on the British livestock sector.[20] The number of ewes kept for breeding was regressed on wool prices deflated by a general index of farm prices and a measure of weather severity (which causes losses in the flocks) for the period 1927 to 1955; the estimated elasticity was +0.20, a figure Jones felt was perhaps unrealistically low.

Shortly after Nerlove's initial publications, Gerald Dean and Earl Heady were the first to apply the dynamic model to the analysis of a meat product when they undertook a study of the responsiveness of American hog raisers.[21] Beginning with a review of the "traditional" cobweb theorem explanation of the hog cycle, they postulated a simple static model with output (in terms of first difference of litters farrowed) expressed as a function of lagged relative hog-to-corn and cattle-to-hog prices, the margin between feeder cattle and slaughter cattle prices, and oats, barley, and sorghum production relative to corn production for spring farrowings, which the authors held to be strongly influenced by the absolute level of the hog-corn price ratio at breeding time in the previous autumn. Fall farrowings, on the other hand, are not significantly affected by breeding-time prices, many sows bred for the spring farrowing merely being carried over and farrowed again in the fall. Thus they postulated a supply model with the number of spring farrowings, output of oats, barley, and sorghum, and the ratio of slaughter steer to corn prices as the independent variables.

Their dynamic model included a Nerlovian price expectation mechanism (both relative hog-corn and cattle-hog prices) and a stock adjustment term. Since the authors were interested in determining whether or not the hog market was undergoing notable changes on the supply side as a result of the agricultural legislation of the 1930s, they tested their models separately for the periods 1924 to 1937 and 1938 to 1956 (omitting 1942-44). The static model was employed for both farrowings, while the dynamic model was used only for the analysis of spring farrowings; both models were applied to aggregate U.S. hog output and that of the 12-state North

Central region (Ohio, Indiana, Illinois, Michigan, Wisconsin, Minnesota, Iowa, Missouri, North Dakota, South Dakota, Nebraska, and Kansas) responsible for close to three-fourths of national production. Supply parameters estimated for both models are shown in Table 9.17 (along with the standard errors).

The initial results using the static model indicated a pronounced upward shift in supply elasticities for both farrowings for the later period, though the change was not significant for fall farrowings. The authors felt the spring results merited further attention, and so adapted the Nerlovian model to allow price expectations to be included in their analysis. The dynamic formulation confirmed the jump in responsiveness and indicated an output adjustment coefficient not significantly different from unity. This latter indication was taken as further confirmation for their hypothesis that the increase in responsiveness was in large part due to the enhanced ability of producers to increase spring farrowings under the impetus of high autumn prices.

A much more recent study of the hog market in North America was conducted by K. D. Meilke, A. C. Zwart, and L. J. Martin.[22] Using quarterly data they examined hog supply in the United States and both eastern and western Canada (Eastern Canada is defined as the Maritime Provinces, Quebec, and Ontario, while the west consists of the Prairie Provinces and British Columbia); they used two models: one of Nerlovian type, containing both adaptive expectations and partial adjustment formulations, the second expressing the price effect in terms of an Almon-type polynomial lag. It was hoped that the two methods of representing prices would allow several distinctions to be made regarding the usefulness of the two models. In particular they expected to be able to compare the Nerlove long-run elasticity with the polynomial lag estimation of total elasticity, to contrast the response patterns suggested by each approach, to find what effect the price specification has on other calculated coefficients, and to determine the relative importance of serial correlation problems.

The Nerlove supply equation used for both the United States and eastern Canada expressed quantity of hogs in terms of lagged hog and feed prices, lagged relative slaughter steer-choice steer calf price, three quarterly intercept dummies, and lagged values of the dependent variable. In western Canada, because of marketing controls on grain, the stock of wheat and barley held on farms was used instead of feed prices; all prices and this stock variable were lagged five periods. The polynomial distributed lag version of the supply model included feed prices lagged five periods, the steer price measurement, the three quarterly dummies, and a lag of

TABLE 9.17

Supply Parameters, U.S. Hogs

Area		Period	Model[a]	Hog-Corn Price	Cattle-Hog Price	Short-Run Elasticity	R^2
Spring farrowing	United States	1924-37	S	366[d] (35)	–	0.50	0.92
		1938-56	D	324[e]	876[e]	0.46	0.91
		1938-56	S	418[d] (36)	–	0.60	0.93
	North Central	1924-37	D	382[e]	–119[e]	0.65	0.76
		1924-37	S	316[d] (35)	–	0.58	0.90
		1938-56	D	289[e]	858[e]	0.53	0.87
		1938-56	S	400[d] (33)	–	0.69	0.93
Fall farrowing	United States	1924-37	D	370[e]	193[e]	0.73	0.79
		1924-37	S	1.38[b,c] (0.64)	–	0.28	0.75
		1938-56	S	4.00[b,d] (1.06)	–	0.30	0.92
	North Central	1924-37	S	8.51[b,c] (4.03)	–	0.41	0.71
		1938-56	S	8.20[b,d] (2.79)	–	0.35	0.89

[a]S indicates static, D dynamic.

[b]Cattle-corn price.

[c]5 percent significance level.

[d]1 percent significance level.

[e]Standard errors not quoted, but authors indicate all elasticities are significant at the 5 percent level or better.

Source: Gerald W. Dean and Earl O. Heady, "Changes in Supply Response and Elasticity for Hogs," Journal of Farm Economics 40 (November 1958).

degree two and length equal to ten periods.* In Tables 9.18 and
9.19 are shown selected elasticity estimates made for the period
1961 to 1972 using ordinary least-squares techniques.

In evaluating their overall results, Meilke, Zwart, and Martin
were generally satisfied. Both models explained a high percentage
of the variation in hog supply in all three submarkets, and again
for both models a fairly consistent pattern relative to independent
variables was found, using expected signs, R^2 and t statistic values
as criteria. The price links were as anticipated—positive for hog
prices and negative for steer and feed prices, though the evidence
for the latter is somewhat mixed. Since feed prices are usually
felt to be a strong influence on hog supply, the authors emphasized
the lack of evidence in this study for such importance.

Though the two models used gave generally consistent results,
the authors indicated a general preference for the polynomial lag
model. This was based on the different response patterns that
emerge from each case (see Figure 9.1). The Nerlove model by
its nature results in a monotonically declining role for prices
beginning with the period selected, perhaps arbitrarily, when the
model is specified. When the degree-two polynomial estimates are
untangled in this case, a more complex U-shaped pattern is seen,
with the influence of prices on both sides of the most important
period indicated. As can be seen, in this case period t - 5 was
selected for inclusion in the Nerlove formulation, while the polynomial lag model indicates that prices seven and eight periods ago
are the most important. The authors hold that such a lag incorporates
both the five-quarter farrowing-to-slaughter period and a pattern
of price expectations prevailing at farrowing.

In the estimation process the authors found problems of serial
correlation for the polynomial lag model only. The results reported
were based on the subsequent use of the Hildreth-Lu method.

Elasticity estimates from each model are comparable if not
identical. The authors conclude that the summed elasticities
through period t - 5 are most like Nerlove's short-run elasticities
but, as can be seen, the former are some 50 to 72 percent higher
than the Nerlove model estimates. Cross-elasticities were low in

---

*When the zero constraint for period t - 1 was applied to the
regression for western Canada the authors reported negative weights
for most years. They then respecified the model, for this case,
with a zero constraint for period t - 3. They commented that though
this formulation proved to give satisfactory results, the reason why
the response pattern in western Canada is different is not apparent
and concluded that further investigation is called for.

TABLE 9.18

Supply Elasticities, U.S. and Canadian Hogs

With Respect to Hog Prices:	United States		Eastern Canada		Western Canada	
	I	II	I	II	I	II
t - 2	–	+0.025	–	+0.048	–	–
t - 3	–	+0.045	–	+0.081	–	–
t - 4	–	+0.059	–	+0.116	–	+0.058
t - 5	+0.160	+0.068	+0.220	+0.136	+0.100	+0.101
t - 6	–	+0.071	–	+0.148	–	+0.129
t - 7	–	+0.069	–	+0.150	–	+0.143
t - 8	–	+0.062	–	+0.143	–	+0.142
t - 9	–	+0.049	–	+0.127	–	+0.126
t - 10	–	+0.030	–	+0.102	–	+0.095
t - 11	–	–	–	+0.068	–	–

Note: I indicates Nerlove model.
II indicates polynomial lag model.
Source: K. D. Meilke, A. C. Zwart, and L. J. Martin, "North American Hog Supply: A Comparison of Geometric and Polynomial Distributed Lag Models," Canadian Journal of Agricultural Economics 22 (July 1974).

TABLE 9.19

Short- and Long-Run Supply Elasticities, U.S. and Canadian Hogs

	United States	Eastern Canada	Western Canada
Nerlove			
Short-run	+0.16	+0.22	+0.10
Long-run	+0.43	+0.89	+0.20
Polynomial Lag			
Quarters 2 Through 4	+0.17	+0.24	+0.06
Quarters 2 Through 5	+0.24	+0.38	+0.16
Long-run	+0.48	+1.12	+0.79

Source: K. D. Meilke, A. C. Zwart, and L. J. Martin, "North American Hog Supply: A Comparison of Geometric and Polynomial Distributed Lag Models," Canadian Journal of Agricultural Economics 22 (July 1974).

FIGURE 9.1

Price Lags, Nerlove and Distributed Lag Models, U.S. and Canadian Hogs

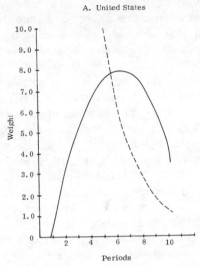

A. United States

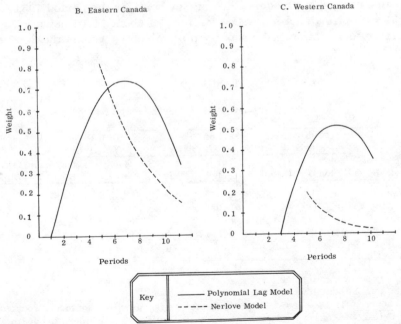

B. Eastern Canada

C. Western Canada

Key

——— Polynomial Lag Model

- - - - - Nerlove Model

Source: K. D. Meilke, A. C. Zwart, and L. J. Martin, "North American Hog Supply: A Comparison of Geometric and Polynomial Distributed Lag Models," Canadian Journal of Agricultural Economics 22 (July 1974).

all cases. Generally negative values smaller in absolute value than about 0.05 were indicated for the effect of steer prices on hog supply in all three markets.

In his two papers on British agriculture Jones considered the output of several kinds of meat.[23] As was mentioned previously, most cattle in Britain are in the dairy herd, but about 20 percent are raised primarily for beef, and of course dairy cows are generally processed as beef after their productive lifetimes. He ran regressions for the period 1924 to 1958 (omitting 1940-45) on three supply equations that include milk, feed, and beef prices with the number of cows, the proportion of calves reared, and the number of calves as the dependent variables. The estimated parameters are shown in Table 9.20. Though the results are somewhat unclear, Jones argued that the long-run elasticity of beef seems to be at least +1.0 and the long-run cross-elasticity with milk prices about +0.4. Focusing in his second paper on the postwar period he used several different formulations incorporating lags of different lengths and both free market and support prices. Parameters calculated for calves, steers, and heifers are shown in Table 9.21. Jones felt his earlier estimates were confirmed, attributing the somewhat higher supply responsiveness to the inclusion of guaranteed prices. He also applied his models to West Germany for the period 1951 to 1964 and estimated a long-run elasticity of about +1.06 using a Nerlove formulation with proportion of calves reared as the dependent variable.

TABLE 9.20

Supply Parameters, U.K. Beef, 1924-58

Dependent Variable	Milk Price Elasticity		Feed Price Elasticity		Beef Price Elasticity		Adjustment Coefficient
	Short-Run	Long-Run	Short-Run	Long-Run	Short-Run	Long-Run	
Cows	0.06[a] (0.03)	0.46	-0.07[a] (0.03)	-0.57	0.10[b] (0.03)	0.88	0.12[a] (0.06)
Calves reared	-0.08 (0.07)	-0.12	-0.10[a] (0.05)	-0.14	0.38[b] (0.11)	0.55	0.69[b] (0.12)
Calves	—	0.34	—	-0.71	—	1.43	—

[a]5 percent significance level.
[b]1 percent significance level.

Source: G. T. Jones, "The Response of the Supply of Agricultural Products in the United Kingdom to Price and Other Factors: Including Consideration of Distributed Lags" (Parts I and II), Farm Economist 9 and 10 (1961, 1962).

TABLE 9.21

Supply Parameters, U.K. Beef, 1955-64

Dependent Variable	Adjustment Coefficient	Beef Elasticities			Milk Elasticities		Feed Elasticities	
		Short-Run		Long-Run	Short-Run	Long-Run	Short-Run	Long-Run
		(Market)	(Support)					
Calves	0.35[a,d]	0.21[b]	0.41[b]	0.94	6.47[b]	0.61	-0.33[b]	-0.50
	(0.15)	(0.07)	(0.12)		(0.18)		(0.13)	
Steers	0.09[d]							
	(0.23)							
	0.22[e]	0.12[a]	-0.01	0.15	0.39[a]	0.55	-0.30[c]	-0.42
	(0.23)	(0.05)	(0.08)		(0.16)		(0.07)	
Heifers	1.06[b,d]							
	(0.41)							
	-0.50[e]	0.15	0.64[a]	1.65	0.23	0.52	-0.27	-0.62
	(0.31)	(0.17)	(0.31)		(0.41)		(0.25)	

[a] 10 percent significance level.
[b] 5 percent significance level.
[c] 1 percent significance level.
[d] 6-month lag.
[e] 12-month lag.

Source: G. T. Jones, "The Influence of Price on Livestock Population over the Last Decade," Journal of Agricultural Economics 16 (December 1965).

To analyze the supply of mutton and lamb Jones regressed the number of ewes available for breeding on one- and two-year lagged prices, a weather index, and a trend variable for the period 1907 to 1958. Two measures of price were used and both were deflated by a general farm price index. The weather index was designed to incorporate the deleterious effect on sheep population of unusually cold and rainy seasons. As can be seen from Table 9.22, two-year lagged prices show more significance when fat-sheep prices (which Jones held to be the more relevant of the two measures) are used. He felt that his long-run elasticity estimates were probably too high but that the true value is probably greater than unity.

However when he later analyzed postwar (1955 to 1964) lamb production, similarly high long-run elasticities were indicated. Jones hypothesized that the generally secondary nature of sheep raising on many farms may explain the greater degree of responsiveness as compared to other livestock products.

Relatively large elasticities were anticipated for the pork market since a sow can produce two litters of six or seven piglets per year. The prices relevant for such prolificity involve lags of less than a year, but before 1940 only annual data was available. Jones used a rather simple model in his first paper relating the number of sows to pork prices (fat pigs or weaners) and feed prices.

TABLE 9.22

Supply Parameters, U.K. Lamb and Mutton

| Period | | Adjustment Coefficient | Short-Run Price[a] Elasticity | | Long-Run Price Elasticity |
			1-Year Lag	2-Year Lag	
1907-58	(1)	0.13[d]	0.04	0.26[d]	2.31
		(0.04)	(0.05)	(0.05)	
	(2)	0.07[c]	0.11[d]	0.09[d]	2.85
		(0.03)	(0.03)	(0.03)	
1955-64	(3)	0.12[b]	0.18	0.30[b]	4.00
		(0.04)	(0.20)	(0.10)	
	(4)	0.35	0.20	0.33	1.51
		(0.23)	(0.20)	(0.11)	
	(5)	0.14	0.11	0.17	2.00
		(0.06)	(0.45)	(0.25)	

[a]Prices are deflated fat lamb price in (1), deflated store sheep price in (2), and a price index for sheep, lambs, hoggets, and wool in (3), (4), and (5).

[b]10 percent significance leve.

[c]5 percent significance level.

[d]1 percent significance level.

Note: Dependent variable was total ewe population in (1) and (2), number of ewes in June in (3) and (4), and number of ewes and shearlings in (5).

Source: G. T. Jones, "The Influence of Price on Livestock Population over the Last Decade," Journal of Agricultural Economics 16 (December 1965).

Table 9.23 shows the resulting parameters, with the long-run elasticities being expectedly high.

In his second paper Jones used both total sow population and actual number of gilts in sow for the dependent variable and considered the changed price situation after the war by regressing on both the guaranteed and flexible portions of the support price separately, including as well the free market pork price. He again obtained high elasticities, especially when gilts are used as the dependent variable.

While examining the supply of eggs Jones also analyzed the supply of poultry for the period 1927 to 1939. He regressed the number of fowls under six months old on meat, egg, and feed prices and calculated a short-run elasticity of about 0.69 and cross-elasticities of about 0.35 and -0.23 with eggs and feed. Indicated is a complementary rather than a competitive relationship between poultry and eggs.

For the postwar period quarterly data from 1960 to 1964 were available. Chick placings for poultry were regressed on current and nine-month lagged prices, feed prices, and 3- and 12-month lagged stock. Though the time period studied was short, the best results indicated short-run responsiveness to current prices of about +1.0, and a long-run price elasticity of about +2.5 with regard to fowl prices and of about -3.5 for feed prices.

Buttimer considered beef as well as milk in his study of Ireland.[24] About one-third of the Irish herd is grown primarily for beef, making this sector almost twice as important, relatively, as it is in Great Britain. During the period of concern, 1953 to 1970, the herd size

TABLE 9.23

Supply Parameters, U.K. Pork

Period	Adjustment Coefficient	Pork Price Elasticities		Feed Price Elasticities	
		Short-Run	Long-Run	Short-Run	Long-Run
1924-39	0.18	0.65[a,e]	3.61	-0.90[e]	-5.00
	(0.14)	(0.20)		(0.13)	
1924-39 and	0.15	0.91[a,e]	6.14	-0.80[e]	-5.43
1951-58	(0.09)	(0.15)		(0.20)	
1949-58	0.18[d]	0.40[b,d]	2.22	-0.13	-0.76
	(0.06)	(0.10)		(0.07)	
1940-56	0.17[e]	0.40[c,e]	2.35	—	—
	(0.02)	(0.03)			

[a]Fat-pig prices.
[b]Weaner prices.
[c]Deflated weaner price.
[d]5 percent significance level.
[e]1 percent significance level.
Source: G. T. Jones, "The Response of the Supply of Agricultural Products in the United Kingdom to Price and Other Factors: Including Consideration of Distributed Lags" (Parts I and II), Farm Economist 9 and 10 (1961, 1962).

grew by more than 60 percent, reflecting the growing importance of Ireland's chief export market, Britain.

The size of the beef herd was expressed as a function of lagged beef prices, a slope shifter representing a government subsidy paid for calves between 1964 and 1968, and another shifter standing for a beef incentive bonus scheme. Other factors included in some of the models tested were a trend variable, lagged milk prices, and the lagged ratio of beef and milk prices (and the inverse of this ratio).

Buttimer encountered collinearity problems between both beef and milk price series and the trend variable, which disappeared when only the beef-to-milk price ratio was included. Nevertheless because Buttimer had hypothesized the relevance of all the included variables, he wanted to obtain a reasonable measure for each coefficient, even if estimating problems arose if all variables were included in the same equation. He felt knowledge of the approximate magnitudes of each factor's effect on beef supply was particularly important in the event changed circumstances should sever the collinearities between prices and the trend variable, a not unlikely occurrence after Ireland's entry into the European Economic Community.

Though Buttimer did not calculate beef supply elasticities, data presented with the article together with his suggested "best" beef price parameter estimates indicate a short-run elasticity of approximately +0.11.

The Powell-Gruen study of the interaction between cereals and livestock in Australia presented estimates of the supply responsiveness of both beef and lamb producers.[25] They found that the latter could be described fairly satisfactorily with the Nerlove supply model used for other commodities. Lamb supply was represented as a function of lagged output, a sheep mortality index, and lagged lamb, wool, and dairy product prices. Estimated parameters from the regression run on this equation are shown in Table 9.24.

However, they found that beef supply needed to be treated in a different manner than the other products in their study. Not only did the Nerlove model break down as an analytic tool in this case, but in their theoretical justification for the beef supply model they could differentiate between short- and long-run expected prices. Beef can be brought to market very quickly; once mature, a brief "fattening-up" period is all that is needed to convert potential future output into present output. Long-term price expectations affect herd size but, coupled with (relatively) low present prices, optimistic long-run expectations should reduce present output. Producers expecting better prices in, for example, a few months

TABLE 9.24

Supply Parameters, Australian Lamb

Short-run elasticity	0.32	Cross-elasticity–wool	-0.12
Long-run elasticity	1.38*	Cross-elasticity–dairy	
Adjustment coefficient	0.07	products	-0.20
		R^2	0.89

*After five-year adjustment.

Source: Alan A. Powell and F. H. Gruen, "The Estimation of Production Frontiers: The Australian Livestock Cereals Complex," Australian Journal of Agricultural Economics 11 (June 1967).

can withhold at least some of their cattle from the market, increasing their inventories on the hoof. Conversely, pessimistic expectations about future prices coupled with more promising current prices can bring cattle to quick sale that might normally be held for a longer period.

This led the authors to attempt to measure supply responsiveness to both "present" and "future" price expectations—both short- and long-run formulations of producer anticipations. Their analysis indicated the hypothesized relationships could be discerned from the available data—long-run expectations affected present market activity negatively, while the link with current prices was positive. The beef-supply equation included lagged beef and dairy product prices, and estimated short-run elasticities were +0.16 and -0.16 for beef and dairy prices, respectively, in a regression where the coefficient of determination was 0.90.

The last of the works to be outlined herein is appropriately another of the Massachusetts Institute of Technology studies that originally prompted this book. Lovell Jarvis concentrated on the chief agricultural commodity of Argentina—beef cattle—but this work is not just a simple adaption of the Nerlovian formulation of price expectations to his analysis.[26] This is the only large-scale study to estimate farmer behavior in a capital-theory manner.

Jarvis considered cattle to be capital goods—which he called "growing machines" or "mother machines," an apt description, though the term might grate a bit as an economist's excess on a more humanistic ear—that are held by their owners only as long as their present discounted value (determined by price expectations) exceeds their slaughter value. Cattle producers are thus essentially portfolio managers who seek the optimal combination of different categories (by age and sex) of animals to complement their noncattle assets, with given existing conditions and expectations of the future.

The Argentine cattle industry is concentrated in the 200,000-square-mile region known as the Pampas—fertile, treeless plains stretching west- and southward from Buenos Aires in the central section of the country. The Pampas provide pasturage for 80 percent of the cattle raised in Argentina and grow 90 percent of the nation's field crops—mostly wheat, corn, sorghum flax, sunflowers, barley, rye, and oats. The agricultural sector as a whole provides 17 percent of gross national product, 90 percent of the value of total exports, and employment of about 20 percent of the labor force; the cattle industry in turn accounts for about one-third of the value of both agricultural output and total exports. Though it has remained relatively stagnant for the last 30 years (and thus severely aggravating balance of payments problems), the cattle industry has increased its share of Pampas acreage from 63 to 75 percent from 1935 to 1963, as land previously devoted to cereal and other crops has been planted in forage crops such as alfalfa.

The traditional production pattern on the Pampas has involved tenancy agreements on large estates—called estancias. The tenant contracts to grow grain on a plot for three to five years, then plant a forage crop and move on to another section of the estancia to raise grain crops for the next three to five years. The cycling of grain lands with periodic pasturage uses has served to regenerate the soil and has allowed future return to grain production.

Government policies regarding the agricultural sector, particularly during the first presidential regime of Juan Peron (1944-55)—such as import restrictions on agricultural inputs, increased minimum wages for farm workers, and a policy of price regulation of domestically consumed food crops designed to favor consumers—contributed to the tendency toward increasing the acreage devoted to the relatively less labor-intensive and more export-oriented cattle industry.

Jarvis postulated that producers seek the optimal slaughter age of each animal, * representing the present discounted value of each animal as

---

*Cattle are classified on the basis of age and sex: calves (0 to 9 months); male yearlings (10-18 months)—often already castrated; female yearlings or heifers (10-18 months)—too young to bear calves; breeding heifers (19-28 months)—about to bear their first calves; cows (28-84 months)—potentially bearing one calf every year; steers (19-30 months)—emasculated and being fattened for slaughter; bulls (28-84 months)—selected and stocked only for breeding purposes.

$$V = W(\theta)\ P(\theta)\ e^{-r\theta} \tag{9.6}$$

where: θ is the age of the animal;
W(θ) is the animal's weight at age θ;
P(θ) is the expected price per kilogram at age θ; and
r is the discount rate.

Solving for the maximum present discounted value (as a function of θ) yields:

$$r = \frac{W\dot{P} + P\dot{W}}{WP} \tag{9.7}$$

that is, an animal is slaughtered at that age when the rate of its increase in value (due to price and weight changes—$\dot{P}$ and $\dot{W}$) is equivalent to the discount rate.

In fact, such a formulation could not be used in the calculations. On the one hand, no accurate measure of a subjective rate of discount was available—considering Argentina's recent problems with inflation, Jarvis postulated that the rate of inflation would most likely prove more influential on producers than any estimated discount rate. On the other hand, the various age-sex categories of cattle have different characteristics, tending to rule out a single approach to all. For example, young animals are more efficient converters of feed to animal protein, indicating that an increase in feed prices would tend to lower the optimal slaughter age. Again, recent world consumption trends have indicated a preference for leaner meat increasing with rising incomes and a willingness to pay premium prices for lean beef, resulting in further influence toward lowering optimal slaughter age. Furthermore, while higher beef prices might hasten the slaughter of older animals, it might also result in fewer calves being slaughtered and more being fattened for later sale as yearlings or steers. On the other hand, cows must be considered in Jarvis' terms, as mother machines, and the discounted value of their potential progeny is of obvious importance.

Jarvis indicated that average gross slaughter weights for the various categories are: calves, 200 to 210 kgs; male yearlings, 325 kgs; yearling heifers, 310 kgs; cows, 430 kgs; steers, 450 kgs; and bulls, 535 kgs. The average percentage of each group that is slaughtered each year is: calves, 7 percent; male yearlings, 20 percent; yearling heifers, 24 percent; cows, 11 percent; steers, 98 percent; and bulls, 10 percent.

In carrying out his estimates Jarvis found that while available data concerning slaughter were quite good, no information about the number of cattle born annually was available directly. Thus he first had to reconstruct this time series of calf births from available figures indicating herd size, slaughter, and other animal deaths.

Initial testing using ordinary least-squares techniques indicated the presence of serial correlation, and therefore inconsistent parameter estimates were obtained. Nonetheless, Jarvis felt he gained information regarding the appropriateness of the specification of the supply models he employed.

Two formulations of the dependent variable were used: number of cattle slaughtered and average slaughter weight in each category. The former was regressed on lagged prices (one to five years) and lagged herd size in each category, percentage of climatological change, and lagged price and climate changes; variants of the model involved different lag structures, real rural wages, changes in exchange rates, rate of inflation (in cost of living terms), and the ratio of rural and nonrural wholesale price indices among others. Slaughter weights were regressed on lagged prices (one to four years), a trend variable, a measure of the effectiveness of the hoof-to-mouth disease vaccination program, and many of the variables enumerated for the number slaughtered regressions. Instrumental variables were employed to avoid problems of inconsistent estimates.

Given the complexity of Jarvis' models it is easily seen that he presented multifarious results from his regression analysis; we confine ourselves to a brief summary. High serial correlation affecting lagged prices (a beef-to-grain ratio) ruled out consideration of these as exogenous variables. Lagged herd levels, export levels, and net change in the rural labor force were among the factors that showed some statistical significance in the regressions run with slaughter numbers as the dependent variable. From these indications Jarvis argued that the government policies that aimed to hold down grain prices either forced farm workers to the cities or farm owners to cattle production. Generally, Jarvis felt that the results of the parameter estimations for each category were quite good, as judged by both the significance of the estimates and the correlation coefficients, as well as the conformance of the statistically significant coefficients with a priori formulation of the supply equations.

Jarvis also examined the possibility of an asymmetrical reaction to price changes—that is, the possibility of a different producer reaction to price increases than to decreases of equal magnitude, since a supply restraint is binding in the first case but not in the second. In general he found less difference between the two sets of response parameter estimates than would be expected if such a differentiation in responsiveness were relevant, indicating either that the case of adjustment for producers switching from cattle to grains and other agricultural activities is less than expected, or that expectations change more slowly when prices fall, so that even

though adjustment <u>can</u> be made faster in response to falling prices,
in fact, such does <u>not</u> happen. Jarvis suggested that cattle producers
might be like smalltime stock-market speculators who consistently
act as optimists who expect price increases to continue and price
declines to be reversed.

In overview Jarvis interpreted his estimates as indicating that
producers do respond to price changes both rapidly and significantly,
if not entirely rationally. He felt their response indicated that
government policies that were designed to increase productivity
and total product should be determined with price sensitivities in
mind, particularly since expansion of agricultural exports seems
to be the most likely way to improve Argentina's chronic balance-
of-trade deficit.

Indications were that producers respond both to the beef-to-grain
relative prices and its rate of change as expected, in both the expected
direction and magnitude. In the short run the response of slaughter
to higher relative prices is <u>negative</u> (except for bulls), as animals
are held for further fattening—price increases for beef give the
cattle high capital values, which postpones the optimal slaughter
age, that is, the age when slaughter and discounted capital values
are equal. Producer expectations seemed to be quite price elastic,
implying that price movements tend to be cumulatively destabilizing.
As a result, policies designed to increase the marketed supply of
beef in the long run (through price stimulation) can be expected to
decrease current supply in the process. Jarvis in fact forecasted
herd size for later years and in comparing them to a benchmark he
found that his model predicted well.

Most of the increase in cattle production in Argentina was
intrasectoral—it was accompanied by a decrease in grain crop
production. If the goal of increasing the real value of net exports
is to be achieved, overall agricultural production, not just that of
beef, must be increased. This requires increased use of modern
techniques and inputs—and Jarvis argued that the Argentine government had yet to do much of either to spur agricultural research or
to ease the restrictions on the import of needed inputs such as farm
machinery.

NOTES

1. Harlow W. Halvorson, "The Supply Elasticity of Milk in
the Short-Run," <u>Journal of Farm Economics</u> 37 (December 1955).

2. Harlow W. Halvorson, "The Response of Milk Production
to Price," <u>Journal of Farm Economics</u> 40 (December 1958).

3. Dean Chen, Richard Courtney, and Andrew Schmitz, "A Polynomial Lag Formulation of Milk Production Response," American Journal of Agricultural Economics 54 (February 1972).

4. Anthony A. Prato, "Milk Demand, Supply, and Price Relationships, 1950-1968," American Journal of Agricultural Economics 55 (May 1973).

5. T. W. Gardner, "The Farm Price and Supply of Milk," Journal of Agricultural Economics 15 (May 1962).

6. T. W. Gardner and Rosemary Walker, "Interactions of Quantity, Price and Policy: Milk and Dairy Products," Journal of Agricultural Economics 23 (May 1972).

7. G. T. Jones, "The Response of the Supply of Agricultural Products in the United Kingdom to Price and Other Factors: Including a Consideration of Distributed Lags," (Part I) Farm Economist 9 (1961).

8. G. T. Jones, "The Influence of Price on Livestock Population over the Last Decade," Journal of Agricultural Economics 16 (December 1965).

9. Brian Hill, "Supply Responses in Crop and Livestock Production," Journal of Agricultural Economics 22 (September 1971).

10. D. J. Buttimer and J. G. MacAirt, "Supply Response in the Irish Creamery Herd 1951-1970," Irish Journal of Agricultural Economics and Rural Sociology 3, no. 3 (1970-71).

11. D. J. Buttimer, "Supply Response in the Irish Dairy and Beef Herds 1953-1970: An Econometric Exercise," Irish Journal of Agricultural Economics and Rural Sociology 4, no. 1 (1972-73).

12. F. H. Gruen et al., Long-Term Projections of Agricultural Supply and Demand in Australia 1965 and 1980 (Clayton, Victoria: Economics Department, Monash University, 1968). Also Alan A. Powell and F. H. Gruen, "The Estimation of Production Frontiers: The Australian Livestock Cereals Complex," Australian Journal of Agricultural Economics 11 (June 1967). For their results for wool, lamb, and beef, see later in this chapter.

13. J. Taplin and P. Smallhorn, "The Supply of Honey in Australia," Quarterly Review of Agricultural Economics 23 (April 1970).

14. Jones, "The Response of the Supply of Agricultural Products" (Part I), op. cit. and (Part II) Farm Economist 10 (1962); and "The Influence of Price on Livestock Population," op. cit.

15. C. A. Robertson, "Supply Response to Price under Certainty, with Reference to the United Kingdom Egg Market, 1954 to 1966," Journal of Agricultural Economics 22 (May 1971).

16. David G. Hartman, "The Egg Cycle and the Ability of Recursive Models to Explain It," American Journal of Agricultural Economics 56 (May 1974).

17. D. L. Dahlberg, "Supply Responses for Wool in South Australia, 1949-61," <u>Australian Journal of Agricultural Economics</u> 8 (June 1964).

18. Powell and Gruen, op. cit.

19. William Witherell, "A Comparison of the Determinants of Wool Production in the Six Leading Producing Countries: 1949-1965," <u>American Journal of Agricultural Economics</u> 51 (1969).

20. Jones, "The Influence of Price on Livestock Population," op. cit.

21. Gerald W. Dean and Earl O. Heady, "Changes in Supply Response and Elasticity for Hogs," <u>Journal of Farm Economics</u> 40 (November 1958).

22. K. D. Meilke, A. C. Zwart, and L. J. Martin, "North American Hog Supply: A Comparison of Geometric and Polynomial Distributed Lag Models," <u>Canadian Journal of Agricultural Economics</u> 22 (July 1974).

23. Jones, "The Response of the Supply of Agricultural Products" and "The Influence of Price on Livestock Population," op. cit.

24. Buttimer, op. cit.

25. Powell and Gruen, op. cit.

26. Lovell Jarvis, "Supply Response in the Cattle Industry: The Argentine Case, 1937-38 to 1966-67" (Ph.D. dissertation, Massachusetts Institute of Technology, 1969), and "Cattle as Capital Goods and Ranchers as Portfolio Managers: An Application to the Argentine Cattle Sector," <u>Journal of Political Economy</u> 82 (May-June 1974).

10

SUPPLY RESPONSIVENESS:
NONPRICE FACTORS

In the previous chapters we have seen many studies of supply response that have been made mostly using the Nerlove model. Yet little or no work has been directed toward any generalization, grounded on empirical work, from what has been learned in all these studies. The results give price elasticities, but nothing or nearly nothing about the conditions that determine the magnitude of these elasticities. Many authors, for example, in reporting on two or more crops and/or regions, have speculated about the reasons for any differences they found, to be sure, but none have attempted any systematic verification of such explanations. Perhaps the most obvious reason none have ventured so far is that few studies resulted in obtaining more than a handful of elasticity estimates, too few observations for any further statistical analysis. Most of the larger studies, on the other hand, had as their object, in addition to generating elasticity information, the testing of various alternative supply models or the consideration of specific supply-related problems, such as the marketable surplus hypothesis. Thus they have included little more substantive evidence regarding an explanation of differences, across crops or regions, of the calculated elasticities than have the briefer works.

What knowledge we have gained from all these efforts is actually applicable only to specific countries, crops, or time periods, or in formulating policies based solely on price criteria (if such a clear distinction could in fact be made and justified). Yet policy decisions, in a given country, frequently have been based out of necessity on scraps of information pertaining to other countries, crops, or times (or, of course, on price criteria alone). It is hardly surprising, then, that such policies have all too often resulted in totally undesired side effects, which might well have been avoided had a more systema-

tic analysis of price responsiveness been available; that is, one
more pertinent to the case in question. If we survey the earlier
Nerlovian works, for example, we find only scattered inclusion
of nonprice variables in the supply model employed. While a large
number of studies have attempted to gauge the effects of changes in
the prices of other crops or of weather (or weather variability) on
output, few other factors are found in more than one or two studies.
Behrman may consider whether Thai rice cultivators are risk-takers
or whether public health expenditures influence output, DeCanio
the role in production of the land tenancy structure, Raj Krishna
that of irrigation systems, and Oury the importance of chemical
fertilizers. But since each researcher has been interested only
in those nonprice variables that he believes to be pertinent to his
particular situation, little information of a widely applicable nature
is available to the policy maker.

If, however, common nonprice factors affecting the degree of
farmer price responsiveness across countries or regions for a
particular crop, or across crops for a particular region, and so
on, can be identified, then the range of reasonably reliable policy
options open to agricultural specialists is considerably widened.
The most optimistic goal would be to identify price elasticity as
a function of various economic and sociological variables. All the
studies we have included above make obvious the complexity of
estimating responsiveness from price, acreage, and other time
series data; not only is adequate information frequently missing,
but shifts in responsiveness due to factors not quantified in most
of these variations of the basic supply model may not even be
realized for years as a result of the time-series approach to
economic analysis that is used. Responsiveness estimates obtained
directly through functional relationships would not only be cheaper
(and far less time consuming—certainly a blessing to any economist
who has ever nearly worn a finger to the bone on the keyboard of
a calculator), but, more importantly, would be more accurate,
more reflective of the dynamic factors in a developing society.

Such optimism, realistically, seems unrealizable. Yet the
goal of identifying the principal nonprice factors shaping responsiveness is obviously still worth pursuing. The daily interaction
between policy maker and peasant—the former who must usually
guess as to the likely reactions of the latter, the latter who must
live (perhaps even more perilously) with the not unlikely mistakes
of the former—compels any effort that might reduce the guessing
and the peril. Again, realistically, we are not likely merely to
be talking along the lines of "anything is better than nothing."
Even a superficial glance at the aggregate data presented in
Tables B.1 and B.2 shows patterns regarding producer elasticities

that are striking despite considerable differences among countries
in which the same crop is grown, or which are discernible in the
same country when diverse crops are considered. A more systematic
approach should be able to uncover some common factors; such an
approach is what we propose to begin in this chapter.

CROP-TO-CROP ELASTICITY

First, let us consider the agriculture of a single country. A
number of reasons suggest themselves as possible explanations as
to why supply elasticities may differ from crop to crop in a relatively
homogeneous country or region, depending upon:

1. Whether the crop is grown primarily for food or cash sale.
The marketable surplus hypothesis, for example, applies essentially
to food crops. Even without resorting to this explanation it seems
obvious that a food crop is likely to be subject to some kind of an
income effect: Higher prices for a primarily subsistence crop mean
higher real income for the cultivator, and even if he chooses to
realize this partly by increasing his cash income, he might also
increase the proportion of the crop that he consumes. On the other
hand, perverse price-output relationships may exist for cash crops
as well as for food crops, but these cannot be explained in marketable
surplus terms; rather, cash needs of the cultivator have to be weighed
against preferences for leisure or for the consumption of additional
quantities of noncash crops.

2. Whether the crop is an annual or a perennial. As has been
discussed above, perennial crop supply often seems best explained
in terms of capital stock adjustments. Short-term responsiveness
to price then depends upon the factors affecting total output only to
the extent of defining a maximum harvest and is more readily
explained in terms of leisure preference. On the other hand, the
determination of long-run responsiveness can be an extremely
complex process dependent upon lagged economic and technical
variables. Annual crops, of course, would be only infrequently
affected by events occurring more than a year or two before their
planting and harvesting and would thus be expected to show both a
greater responsiveness to yearly variations in price and other
variables and a faster adjustment to long-term trends in the same
factors. But when a stock of producing units is involved, as in the
case of perennials or livestock, the farmer adjusts only at the
margin.

3. The number of crops that can be harvested in a year. Here also the time element should result in greater responsiveness to seasonal changes in variables and in a faster adjustment to long-term trends when more than one crop per year is possible, though the differences might not be as notable as in the case of perennial versus annual crops. However, in a situation where, for example, the cultivator has the choice to plant (or not plant) a second or even a third crop, whether his alternative is to sow a different crop or to leave a field fallow, then obviously the possibility of multiple cropping should mean greater responsiveness to price incentives than in a situation where mere survival under conditions of subsistence output depends upon a rigid pattern of land use throughout the year.

4. The competition of other crops for available inputs. In this case the relative importance of the different crops to the cultivator is of particular relevance in assessing the effect on responsiveness. Certainly a relatively minor crop competing for labor, land, water, and so on with a basic crop like rice, at any period crucial to both, should show a different pattern of responsiveness than if no such competition was present or if the conflict was with another minor crop. The relative importance of the crop being examined may also lead to variations in the degree of responsiveness, depending upon whether the price variation is upward or downward from some or other long-term trend in prices. A minor crop competing with other crops for inputs might show a precipitous drop in output brought to market in the face of a price decline, while even a considerable price increase might not elicit much additional supply because of the peasantry's other commitments. A more important crop might show a responsiveness that would reverse this situation simply by virtue of the cultivator's customary dependence upon such a crop and his appreciation of its importance. A really dominant crop, on the other hand, may show only slight supply responsiveness regardless of the direction of any price change; an increase in price may conflict with inherent physical limitations on an increase in the crop's output: most of the land suitable for its cultivation, for example, may already be used for this purpose. Of course, all of these are relatively short-term considerations, since a minor crop can grow to major importance (or a major crop notably diminish in significance) in only a short period of time.

5. The time needed to harvest the crop or to perform any other vital endeavor for its cultivation. Even if competition for inputs with other crops is not directly felt, the physical limitations on available manpower may be crucial. Some items—for example, certain better grades of coffee beans—must be harvested within very short specific periods lest they lose much of their premium

quality. Higher prices might induce a cultivator to work around the
clock or to hire an extra hand or two, but this might not result in
a much larger harvest if he normally worked a 20-hour day during
the harvest or if he had to hire unskilled help. The same time
factor can bring with it diminishing returns even if the task in
question is not one that must be accomplished within such rigid
bounds. For example, the time needed to travel between widely
scattered plots of land becomes a limiting factor, even when the
tasks to be done are brief or the schedule to be adhered to is flexible,
and might affect a cultivator's decision as to how many of his parcels
will be planted in a particular crop.

6. The effect of differences in plot size. Almost by definition,
essentially subsistence farmers are not very market oriented, and
though the size of the average landholding is not the only factor to
be considered in calculating how large a proportion of the agricultural
sector is actually subsistence in character, it is one of the more
important ones. The responsiveness of food crop producers then
may well be different according to holding size, whereas this may
not be important for cash crops. It should be emphasized that it
is not only the total size of the average peasant's holdings that is
of importance here, but also a consideration of how the holding is
divided. Obviously, one would expect some variation in the responsiveness of peasants who hold, respectively, two undivided acres
of mediocre land, one acre of good land and a second nearby acre
of lower quality, and 20 or so widely scattered plots of different
character totalling two acres.

7. The effect of fluctuations in price and yield. Even in a
homogeneous society the degree to which a peasant is likely to be
a risk-taker will be dependent upon how close he feels he is to the
bare margin needed for survival. With subsistence the keystone,
the implications of risks due to variations in price and yield for
responsiveness would be shaped by the relative prosperity of the
average cultivator and on the role the crop in question plays in
determining that prosperity. Even the smallest landholder might
take a chance with a crop grown on a few square meters that might
otherwise go untilled, while the most prosperous may tire of
excessive volatility and at least hedge his bets through crop diversification.

8. The importance of climatological variability. Certainly,
rainfall, sunshine, and so on during the present growing season
directly affect output and, through this, future price expectations
and planting decisions. But this is not the relationship between
climate and responsiveness of interest here. Different crops
display varying degrees of tolerance to changes in climate. All
other things being equal, one would expect greater price responsiveness shown for the output of hardier crops. As in the case of risks

due to price and yield, some variation in the responsiveness shown by peasants of different income levels may be present.

9. The need for large investments in any part of the cultivation process or the underlying infrastructure. Here no clear-cut expectations about the relationship between investment and responsiveness emerges. One could argue that a massive investment expenditure such as a resettlement project or a new irrigation network implies a major break in the region's traditional agricultural behavior patterns and the introduction of a bias in favor of market-oriented cultivation; therefore, greater price responsiveness should be found following such investment. Similarly, investment of a less widespread nature, such as a peasant's purchase of a pump or other small machine, implies some preconditioning on his part toward market agriculture and a consequent greater degree of responsiveness. On the other hand, if investment is to have a notable effect on output, it frequently must be of some sizable minimum amount. The presence of such a threshold—whether it faces a ministry that lacks £100 million to build a dam or a peasant who does not have £10 to buy a new plow—as a prerequisite for the expansion of the output of a particular crop may simply mean little or no price responsiveness as long as the needed investment funds are lacking and quite possibly a diversion of attention to crops not demanding similar investments, crops that might as a result display a greater degree of supply responsiveness.

10. The existence of national and/or international agreements or restrictions covering the cultivation or marketing of a crop. Such agreements can considerably reduce the risk due to price variation and thus lead to greater price responsiveness among a peasantry conservative by habit or out of necessity. However, such arrangements frequently do more than place a floor under prices. The coffee and cocoa marketing boards that have proliferated in producing countries in recent years impose farm prices that in most years are less-than-prevailing free market prices. In the face of considerable divergence over time between these prices or between the prices producers realize for their produce and those they pay for their inputs and consumption goods then marketing boards conceivably may lead to greater cultivation of alternative uncontrolled commodities and to a slackening of the price responsiveness shown for the original crop.

COUNTRY-TO-COUNTRY ELASTICITY

Similarly, there are a number of reasons that might explain why the elasticity of supply may vary for the same crop from country to country. Among these we can include differences in:

1. Social systems. Since we are concerned with price responsiveness, which enjoys a collateral kinship with the profit motive,
then the presence of a social system that is generally favorable to
the development of so-called capitalist or protocapitalist characteristics would seem encouraging with regard to market orientation.
Individual, as opposed to communal, ownership or operation of
land,* the attachment of prestige to the acquisition of productive
material wealth, an ethos that imposes no serious religious or
philosophical strictures on change—these and other social conditions
might favorably affect price responsiveness.

2. Tenancy structures. If a peasant is to react positively to
price changes he must be able to enjoy some notable part of the
change. If the rent structure contrives in a Ricardian way to keep
the cultivator in a subsistence existence, then price responsiveness
could be exhibited only by the landlord, and the latter's ability to
translate this into output changes would depend upon whatever other
power over his tenants he could exert (for example, eviction of
less-productive tenants, and so on).[1] Otherwise, some reasonable
sharing with the cultivator of the extra revenues due to higher prices
would best serve the landlord's income goals. (To no small extent
one could substitute "the state" for "landlord" and "land taxes" for
"rents" and make essentially the same argument.) Other aspects
of the tenancy system that would affect price responsiveness are
the effectiveness with which the landlords fill ancillary production
roles, such as those of purveyors of technological improvements
and the providers and maintainers of simple machinery.

3. Levels of education. As was indicated in Chapter 2, the
motivation for rural literacy programs is the belief that a literate
peasant will play a more significant role in the agricultural market.
It would seem, however, that literacy measures alone are inadequate.
Though probably no more suitable and widely applicable measure
of the level of education among the peasants themselves may be
available, price responsiveness is likely to be considerably affected
by the training and skills of other elements in the population, such
as the agricultural bureaucracy.

_____

*The importance of this in expanding agricultural output has
been disputed by Tanzanian President Julius Nyerere. He holds
that traditional African communal patterns of land ownership favor
socialism and socialist incentives as a means of improving economic
performance. See "Ujamaa—The Basis of African Socialism," in
Ujamaa: Essays on Socialism (Dar-es-Salaam: Oxford University
Press, 1968).

4. Income level. Again as mentioned earlier in the discussion of the influence of risk on responsiveness, higher income level should indicate a greater degree of market orientation, if for no other reason than that higher income indicates an existence above bare subsistence and, therefore, a more likely involvement in market-based cultivation.

5. Average farm size. All other things being equal, this is of course another measure of productive wealth and income level, and producers of the same crop would be expected to be more sensitive to the market in countries where farms are larger. However, a number of other considerations (such as the next two points) must be made, since a notable variation in the importance of differences in land distribution can occur from region to region.

6. The quality of the land. The few acres, for example, that can assure an Egyptian farmer an almost middle-class existence wouldn't even be able to promise survival to his Iraqi counterpart.

7. Weather conditions, particularly weather variability. Differences in climate not only determine what crops can be grown in an area and their quality but also affect the degree of risk involved in the cultivation of any crop.

8. Government policies regarding credit, price stability, and so on, and on the condition of the infrastructure. Here of course are a whole spectrum of policies and programs that may increase yields, promote the awareness of new crops or strains, reduce risks, increase the cultivator's share of agricultural income, and so on—all with the economic intent of improving the amount and the value of agricultural output. That countries which pursue different policies should have different performance records in fulfilling this intention is not unexpected. The question as to why two or more countries with the same policies administered by more or less equivalent supporting bureaucracies for about the same length of time should have realized vastly different results requires analysis of the underlying factors that determine basic peasant behavior patterns.

The above is only a partial listing of the factors that might affect the magnitude of supply elasticity in any cross-crop and cross-regional analysis. An attempt to learn what influence some of these might have on elasticity now leads us to the postulation of a hypothesis that relates certain factors to market responsiveness (elasticity) and then to the testing of this hypothesis using the results of several earlier Nerlovian supply analyses.

As has been mentioned previously, only a few of the hundred or so supply studies we initially surveyed seemed useful in any attempt to isolate the effects of nonprice considerations on peasant responsiveness. These studies, listed in Table 10.1, were selected by following two pragmatic, if somewhat arbitrary, guidelines: (1) the degree of disaggregation the author reported for his parameter estimates and other pertinent data; and (2) the availability of statistical information about those factors that we incorporated into our hypothesis in order to examine their effect on elasticity. As regards the first guideline, we wished to avoid the problem of lumping together areas as diverse in size and population as countries and counties. Furthermore, in order to secure as large a data population as possible, we naturally preferred the more disaggregated studies, and the Behrman and Nowshirvani studies alone offered a large data base as a beginning. The Fisher-Temin and Swift papers added more information about wheat producers, already prominently included in Nowshirvani's work. The DeCanio paper offered another cash crop for some contrast, and the other Indian studies were complementary both regarding crops and geography. All these works, furthermore, were carried out on a scale (population, output, and so on) of the basic unit considered that was comparable with the first two studies. Finally, the several studies together offer a continuum regarding the status of economic development, from Gangetic plain states through Southeast Asian "rice bowl" to modern Chile and nineteenth-century North America. Though obvious discrete differences exist between Uttar Pradesh and Illinois, the intervening areas smooth out the gap to some extent.

As regards (2), the availability of compatible data from diverse countries and time periods was a very serious problem. Not only were some factors originally hypothesized as important considerations in an analysis of supply responsiveness eliminated from our study because of a lack of available data, as will be mentioned below, but some of the studies discussed in the earlier sections, in which relatively disaggregated parameter estimates were presented, similarly proved unusable. For example, it will be noted that we did not include any perennial crops in this attempt. Unfortunately, only for Brazilian coffee were we able to find adequate supporting statistical information: four producing states, four supply elasticities—certainly not enough for separate regression estimates to be made, and, if the coffee data were lumped with that for the annual crops, the former would be but a tiny percentage of the total observations. Yet perennials, because of their so obvious differences with annuals, made a strong case for their inclusion in order to provide contrasts with annuals and, possibly even to uncover some similarities.

TABLE 10.1

Responsiveness Study, Elasticity Sources

Author and Title	Country	Crops	Time Period
Jere Behrman: <u>Supply Response in Underdeveloped Agriculture</u>	Thailand (50 provinces)	Rice, maize, cassava, and kenaf	1937–63
Vahid Nowshirvani: "Agricultural Supply in India"	India (41 districts)–Bihar and Uttar Pradesh	Rice, wheat, barley, sugar, and groundnuts	1952–64
V. Rajagopalan: "Supply Response for Irrigated Crops in Madras State"	India (10 districts)–Madras	Rice, cumbu, ragi, sugar, groundnuts, and cotton	1939–61
Jawahar Kaul: "A Study of Supply Responses to Price of Punjab Crops"	India (9 districts)–Punjab	Wheat, gram, and bajra	1951–64
K. L. Rathod: "Farmers' Aversion to Risk–A Case of Sugarcane in Western Uttar Pradesh"	India (9 districts)–Uttar Pradesh	Sugar	1950–68
J. Mahender Reddy: "Estimation of Farmers' Supply Response–A Case Study of Groundnut"	India (Kurnool district)	Groundnut	1931–43
Franklin Fisher and Peter Temin: "Regional Specialization and the Supply of Wheat in the United States"	United States (17 states)	Wheat	1867–1914
Jeannine Swift: "An Economic Study of the Chilean Agrarian Reform"	Chile (5 provinces)	Wheat	1942–64
Stephen DeCanio: "Tenancy and the Supply of Southern Cotton 1883–1914"	United States (10 states)	Cotton	1882–1914

Source: Compiled by the authors.

HYPOTHESIS

In formulating our hypothesis several factors were considered as likely to have some effect on the magnitude and direction of peasant responsiveness to prices, as measured by short- and long-run supply elasticities. These factors can be classified as technical, social, and political.

Among the first group are soil fertility or crop yield, the degree of risk in the cultivation of a particular crop, the prevalence of irrigation, the relative importance of the crop being examined within the agricultural sector as a whole, the availability of arable but unused land, and the lifetime of the crop.

Fertility, measured in terms of output per unit area, would seem logically to affect responsiveness positively—with everything else the same, peasants with the more fertile holdings would respond more to market incentives and plant more land in the crop because they can earn more per acre planted. Risk, on the other hand, would seem to be a negative factor, at least in areas where actual or near-subsistence-level farming is involved; for more prosperous cultivators, who might perhaps be considered embryonic entrepreneurs, risk might well be positively related to market responsiveness.*
We differentiated between risks due to variations in price, yield, and rainfall, using as a measure in each case the standard deviation as a percentage of the mean value. Irrigation was expected to have a positive effect on supply response.

On the other hand, there seems to be no clear-cut consensus, in advance of the regression analysis, as to the likely effect on supply elasticity of the relative importance of the crop being examined within the agricultural sector as a whole. For example, a minor crop might show more price responsiveness (as Nowshirvani reported for sugar in Uttar Pradesh) since the farmer need only press a few square meters into its cultivation in order to increase output considerably, or because, in the case of more important crops, increasingly less suitable land is devoted to a crop as its production

---

*This was recently argued by John Weeks in "Uncertainty, Risk and Wealth and Income Distribution in Peasant Agriculture," Journal of Development Studies 7 (October 1970). Arguing that the poorest farmers face as much risk as they dare in the inherent marginality of their holdings, Weeks holds they avoid any innovative techniques available; these thus are adopted only by more prosperous farmers. Agricultural bureaucrats, impressed by the latter group's "economic rationality" and seeing their prejudices about resistance to change among poorer cultivators confirmed, then continue and expand the

increases beyond the capacity of the top-grade acreage. On the other hand, price inducements regarding such a minor crop might not noticeably impress a conservative peasant, nor might he have much knowledge about increasing the yield of such a crop, unless perhaps a government agency were pressing the crop's cause.

By contrast, a major crop, due to its very importance, ought to evoke a positive supply response to changes in price. Certainly its cultivators will be aware of such changes and are more likely to be acquainted with any available yield-enhancing methods affecting such a crop than one that is quite minor in the region's agriculture. Yet a major crop might well be so important that almost all land suitable for its cultivation is already so used, with little acreage available for output response to positive changes in price. (This might, for example, be the case in much of Thailand, where rice claims more than 80 percent of the cultivated acreage in many provinces.) Changes in output due to yield improvements are of course possible, though these are often dependent on the inspiration of some outside agent.

In addition it is in this particular case of a major crop that the so-called marketable surplus hypothesis needs to be considered. In one version of this hypothesis it is argued that a peasant's cash requirements are relatively stable, so that the marketable surplus will vary inversely with crop price, consumption then being the residual.[2] In a second version the point is made that this argument is certainly unlikely to hold true among peasants producing at the absolute level of subsistence and for whom consumption is fixed, not residual, though those who have somewhat higher real incomes may well show more flexibility in their desire regarding increased consumption of produce versus sales for cash and the consumption of other goods.[3]

The availability of unused arable land would be expected to have a positive effect on responsiveness. However, statistics regarding such land include fallow acreage, which is for the most part land that, given the available agricultural technology, must periodically be so designated in order to regenerate its bearing capabilities. Thus cultivators are not free to ignore fallow requirements in order to increase a crop's output, whereas the presence of uncultivated

---

very programs in which only the rich can participate. Weeks maintained that only an attempt to collectivize risk would be likely to spread innovation to the marginal peasants—that one method to do this would be offer the latter some form of "disaster" insurance, though he allowed an extensive program might be beyond the administrative and resource capabilities of most developing countries.

arable land not in fallow would clearly seem to make them more responsive. Despite the ambiguity of the available figures, this factor was included in our analysis. (Mitigating any possible confusion was the consideration that if large amounts of fallow land are present and if cultivators have the frequently available option of adopting new soil-regenerating techniques that reduce the necessary acreage left fallow, then greater response flexibility should be present than when little fallow is present.)

However, eliminated from consideration was any determination of the role played in determining price responsiveness by the distinction between annual and perennial crops, as was mentioned previously. Although a number of studies of perennial crops have been published, most of these present their results in a relatively aggregated manner compared to the works on annual crops. As a result the number of observations of price elasticities for perennials were too few, far too few relative to the approximately 320 observations available for annuals to make any statistically meaningful distinctions between perennials and annuals; thus we limited our work to the latter.

Social factors considered likely to be significant were farm income, rural male literacy, and land distribution (as measured by average size of holding per cultivator family). All three factors were postulated as having likely positive effects on responsiveness.

The political factor most prominent in this discussion would be the presence (or absence) of any active governmental policy of encouraging the cultivation of a particular crop. Within the scope of this study, however, we did not feel justified in including a measure of this factor in the face of a lack of any hard facts on which to base rational judgments about sundry governmental programs, some of which exist in reality only on paper, while the rest are quite obviously of vastly different intent and effectiveness. Another political factor of likely significance is the land distribution system as seen in terms of the tenancy structure. The assumption is that, all other things being equal, the more land in the hands of owner-cultivators the greater the degree of market responsiveness.

In summary, the hypothesis as tested, with the expected sign of the effects shown in parentheses, is that peasant supply responsiveness (as measured in terms of short- and long-run elasticity of supply) is a function of: F—fertility or yield, in pounds per acre (positive); R_p—risk due to price variation, measured as standard deviation of price as a percentage of mean price; R_f—risk due to yield variation, measured analogously to that in price (both possibly negative, though a positive relationship might be found for more prosperous cultivators); R_w—risk due to rainfall variation (negative, with magnitude greater for less hardy crops); I—percentage of cultivated land under irrigation (positive); P—importance of the crop under consideration relative to all other crops, measured as the percentage of cultivated arable land devoted to the crop being considered (expectation unclear); U—the availability of uncultivated arable land expressed as a ratio of such acreage to that under cultivation (positive); Y—farm income, measured in terms of gross returns (positive); L—rural male literacy (positive); S—mean plot size, in acres per cultivator family (positive); and finally, T—land tenure system, in terms of percentage of land holdings in hands of owner-cultivators (positive).

Our source materials for the information used in this section were the original works themselves and the documents listed in Table 10.2. Measures of some of the variables were not available in comparable terms for all regions; thus the hypothesis was tested in various forms for different data samples. Specifically, rainfall, uncultivated land, and land ownership figures were available only for Thailand and India, while measures of farm income (lacking only for Chile) were not everywhere expressed in the same terms. Therefore, this factor was included only when the hypothesis was tested for single country samples.*

---

*It should be stressed that our approach to the analysis of the effects of these various factors on cultivator responsiveness is essentially aggregative. Elasticity estimates are available, from the studies used, on a geographic basis; response in each region is then related to the technical, social, and political variables as measured for these regions.

Several microeconomically oriented studies of responsiveness have been published in recent years. Those of K. L. Sharma and M. P. Gupta and of Kalpana Bardhan (see Appendix A) focused on market sales on the village level. Sharma and Gupta went even further, grouping cultivators within a village according to wealth (expressed in terms of landholdings) in order to uncover any difference in degree of market participation among the groups. A similar procedure was followed by Mubyarto (see Chapter 5) using data from Java.

Another paper taking this approach has been put forward by David E. Pfanner.[4] His interest focused on the role of agricultural credit in the village economy, and he found that while nearly all cultivators required credit in the cycle of agricultural operations, notable differences in the extent credit was used and in the costs incurred were apparent within the village.

TABLE 10.2

Data Sources

Country	Publication	
Thailand	Agricultural Statistics of Thailand	Agricultural Statistic Section, Division of Agricultural Economics, Ministry of Agriculture
	Census of Agriculture 1963	National Statistical Office
	Bulletin of Statistics (quarterly)	Central Statistical Office, Office of the National Economic Development Board
India	Census of India 1961	Government of India Census Commission
	Statistical Abstract of the Indian Union (annual)	Central Statistical Organization, Department of Statistics
	Indian Agricultural Statistics (annual)	Directorate of Economics and Statistics, Ministry of Food and Agriculture
	Indian Crop Calendar	Directorate of Economics and Statistics, Ministry of Food and Agriculture
	Agricultural Situation In India (monthly)	Economics and Statistical Advisor, Ministry of Food and Agriculture
	World Weather Records	United States Department of Commerce
Chile	III Censo Nacional Agricola Ganadero	Servicio Nacional de Estadistica y Censos
	Estadistica Chilena (bimonthly)	Servicio Nacional de Estadistica y Censos
	XIII Censo de Poblacion	Direccion de Estadistica y Censos
United States	Eleventh Census of the United States 1890	Census Office, Department of the Interior
	Population Redistribution and Economic Growth, United States 1870–1950	Simon Kuznets, Ann Ratner Miller, and Richard A. Easterlin

Source: Compiled by the authors.

RESULTS

Parameter estimates for equations representing both short- and long-run elasticities as functions of the above-enumerated independent variables were obtained using both ordinary least-squares techniques and the method suggested by Eric Hanushek.[5] The latter takes some account of the presence of sampling error in observations used as dependent variables, as is the case when such a variable is itself derived from separately estimated regression coefficients. Our dependent variables, the short- and long-run elasticities, were of course derived from parameter estimates of the Nerlove supply response model. Since the standard errors associated with these estimates were reported in the studies we utilized, we could use the added information suggested by Hanushek as a means for considering the relative accuracy of data serving as input into regression analysis.

Generally the corresponding parameter estimates obtained using each method had similar signs and magnitudes; in only a handful of cases were there any notable differences in either regard when estimates from both regression procedures were simultaneously statistically significant. In addition the Hanushek estimates showed a consistently greater degree of significance, and this method gives asymptotically efficient estimates of the coefficients. The Hanushek parameter estimates are shown in Tables 10.3 and 10.4, and short- and long-run elasticities for the total sample and for the three principal national subsamples (Thailand, India, and the United States) are shown in Tables 10.5 and 10.6 for the major crops considered, and in Tables 10.7, 10.8, 10.9, and 10.10 for geographical breakdowns of rice and wheat. All regression estimates for India, including those made for samples made up of the available cereal and cash crop data, are presented in Tables 10.11 and 10.12.

If we consider in turn the factors involved in our hypothesis, we immediately encounter unexpected indications in the estimated parameters for the soil fertility variable (incorporated in terms of thousands of pounds of output per acre). Positive and statistically significant estimates were found (Tables 10.5 and 10.6) for sugar and wheat, but equal strength was uncovered for a negative link between soil fertility and price responsiveness for rice, barley, and cotton. The evidence is further complicated when geographically based regressions are considered. For rice the only significant estimate was found for short-run Indian responsiveness and this was positive, while in the long-run case, significance was indicated only for the negative Thai estimate. The significance of the wheat parameters did not extend to the geographically disaggregated samples, and three of the four estimates had perverse signs.

TABLE 10.3

Short-Run Supply Responsiveness
Parameter Estimates

Sample Description	All Crops	Thailand, All Crops	India, All Crops	United States, All Crops
Sample size	315	68	215	27
Constant	-0.415^e	-1.233^e	-0.005^b	-0.0003^e
	(6.10)	(6.00)	(1.37)	(2.78)
Fertility	–	–	–	–
Price risk	$+0.007$	$+0.093^e$	-0.0008	-0.002
	(1.01)	(4.61)	(0.24)	(0.37)
Fertility risk	$+0.016^d$	$+0.027^a$	-0.005^c	$+0.001$
	(2.01)	(1.23)	(1.65)	(0.22)
Weather risk	–	$+0.088^e$	-0.007^e	–
		(3.35)	(4.77)	
Irrigation	$+0.0065^e$	$+0.011^b$	$+0.0006$	$+0.154^e$
	(2.69)	(1.32)	(0.34)	(10.31)
Cultivated area in crop	-0.023^e	-0.015^e	-0.024^e	-0.002^a
	(7.16)	(2.95)	(5.66)	(1.22)
Unutilized land	–	$+0.0035$	$+0.007^c$	–
		(1.03)	(3.79)	
Farm income	–	$+0.582^e$	$+0.073^e$	-0.0004^e
		(3.30)	(6.69)	(3.91)
Male literacy	$+0.032^e$	-0.016	$+0.010^e$	$+0.006^d$
	(9.04)	(0.57)	(2.78)	(2.59)
Mean plot size	-0.0075^e	-0.015	$+0.0002$	$+0.0009^d$
	(4.21)	(0.15)	(0.02)	(2.12)
Crop area owner cultivated	–	$+0.018^b$	$+0.004^c$	–
		(1.64)	(1.78)	
R^2	0.714	0.928	0.994	0.999
F statistic	128.2^e	73.48^e	3213.3^e	716061.0^e
	(6, 308)	(10, 57)	(10, 204)	(7, 19)

[a]30 percent significance level.
[b]20 percent significance level.
[c]10 percent significance level.
[d]5 percent significance level.
[e]1 percent significance level.
Source: Compiled by the authors.

TABLE 10.4

Long-Run Supply Responsiveness
Parameter Estimates

Sample Description	All Crops	Thailand, All Crops	India, All Crops	United States, All Crops
Sample size	315	68	215	27
Constant	−9.480[e]	−61.12[e]	−0.078[e]	−0.013[d]
	(10.56)	(15.27)	(3.26)	(2.04)
Fertility	−	−	−	−
Price risk	+0.076[e]	+0.433[e]	+0.086[e]	−0.023
	(3.16)	(8.33)	(11.94)	(0.75)
Fertility risk	+0.040[b]	+0.113[d]	−0.020[e]	−0.029[a]
	(1.42)	(2.27)	(3.20)	(1.12)
Weather risk	−	+0.007	−0.023[e]	−
		(0.11)	(5.19)	
Irrigation	+0.025[e]	+0.012	+0.002	+0.011
	(3.06)	(0.60)	(0.46)	(0.19)
Cultivated area in crop	−0.078[e]	−0.029[d]	−0.020[d]	−0.0016
	(7.32)	(2.44)	(2.28)	(0.12)
Unutilized land	−	+0.0007	+0.042[e]	−
		(0.10)	(5.62)	
Farm income	−	−0.925[d]	+0.261[e]	−0.025
		(2.05)	(10.97)	(0.93)
Male literacy	+0.146[e]	+0.105[c]	−0.040[d]	+0.024[d]
	(10.78)	(1.74)	(2.12)	(2.04)
Mean plot size	−0.034[e]	+0.101	−0.233[e]	+0.0015[b]
	(4.76)	(0.44)	(16.14)	(1.38)
Crop area owner cultivated	−	+0.040[b]	+0.012[d]	−
		(1.50)	(2.17)	
R^2	0.685	0.925	0.999	0.999
F statistic	111.4[e]	70.24[e]	73164.4[e]	2922.8[e]
	(6,308)	(10,57)	(10,204)	(7,19)

[a]30 percent significance level.
[b]20 percent significance level.
[c]10 percent significance level.
[d]5 percent significance level.
[e]1 percent significance level.
Source: Compiled by the authors.

TABLE 10.5

Short-Run Supply Responsiveness
Parameter Estimates, by Crop

Sample Description	All Rice	All Wheat	All Barley	All Sugar	All Cotton
Sample size	95	66	34	45	16
Constant	-0.159^e	-0.131^e	-0.013^a	-0.071^e	$+0.827$
	(7.56)	(9.68)	(1.15)	(4.91)	(0.75)
Fertility	-0.558^e	$+0.453^e$	-0.291^e	$+0.016^e$	-4.133^c
	(2.97)	(2.69)	(2.91)	(3.28)	(2.00)
Price risk	$+0.0018$	$+0.002$	-0.013^e	$+0.007^c$	-0.012
	(0.21)	(0.45)	(4.39)	(1.88)	(0.74)
Fertility risk	$+0.019^e$	$+0.010^e$	$+0.007^c$	$+0.006^c$	$+0.066^b$
	(3.67)	(2.68)	(1.79)	(1.82)	(1.77)
Weather risk	$+0.004$	–	$+0.006^b$	$+0.004^c$	–
	(0.54)		(1.54)	(1.80)	
Irrigation	$+0.002^a$	-0.0001	$+0.0012^b$	-0.003^e	-0.026^c
	(1.13)	(0.14)	(1.55)	(3.45)	(2.25)
Cultivated area in crop	$+0.006^e$	$+0.005^c$	-0.003^a	$+0.007$	-0.007
	(2.66)	(1.67)	(1.18)	(0.73)	(0.85)
Unutilized land	-0.0007	–	$+0.0006$	-0.010^e	–
	(0.79)		(0.50)	(4.43)	
Farm income	–	–	-0.136	$+0.098$	–
			(0.81)	(0.53)	
Male literacy	$+0.0026$	$+0.0067^d$	-0.003^a	-0.0012	-0.0043
	(0.49)	(2.39)	(1.31)	(0.23)	(0.35)
Mean plot size	-0.015	-0.0005	$+0.009$	-0.029	-0.0041^b
	(0.72)	(0.82)	(0.84)	(0.79)	(1.82)
Crop area owner cultivated	$+0.006^d$	–	$+0.005^d$	$+0.004^c$	–
	(2.37)		(2.56)	(1.79)	
R^2	0.819	0.920	0.985	0.906	0.694
F statistic	37.88^e	95.55^e	131.5^e	29.04^e	2.586^b
	(10, 84)	(7, 58)	(11, 22)	(11, 33)	(7, 8)

[a] 30 percent significance level.
[b] 20 percent significance level.
[c] 10 percent significance level.
[d] 5 percent significance level.
[e] 1 percent significance level.
Source: Compiled by the authors.

TABLE 10.6

Long-Run Supply Responsiveness
Parameter Estimates, by Crop

Sample Description	All Rice	All Wheat	All Barley	All Sugar	All Cotton
Sample size	95	66	34	45	16
Constant	-0.631^e	-0.610^e	-0.082^e	-0.741	-4.903^c
	(8.52)	(6.69)	(6.40)	(0.17)	(1.98)
Fertility	-0.415^b	$+0.318$	-0.497^e	$+0.059^b$	-6.761^a
	(1.29)	(0.88)	(3.59)	(1.68)	(1.13)
Price risk	$+0.0076$	$+0.010^a$	-0.011^d	$+0.015$	$+0.042$
	(0.53)	(1.15)	(2.46)	(0.44)	(1.00)
Fertility risk	$+0.0072$	$+0.017^c$	-0.003	-0.039^b	$+0.275^e$
	(0.78)	(1.92)	(0.50)	(1.32)	(5.45)
Weather risk	$+0.064^e$	—	$+0.011^e$	-0.032^a	—
	(4.80)		(3.40)	(1.26)	
Irrigation	$+0.0032^a$	$+0.0008$	$+0.0042^e$	$+0.0056$	-0.020
	(1.09)	(0.38)	(3.37)	(0.57)	(0.56)
Cultivated area in crop	$+0.015^e$	$+0.022^e$	$+0.0042$	$+0.013$	-0.0049
	(4.01)	(4.74)	(1.04)	(0.19)	(0.22)
Unutilized land	$+0.0007$	—	-0.0017^a	-0.012	—
	(0.51)		(1.23)	(0.57)	
Farm income	—	—	$+0.158$	-0.004^e	—
			(0.64)	(2.93)	
Male literacy	$+0.020^d$	$+0.016^e$	$+0.007^c$	$+0.004$	$+0.045^b$
	(2.52)	(3.56)	(1.76)	(0.09)	(1.50)
Mean plot size	-0.127^e	-0.002^d	$+0.012$	$+0.926^e$	-0.011^c
	(3.93)	(2.22)	(0.63)	(3.72)	(2.13)
Crop area owner cultivated	-0.007^b	—	$+0.0025$	-0.0003	—
	(1.49)		(0.92)	(0.01)	
R^2	0.872	0.794	0.955	0.425	0.845
F statistic	57.20^e	31.99^e	42.71^e	2.217^d	6.246^e
	(10, 84)	(7, 58)	(11, 22)	(11, 33)	(7, 8)

[a]30 percent significance level.
[b]20 percent significance level.
[c]10 percent significance level.
[d]5 percent significance level.
[e]1 percent significance level.
Source: Compiled by the authors.

TABLE 10.7

Short-Run Supply Responsiveness
Parameter Estimates, Rice

Sample Description	All Rice	Thai Rice	Indian Rice
Sample size	95	50	45
Constant	-0.159[e]	-0.200[e]	-0.017[e]
	(7.56)	(6.75)	(4.10)
Fertility	-0.558[e]	-0.236	+0.501[e]
	(2.97)	(0.97)	(3.26)
Price risk	+0.0018	–	-0.0022
	(0.21)		(0.59)
Fertility risk	+0.019[e]	+0.030[e]	+0.0015
	(3.67)	(4.16)	(0.48)
Weather risk	+0.004	-0.012[a]	+0.0059
	(0.54)	(1.10)	(0.59)
Irrigation	+0.002[a]	-0.0069[d]	-0.0018[b]
	(1.13)	(2.23)	(1.44)
Cultivated area in crop	+0.006[e]	+0.010[e]	+0.0011
	(2.66)	(3.30)	(0.68)
Unutilized land	-0.007	-0.00065	-0.0011
	(0.79)	(0.70)	(0.84)
Farm income	–	-0.049	-0.298[c]
		(0.76)	(1.72)
Male literacy	+0.0026	+0.022[d]	+0.0005
	(0.49)	(2.61)	(0.14)
Mean plot size	-0.015	-0.059[c]	+0.020[a]
	(0.72)	(1.97)	(1.08)
Crop area owner cultivated	+0.006[d]	-0.006[a]	-0.0018
	(2.37)	(1.63)	(0.63)
R^2	0.819	0.896	0.592
F statistic	37.88[e]	33.56[e]	4.350[e]
	(10,84)	(10,39)	(11,33)

[a] 30 percent significance level.
[b] 20 percent significance level.
[c] 10 percent significance level.
[d] 5 percent significance level.
[e] 1 percent significance level.
  Source: Compiled by the authors.

TABLE 10.8

Long-Run Supply Responsiveness
Parameter Estimates, Rice

Sample Description	All Rice	Thai Rice	Indian Rice
Sample size	95	50	45
Constant	-0.631[e]	-0.618[e]	+0.0016
	(8.52)	(5.28)	(0.61)
Fertility	-0.415[b]	-0.554[b]	-0.021
	(1.29)	(1.38)	(0.07)
Price risk	+0.0076	–	-0.0062
	(0.53)		(0.87)
Fertility risk	+0.0072	+0.018[b]	-0.003
	(0.78)	(1.39)	(0.56)
Weather risk	+0.064[e]	+0.014	+0.009
	(4.80)	(0.70)	(0.78)
Irrigation	+0.0032[a]	-0.0047	-0.0048[c]
	(1.09)	(0.92)	(2.01)
Cultivated area in crop	+0.015[e]	+0.014[e]	+0.0037
	(4.01)	(2.81)	(1.04)
Unutilized land	+0.0007	-0.0017[a]	+0.0013
	(0.51)	(1.09)	(0.53)
Farm income	–	+0.130[a]	+0.019
		(1.23)	(0.68)
Male literacy	+0.020[d]	+0.061[e]	-0.007[a]
	(2.52)	(4.39)	(1.29)
Mean plot size	-0.127[e]	-0.249[e]	+0.053[a]
	(3.93)	(5.07)	(1.60)
Crop area owner cultivated	-0.007[a]	-0.017[d]	-0.0028
	(1.49)	(2.44)	(0.59)
R^2	0.872	0.920	0.818
F statistic	57.20[e]	44.79[e]	13.49[e]
	(10, 84)	(10, 39)	(11, 33)

[a] 30 percent significance level.
[b] 20 percent significance level.
[c] 10 percent significance level.
[d] 5 percent significance level.
[e] 1 percent significance level.

Source: Compiled by the authors.

TABLE 10.9

Short-Run Supply Responsiveness
Parameter Estimates, Wheat

Sample Description	All Wheat	Indian Wheat	U.S. Wheat
Sample size	66	44	17
Constant	−0.131[e]	−0.070[e]	−0.008[d]
	(9.68)	(3.18)	(2.53)
Fertility	+0.453[e]	−0.397	−0.072
	(2.69)	(0.69)	(0.34)
Price risk	+0.002	+0.0042	+0.0004
	(0.45)	(0.30)	(0.03)
Fertility risk	+0.010[e]	+0.012[b]	−0.027[d]
	(2.68)	(1.46)	(2.60)
Weather risk	−	−0.0018	−
		(0.19)	
Irrigation	−0.0001	−0.0011	0.097[e]
	(0.14)	(0.47)	(3.42)
Cultivated area in crop	+0.005[c]	−0.0059	+0.0032
	(1.67)	(0.54)	(0.57)
Unutilized land	−	−0.0004	−
		(0.19)	
Farm income	−	+0.056	+0.007
		(0.94)	(0.40)
Male literacy	+0.0067[d]	+0.00065	+0.009[a]
	(2.39)	(0.06)	(1.43)
Mean plot size	−0.0005	−0.015	+0.0043
	(0.82)	(0.43)	(0.72)
Crop area owner cultivated	−	+0.0068	−
		(1.23)	
R^2	0.920	0.856	0.999
F statistic	95.55[e]	17.35[e]	3534.5[e]
	(7, 58)	(11, 32)	(8, 8)

[a]30 percent significance level.
[b]20 percent significance level.
[c]10 percent significance level.
[d]5 percent significance level.
[e]1 percent significance level.
  Source: Compiled by the authors.

TABLE 10.10

Long-Run Supply Responsiveness
Parameter Estimates, Wheat

Sample Description	All Wheat	Indian Wheat	U.S. Wheat
Sample size	66	44	17
Constant	-0.610[e]	-0.120[e]	-0.125[d]
	(6.69)	(5.03)	(2.48)
Fertility	+0.318	+0.117	-0.223
	(0.88)	(0.24)	(0.41)
Price risk	+0.010[e]	-0.0018	-0.012
	(1.15)	(0.20)	(0.26)
Fertility risk	+0.017[c]	+0.013[c]	-0.038[e]
	(1.92)	(1.82)	(1.27)
Weather risk	–	-0.0093[a]	–
		(1.27)	
Irrigation	+0.0008	-0.0027[a]	-0.037
	(0.38)	(1.15)	(0.40)
Cultivated area in crop	+0.022[e]	+0.0088[a]	-0.011
	(4.74)	(1.15)	(0.49)
Unutilized land	–	-0.0057[d]	–
		(2.53)	
Farm income	–	+0.016	-0.050
		(0.41)	(0.95)
Male literacy	+0.016[e]	-0.0053	+0.030[a]
	(3.56)	(0.59)	(1.39)
Mean plot size	-0.002[d]	-0.0075	+0.0026[a]
	(2.22)	(0.20)	(1.37)
Crop area owner cultivated	–	+0.015	–
		(3.41)	
R^2	0.794	0.921	0.988
F statistic	31.99[e]	33.68[e]	82.24[e]
	(7,58)	(11,32)	(8,8)

[a]30 percent significance level.
[b]20 percent significance level.
[c]10 percent significance level.
[d]5 percent significance level.
[e]1 percent significance level.
Source: Compiled by the authors.

The strength of the negative link indicated between fertility and responsiveness for barley is the first indication of the rather inverted outlook its cultivators take. As has been indicated previously, barley is generally considered an inferior crop relative to its chief (Indian) competitor, wheat; not only does it command a lower market price, but it is a less prestigious consumption item than wheat.[6] Since soil good for one is good for the other, barley tends to be planted on the more marginal acreage, and thus to the extent such soils are available, price responsiveness quite rationally could be expected to be favorably affected—that is, positive acreage responsiveness to price is likely when there is inferior marginal

TABLE 10.11

Short-Run Supply Responsiveness
Parameter Estimates, India

Sample Description	All India	Indian Cereals	Indian Rice	Indian Wheat	Indian Barley	Indian Cash	Indian Sugar
Sample size	215	150	45	44	34	65	45
Constant	−0.005	−0.039	−0.017	−0.070	−0.013	+0.101	−0.071
	(1.37)	(3.50)	(4.10)	(3.18)	(1.15)	(1.27)	(4.91)
Fertility	−	−	+0.501^e	−0.397	−0.291^e	−	+0.016^e
			(3.26)	(0.69)	(2.91)		(3.28)
Price risk	−0.0008	−0.015^e	−0.0022	+0.0042	−0.013^e	−0.0025	+0.007^c
	(0.24)	(3.43)	(0.59)	(0.30)	(4.39)	(0.47)	(1.88)
Fertility risk	−0.005^c	+0.007^c	+0.0015	+0.012^b	+0.007^c	+0.0005	+0.006^c
	(1.65)	(1.95)	(0.48)	(1.46)	(1.79)	(0.06)	(1.82)
Weather risk	−0.007^e	−0.011^e	+0.0059	−0.0018	+0.006^b	−0.0003	+0.004^c
	(4.77)	(6.67)	(0.59)	(0.19)	(1.54)	(0.13)	(1.80)
Irrigation	+0.0006	−0.00008	−0.0018^b	−0.0011	+0.0012^b	−0.0015	−0.003^e
	(0.34)	(0.07)	(1.44)	(0.47)	(1.55)	(0.78)	(3.45)
Cultivated area in crop	−0.024^e	−0.008^d	−0.0011	−0.0059	−0.003^a	+0.0037	+0.007
	(5.66)	(2.39)	(0.68)	(0.54)	(1.18)	(0.39)	(0.73)
Unutilized land	+0.007^e	+0.004^e	−0.0011	−0.0004	+0.0006	+0.0004	−0.010^e
	(3.79)	(2.79)	(0.84)	(0.19)	(0.50)	(0.12)	(4.43)
Farm income	+0.073^e	+0.083^e	−0.298^c	+0.056	−0.136	−0.035^c	+0.098
	(6.69)	(6.57)	(1.72)	(0.94)	(0.81)	(1.98)	(0.53)
Male literacy	+0.010^e	−0.0008	+0.0005	+0.00065	−0.003^a	+0.015^c	−0.0012
	(2.78)	(0.21)	(0.14)	(0.06)	(1.31)	(1.99)	(0.23)
Mean plot size	+0.0002	−0.012	+0.020^a	−0.015	+0.009	+0.074^e	−0.029
	(0.02)	(0.94)	(1.08)	(0.43)	(0.84)	(2.66)	(0.79)
Crop area owner cultivated	+0.004^b	+0.013^e	−0.0018	+0.0068^a	+0.005^d	−0.0052^a	+0.004^b
	(1.78)	(6.21)	(0.63)	(1.23)	(2.56)	(1.30)	(1.79)
R^2	0.994	0.927	0.592	0.856	0.985	0.397	0.906
F statistic	3213.3^e	175.8^e	4.350^e	17.35^e	131.5^e	3.559^e	29.04^e
	(10,204)	(10,139)	(11,33)	(11,32)	(11,22)	(10,54)	(11,33)

[a]30 percent significance level.
[b]20 percent significance level.
[c]10 percent significance level.
[d]5 percent significance level.
[e]1 percent significance level.
Source: Compiled by the authors.

TABLE 10.12

Long-Run Supply Responsiveness
Parameter Estimates, India

Sample Description	All India	Indian Cereals	Indian Rice	Indian Wheat	Indian Barley	Indian Cash	Indian Sugar
Sample size	215	150	45	44	34	65	45
Constant	-0.078	-0.298	+0.0016	-0.120	-0.082	+1.565	-0.741
	(3.26)	(7.86)	(0.61)	(5.03)	(6.40)	(0.78)	(0.17)
Fertility	—	—	-0.021	+0.117	-0.497[e]	—	+0.059[c]
			(0.07)	(0.24)	(3.59)		(1.69)
Price risk	+0.086[e]	+0.056[e]	-0.0062	-0.0018	-0.011[d]	-0.0011	+0.015
	(11.94)	(5.53)	(0.87)	(0.20)	(2.46)	(0.06)	(0.44)
Fertility risk	-0.020[e]	-0.044[e]	-0.003	+0.013[c]	-0.003	-0.003[a]	-0.039[b]
	(3.20)	(3.90)	(0.56)	(1.82)	(0.50)	(1.22)	(1.32)
Weather risk	-0.023[e]	-0.013[e]	+0.009	-0.0093[a]	+0.011[e]	-0.017[c]	-0.032[a]
	(5.19)	(2.80)	(0.78)	(1.27)	(3.40)	(1.75)	(1.26)
Irrigation	+0.002	-0.009[d]	-0.0048[c]	-0.0027[a]	+0.0042[e]	+0.070[b]	+0.0056
	(0.46)	(2.44)	(2.01)	(1.15)	(3.37)	(1.34)	(0.57)
Cultivated area in crop	-0.020[d]	-0.007	+0.0037	+0.0088[a]	+0.0042	+0.044[b]	+0.013
	(2.28)	(0.83)	(1.04)	(1.15)	(1.04)	(1.33)	(0.19)
Unutilized land	+0.042[e]	+0.014[e]	+0.0013	-0.0057[d]	-0.0017[a]	+0.019[c]	-0.012
	(5.62)	(2.61)	(0.53)	(2.53)	(1.23)	(1.74)	(0.57)
Farm income	+0.261[e]	+0.0019[e]	+0.019	+0.016	+0.158	-0.193[d]	-0.004[d]
	(10.67)	(6.52)	(0.68)	(0.41)	(0.64)	(2.61)	(2.93)
Male literacy	-0.040[d]	+0.031[d]	-0.007[a]	-0.0053	+0.007[b]	+0.0024	+0.004
	(2.12)	(2.34)	(1.29)	(0.59)	(1.76)	(0.09)	(0.09)
Mean plot size	-0.233[e]	-0.220[e]	+0.053[b]	-0.0075	+0.012	+0.448[e]	+0.926[e]
	(16.14)	(11.04)	(1.60)	(0.20)	(0.63)	(2.88)	(3.72)
Crop area owner cultivated	+0.012[d]	+0.014[d]	-0.0028	+0.015[e]	+0.0025	-0.015	-0.0003
	(2.17)	(2.45)	(0.59)	(3.41)	(0.92)	(0.65)	(0.01)
R^2	0.999	0.987	0.818	0.921	0.955	0.573	0.425
F statistic	73164.4[e]	1042.3[e]	13.49[e]	33.68[e]	42.71[e]	7.235[e]	2.217[d]
	(10,204)	(10,139)	(11,33)	(11,32)	(11,22)	(10,54)	(11,33)

[a]30 percent significance level.
[b]20 percent significance level.
[c]10 percent significance level.
[d]5 percent significance level.
[e]1 percent significance level.
Source: Compiled by the authors.

land available for barley planting. In short, barley, according to
Nowshirvani, is a likely candidate for "perverse" behavior. However, no such explanation can presently be offered for the negative
estimates indicated for other crops.

The element of risk reflected in uncertainty over price and yield
seems to be positively related to responsiveness; most of the
statistically significant parameter estimates are of this sign. The
only possibly notable exception can be seen if we contrast Indian
short- and long-run responsiveness (see Tables 10.11 and 10.12).
Negative significant parameters are indicated more often than not
in the latter case. This could be interpreted as evidence that

Indian cultivators, considerably closer to subsistence than their
compatriots in contemporary Thailand or nineteenth-century America,
are not unnaturally less entrepreneurial in their reactions toward
risk. (In the context of this study, most Indian cultivators are from,
relatively speaking, the poorest areas of the country: namely,
Nowshirvani's focus of concern—Bihar and Uttar Pradesh.) However,
since positive parameters were frequently found for India, particularly when short-run elasticity was the dependent variable, even
her peasants cannot be considered outside the stream of risk-taking,
profit-maximizing explanations of cultivator behavior. Rather,
they appear as likely more conservative, more cognizant of the
precarious nature of survival/nonsurvival agriculture than the
more prosperous farmers of Thailand and North America.

Weather risk is distinct from that associated with price—the
latter indicating entrepreneurial outlook, the former being a case
of an "act of God" even in such relatively weather-insulated areas
as the extensively irrigated parts of twentieth-century California.
Yield risk occupies somewhat of a middle ground between that
derived from price and weather fluctuations; obviously it is affected
by weather shifts—but cultivators have considerable independence
in this regard. They can vary such yield-enhancing inputs as
natural and synthetic fertilizers, the purchase of available irrigation
water, the use of nontraditional inputs such as advanced seeds or
machinery, depending upon whether they react to the potential
changes in per acre yield (and income returns) that are linked to
the definite changes in per acre costs incurred in the use of one or
more of these factors.* If weather risk is considered in isolation
from price and yield risk, the argument is proposed that, ceteris
paribus, weather risk exercises a negative influence on price

---

*The overlapping nature of price, yield, and weather risk measures,
all used together in most of the regressions, brings up the estimating
problem of multicollinearity, introduced by the simultaneous inclusion
in regression analysis, of one or more variables highly correlated
with one another.

The correlation coefficients indicated between the various
independent variables were almost universally low: of the factors
for which data were available in all the principal subsamples, only
between average holding size and rural male literacy is the correlation coefficient of any notable size, and here only about +0.56.

In the several various subsamples for which regressions were
run, correlation coefficients were also calculated; however, no
obvious patterns of large correlation coefficients between individual
independent variables were discernible. This point is not cited to

responsiveness; however, there is considerable difference in the
magnitude of such an effect depending upon the hardiness (with
respect to rainfall) of the crop. In fact, "dry" crops might even
show positive links between weather variability and price responsiveness.

Unfortunately, important data limitations affect the gains derived
from including this variable. The only really dry crops for which
data were available were Indian groundnuts and cotton, and in neither
case were sufficient elasticity estimates reported to allow separate
regressions to be performed that would effectively isolate this
particular situation. As a result, the frequently statistically
insignificant weather risk parameter estimates indicated in Tables
10.3 through 10.12 give us no really solid evidence. Though barley
proceeds are somewhat less dependent upon rainfall than those from
wheat, for example, in India, negative coefficients are indicated
for both cases, though a considerably greater degree of statistical
significance is found for the "perverse" (and relatively drier) barley
crop. Certainly, with regard to this variable, a more sophisticated
degree of examination is demanded.

At this point it seems relevant to point out that the bounds imposed
on our study, as reported in this chapter, by the use of elasticity
data discussed in the earlier Nerlove supply model studies enumerated
in Chapters 5 through 8, has prompted considerable further work
by one of the authors. The need is apparent for supply analysis
of selected crops, within a relatively homogeneous environment
from the viewpoint of data availability—an analysis conducted that
considers the need, if our responsiveness hypothesis is to be
adequately tested, for elasticity estimates from a geographically,
climatically, and economically diverse group of regions, relating
to a wide cross-section of crops. Such elasticity estimates allow
the testing of our responsiveness hypothesis under circumstances
where the other included independent variables are bureaucratically
computed and reported under similar definitional circumstances.

For all these reasons, the study reported by John Thomas
Cummings was undertaken.[7] This study, from the viewpoint of
the present work, is definitely tentative. It was limited to India
and Pakistan in order to homogenize data reporting along the lines
set forth in the former Indian Empire; it includes crops selected,

----

indicate that the potential for multicollinearity problems is insignificant, but only that no patterns, among the various samples for
which regressions were carried out, emerged to indicate likely
multicollinearity problems across the subsamples for which we
tested our responsiveness hypothesis.

complementarily and additively, in relation to already available
studies. Supply elasticities are estimated, across the subcontinent,
for the cereals, rice, wheat, and barley that have been previously
calculated for parts of India/Pakistan by other authors. In addition,
six cash crops (two fibers—cotton and jute; three oilseeds—groundnuts,
sesamum, and rape [mustard seed]; and tobacco) are analyzed;
these include both predominantly wet (jute) and dry (cotton and groundnuts) crops. It must be emphasized that the current state of the
material of this study precludes its total inclusion herein; however,
the supply analysis being complete is reported above in Chapters 5
and 6. Later references in this chapter in regard to the need for
further supply analysis within a controlled geographic environment
are to be considered within this context.

Irrigation facilities, the authors hypothesized, should positively
influence the responsiveness of cultivators, allowing them greater
flexibility to vary acreage in response to market changes by compensating for deficiencies related to the availability of water. Not only
does irrigation permit the production of crops not easily or profitably
grown under natural conditions but it expands the overall crop
productivity, potentially increasing the proportion of output even
of basic subsistence crops that can be brought to market.*

The estimated coefficients had the expected signs in all the
cross-crop samples tested (Tables 10.3 and 10.4), but negative
and often statistically significant parameters were indicated for
isolated individual crops. The results show some rather curious
anomalies: For example, positive signs are found for rice when
India and Thailand are pooled (and for both short- and long-run
cases, the estimates are statistically significant, at least at the
30 percent level), while negative relationships emerge for both
Indian and Thai rice considered separately (with significance at

_____

*Within the context of this study a wide variation exists in the
importance of irrigation in the crop districts considered. Little or
no irrigation figured in the U.S. wheat and cotton states included in
the Fisher-Temin and DeCanio papers, while close to half of the
acreage in the Thai and Indian districts was irrigated. However
within the latter countries, considerable variation was found from
crop to crop. Thai rice was more than 49 percent irrigated (in
50 districts), while the average for irrigated kenaf (8 districts) was
only about 28 percent. In India the average sugar district (out of
45 districts) saw better than 67 percent of the crop so watered,
while the figures for wheat (44 districts), barley (34 districts),
bajra (14 districts), and groundnuts (14 districts) were 46, 22, 17,
and 8 percent respectively.

the 20 percent level or better in three out of four cases). Similarly, a strongly significant negative parameter was calculated for short-run responsiveness of Indian sugar, the most irrigated of all the crops included herein (though the long-run regression yielded a positive estimated coefficient with no appreciable significance). Since Indian wheat and barley regressions yield negative and positive parameter estimates for these crops (relatively) highly and moderately irrigated, respectively, one might suggest reasonably that irrigation's hypothesized positive effect on responsiveness is felt for crops where such facilities are less prevalent, whereas for more irrigation-dependent crops (sugar, rice, and wheat) the negative estimated coefficients (that is, less responsiveness in the most irrigated districts) could point to a diminishing returns effect for irrigation facilities. It must be stressed that the evidence presented here only suggests this possibility; more explicit contrast between crops relatively highly dependent and independent of the need for fairly steady water inputs is needed before this suggestion could become a conclusion.

With regard to the next independent variable included in our hypothesis, the proportion of cultivated land devoted to the crop in question, we originally formulated no definite preconception but suggested that cultivator behavior might be quite different for major and minor crops.* Estimates based on aggregate cross-crop samples (Tables 10.3 and 10.4) unanimously yield negative parameter estimates (all but one statistically significant at the 30 percent level or better) for this factor, pointing to greater responsiveness, overall, in districts where a given crop is less dominant.

However, if we examine individual crops in India (Tables 10.11 and 10.12), mild evidence is offered for a distinction between cereal (relatively major in acreage terms) and cash (relatively minor) crops—negative and positive crop importance-to-responsiveness links, respectively. This evidence is somewhat bolstered by the positive (and at least somewhat statistically significant) parameter estimates indicated for both the short- and long-run responsiveness of barley—the least important cereal crop analyzed separately. On

----

*For the crop districts represented in our responsiveness regressions the relative importance of the crops varies considerably; for example, in Thai districts the average proportion devoted to rice is nearly 87 percent, while in India this figure drops to 33 percent. Other situations include 15 percent for Indian wheat, 12 percent for U.S. wheat, 10, 12, 5, and 10 percent for Indian barley, bajra, sugar, and groundnuts, respectively, and 26 percent for U.S. cotton.

the other hand, the regressions performed for both Thai and Indian
rice indicate positive coefficients for the crop, which is far and
away the most important in both countries (claiming approximately
75 and 25 percent of the acreage in each, respectively); the Thai
coefficients are strongly significant, however, unlike those obtained
for the Indian samples.

It should be remembered that Thai rice represents a truly
unique case among the crops herein represented. No other crop
so completely dominates the agriculture of the region for which the
elasticity estimates were originally made; in some Thai districts
practically every cultivated acre is planted in rice—as the overall
average testifies, Thailand is truly Southeast Asia's "rice bowl."
These districts do not grow rice merely for subsistence purposes
or even for internal Thai consumption—rice is the country's most
important export and Thailand is one of the world's major suppliers.
In India, on the other hand, rice is essentially a nonmarket crop;
the nation is often a net rice importer (even in relatively good years,
as population pressures mount), though many areas, particularly
in the south and in Bengal, are nearly as productive as Thailand.
However, our available elasticity inputs come from Nowshirvani's
study of Bihar and Uttar Pradesh—two of the poorest and most
crowded states in the federal union. Some marketable surplus
emerges from these areas in most years, but their peasants always
hover on the margin of survival. Their rice output is first claimed
by their families; in good years much can reach the market—in
Thailand, even in years when the yields are reduced, peasants grow
enough to feed themselves <u>and</u> deliver the major portion of the crop
to the marketplace.

In short we face a three-, not a twofold, distinction. Relatively
minor crops (for example, 7 or 8 percent of cultivated area or less),
either cash or food in nature, are essentially marginal—their cultivation can be changed considerably with only minor shifts in acreage.
Furthermore, if the crop is not too specific in its input demands,
the potential available to make such shifts is greatly enhanced—for
example, planting a few more square meters with a few extra
cultivator hours squeezed from other activities.

More important crops, especially those that are major present
consumption items, are often essentially traditional in their
cultivation—they may have a long history of being cultivated, year
in and year out, to approximately the same extent; they are thus
generally grown on the acreages most suitable for their production,
and short of some relatively drastic change in available inputs
(like new irrigation facilities or improved seed or fertilizer) it is
difficult to alter considerably total output. All in all, long-run

responsiveness shifts might be large, but in the short run, changes
are likely moderate.

In the third category are overwhelmingly dominant crops, which
may or may not be consumption cereals (like rice)—their very
importance, ipso facto, has resulted in their claim (at one time
or another) to nearly all acreage suitable for their production. On
the other hand, the likely concomitant dominant role played by
market forces in the cultivation of such a role could well result in
greater responsiveness of total output to price changes in such
yield-per-acre-enhancing areas as the use of fertilizer, rented
machinery, or hired labor, or of acreage (to price changes), because
of a greater sensitivity to market forces in general, and to those
affecting alternative economic activities in particular. Consideration
of the importance of this latter effect, for example, leads to the
possibility that a crop like rice is planted to the utmost whenever
relative rice returns per acre dramatically increase, but market-
sensitive farmers are open to other uses for rice land whenever
market impetuses move in the opposite direction—though obviously
such shifts are subject to technical limitations imposed by the technical characteristics of available essential inputs.

Again in this case the data available for our analysis result
more in suggestion than hard evidence—distinctions between cultivator behavior with regard to "minor" versus "major" (cash as opposed
to cereal) crops. A greater degree of responsiveness is indicated
among the former the less important a crop is in a given region—
that is, the more marginal the crop, the more possible it is to
increase its output with fairly minor shifts in input allocations.
For the latter the cultivators in districts where the crop is relatively
more important seem more market sensitive, but a distinction is
indicated, perhaps, between districts where a major crop's domina-
tion is moderate versus more or less overwhelming—a distinction
possibly clearly indicated by the case of a basic subsistence crop
raised, in the first case, predominantly for home consumption,
and in the second, largely for the cash market (though both domestic
and market destinations may be significant in each case).

Again we see the need for regression analysis with a data base
designed to heighten the presence of input from hypothetically distinct
regions—here, for example, we might find useful elasticity estimates
from Indian districts where the major cereal is grown in sufficient
abundance to be as much, in most years, a market crop as a consumption item—certainly not the case with regard to Bihar and Uttar
Pradesh rice or wheat.

Data for the next independent variable, the availability of arable
but uncultivated land, were available on a more or less comparable

basis only for India and Thailand;* this unfortunately omits our only
real case of the so-called frontier agricultural economy—that of
nineteenth-century North America, as illustrated in the studies of
Fisher and Temin for wheat and DeCanio for cotton. Statistically
significant exceptions to positive parameter estimates were rather
uncommon—thus generally indicating a relationship between greater
responsiveness and the availability of uncultivated, but potentially
useful, land. Such evidence is certainly not overwhelming. In
many of our regressions the estimated coefficients show no great
degree of significance in either direction.

Available farm income figures are subject to certain data
limitations that cloud somewhat our original conceptual relationship
of income with market responsiveness. (No attempt was made to
convert income [or rather cultivator family gross returns] to
comparable intercountry terms. Income measurements thus were
included only in the single country—Thailand, India, United States—
samples.) For India and Thailand available income figures are
actually estimates of cultivator returns, without consideration of
input costs; official estimates by district have been published for
many Indian states (including Bihar and Uttar Pradesh), but in the
case of Thailand similar figures are available only for more aggregated regions.

The estimated coefficients that are statistically significant
generally indicate the expected positive relationship between income
and responsiveness. While negative estimates were found, no
specific pattern regarding these exceptions appears.

---

*Figures for such land in both countries include fallow acreage—
potential left uncultivated out of a need for the land to regenerate
itself with a season where, at most, an animal forage crop is planted.
Under modern techniques the need for extensive relatively nonproductive fallow plantings can be considerably reduced; even profitable
crops can cyclically serve this soil-regenerative process. Thus
we make the assumption that land left fallow (in the traditional sense)
is potentially available for economically rewarding purposes, whether
through planting in alternative, soil-enhancing crops or through the
use of artificial fertilizers. In many cases (perhaps, most prominently, that of post-World War II India) this potential may be unrealizable.
However, to no small extent we must remain the victim of both the
data that is available and makes no distinction between fallow and
other cultivable unplanted acreage and the potential for reducing
the traditional fallow proportion, a potential not precisely measurable
but nonetheless present given general acceptable "modern" planting
techniques.

Rural male literacy is positively linked to market responsiveness (with the coefficient ranging from about 0.006 to 0.15) by almost all the statistically significant parameter estimates. Considerable variation in literacy exists for the three regions involved in this study—from a low of 29 percent in India to 71 percent in Thailand and 89 percent in the United States. No particular difference is noted between the Indian subgroups (food crops, rice, wheat, barley, cash crops, and sugar) of districts—all are between 27 and 30 percent. The few exceptions are isolated and show no discernible pattern regarding area, crop, or short- versus long-run responsiveness.

We had hypothesized that, ceteris paribus, cultivators with bigger holdings would be more responsive, and, by and large, this is indicated by the regression results, though those run on the total data base do yield negative and significant coefficients. Again regional differences are great—an average of more than 147 acres in the United States, 9.5 acres in Thailand, and 4.9 acres in India. These discrepancies undoubtedly result in relatively useless estimated coefficients for samples in which U.S. data plays an important role—namely, the all-wheat and all-cotton samples. Again as with literacy, no significant differences were found for Indian subsamples—ranging from 4.6 to 5.4 acres for rice and sugar to wheat, respectively. The latter are also indicated for most Thai-related samples, while for most of those drawn on Indian or U.S. data positive relationships were found. In the case of Thailand this could be interpreted as evidence for the Sharma-Gupta version of marketable surplus (see Chapter 1); that is, in a given situation a cultivator family defines its own threshold level of subsistence inversely in proportion to wealth (with mean plot size in this case taken as a measure of that wealth). If the degree of correlation between crop fertility and mean plot size was high, then of course potential multicollinearity problems would affect the parameter estimates for both variables. However, the correlation coefficient was only -0.18 in this case. For Indian rice districts the coefficient was almost the same: -0.19.

Since most of our Indian data is drawn from the poorest parts of the country, our cross-section regarding this variable includes few districts where farms are large enough to consider their holders as members of the economically better-off groups that Sharma and Gupta used to contrast with subsistence-level family behavior. On the other hand we include Thai districts where average holdings of comparable quality land (in yield-per-acre terms) range from less than 4 to more than 16 acres per family. If additional elasticity data were available from more well-endowed districts then perhaps further evidence of Sharma and Gupta's wealth-consumption effect would be found.

Finally, the only notable exceptions noted for the expected positive relationship between responsiveness and the proportion of land owned by the cultivator is found for rice, particularly in Thailand. Figures regarding owner-cultivated land were not available for nineteenth-century United States on a comparable basis to India and Thailand—though DeCanio focused on post-Civil War cotton production, among other reasons, because of the importance of tenant farming, while on the other hand, the Fisher-Temin study involved the "great frontier"—the Great Plains states where any citizen could stake out his own claim, far from any landlords. In modern India and Thailand not too much difference was indicated in the aggregate—about 84 percent of all holdings being owner-cultivated in Thailand, 79 percent in India. However, within each country considerable variation exists. Owner-operated holdings are far and away the rule in Thailand—in nearly three-quarters of the districts this proportion is 75 percent or higher, whereas a greater degree of tenancy is found somewhat more often in Indian (that is, Bihar and Uttar Pradesh) rice districts. Thai rice, it must be admitted, again presents us with a peculiarity, as was found in the case of mean landholding size. However, the results would be compatible with the Sharma-Gupta marketable surplus hypothesis if districts with high proportions of owner-cultivated holdings are also high cultivator "wealth" districts. (The correlation coefficient between owner-operated holdings and cultivator family gross earnings, the closest indicator for wealth available, is, however, very close to zero. The earnings data for Thailand is notably less disaggregated than that for India. This together with the fact that gross earnings are possibly not all that good an indicator of wealth, conceptually speaking, anyway, means we have no evidence one way or the other as to whether wealth and the degree of owner-operated holdings are significantly correlated.)

SUMMARY OF RESULTS

In assessing the overall performance of our original hypotheses it seems fair to say they held up reasonably well, though the results raise a number of still-unanswered questions. Regarding the degree of price and yield-related risk, the availability of irrigation facilities, cultivator family income, rural male literacy, average size of landholding, and the proportion of owner-cultivated acreage, the regression evidence is largely compatable with the basic hypotheses. Given the distinction made above between "wet" and "dry" crops, the estimated coefficients for weather-related risk are con-

fusing. Furthermore, our proposed relationship between the proportion of unutilized cultivable land and market responsiveness is
generally contrary to what was expected—that is, a positive link.
As mentioned above our analysis lacked the proper data for this
variable from the only regions for which elasticity estimates were
available and where such land was likely in plentiful supply—the U.S.
Western states; thus we maintain the negative evidence, while
obviously requiring consideration, is not conclusive with regard
to this portion of the basic hypothesis.

As regards our measure of the relative importance of the crop
in question, we had made no clear prognostication, but rather
indicated a likely possibility of differences in the tie with responsiveness depending upon whether the crop was minor or major in
importance. Some corroborating evidence for this was found, as
argued above, but our results were not conclusive. Nor was this
in fact the only question left hanging. In the case of the role that
the size of landholdings play in cultivator responsiveness, some
evidence was indicated for the Sharma-Gupta marketable surplus
hypothesis, but the need for stronger indications is obvious—
specifically within a framework where the data base is selected
for the compatability of the needed supportive data (given our difficulty above in finding time-series information for the several
exogenous variables proposed as relevant for our responsiveness
hypothesis and the likelihood of easing these problems if the data
base to be tested were relatively homogenous from the bureaucratic
and statistic point of view).

POLICY IMPLICATIONS

As to policies, it has been hard to discuss specific cases given
this mass of information involving so many different crops and
world locations. However, a broad discussion of the results may
be useful. In essence governments have tried to increase agricultural
output by relying on market forces. For example, by supporting the
price of a crop a government may hope to increase production.
However, if such a policy is to be effective and accurate the authorities must have an estimate of the price elasticity of supply, otherwise
the government would be "shooting in the dark." Clearly if the
price elasticity is both positive and significant, then the government
may be successful in increasing output; and by knowing the size of
this elasticity the policy maker would have an idea as to how much
of a price support is necessary. (We have supplied most available
information on the size of price elasticities.) In this sense a large

positive and significant price elasticity of supply would be desirable. A large elasticity would require a small price support in order to get a large output effect. However, very large elasticities could cause stability problems and these also may be undesirable. And a highly significant elasticity would result in a more certain or likely end result. We should note, however, that any such price support may adversely affect industrialization by turning the terms of trade; that is, how such policies are handled is also important. It is not enough to have a large and significant elasticity, the authorities must also take into account the possible effects, on other sectors, of price policies to increase agricultural output. Thus depending on the form of price policies adopted, additional measures may be necessary to balance any possible adverse effects.

However, what if the elasticity is either insignificant or significant but very small in magnitude? Are there policies that can increase the size of the supply response? In this chapter we have attempted to estimate what factors affect the size of the price elasticity of supply. This information has at least two potential uses. First, if agriculturists know the relationship between various factors and the size of this elasticity, then instead of estimating the elasticity directly, a lengthy process, they could obtain its magnitude indirectly by multiplying cash of the estimated coefficients by the corresponding value of the variables in question. Second, and more important, if a relatively large (again not too large) and significant elasticity is desirable, as discussed above, these results may help in changing an insignificant and/or small elasticity to the desired level.

Our results indicate four broad areas of government policy to increase price responsiveness on the part of farmers. First, the higher the level of their incomes, the more responsive are farmers; this policy is hardly useful for a poor country as in essence it says that if you were richer then you could increase output more; but in order to get richer, you have to increase output—a vicious chain. Second, the increased availability of inputs such as irrigation will enhance price responsiveness; the impact of this factor varies greatly across countries and crops. Third, governments can increase price responsiveness substantially by educating the rural population. And fourth, given the positive effect on elasticity of both larger landholdings and owner-cultivated land, a special kind of land reform is indicated. That is land reform, which of course results in more owner-cultivated land, where the distributed parcels are not too small. Such policies will increase the market responsiveness of farmers and may then enable the governments of developing nations to more easily increase agricultural output in a "hungry world."

CONCLUSION

In conclusion, at this time established quasiacademic practice might call for emphasizing our successes and minimize our less-than-optimum results while mentioning doubtful indications only in circular terms. Unfortunately, to some extent, this must be what we do at this point.

We believe it is only fair to recall our initial intention as stated in the title of this work and in Chapter 1. We set out to draw together the evidence that economists have presented during the last decade and a half regarding agricultural supply responsiveness in reaction to the tools formulated by Marc Nerlove and the dozens of economists who have tested, modified, and criticized the basic Nerlovian model. This goal we believe was achieved in Chapters 5 through 9.

In this chapter we set out our responsiveness hypothesis—then and now, on a tentative basis. Its tentative value, we hold, is proven; also proven is the need for further testing.

We indicated no clear-cut prejudgment on the likely direction of the relationship between responsiveness and the two risk variables and the relative importance of the crop being considered. The calculations provide evidence for the argument that the further a peasant is from the subsistence level the more likely he will be a risk-taker. Similarly, cultivators seem more price responsive the more minor the crop is in their respective "investment portfolios."

It also seems that the version of marketable surplus offered by the Sharma and Gupta (cum Krishnan) version of the marketable surplus hypothesis is strengthened, at least as regards a crop that is both a major consumption and market crop.

Thus, despite the dozens of applications of the Nerlove model enumerated above, post facto we face the need for a considerably widened field of elasticity estimates in order to test our cultivator responsiveness hypothesis within a sphere where the other relevant variables are measurable under circumstances that are more or less similar. In short our analysis, we believe, represents a beginning—a first attempt using the results of existing price-response studies to confirm the existence of our hypothesized relationships—those between a number of likely technical, social, and political factors and peasant supply responsiveness. We have already mentioned that a wider study undertaken by one of the present authors is aimed at obtaining the further evidence that seems to be needed for a better testing (as defined above) of our hypothesis.[8]

Our responsiveness argument requires further analysis, no doubt, on the macroeconomic level already utilized; we must utilize a wider cross-section regarding the relevant independent variables within a framework where the data is compiled under more or less consistent conditions. However, a very basic point must be made at this time: Since the required statistical information is regionally compiled, the testing of our responsiveness hypothesis is cross-sectional by nature and aggregative by necessity. A fundamental objection can be raised to this essentially macroeconomic approach. Aggregate data naturally represents average measures that can easily mask large differences within the group or region that, if known, could significantly effect the results. For example, we might postulate that higher farm income, ceteris paribus, calls forth greater responsiveness from cultivators. However, one can question the wisdom of testing such a hypothesis using income data that might in one district be relatively high, as would be so if it were the average of a tiny feudal landowning class and a barely surviving mass of quasi serfs (neither of which groups might be much influenced by modern market forces), and in another region be somewhat lower but represent the earnings of cultivators derived from a fairly equitable distribution of acreage.

On the other hand, microeconomically oriented studies of farmers' responsiveness allow the researcher the opportunity to obtain in-depth knowledge of the sample being considered, often as the result of personal observation.[9] If sufficient data were available from such studies to allow testing of hypotheses expressing responsiveness in terms of various market and nonmarket factors, the analysis could take account of peculiarities noted about the samples and make use of data gathered by, and according to, the specifications of the researcher.

The value of the Nerlovian model as an analytical tool must certainly be recognized; all these scores of studies published in the last dozen years have greatly extended the boundaries of the reliable information available to the formulators of agricultural policies.*

————

*The signs of the coefficients estimated in these regressions are of course of interest to policy makers. But just as important as the direction are the magnitudes of the links between the independent variables and the dependent variable, cultivator responsiveness. Responsiveness elasticities can be calculated from our data: the ratio of the change (in percentage terms) is responsiveness to that in each of the exogenous factors in turn.

In our case these ratios are available but we have left them unexpressed. A determination of these responsiveness elasticities, we believe, demands a more appropriate selection of geographic districts and of relevant crops. Should regressions on the supply data for such crop districts yield statistically significant parameter

Recognition, however, must also be made of the limitations imposed on what we can gain from this kind of essentially macro-economic supply analysis. Most of the Nerlove-based studies have been undertaken in the spirit inspired by W. Arthur Lewis' monumental work[10]—as a result of the recent awakening, in the late 1950s, to the importance of agriculture in the process of economic development, of the realization that the success of any industrialization program would depend upon mobilizing the surplus of a healthy agricultural sector.

We began this work with mention of the 1974 United Nations Food Conference; its delegates came together knowing that the fat years have already turned lean. In the past a trial-and-error process could perhaps be afforded in testing the effectiveness of empirically derived government agricultural policies. But today and in the future we cannot be satisfied with such a process; we must have better information about how to influence cultivator responsiveness. In a period of shortages, mistaken or ineffective policies will not merely slow the rate of growth in the modern sectors of developing economies but may mean a lengthy hiatus or even a reversal of the movement away from bare subsistence standards.

The specter of massive famine in India, Bangladesh, or sub-Saharan Africa can no longer be dismissed as wolf-crying. The right combination of ill-conceived governmental action and prolonged bad luck in weather patterns would spark famines of catastrophic proportions—a worldwide nightmare coming with little advance notice and less prospect of easing its grief from the now nearly bare cupboards of the traditional food-surplus nations.

If econometric analysis is to provide any guidance along the narrow path that policy makers must tread in the future, we must take counsel from the evidence that exists. Even more critically, a new generation of evidence must be uncovered and evaluated. We believe that this study of the factors affecting responsiveness is a first step in adding a range of macroeconomic tools to the decision process. However, the essential complementary micro-economic approach has yet to begin on the scale necessary to provide reliable answers and to equip policy makers with further policy tools to increase agricultural output.

---

estimates, then meaningful responsiveness elasticities would be based on a large and varied sample. These would be more reliable policy guides than those elasticities that could be calculated from the limited sample available at this time.

NOTES

1. Some evidence that this can be done by landlords is offered by E. R. J. Owen in Cotton and the Egyptian Economy 1820-1914 (London: Oxford University Press, 1969); see pp. 264-68.

2. P. N. Mathur and H. Ezekiel, "Marketable Surplus of Food and Price Fluctuations in a Developing Economy," Kyklos 14 (1961).

3. T. N. Krishnan, "The Marketed Surplus of Foodgrains: Is It Inversely Related to Price?" Economic Weekly 17 (annual number, February 1965).

4. David E. Pfanner, "A Semisubsistence Village Economy in Lower Burma," in Subsistence Agriculture and Economic Development, ed. Clifton R. Wharton (Chicago: Aldine, 1969).

5. Eric A. Hanushek, "Efficient Estimators for Regressing Regression Coefficients," American Statistician 28 (May 1974).

6. All barley data available come from India, and are found in the work of Vahid Nowshirvani, "Agricultural Supply in India: Some Theoretical and Empirical Studies" (Ph.D. dissertation, Massachusetts Institute of Technology, 1962).

7. John Thomas Cummings, "Supply Response in Peasant Agriculture: Price and Non-Price Factors" (Ph.D. dissertation, Tufts University, 1974).

8. Cummings, op. cit.

9. Studies such as those of K. L. Sharma and M. P. Gupta, "Study of Farm Factors Determining Market Surplus of Bajra in Jaipur District," Indian Journal of Agricultural Economics 25 (October-December 1970); Kalpana Bardhan, "Price and Output Response of Marketed Surplus of Foodgrains: A Cross-Sectional Study of Some North Indian Villages," American Journal of Agricultural Economics 52 (February 1970); and David Pfanner, op. cit.

10. W. Arthur Lewis, Theory of Economic Growth (London: George Allen and Unwin, 1955).

In any discussion of the production of basic food crops in developing economies, an extremely fundamental question relative to the link between total production and the marketed portion must be resolved. Almost all cultivators retain some part of their output for domestic use, for seed, or as a result of wastage. When conditions approaching those of subsistence agriculture result, however, this retained fraction swells and conceivably might consist, in extremo, of all the crop that is produced. Should cultivators be in such a situation they can hardly be much affected by market fluctuations since they are isolated from this sector of the national economy.

We have touched upon this subject above in Chapter 1, mentioning the theses of Mathur and Ezekiel, Krishnan, and Olson.[1] The first authors held that cultivators, in generally subsistence economies, have fairly steady annual cash requirements; thus, what they market out of their produce (the marketed or marketable surplus) varies inversely with price in rather rigid fashion. Consumption, which is the residual, is clearly dominant in this regard, once cash needs have been met. But Krishnan argued that such an approach falters when cultivators on the barest subsistence level are discussed; for them, minimum consumption, not cash needs, must be the starting point, since survival is the most essential goal. He allowed that for peasants above the bare minimum level of production of food crops it may be valid to consider consumption as residual rather than fixed. In such circumstances, then, the question of marketable surplus again arises.

Krishnan, along with Olson, then explained variation in this surplus in terms of a real income effect. As prices for the crops grown rise, so does real income; when these crops are cereals and other basic consumption items, an income-consumption effect is likely to occur. Price increases swell the real income of the peasantry, and the income effect on their demand for consumption of these goods counterbalances the influence price increases might have on the amount they bring to the market.

More recently, J. T. Cummings, presenting district-level elasticity estimates from all parts of India, compared the responsiveness shown by cultivators in poor districts with that indicated in richer areas.[2] He suggested that when both minimum consumption and minimum cash needs can be met from total output, farmers then, if they still have a surplus, respond positively to market incentives.

These studies do not generally provide definitive evidence relative to their arguments. However, several studies have considered the specific subject in some detail. In some cases (for example, Behrman and Nowshirvani) the authors' arguments relative to this topic have been incorporated in the general discussion of their works. In others, particularly those that are limited to consideration of marketable surplus, no mention of their work has been made. Thus, in this appendix we will examine a selection of some such recent studies.

Emphasis tends to be on an essentially microeconomic approach as the most likely to generate evidence regarding one or another of the various explanations. For example, the Mathur-Ezekiel hypothesis was tested by V. M. Dandekar using the district-level data from India's Maharashta state that Mathur had quoted in another study.[3] Dandekar pointed out that the relationship between prices and the marketed portions of the wheat, jowar, and other cereal crops was both positive in sign and significant in size. He then emphasized that the most influential factor relative to the marketed share seems to be the size of the cultivator's holding.

Many other efforts carried out in the 1960s aimed at illustrating the same point. Beginning with a number of papers presented at the 1961 meeting of the Indian Society of Agricultural Economics, studies on the village level that differentiated between cultivators based on their holding size, incomes, relative crop mix, and other pertinent variables have had as their purpose the identification of the portion of the crop of concern that is marketed.[4] For example, G. C. Mandal reported on rice cultivators in eight villages scattered across three northeastern Indian states. B. Misra and S. P. Sinha looked at a single Bihari village, while C. P. Shastri looked at three villages, each in a different part of that state. Rao examined marketed food grains in ten southern villages located in Andhra Pradesh (4 villages), Kerala (1), Madras (3), and Mysore (2), while Srinivasan chose a small sample of wheat growers in a village in Madhya Pradesh. Generally, they portray a picture of considerably greater market participation on the part of richer farmers (as measured by the criterion of landholdings) and of cultivators of the traditional market crops (that is, noncereals). Several of these and other papers also try to identify the various nonmarket destinations of the crops being analyzed, including the portion used for family and livestock consumption, payments in kind and/or barter, and future seed requirements.

In the rapporteur's report on this session, the overall impression conveyed by the participants was termed disconcerting.[5] They

had shown no evidence that the marketed surplus was increasing;
rather, the indications were that it had stagnated or even declined
in the face of generally found increases in food crop production.
Though they (and other researchers concerned with the Indo-Pakistani
subcontinent) conceded that data measurement difficulties were
considerable and might well make it impossible to make definitive
statements regarding trends, nevertheless their evidence was hardly
encouraging to economic planners who mostly emphasized industrialization policies in the 1950s and early 1960s, leaving the agricultural
sector to care for itself.

Other papers have marked the later years relative to the subcontinent; among them are those of Bhalerao and Lal for maize
cultivation in Uttar Pradesh,[6] and two studies on Pakistan by Khan
and Chowdhury, and Raquibuzzaman.[7]

Among the more recent studies of marketed surplus is that of
K. L. Sharma and M. P. Gupta, who concentrated on a single
district.[8] Therein they selected randomly a sample of 65 peasant
families with landholdings running the spectrum from the smallest
to largest in the area. Grouping these families by size of landholding,
and regressing marketed bajra on family size and total bajra output,
they found similar statistically significant response patterns (negative
and positive coefficients for family size and total output, respectively)
for all subgroups except the poorest (holdings less than about 6.5
acres), which reported no market surplus. The "threshold" level
of retained bajra per family member (that is, before any sales are
made) seems to increase notably with the size of the family's landholding, rising from about 74 kg per person on holdings between
6.5 to 13 acres, to 140 kg per person on holdings between 13 and
19 acres, and to 154 kg in holdings larger than 19 acres—evidence
certainly of strong positive wealth (if not income) elasticity of
demand among cultivators for their own produce.

P. N. Bhargava and V. S. Rustogi set out to determine two
relationships: that between gross output and marketed surplus and
between the portion disposed and holding size, using data for rice
cultivation in the Burdwan district of West Bengal.[9] To cover the
region they divided it into 12 zones and then chose 12 villages
randomly in each zone. Their survey efforts then were based on
8 cultivators chosen from each village. The surplus thus determined
was then regressed on overall crop production. For holdings varying
between less than 1 hectare to more than 4 hectares they found that
the marketed portion ranges upward from 12 to over 60 percent
of the cultivated area, and elasticities of sale with respect to production rose from about +1.2 for the smallest holdings to about +2.2
for the largest.

G. L. Mandal and M. G. Ghosh selected villages from both relatively advanced and relatively backward areas—two villages in West Bengal and two in Orissa.[10] They then looked at the market behavior of both small- and largeholders in each state. Rice cultivation predominated in all four villages, but landholding patterns were somewhat different, with considerably more land in largeholdings in the Orissa villages. In all cases they found the marketed share of rice output to increase with holding size, but in each size category Bengali cultivators showed much higher marginal propensities to sell than did Orissans.

An even more detailed study has been presented by Kalpana Bardhan.[11] She examined data from 27 villages in Uttar Pradesh and the Punjab, expressing market surplus of cereals and pulses as a function of total food grain output per adult cultivator, average price of food grains for the cultivator from noncrop sources, an index of the concentration of landholdings and nonsales disposals (for example, rental payments in kind) minus other receipts of food grains. Her results showed a notable effect on marketed surplus of total output (positive), prices (negative), and noncrop income (negative)—the latter showing less statistical significance than the first two. The other variables showed little significance (with positive coefficients indicated for value of commercial crops and the degree of concentration of landholdings among the wealthier classes and negative for nonsales disposals minus other receipts of food grains).

Bardhan also tried to differentiate between economic classes by several methods. Perhaps the most important economic difference to emerge as a result of the regressions run on the wealthier subgroups was the indication that while the price elasticity of marketed surplus remained negative it was both smaller in magnitude and much less statistically significant than for the general sample.

With sales (S) defined as total output of food grains (O_f) minus consumption (C_f assumed to be a function of total income [O] and the price of food grains [P_f]) and net other disposal of food grain (that is, payments in kind minus receipts in kind) (N):

$$S = O_f - C_f(O, P_f) - N \tag{A.1}$$

or in proportional terms:

$$s = \frac{S}{O_f} = 1 - \frac{C_f(O, P_f)}{O_f} - \frac{N}{O_f} \tag{A.2}$$

and

$$\frac{\partial s}{\partial P_f} = - \frac{C_f}{O} \left[\frac{\partial C_f}{\partial O} \times \frac{O}{C_f} - \frac{\sigma_f}{P_f O_f} O \right] = \frac{C_f}{O} \left[\frac{\sigma_f}{P_f O_f} O - e_f \right] \qquad (A.3)$$

where σ_f and e_f are the cultivators' price and income elasticity of demand for food grains, respectively. Thus the likelihood of a negative price elasticity of marketed surplus $\left[\dfrac{\partial s}{\partial P_f} \times \dfrac{P_f}{s} \right]$ declines as e_f shrinks and/or as the importance of food grains in determining farm income (that is, the ratio O_f/O) diminishes. For the data Bardhan examines she notes O_f/O is only slightly smaller for the richer subgroups than for the whole, but that all available studies point to a negative income-elasticity of demand.

In another article written with Pranab Bardhan, Bardhan points out that her earlier estimates using village level cross-sectional data yielded only short-run elasticity estimates.[12] On the other hand, policy formulation requires information on long-run responsiveness, and for this, time-series data must be used. In this regard microlevel data was not available, so they used national consumption, output, and distribution figures.

The Bardhans took per capita cereals consumption (C_x) to be a function of per capita income (I) and the price of cereals relative to those of all other foodstuffs (P_x/P_y), while per capita output (O_x) was defined in terms of cereal prices relative to those of alternative agricultural commodities (P_x/P_z), and a proxy variable mostly representing technological change (A). Then the marketed surplus of cereals (s) is:

$$s = 1 - \frac{C_x(I, P_x/P_y)}{O_x(P_x/P_z, A)} \qquad (A.4)$$

and per capita agricultural income is:

$$I = P_x O_x (P_x/P_z, A) + P_z O_z (P_z/P_x, A) \qquad (A.5)$$

where O_z is per capita output of noncereal commodities. Marketed surplus then can be expressed as a function of two price ratios (P_x/P_y and P_z/P_x) and the proxy variable. They argued that the coefficients of the first two are most likely positive and negative respectively, while that for the third would be positive if technological change leads to more rapid growth in cereals output than for noncereals, and negative if noncereals benefit more.

Using two different measures of the cereals consumption of the nonagricultural population they estimated a logarithmic form of the marketed surplus. Their signs confirmed the initial hypothesis and indicate a marketed supply elasticity of close to unity relative to the ratio of cereals prices and those of all food products that can be bought with the proceeds of agricultural sales; on the other hand, the expected negative elasticity relative to the commercial crop-cereals price ratio is considerably smaller than unity.

Walter Haessel has recently pointed out that unless it is assumed that the prices farmers receive are exogenous and not determined by what they have marketed, then Bardhan's application of ordinary least-squares techniques will not yield consistent estimates.[13] He argues that such an assumption would be very tenuous given the basic self-sufficiency in grain of most Indian villages and suggests a model that includes allowance for home consumption demand, the supply marketed, and the price determined in a closed village.

Haessel found positive price elasticities using his model, as opposed to Bardhan's negative values. In addition the larger farmers were generally more market responsive than the group as a whole. The high value of the elasticity of marketings with respect to output was cited as evidence of a tendency for the market's share to increase faster than output, a favorable circumstance to policy makers who hope to influence the market through such devices as yield-enhancing seed and fertilizer.

NOTES

1. P. N. Mathur and H. Ezekiel, "Marketable Surplus of Food and Price Fluctuations in a Developing Economy," Kyklos 14 (1961); T. N. Krishnan, "The Marketed Surplus of Foodgrains: Is It Inversely Related to Price?" Economic Weekly 17 (annual number, February 1965); and R. O. Olson, "The Impact and Implications of Foreign Surplus Disposal on Underdeveloped Economies," Journal of Farm Economics 42 (December 1960).

2. John Thomas Cummings, "Supply Response in Peasant Agriculture: Price and Non-Price Factors" (Ph.D. dissertation, Tufts University, 1974).

3. V. M. Dandekar, "Prices, Production and Marketed Surplus of Foodgrains," Indian Journal of Agricultural Economics 19 (July-December 1964); P. N. Mathur, "Differential Effects of Price Increases on Small and Big Cultivators—A Case Study," Artha Vijnuna 4 (1962).

4. All these papers, published in the Indian Journal of Agricultural Economics 16 (January-March 1961) are listed in the bibliography. For economy of space their titles are not listed at this point. Other papers also listed in the bibliography are concerned with related aspects of the problems surrounding the question of marketable surplus.

5. M. B. Desai, "Rapporteur's Report on Problems of Marketable Surplus in Indian Agriculture," Indian Journal of Agricultural Economics 16 (January-March 1961).

6. M. M. Bhalerao and Sant Lal, "Marketable Surplus in Maize," Indian Journal of Economics 20 (July-September 1965).

7. Azizur Rahman Khan and A. H. M. Naruddin Chowdhury, "Marketable Surplus Function: A Study of the Behavior of West Pakistan Farmers," Pakistan Development Review 2 (Autumn 1962); Mohammad Raquibuzzaman, "Marketed Surplus Function of Major Agricultural Commodities in Pakistan," Pakistan Development Review 6 (1966).

8. K. L. Sharma and M. P. Gupta, "Study of Farm Factors Determining Market Surplus of Bajra in Jaipur District," Indian Journal of Agricultural Economics 25 (October-December 1970).

9. P. N. Bhargava and V. S. Rustogi, "Study of Marketable Surplus of Paddy in Burdwan District," Indian Journal of Agricultural Economics 27 (July-September 1972).

10. G. C. Mandal and M. G. Ghosh, "A Study of Marketed Surplus of Paddy at the Farm Level in Four East Indian Villages," Indian Journal of Agricultural Economics 23 (July-September 1968).

11. Kalpana Bardhan, "Price and Output Response of Marketed Surplus of Foodgrains: A Cross-Sectional Study of Some North Indian Villages," American Journal of Agricultural Economics 52 (February 1970).

12. Pranab Bardhan and Kalpana Bardhan, "Price Response of Marketed Surplus of Foodgrains," Oxford Economic Papers 23 (July 1971).

13. Walter Haessel, "The Price and Income Elasticities of Home Consumption and Marketed Surplus of Foodgrains," American Journal of Agricultural Economics 57 (February 1975).

TABLE B.1

Supply Elasticities, by Crop and Region

Crop	Region	Period	Author	Short-Run Elasticity	Long-Run Elasticity
RICE	Punjab	1914-46	Raj Krishna	+0.31	+0.59
	Punjab	1951-64	Kaul	+0.24	+0.40
	Punjab	1960-69	Kaul and Sidhu	+0.19 to 0.24	+0.64 to 0.68
	Punjab	1950-66	Cummings	+0.03	+0.05
	Punjab	1955-66	Askari and Cummings	+0.18	+0.42
	Punjab	1948-65	Maji, Jha, and Venkataraman	+0.11 to 0.49	+0.38 to 0.67
	Haryana	1950-70	Singh, Singh, and Rai	+0.83	-
	Uttar Pradesh (6 divisions)	1909-38	Nowshirvani	-	-0.36 to +0.60
	Uttar Pradesh (14 districts)	1953-63	Nowshirvani	-	-0.11 to +0.27
	Bihar	1953-63	Nowshirvani	-	+0.12
	Bihar (12 districts)	1953-63	Nowshirvani	-	+0.01 to 0.22
	Bihar-Orissa	1900-39	Parikh	+0.16 to 0.24	-
	Orissa	1938-51	NCAER	+0.05	-
	Madras (Tamil Nadu)	1900-39	Parikh	-0.14	-0.15
	Madras (Tamil Nadu)	1937-66	Subramanian	negative	-
	Madras (Tamil Nadu)	1939-61	Rajagopalan	+0.11	-
	Madras (Tamil Nadu)	1938-57	NCAER	+0.28	-
	Madras (Tamil Nadu)	1946-67	Cummings	+0.08	+0.08
	Madras (Tamil Nadu)	1952-65	Askari and Cummings	-0.26	+0.76
	Madras (Tamil Nadu)	1947-65	Madhavan	-0.05 to +0.03	-0.07 to +0.04
	Andhra Pradesh	1950-67	Cummings	+0.48	+0.62
	Andhra Pradesh	1952-67	Askari and Cummings	+0.46	+0.66
	Himachal Pradesh	1949-66	Cummings	-0.07	-0.06
	Tripura	1949-67	Cummings	+0.01	+0.01
	Assam	1938-57	NCAER	+0.10	-
	Assam	1950-67	Cummings	+0.07	+0.07
	Gujarat	1954-67	Cummings	-0.07	-0.07
	Kerala	1951-66	Cummings	-0.14	-0.12
	Kerala	1955-67	Askari and Cummings	-0.14	-0.10
	Maharashta	1955-67	Cummings	-0.12	-0.14
	Mysore	1951-67	Cummings	+0.06	+0.07
	Mysore	1953-65	Askari and Cummings	-0.08	-0.12
	Bengal	1911-38	S. Krishna	+0.06	+0.19
	West Bengal	1938-57	NCAER	+0.30	-
	West Bengal (autumn rice)	1949-66	Cummings	+0.37	+0.38

Crop	Region	Period	Author	Short-Run Elasticity	Long-Run Elasticity
RICE (continued)	West Bengal (winter rice)	1949-66	Cummings	+0.09	+0.08
	India	1938-57	NCAER	+0.22	−
	Pakistan (West)	1949-68	Cummings	+0.12	+0.17
	Pakistan (West)	1950-68	Askari and Cummings	−0.03	−0.07
	Bangladesh	1948-63	Hussain	+0.03 to 0.09	−
	Bangladesh	1949-68	Cummings	+0.13	+0.19
	Bangladesh	1950-68	Askari and Cummings	+0.23	+1.28
	Egypt	1920-40	Askari, Cummings, and Harik	−0.21	−0.24
	Egypt	1953-72	Askari, Cummings, and Harik	+0.08	+0.08
	Iraq	1950-60	Askari, Cummings, and Harik	+2.68	+2.71
	Iraq	1961-71	Askari, Cummings, and Harik	+0.66	+1.57
	Thailand	1937-63	Behrman	+0.17 to 0.18	+0.19 to 0.43
	Thailand (50 provinces)	1937-63	Behrman	+0.19[a]	+0.28[a]
	Thailand (50 provinces)	1937-63	Behrman	+0.08 to 0.33[b]	+0.16 to 0.45[b]
	Thailand	1951-65	Aromdee	+0.31	+0.20
	West Malaysia	1951-65	Aromdee	+0.23 to 0.25	+1.35
	Japan	1951-65	Aromdee	0	0
	Philippines	1910-41	Mangahas, Recto, and Ruttan	+0.01 to 0.26	+0.02 to 1.16
	Philippines	1948-64	Mangahas, Recto, and Ruttan	neg.	neg.
	Philippines Ilocos	1953-64	Mangahas, Recto, and Ruttan	+0.04 to 0.28	+0.51
	Philippines Cayagan Valley	1953-64	Mangahas, Recto, and Ruttan	neg.	neg.
	Philippines Central Luzon	1953-64	Mangahas, Recto, and Ruttan	neg. to +0.55	neg. to +2.15
	Philippines South Tagalog	1953-64	Mangahas, Recto, and Ruttan	+0.19 to 1.95	+0.42 to 2.06
	Philippines Bicol	1953-64	Mangahas, Recto, and Ruttan	+0.01 to 2.00	−
	Philippines East Visayas	1953-64	Mangahas, Recto, and Ruttan	+0.15 to 0.26	+0.15 to 0.32
	Philippines West Visayas	1953-64	Mangahas, Recto, and Ruttan	+0.09 to 3.20	+3.52
	Philippines North and East Mindanao	1953-64	Mangahas, Recto, and Ruttan	neg. to +0.22	−
	Philippines South and West Mindanao	1953-64	Mangahas, Recto, and Ruttan	neg. to +1.52	neg. to +0.93
	Java and Madura	1951-62	Mubyarto	+0.30	−
	Peru	1944-64	Merrill	+0.50	−

(continued)

Crop	Region	Period	Author	Short-Run Elasticity	Long-Run Elasticity
WHEAT	Bombay-Sind	1900-39	Parikh	neg.	neg.
	Bombay	1938-57	NCAER	+0.64	–
	Gujarat	1954-67	Cummings	+0.93	+1.00
	Maharashta	1955-67	Cummings	+0.24	+0.33
	Punjab (dry farming)	1914-46	Raj Krishna	0	+0.22
	Punjab (irrigated)	1914-46	Raj Krishna	+0.08	+0.14
	Punjab	1900-39	Parikh	+0.06	+0.10
	Punjab (dry farming)	1951-64	Kaul	+0.25	+0.27
	Punjab (irrigated)	1951-64	Kaul	+0.08	+0.09
	Punjab	1950-67	Cummings	+0.10	+0.13
	Punjab	1955-65	Askari and Cummings	-0.01	-0.01
	Punjab	1948-65	Maji, Jha, and Venkataraman	+0.11 to 0.67	+0.51 to 1.02
	Madhya Pradesh-Berar	1900-39	Parikh	neg.	neg.
	Haryana	1950-70	Singh, Singh, and Rai	+0.60	–
	Delhi	1953-67	Askari and Cummings	+0.25	+0.28
	Himachal Pradesh	1953-66	Askari and Cummings	+0.04	+0.04
	Uttar Pradesh	1904-39	S. Krishna	+0.05	+0.19
	Uttar Pradesh (6 divisions)	1909-38	Nowshirvani	–	-0.11 to -0.57
	Uttar Pradesh	1953-62	Nowshirvani	–	-0.13 to +0.76
	Uttar Pradesh	1938-57	NCAER	+0.06	–
	Uttar Pradesh	1950-62	Rao and Krishna	+0.03 to 0.21	+0.09 to 0.64
	Bihar (3 districts)	1952-64	Nowshirvani	–	+0.41
	Mysore	1954-67	Cummings	+0.23	+0.33
	Mysore	1955-67	Askari and Cummings	+0.48	+0.52
	Rajasthan	1954-68	Askari and Cummings	+0.13	+0.29
	Rajasthan	1951-68	Cummings	+0.02	+0.03
	West Bengal	1946-67	Cummings	+0.23	+0.20
	India	1938-57	NCAER	+0.16	–
	Pakistan (West) (dry farming)	1933-59	Falcon	0	–
	Pakistan (West) (irrigated)	1933-59	Falcon	+0.10 to 0.20	–
	Pakistan (West)	1949-68	Cummings	+0.10	+0.22
	Pakistan (West)	1950-68	Askari and Cummings	+0.07	+0.21
	Egypt	1920-40	Askari, Cummings, and Harik	+0.01	+0.01
	Egypt	1953-72	Askari, Cummings, and Harik	+0.91	+0.44
	Syria	1947-60	Askari, Cummings, and Harik	-0.02	-0.03

Crop	Region	Period	Author	Short-Run Elasticity	Long-Run Elasticity
WHEAT (continued)	Syria	1961–72	Askari, Cummings, and Harik	+0.64	+3.23
	Iraq	1951–60	Askari, Cummings, and Harik	+0.40	−4.42
	Iraq	1962–71	Askari, Cummings, and Harik	−0.85	−0.34
	Jordan	1955–67	Askari, Cummings, and Harik	+0.20	+0.23
	Lebanon	1951–72	Askari, Cummings, and Harik	+0.27	+0.39
	Hungary	1871–93	Eddie	+0.09	−
	Hungary (7 districts)	1893–1913	Eddie	−0.10 to +0.23	−
	France	1946–61	Oury	+0.63	−
	United Kingdom	1924–39	Jones	+0.33 to 0.41	+0.46 to 0.98
	United Kingdom	1955–66	Colman	+0.17	−
	United Kingdom (spring wheat)	1955–66	Colman	+0.41	−
	United States (17 states)	1867–1914	Fisher and Temin	+0.11[a]	+0.80[a]
	United States (17 states)	1874	Cooley and DeCanio	+0.12[a]	+0.18[a]
	United States (17 states)	1914	Cooley and DeCanio	+0.08[a]	+0.11[a]
	United States	1909–32	Nerlove	+0.47 to 0.93	−
	Canada	1947–66	Schmitz	+0.42 to 0.75	+0.62 to 1.30
	Argentina	1948–65	Freire	+0.57	−
	Chile	1942–64	Swift	+0.37	+3.65
	Australia	1947–64	Powell and Gruen	+0.18	+0.85
	New South Wales (old districts)	1947–62	Duloy and Watson	+0.33 to 0.47	+0.66 to 1.07
	New South Wales (new districts)	1947–62	Duloy and Watson	+0.16 to 1.13	−0.13 to +7.95
	New Zealand	1945–65	Guise	+0.96	+1.58
BARLEY	Punjab	1914–46	Raj Krishna	+0.39	+0.50
	Punjab	1951–64	Kaul	+0.53	+0.60
	Punjab	1950–67	Cummings	+0.22	+0.27
	Punjab	1955–66	Askari and Cummings	−0.63	+0.94
	Haryana	1950–70	Singh, Singh, and Rai	+0.58	−
	Uttar Pradesh (1 division)	1909–39	Nowshirvani	−	+0.31
	Uttar Pradesh (4 divisions)	1953–63	Nowshirvani	−	+0.04 to 0.50
	Uttar Pradesh	1938–57	NCAER	+0.16	−
	Bihar	1953–63	Nowshirvani	−	+0.17 to 0.40
	Rajasthan	1950–68	Cummings	+0.67	+1.46
	Rajasthan	1954–68	Askari and Cummings	+0.31	+1.19
	Delhi	1948–67	Cummings	+0.52	+0.69

(continued)

Crop	Region	Period	Author	Short-Run Elasticity	Long-Run Elasticity
BARLEY (continued)	Delhi	1953-67	Askari and Cummings	+0.53	-3.60
	Himachal Pradesh	1949-66	Cummings	-0.10	-0.26
	Himachal Pradesh	1953-65	Askari and Cummings	-0.22	-1.20
	India	1938-57	NCAER	+0.16	–
	Pakistan (West)	1951-68	Cummings	+0.03	+0.02
	Pakistan (West)	1954-68	Askari and Cummings	+0.01	+0.01
	Syria	1947-60	Askari, Cummings, and Harik	-0.15	-0.24
	Syria	1953-72	Askari, Cummings, and Harik	-0.57	-0.57
	Iraq	1951-60	Askari, Cummings, and Harik	+0.16	-0.28
	Iraq	1962-71	Askari, Cummings, and Harik	-0.05	-0.19
	Jordan	1955-67	Askari, Cummings, and Harik	-0.61	-0.45
	Lebanon	1951-72	Askari, Cummings, and Harik	+0.27	+0.22
	Hungary	1871-93	Eddie	+0.14	–
	Hungary (7 districts)	1893-1913	Eddie	-0.42 to +0.47	–
	United Kingdom	1924-39	Jones	+0.57 to 0.63	+1.75 to 2.71
	United Kingdom	1955-66	Colman	+0.57	–
	United Kingdom	1955-69	Colman	+0.78	–
	United States	1909-32	Brandow	+1.32	–
	Canada	1947-66	Schmitz	0	0
MAIZE	Punjab	1914-46	Raj Krishna	+0.23	+0.56
	Punjab	1960-69	Kaul and Sidhu	+0.11 to 0.13	+0.14 to 0.16
	Punjab	1948-65	Maji, Jha, and Venkataraman	+0.28 to 0.56	+0.35 to 0.66
	Haryana	1950-70	Singh, Singh, and Rai	+0.33	–
	Egypt	1920-40	Askari, Cummings, and Harik	-0.16	-0.25
	Egypt	1953-72	Askari, Cummings, and Harik	+0.04	+0.09
	Sudan	1951-65	Medani	+0.23	+0.56
	Syria	1947-60	Askari, Cummings, and Harik	+0.51	+0.69
	Syria	1961-72	Askari, Cummings, and Harik	+2.27	+2.16
	Jordan	1955-66	Askari, Cummings, and Harik	-0.21	-0.25
	Lebanon	1953-72	Askari, Cummings, and Harik	+0.13	+0.29
	Philippines	1910-41	Mangahas, Recto, and Ruttan	neg. to +0.12	neg. to +0.11
	Philippines	1946-64	Mangahas, Recto, and Ruttan	neg. to +0.23	+0.42 to 1.14

Crop	Region	Period	Author	Short-Run Elasticity	Long-Run Elasticity
MAIZE (continued)	Philippines Ilocos	1946–64	Mangahas, Recto, and Ruttan	+0.04 to 0.09	+0.06 to 0.33
	Philippines Cagayan Valley	1946–64	Mangahas, Recto, and Ruttan	neg. to +0.17	neg. to +0.43
	Philippines Central Luzon	1946–64	Mangahas, Recto, and Ruttan	neg.	neg.
	Philippines South Tagalog	1946–64	Mangahas, Recto, and Ruttan	neg. to +0.60	neg. to +0.47
	Philippines Bicol	1946–64	Mangahas, Recto, and Ruttan	neg. to +0.29	neg. to +0.26
	Philippines East Visayas	1946–64	Mangahas, Recto, and Ruttan	neg. to +0.67	neg. to +0.97
	Philippines West Visayas	1946–64	Mangahas, Recto, and Ruttan	+0.03 to 1.66	+0.04
	Philippines North and East Mindanao	1946–64	Mangahas, Recto, and Ruttan	neg.	neg.
	Philippines South and West Mindanao	1946–64	Mangahas, Recto, and Ruttan	neg. to +0.13	neg.
	Thailand (4 provinces)	1949–63	Behrman	+0.27 to 4.47	+0.41 to 14.17
	Hungary	1877–93	Eddie	neg.	—
	Hungary (7 districts)	1893–1913	Eddie	−0.14 to +0.16	—
	United States	1909–32	Nerlove	+0.09 to 1.02	—
RYE	Hungary	1871–93	Eddie	+0.16	—
	Hungary	1893–1913	Eddie	+0.19	—
	Hungary (7 districts)	1893–1913	Eddie	+0.05 to 1.07	—
OATS	United Kingdom	1924–39	Jones	+0.11	+0.16
	United Kingdom	1946–58	Jones	+0.18	+0.24
	United Kingdom	1955–66	Colman	+1.56	—
	Hungary	1871–93	Eddie	+0.13	—
	Hungary (7 districts)	1893–1913	Eddie	−0.02 to +0.32	—
FEED GRAINS	France	1946–61	Oury	+0.77	—
	Australia	1947–64	Powell and Gruen	+0.14	+0.81
CASSAVA	Thailand (1 province)	1955–63	Behrman	+1.09	+1.09
BAJRA	Punjab	1914–46	Raj Krishna	+0.09	+0.36
	Punjab	1951–64	Kaul	−0.05	−0.06
	Punjab (4 districts)	1951–64	Kaul	−0.01 to −0.50	−0.02 to −1.58
	Haryana	1950–70	Singh, Singh, and Rai	pos.	—
	Madhya Pradesh	1951–64	Kaul	−0.08	−0.16
CUMBU	Madras (Tamil Nadu)	1947–65	Madhavan	−0.22 to +0.03	−2.50 to +0.15
	Madras (Tamil Nadu)	1951–65	Rajagopalan	+0.83 to 0.90	—

(continued)

Crop	Region	Period	Author	Short-Run Elasticity	Long-Run Elasticity
RAGI	Madras (Tamil Nadu)	1947-65	Madhavan	+0.09 to 0.15	+0.16 to 0.31
	Madras (Tamil Nadu)	1951-65	Rajagopalan	pos.	—
JOWAR	Punjab	1914-46	Raj Krishna	0	-0.58
	Sholapur (Maharashta)	1938-57	NCAER	+0.50	—
	Madhya Pradesh	1951-64	Kaul	-0.04	-0.06
SORGHUM	Madras (Tamil Nadu)	1947-65	Madhavan	+0.02 to 0.20	+0.03 to 0.28
	Sudan	1951-65	Medani	+0.31	+0.59
	Sudan (traditional farms)	1966-69	Medani	+0.10 to 0.21	+0.23 to 0.31
	Sudan (modern farms)	1966-69	Medani	+0.50	+0.63 to 0.70
GRAM	Punjab	1914-66	Raj Krishna	0	-0.33
	Punjab	1951-64	Kaul	-0.30	-0.65
	Punjab (3 districts)	1951-64	Kaul	-1.00 to +0.49	-1.52 to +1.38
	Haryana	1950-70	Singh, Singh, and Rai	pos.	—
	Andhra Pradesh	1957-67	Bahadur and Haridasan	+0.06 to 0.67	—
GREEN GRAM	Andhra Pradesh	1957-67	Bahadur and Haridasan	+0.18 to 0.41	—
	Iraq	1950-60	Askari, Cummings, and Harik	-0.27	-0.69
	Iraq	1961-70	Askari, Cummings, and Harik	-0.24	-0.32
VETCH	Syria	1947-60	Askari, Cummings, and Harik	-0.23	-0.22
	Syria	1961-72	Askari, Cummings, and Harik	-0.50	-0.53
	Jordan	1955-67	Askari, Cummings, and Harik	-0.37	-0.62
MILLET	Syria	1947-60	Askari, Cummings, and Harik	+0.94	+0.54
	Syria	1961-72	Askari, Cummings, and Harik	+1.21	+1.60
	Iraq	1953-60	Askari, Cummings, and Harik	-0.85	-0.75
	Iraq	1961-71	Askari, Cummings, and Harik	-0.84	-3.30
	Sudan	1951-65	Medani	+0.09	+0.36
GIANT MILLET	Iraq	1954-60	Askari, Cummings, and Harik	-25.57	-8.00
	Iraq	1961-71	Askari, Cummings, and Harik	+0.88	+1.85
BEANS	Great Britain	1938-58	Jones	+0.39	+0.53
BROAD BEANS	England and Wales	1936-58	Jones	+0.16	+0.47
	Egypt	1920-40	Askari, Cummings, and Harik	+0.01	+0.01
	Egypt	1953-72	Askari, Cummings, and Harik	+0.19	+0.14

Crop	Region	Period	Author	Short-Run Elasticity	Long-Run Elasticity
BROAD BEANS (continued)	Syria	1950–60	Askari, Cummings, and Harik	-0.02	-0.04
	Syria	1961–72	Askari, Cummings, and Harik	-0.04	-0.07
	Jordan	1955–67	Askari, Cummings, and Harik	-0.77	-1.11
	Lebanon	1958–72	Askari, Cummings, and Harik	+0.54	+0.68
LIMA BEANS	United States	c	Nerlove and Addison	+0.10	+1.70
SNAP BEANS	United States	c	Nerlove and Addison	+0.15	d
LENTILS	Syria	1947–60	Askari, Cummings, and Harik	-0.44	-1.19
	Syria	1961–72	Askari, Cummings, and Harik	-0.80	-0.56
	Iraq	1950–60	Askari, Cummings, and Harik	-0.19	-0.18
	Iraq	1961–71	Askari, Cummings, and Harik	+6.49	+0.32
	Jordan	1955–67	Askari, Cummings, and Harik	-0.30	-0.46
	Lebanon	1955–72	Askari, Cummings, and Harik	-0.28	-0.54
CHICK-PEAS	Syria	1947–60	Askari, Cummings, and Harik	-1.04	-1.27
	Syria	1961–72	Askari, Cummings, and Harik	+0.43	+0.51
	Jordan	1955–67	Askari, Cummings, and Harik	+0.10	+0.09
	Lebanon	1955–72	Askari, Cummings, and Harik	+0.68	+1.70
PEAS	United States	c	Nerlove and Addison	+0.31	+4.40
	Great Britain	1938–58	Jones	+0.65	+3.10
CABBAGE	United States	c	Nerlove and Addison	+0.36	+1.20
	England and Wales	1928–58	Jones	+0.30	+0.83
CARROTS	United States	c	Nerlove and Addison	+0.14	+1.00
	England and Wales	1928–58	Jones	+0.39	+1.77
CUCUMBERS	United States	c	Nerlove and Addison	+0.29	+2.20
LETTUCE	United States	c	Nerlove and Addison	+0.03	+0.16
KALE	United States (Virginia)	c	Nerlove and Addison	+0.20	+0.23
SPINACH	United States	c	Nerlove and Addison	+0.20	+4.70
CELERY	England and Wales	1928–58	Jones	+0.10	+0.71
	United States	c	Nerlove and Addison	+0.14	+0.95
PEPPERS	United States	c	Nerlove and Addison	+0.07	+0.26

(continued)

Crop	Region	Period	Author	Short-Run Elasticity	Long-Run Elasticity
CAULIFLOWER	United States	c	Nerlove and Addison	+0.14	+1.10
	England and Wales	1928-58	Jones	+0.05	+0.42
SPROUTS	England and Wales	1928-58	Jones	+0.20	+0.59
SHALLOTS	United States (Louisiana)	c	Nerlove and Addison	+0.12	+0.31
ARTICHOKES	United States (California)	c	Nerlove and Addison	-0.04	-0.14
BEETS	United States	c	Nerlove and Addison	+0.13	+1.00
EGGPLANT	Jordan	1955-66	Askari, Cummings, and Harik	-0.67	-4.47
	United States	c	Nerlove and Addison	+0.16	+0.34
TOMATOES	Jordan	1955-67	Askari, Cummings, and Harik	-0.01	+0.01
	United States	c	Nerlove and Addison	+0.16	+0.90
	England and Wales	1936-58	Jones	+0.17	+1.05
ONIONS	Egypt	1920-40	Askari, Cummings, and Harik	+0.05	+0.06
	Egypt	1953-72	Askari, Cummings, and Harik	+0.16	+0.13
	Syria	1950-60	Askari, Cummings, and Harik	-0.20	-0.18
	Syria	1961-72	Askari, Cummings, and Harik	+0.09	+0.14
	Lebanon	1953-72	Askari, Cummings, and Harik	+0.42	+0.46
	United States	c	Nerlove and Addison	+0.34	+1.00
	England and Wales	1928-58	Jones	+0.59	+1.64
POTATOES	Syria	1950-60	Askari, Cummings, and Harik	+0.34	+0.35
	Syria	1961-72	Askari, Cummings, and Harik	-0.35	-0.35
	Jordan	1955-67	Askari, Cummings, and Harik	+0.37	+0.56
	Lebanon	1953-72	Askari, Cummings, and Harik	+0.54	+0.58
	South Australia	1952-63	Mules and Jarrett	+0.36	+1.09
	Great Britain	1884-1914	Jones	+0.11	+0.31
	England and Wales	1924-37	Jones	+0.11	+0.33
VEGETABLES	Great Britain	1924-58	Jones	+0.32	+1.45
	Great Britain	1946-57	Jones	+0.30	+0.94
CANTELOUPE	United States	c	Nerlove and Addison	+0.02	+0.04
WATERMELON	United States	c	Nerlove and Addison	+0.23	+0.48
STRAWBERRIES	Great Britain	1924-58[e]	Jones	+0.20	+0.60
	Great Britain	1946-58	Jones	+0.30	+1.03

Crop	Region	Period	Author	Short-Run Elasticity	Long-Run Elasticity
GOOSEBERRIES	Great Britain	1946-58	Jones	+0.10	+0.91
RASPBERRIES	Great Britain	1946-58	Jones	+0.21	+1.40
BLACK CURRANTS	Great Britain	1946-58	Jones	+0.29	+1.16
SOFT FRUITS	Great Britain	1924-58[e]	Jones	+0.18	+0.58
	Great Britain	1946-58	Jones	+0.30	+1.00
SESAMUM	Andhra Pradesh	1955-68	Cummings	+0.29	+0.23
	Bihar	1953-67	Cummings	-0.74	-0.39
	Gujarat	1955-68	Cummings	+0.08	+0.10
	Kerala	1958-68	Cummings	-0.30	-0.68
	Maharashta	1955-68	Cummings	+0.23	+0.30
	Mysore	1955-68	Cummings	+0.03	+0.04
	Punjab	1949-67	Cummings	-0.93	-2.33
	Rajasthan	1951-68	Cummings	+0.37	+0.34
	Madras (Tamil Nadu)	1947-65	Madhavan	+0.42 to 0.48	+0.31 to 0.32
	Madras (Tamil Nadu)	1949-67	Cummings	-0.15	-0.21
	Assam	1949-67	Cummings	-0.42	-0.98
	Tripura	1954-67	Cummings	+0.40	+0.56
	Pakistan (West)	1951-67	Cummings	-0.09	-0.09
	Bangladesh (winter)	1953-64	Cummings	+0.21	+0.60
	Bangladesh (summer)	1953-64	Cummings	-0.28	-0.20
	Syria	1947-60	Askari, Cummings, and Harik	-1.04	-0.79
	Syria	1961-72	Askari, Cummings, and Harik	+0.58	+0.99
	Iraq	1950-60	Askari, Cummings, and Harik	-0.80	-1.00
	Iraq	1961-71	Askari, Cummings, and Harik	+2.30	+2.76
	Jordan	1955-67	Askari, Cummings, and Harik	-0.64	-0.45
	Sudan	1951-65	Askari, Cummings, and Harik	+0.59	+1.08
RAPE AND MUSTARD	Haryana	1950-70	Singh, Singh, and Rai	0	—
	Pakistan (West)	1950-62	Cummings	+0.38	+0.48
	Bangladesh	1950-62	Cummings	+0.23	+0.42
RAPESEED	Canada	1951-67	Paddock	+2.35	—
GROUNDNUTS	Punjab	1953-68	Boon-raung et al.	+0.60	—
	Punjab	1951-67	Cummings	+0.89	+4.05
	Punjab	1953-66	Askari and Cummings	+0.18	+0.85
	Punjab	1960-69	Kaul and Sidhu	+0.51 to 0.78	+3.05 to 3.25
	Uttar Pradesh	1953-64	Nowshirvani	—	+0.89
	Uttar Pradesh	1953-68	Boon-raung et al.	+0.31	—
	Bombay-Sind	1900-39	Parikh	+0.40 to 0.51	+5.27 to 19.24
	Bombay	1938-57	NCAER	+0.21	—
	Bombay	1953-68	Boon-raung et al.	+0.24	—
	Gujarat	1955-67	Cummings	-0.11	-0.11
	Maharashta	1955-68	Cummings	-0.14	-0.14
	Maharashta	1956-67	Askari and Cummings	+0.10	+0.33

(continued)

Crop	Region	Period	Author	Short-Run Elasticity	Long-Run Elasticity
GROUNDNUTS (continued	Madhya Pradesh	1953-68	Boon-raung et al.	-0.23	—
	Mysore	1953-67	Cummings	-0.06	-0.06
	Mysore	1955-66	Askari and Cummings	-0.17	-0.15
	Mysore	1953-68	Boon-raung et al.	-0.11	—
	Madras (Tamil Nadu)	1900-39	Parikh	+0.80	+3.71
	Madras (Tamil Nadu)	1938-57	NCAER	+0.23	—
	Madras (Tamil Nadu)	1947-65	Madhavan	+0.03 to 0.34	+0.04 to 0.65
	Madras (Tamil Nadu)	1951-65	Rajagopalan	+0.50	—
	Madras (Tamil Nadu)	1950-67	Cummings	-0.01	-0.01
	Madras (Tamil Nadu)	1953-68	Boon-raung et al.	+0.15	—
	Pondicherry	1958-68	Cummings	+0.16	+0.14
	Andhra Pradesh	1951-67	Cummings	+0.69	+0.52
	Andhra Pradesh	1953-66	Askari and Cummings	-0.07	+0.23
	Andhra Pradesh	1953-68	Boon-raung et al.	+0.35	—
	Andhra Kurnool	1931-43	Reddy	+0.76	—
	Rajasthan	1953-68	Boon-raung et al.	+0.62	—
	Rajasthan	1950-68	Cummings	-0.47	-0.57
	Rajasthan	1954-68	Askari and Cummings	-0.31	-1.24
	India	1938-57	NCAER	+0.22	—
	India	1953-68	Boon-raung et al.	+0.22	—
	Sudan	1951-65	Medani	+0.72	+1.62
	Nigeria	1948-67	Olayide	+0.24 to 0.79	—
SOYBEANS	United States	1946-66	Houck and Subotnik	+0.84	—
	United States Lake States	1946-66	Houck and Subotnik	+0.91	—
	United States Corn Belt	1946-66	Houck and Subotnik	+0.50	—
	United States Plains States	1946-66	Houck and Subotnik	+2.10	—
	United States Delta States	1946-66	Houck and Subotnik	+0.75	—
	United States Atlantic States	1946-66	Houck and Subotnik	+1.70 to 3.30	—
FLAXSEED	Argentina	1948-65	Freire	+1.10	—
	Canada	1947-66	Schmitz	+0.08 to 0.19	—
LINSEED	Iraq	1950-60	Askari, Cummings, and Harik	+2.33	+2.44
	Iraq	1961-71	Askari, Cummings, and Harik	-2.85	-14.23
COTTON	Punjab (Desi variety)	1922-43	Raj Krishna	+0.59	+1.08
	Punjab (American variety)	1922-43	Raj Krishna	+0.78	+1.62

Crop	Region	Period	Author	Short-Run Elasticity	Long-Run Elasticity
COTTON (continued)	Punjab (American)	1900-39	Parikh	+0.43	+9.74
	Punjab (American)	1951-64	Kaul	+0.34	+2.84
	Punjab (Desi)	1951-64	Kaul	+0.29	+1.19
	Punjab (Desi)	1960-69	Kaul and Sidhu	+0.45 to 0.68	+0.79 to 1.17
	Punjab	1950-68	Cummings	+0.37	+0.56
	Haryana	1950-70	Singh, Singh, and Rai	+0.62	–
	Bombay	1904-39	S. Krishna	+0.15	+0.25
	Gujarat	1954-68	Cummings	+0.05	+0.08
	Madhya Pradesh-Berar	1900-39	Parikh	+0.10 to 0.12	+0.16 to 0.72
	Madras (Tamil Nadu)	1947-65	Madhavan	+0.01 to 0.31	+0.02 to 0.54
	Madras (Tamil Nadu)	1939-65	Rajagopalan	+1.28	–
	Madras (Tamil Nadu)	1955-67	Askari and Cummings	+0.02	+0.02
	Madras (districts)	1950-67	Cummings	-0.28 to +0.65	-0.42 to +1.06
	Andhra Pradesh	1951-69	Cummings	+0.07	+0.11
	Andhra Pradesh	1953-68	Askari and Cummings	+0.40	+0.64
	Kerala	1957-68	Cummings	-0.39	-0.41
	Mysore	1953-69	Cummings	+0.29	+0.33
	Mysore	1955-67	Askari and Cummings	+0.33	+0.54
	Assam	1951-69	Cummings	-0.09	-0.11
	Assam	1954-68	Askari and Cummings	+0.12	+0.25
	Tripura	1951-69	Cummings	+0.20	+0.29
	Tripura	1955-69	Askari and Cummings	+0.01	+0.03
	India	1938-57	NCAER	+0.75	–
	India	1948-61	Raj Krishna	+0.64	+1.33
	Pakistan (West)	1933-59	Falcon	+0.41	–
	Pakistan (West)	1949-62	Mohammad	+0.53	–
	Pakistan (Desi)	1950-67	Cummings	+0.41	+0.28
	Pakistan (American)	1950-67	Cummings	+0.40	+0.47
	Egypt	1899-1937	Stern	+0.38[a]	–
	Egypt	1914-37	Stern	+0.52[a]	–
	Egypt	1920-40	Askari, Cummings, and Harik	-3.36	-5.18
	Egypt	1953-72	Askari, Cummings, and Harik	-0.09	-0.08
	Syria	1948-60	Askari, Cummings, and Harik	+1.12	+0.83
	Syria	1961-72	Askari, Cummings, and Harik	+1.49	+1.09
	Iraq	1950-60	Askari, Cummings, and Harik	+1.95	+1.62
	Iraq	1961-71	Askari, Cummings, and Harik	-0.85	-1.44

(continued)

Crop	Region	Period	Author	Short-Run Elasticity	Long-Run Elasticity
COTTON (continued)	Sudan	1951-65	Medani	+0.39	+0.50
	Nigeria	1948-67	Olayide	+0.03 to 0.04	–
	Nigeria	1948-67	Oni	+0.38	+0.28
	Uganda	1922-38	Frederick	+0.25	–
	Uganda Buganda	1922-38	Frederick	+0.67 to 0.73	–
	Uganda Buganda	1945-66	Alibaruho	+0.50	+0.63
	Uganda Eastern region	1945-66	Alibaruho	+0.23	+0.44
	Uganda Western region	1945-66	Alibaruho	+0.26	+0.62
	Uganda Northern region	1945-66	Alibaruho	+0.02	+0.07
	United States (10 states)	1883-1914	DeCanio	+0.13 to 0.34	+0.23 to 0.85
	United States (10 states)	1874	Cooley and DeCanio	+0.08 to 0.29	+0.12 to 0.60
	United States (10 states)	1914	Cooley and DeCanio	+0.06 to 0.33	+0.08 to 0.60
	United States Southeast	1905-32	Brennan	+0.33	–
	United States Delta	1905-32	Brennan	+0.31	–
	United States Southwest	1905-32	Brennan	+0.37	–
	United States	1909-32	Nerlove	+0.20 to 0.67	–
KENAF	Thailand (8 provinces)	1954-63	Behrman	+0.88 to 7.71	+1.19 to 42.60
JUTE	Bengal (undivided)	1912-39	Rabbani	+0.48 to 0.78	+0.84 to 0.90
	Bengal (undivided)	1911-39	Stern	+0.68	+1.03
	Bengal (undivided)	1911-38	S. Krishna	+0.49 to 0.57	+1.16 to 1.29
	West Bengal	1900-39	Parikh	+0.01	+0.12
	West Bengal	1951-62	Rabbani	+0.70	+0.71 to 0.74
	West Bengal	1958-70	Bansil	0	–
	West Bengal	1949-69	Cummings	+0.40	+0.35
	West Bengal	1954-69	Askari and Cummings	+0.58	+0.89
	Assam	1951-61	Rabbani	+0.41 to 0.43	+0.51 to 0.57
	Assam	1949-69	Cummings	+0.07	+0.05
	Bihar	1949-62	Rabbani	+0.78 to 0.80	+0.88 to 0.97
	Bihar	1946-69	Cummings	+0.12	+0.13
	Bihar	1955-69	Askari and Cummings	+0.57	+0.65
	Orissa	1950-62	Rabbani	+0.75 to 0.79	+0.77 to 0.88
	Bihar and Orissa	1900-39	Parikh	+0.51	+0.78
	Uttar Pradesh	1957-68	Cummings	+0.14	+0.14
	Tripura	1949-69	Cummings	+0.80	+1.60
	Tripura	1952-69	Askari and Cummings	+1.03	-33.25
	India (undivided)	1911-39	Rabbani	+0.38 to 0.47	+0.65 to 0.80

Crop	Region	Period	Author	Short-Run Elasticity	Long-Run Elasticity
JUTE (continued)	India (undivided)	1921–39	Rabbani	+0.49 to 0.50	+0.93 to 1.00
	India (undivided)	1911–38	Venkataraman	+0.46	+0.73
	India	1951–62	Rabbani	+0.74 to 0.76	+0.96 to 0.99
	Bangladesh	1931–54	Clark	+0.60	–
	Bangladesh	1931–47	Rabbani	+1.35	+1.67
	Bangladesh	1949–63	Rabbani	+0.39 to 0.40	+0.65 to 0.66
	Bangladesh	1948–63	Hussain	+0.36 to 0.38	–
	Bangladesh	1948–66	Huq	+0.35	+0.83
	Bangladesh	1949–68	Cummings	+0.40	+0.48
	Bangladesh	1952–68	Askari and Cummings	-0.16	-0.23
SISAL	Tanzania	1945–67	Gwyer	+0.42 to 0.50	+0.24 to 0.42
TOBACCO	Andhra Pradesh	1940–67	Rao and Singh	+0.25	+0.42
	Andhra Pradesh	1950–66	Cummings	+0.18	+0.19
	Andhra Pradesh (3 districts)	1954–66	Askari and Cummings	-0.08 to +0.13	-0.09 to +0.24
	Assam	1955–68	Cummings	-0.26	-0.33
	Assam	1956–67	Askari and Cummings	-0.30	-0.26
	Bihar	1950–68	Cummings	-0.07	-0.08
	Bihar	1954–67	Askari and Cummings	+0.05	+0.06
	Gujarat	1954–67	Cummings	+0.16	+1.00
	Gujarat (2 districts)	1953–67	Askari and Cummings	-0.55 to +0.34	-1.67 to +0.85
	Maharashta	1954–68	Cummings	-0.08	-0.12
	Mysore	1953–68	Cummings	-0.04	-0.05
	Mysore	1955–67	Askari and Cummings	+0.06	+0.07
	Madras (Tamil Nadu)	1949–67	Cummings	+0.22	+0.25
	Madras (Tamil Nadu)	1953–67	Askari and Cummings	+0.16	+0.22
	India	1938–57	NCAER	+0.71	–
	Pakistan (West)	1950–66	Cummings	-0.13	-0.14
	Pakistan (West)	1951–67	Askari and Cummings	-0.08	-0.11
	Bangladesh	1950–66	Cummings	+0.51	+0.53
	Bangladesh	1951–67	Askari and Cummings	+0.15	+0.24
	Nigeria	1945–64	Adesimi	+0.60	+0.82
	Malawi	1926–60	Dean	+0.48	–
SUGAR	Uttar Pradesh (6 divisions)	1909–42	Nowshirvani	+0.19 to 1.47	+0.24 to 2.46
	Uttar Pradesh (6 divisions)	1953–64	Nowshirvani	-0.04 to +0.63	-0.29 to +1.19
	Uttar Pradesh	1900–39	Parikh	+0.40	+0.91
	Uttar Pradesh	1950–68	Rathod	+0.25	–
	Uttar Pradesh (11 districts)	1950–68	Rathod	+0.12 to 0.85	–
	Punjab	1900–39	Parikh	+0.57	+1.36
	Punjab	1915–43	Raj Krishna	+0.34	+0.60

(continued)

Crop	Region	Period	Author	Short-Run Elasticity	Long-Run Elasticity
SUGAR	Punjab	1951-64	Kaul	+0.09	+0.73
(continued)	Madhya Pradesh	1951-64	Kaul	+0.84	+0.88
	Bihar	1951-64	Nowshirvani	−	+1.38
	Bihar Tirkut division	1933-64	Jha	+0.35	+0.44
	Bihar Tirkut division	1950-64	Jha	+0.65	+0.79
	Andhra Pradesh	1952-64	Subbarao	+0.50	−
	Madras (Tamil Nadu)	1900-39	Parikh	+0.30 to 0.39	+1.08 to 1.51
	Madras (Tamil Nadu)	1947-65	Madhavan	+0.52 to 0.63	+0.66 to 1.21
	Madras (Tamil Nadu)	1951-65	Rajagopalan	+0.68 to 0.74	−
	Philippines	1914-64	Askari	+0.08 to 0.13	+0.13 to 0.16
COCOA	Ghana (old areas)[f]	1949-62	Bateman	+0.39	+0.77
	Ghana (medium areas)[f]	1949-62	Bateman	+0.42 to 0.51	+1.28
	Ghana (new areas)[f]	1949-62	Bateman	+0.61 to 0.87	+1.06
	Ghana	1947-63	Behrman	−	+0.71
	Nigeria	1947-63	Behrman	−	+0.45
	Nigeria	1948-67	Olayide	+0.15 to 0.20	−
	Ivory Coast	1947-63	Behrman	−	+0.80
	Cameroon	1947-63	Behrman	+0.68	+1.81
	Brazil	1947-63	Behrman	+0.53	+0.95
	Ecuador	1947-63	Behrman	−	+0.28
	Dominican Republic	1947-63	Behrman	+0.03	+0.15
	Venezuela	1947-63	Behrman	+0.12	+0.38
COFFEE	Uganda	1926-38	Frederick	+0.63	−
	Uganda Buganda	1926-38	Frederick	+0.42	−
	Kenya	1946-64	Maitha	+0.15	+0.38
	Kenya (estates)	1946-64	Maitha	+0.16	+0.40
	Kenya (small-holders)	1946-64	Maitha	+0.20	+0.51
	Kenya	1946-64	Ford	−	+0.38
	Kenya (estates)	1946-64	Ford	−	+0.47
	Kenya (small-holders)	1946-64	Ford	−	+0.59
	Africa	1943-60	Bacha	+0.14 to 0.24	+0.37 to 0.60
	Brazil	1948-64	Behrman and Klein	+0.10	+0.11
	Brazil Sao Paulo	1930-55	Arak	+2.02 to 2.28[g]	−
	Brazil Sao Paulo	1925-33 and 1951-61	Bacha	+0.23	+1.00
	Brazil Sao Paulo	1948-70	Saylor	+0.10 to 0.16	+0.51 to 0.64
	Brazil Parana	1945-62	Arak	−	+0.96
	Brazil Parana	1945-62	Bacha	−	+0.71

404

Crop	Region	Period	Author	Short-Run Elasticity	Long-Run Elasticity
COFFEE (continued)	Brazil Minhas Gerais	1927–59	Arak	+0.08	+0.54
	Brazil Espirito Santo	1927–59	Arak	+0.20	+0.28
	Colombia	1939–64	Bacha	+0.07	+0.45
	Colombia	1947–65	Bateman	–	+0.47g
	Colombia	1952–65	Bateman	–	+0.84g
	Latin America (excluding Brazil and Colombia)	1943–60	Bacha	+0.28	+0.52
	Jamaica	1953–68	Williams	+0.70 to 0.82	–
TEA	India	1921–61	Rajagopalan	+0.02 to 0.06	+0.09 to 0.16
RUBBER	Malaysia (smallholders)	1948–61	Chan	+0.12 to 0.34	–
	Malaysia (estates)	1948–61	Chan	0	–
	Malaysia (smallholders)	1953–60	Stern	+0.20	–
	Malaysia (estates)	1953–60	Stern	0	–
	Malaysia (smallholders)	1949–63	Behrman	+0.18 to 0.23	+0.21
	Malaysia (estates)	1949–63	Behrman	-0.09 to +0.09	+0.15
	Thailand	1947–65	Behrman	+0.04 to 0.41	+0.19
	Indonesia (smallholders)	1949–64	Behrman	-0.02 to +0.33	+0.03
	Indonesia (estates)	1949–64	Behrman	0 to +0.05	+0.40
	Nigeria	1948–67	Olayide	+0.17 to 0.24	+0.21 to 0.94
	Liberia	1950–72	Ghoshal	+0.14	+0.22
PALM OIL	Nigeria	1948–67	Olayide	+0.22 to 0.26	–
	Nigeria	1949–64	Oni	+0.20 to 0.35	–
	Nigeria, Eastern Nigeria	1949–64	Oni	+0.40 to 0.70	–
PALM KERNELS	Nigeria	1948–67	Olayide	+0.05 to 0.10	–
	Nigeria	1949–64	Oni	+0.22 to 0.28	–
	Nigeria, Eastern Nigeria	1949–64	Oni	+0.28 to 0.39	–
HONEY	Western Australia	1952–63	Taplin and Smallhorn	+0.13	+0.35h
	New South Wales	1952–63	Taplin and Smallhorn	0	–
EGGS	United Kingdom	1927–39	Jones	+0.28 to 0.57	+1.17 to 1.36
	United Kingdom	1955–63	Jones	+0.55	+1.66
	United Kingdom	1954–66	Robertson	+1.52	+2.42
	United States	1927–57	Jones	+0.42	+1.35
MILK	Australia	1947–64	Powell and Gruen	+0.19	+0.42
	Ireland	1951–68	Buttimer and MacAirt	+0.25 to 0.30	–
	Ireland	1953–70	Buttimer	+0.37	–
	United Kingdom	1924–58e	Jones	+0.06	+0.46

(continued)

Crop	Region	Period	Author	Short-Run Elasticity	Long-Run Elasticity
MILK (continued)	United Kingdom	1955-64	Jones	+0.17 to 0.23	+0.27 to 1.05
	United Kingdom	1965-70	Hill	+0.10	–
	United Kingdom	1957-68	Gardner and Walker	+0.22	+0.66
	England and Wales	1948-58	Gardner	+0.13	+1.42
	Greece (cows)	1952-65	Papaioannou and Jones	+0.49 to 0.59	+1.30
	Greece (sheep)	1952-65	Papaioannou and Jones	+0.58 ⎫	+1.50 to 2.00
	Greece (goats)	1952-65	Papaioannou and Jones	+0.39 ⎭	
	United States	1931-54	Halvorson	+0.03[i]	–
	United States	1931-54	Halvorson	+0.14[j]	–
	United States North Atlantic	1931-54	Halvorson	+0.09[i]	–
	United States North Atlantic	1931-54	Halvorson	+0.21[j]	–
	United States East North Central Atlantic	1931-54	Halvorson	+0.03[i]	–
	United States East North Central Atlantic	1931-54	Halvorson	+0.10[j]	–
	United States West North Central Atlantic	1931-54	Halvorson	+0.05[i]	–
	United States West North Central Atlantic	1931-54	Halvorson	+0.11[j]	–
	United States South Atlantic	1931-54	Halvorson	-0.01[i]	–
	United States South Atlantic	1931-54	Halvorson	+0.22[j]	–
	United States South Central Atlantic	1931-54	Halvorson	+0.06[i]	–
	United States South Central Atlantic	1931-54	Halvorson	+0.19[j]	–
	United States West Atlantic	1931-54	Halvorson	+0.03[i]	–
	United States West Atlantic	1931-54	Halvorson	+0.18[j]	–
	United States	1927-57	Halvorson	+0.13 to 0.17	+0.40 to 0.44
	United States	1941-57	Halvorson	+0.18 to 0.31	+0.15 to 0.89
	United States	1958-68	Prato	0	–
	California	1953-68	Chan, Courtney, and Schmitz	+0.38	+2.54
WOOL	Australia	1949-65	Witherell	+0.07 to 0.08	+0.13 to 0.28
	Australia	1947-64	Powell and Gruen	+0.07	+0.33
	South Australia	1949-61	Dahlberg	+0.08	–
	New Zealand	1949-65	Witherell	+0.03	+0.72
	South Africa	1949-65	Witherell	+0.08	+0.76

Crop	Region	Period	Author	Short–Run Elasticity	Long–Run Elasticity
WOOL	Great Britain	1927–55	Jones	–	+0.20
(continued)	Argentina	1950–64	Witherell	+0.04	+0.20
	Uruguay	1950–64	Witherell	+0.21	+0.48
	United States	1948–65	Witherell	+0.14 to 0.15	+0.32 to 0.35
BEEF	Australia	1947–64	Powell and Gruen	+0.16	–
	United Kingdom	1924–58	Jones	+0.10 to 0.38	above +1.00
	West Germany	1951–64	Jones	–	+1.06
	Ireland	1953–70	Buttimer	+0.11	–
	Greece (veal)	1952–65	Papaioannou and Jones	+0.33 to 0.43	–
LAMB	Australia	1947–64	Powell and Gruen	+0.32	+1.38
	United Kingdom	1907–58	Jones	+0.30	+2.31
	United Kingdom	1955–64	Jones	+0.28 to 0.50	+1.51 to 4.00
	Greece	1952–65	Papaioannou and Jones	+0.49	–
GOATS	Greece	1952–65	Papaioannou and Jones	+0.63	–
PORK	United Kingdom	1924–39	Jones	+0.65	+3.61
	United Kingdom	1949–58	Jones	+0.40	above +2.00
	United States	1924–37	Dean and Heady	+0.46[k]	–
	United States	1924–37	Dean and Heady	+0.28[l]	–
	United States	1937–56[m]	Dean and Heady	+0.60[k]	–
	United States	1938–56[m]	Dean and Heady	+0.30[l]	–
	United States	1961–72	Meilke, Zwart, and Martin	+0.24	+0.48
	Canada Eastern provinces	1961–72	Meilke, Zwart, and Martin	+0.38	+1.12
	Canada Western provinces	1961–72	Meilke, Zwart, and Martin	+0.16	+0.79
POULTRY	United Kingdom	1927–39	Jones	+0.69	–
	United Kingdom	1960–64	Jones	+1.00	+2.50

[a]Median value.
[b]Lower and upper bounds of second and third quartiles, respectively.
[c]Nerlove-Addison time periods variously begin between 1919 and 1929, and all end in 1955.
[d]Infinite value indicated.
[e]Omitting 1940 to 1945.
[f]Refers to how long cocoa has been cultivated in the region.
[g]Elasticity of new plantings.
[h]From stocks.
[i]Summer production.
[j]Winter production.
[k]Spring farrowing.
[l]Fall farrowing.
[m]Omitting 1942 to 1944.

Source: Compiled by the authors.

TABLE B.2

Supply Elasticities, by Numerical Range

Less Than Zero

Rice: Uttar Pradesh,[a] Himachal Pradesh,[b] Gujarat,[b] Maharashta,[b] Madras,[b,c] Kerala,[b] Egypt[b,c]

Wheat: Uttar Pradesh,[a,c] Madhya Pradesh-Berar,[b,c] Bombay-Sind,[b,c] Iraq[b]

Barley: Himachal Pradesh,[b] Syria,[b] Iraq,[b] Jordan[b]

Maize: Jordan,[b] Egypt[b,c]

Bajra: Punjab,[b] Madhya Pradesh[b]

Jowar: Punjab,[b] Madhya Pradesh[b]

Vetch: Syria,[b] Jordan[b]

Millet: Iraq[b]

Broadbeans: Syria,[b] Jordan[b]

Lentils: Syria,[b] Jordan,[b] Lebanon[b]

Eggplant: Jordan[b]

Artichokes: California[b]

Potatoes: Syria[b]

Sesamum: Pakistan,[b] Jordan[b]

Groundnuts: Rajasthan,[b] Bihar,[b] Kerala,[b] Assam,[b] Gujarat,[b] Maharashta,[b] Mysore,[b] Madhya Pradesh

Linseed: Iraq[b]

Cotton: Kerala,[b] Egypt,[b] Iraq[b]

Tobacco: Maharashta,[b] Assam,[b] Pakistan[b]

Zero to One-Third

Rice: Assam,[b] Bihar,[a] Mysore,[b] Punjab, West Bengal,[b] Tripura,[b] Pakistan,[b] Bangladesh,[b] Thailand, West Malaysia, Japan,[b] Philippines, Egypt[b,d]

Wheat: Mysore, Punjab,[b] Rajasthan,[b] West Bengal,[b] Maharashta,[b] Himachal Pradesh,[b] Pakistan,[b] Hungary, Jordan,[b] Lebanon, Egypt,[b,c] United States

Barley: Pakistan,[b] Lebanon,[b] Canada

Maize: Punjab, Egypt,[b,d] Lebanon,[b] Sudan, Philippines, United States

Rye: Hungary

Oats: Hungary, United Kingdom[b]

Feed grains: Australia

Bajra: Haryana

Gram: Haryana, Andhra Pradesh

Ragi: Madras[b]
Sorghum: Madras,[b] Sudan[b]
Beans: United States
Broad beans: Egypt[b]
Chick peas: Jordan[b]
Onions: Egypt,[b] Syria[b]
Cauliflower: United Kingdom, United States
Celery: United Kingdom, United States
Carrots: United States
Peppers: United States[b]
Shallots: United States (Louisiana)[b]
Spinach: United States
Lettuce: United States[b]
Kale: United States[b]
Sprouts: United Kingdom
Eggplant: United States[b]
Tomatoes: Jordan,[a] United Kingdom, United States
Potatoes: United Kingdom[b]
Watermelon: United States
Canteloupe: United States[b]
Berries: United Kingdom
Soft Fruits: United Kingdom
Sesamum: Andhra Pradesh,[b] Bombay,[b] Mysore,[b] Madras,[b]
Bangladesh[b]
Rape and Mustard: Haryana, Bangladesh
Groundnuts: Uttar Pradesh, Madras, Pondicherry[b]
Flaxseed: Canada
Cotton: Madhya Pradesh-Berar,[c] Andhra Pradesh,[b] Mysore,[b]
Assam,[b] Gujarat,[b] Madras, Tripura,[b] Uganda, United States[b]
Jute: Uttar Pradesh[b]
Sisal: Tanzania
Tobacco: Andhra Pradesh,[b] Gujarat, Madras,[b] Bihar,[b]
Mysore,[b] Bangladesh[b]
Sugar: Punjab,[d] Philippines[b]
Cocoa: Ecuador,[a] Dominican Republic,[b] Venezuela, Nigeria
Coffee: Brazil, Colombia, Kenya
Tea: India[b]
Palm Oil and Kernels: Nigeria
Rubber: Malaysia,[b] Thailand,[b] Indonesia,[b] Nigeria, Liberia[b]
Honey: New South Wales
Milk: England and Wales, Ireland, Australia, United States

(continued)

Zero to One-Third (continued)

Wool: Australia,[b] Argentina,[b] Uruguay, South Africa, United States, United Kingdom[b]
Lamb: Australia
Beef: Australia, Ireland
Pork: Canada (west)

One-Third to Two-Thirds

Rice: Punjab,[a] Bihar-Orissa,[a] Peru,[b] Java, Iraq
Wheat: Uttar Pradesh,[a,d] Bihar,[a] Egypt,[a,d] Syria, Lebanon,[a] New South Wales, United Kingdom,[b] France, Argentina, Chile
Barley: Rajasthan, Uttar Pradesh,[a] Bihar,[a] Delhi, Punjab,[b] United Kingdom
Maize: Punjab, Hungary, Sudan[a]
Jowar: Maharashta
Gram: Andhra Pradesh
Beans: Lebanon,[b] United Kingdom[b]
Cabbage: United Kingdom, United States
Carrots: United Kingdom
Cauliflower: United Kingdom[a]
Sprouts: United Kingdom[a]
Potatoes: South Australia, Jordan,[b] Lebanon,[b] United Kingdom[a]
Peas: United Kingdom, United States
Chick peas: Syria,[b] Lebanon
Onions: Lebanon,[b] United Kingdom, United States
Vegetables: United Kingdom
Watermelons: United States[a]
Strawberries: United Kingdom[a]
Soft Fruits: United Kingdom[a]
Sesamum: Rajasthan, Syria, Sudan
Rape and Mustard: Pakistan,[b] Bangladesh[a]
Groundnuts: Bombay-Sind,[c] Andhra Pradesh,[b] Punjab, Tripura,[b] Rajasthan, Nigeria
Cotton: Punjab, Pakistan, Uganda,[a] Nigeria, Sudan[a]
Jute: India-Bangladesh: old areas[b]
Sisal: Tanzania[a]
Tobacco: Nigeria, Malawi
Sugar: Punjab, Uttar Pradesh, Bihar, Madras, Andhra Pradesh
Cocoa: Ghana: old areas, Nigeria,[a] Venezuela,[a] Brazil
Coffee: Brazil: new areas,[a] Colombia,[a] Uganda, Kenya[a]
Honey: Western Australia
Eggs: United Kingdom, United States

Milk: Australia,[a] United Kingdom,[a] Greece, United States[a]
Wool: Uruguay,[a] United States[a]
Lamb: United Kingdom, Greece
Goats: Greece
Beef: United Kingdom, Greece
Pork: United States, Canada (east)

Two–Thirds to One

Wheat: Gujarat,[b] Egypt,[a] New South Wales,[a] New Zealand, United States,[a] Canada[b]
Feed grains: Australia,[a] France
Cumbu: Madras
Chick peas: Lebanon
Celery: United Kingdom,[a] United States[a]
Cabbage: United Kingdom[a]
Tomatoes: United States[a]
Gooseberries: United Kingdom[a]
Soft Fruits: United Kingdom[a]
Sesamum: Syria[a]
Groundnuts: Uttar Pradesh,[a] Kurnool (Andhra Pradesh), Sudan
Soybeans: United States
Cotton: Buganda
Jute: India–Bangladesh: new areas
Tobacco: Gujarat,[a] Nigeria[a]
Sugar: Uttar Pradesh,[a] Punjab,[a,d] Madhya Pradesh,[b] Bihar[a]
Cocoa: Ghana: new areas, Ivory Coast,[a] Cameroons, Brazil[a]
Coffee: Jamaica
Wool: South Africa,[a] New Zealand,[a] United States[a]
Pork: Canada (west)[a]
Poultry: United Kingdom

More Than One

Rice: West Malaysia,[a] Iraq[a]
Wheat: Syria,[a] New Zealand,[a] Chile[a]
Barley: Rajasthan,[a] United Kingdom,[a] United States
Maize: Thailand,[b] Syria[b]
Millet: Syria[b]
Cassava: Thailand[b]
Beans: United States[a]

(continued)

More Than One (continued)

Cabbage: United States[a]
Carrots: United Kingdom,[a] United States[a]
Cucumbers: United States[a]
Cauliflower: United States[a]
Spinach: United States[a]
Tomatoes: United Kingdom[a]
Onions: United Kingdom,[a] United States[a]
Potatoes: South Australia[a]
Vegetables: United Kingdom[a]
Raspberries: United Kingdom[a]
Blackcurrants: United Kingdom[a]
Sesamum: Iraq,[b] Sudan[a]
Groundnuts: Madras,[a] Bombay-Sind,[a] Punjab,[a] Sudan[a]
Flax: Argentina
Rapeseed: Canada
Cotton: Punjab,[a] Madras,[a] Syria[b]
Kenaf: Thailand[b]
Sugar: Bihar,[a] Madras,[a] Punjab,[a] Uttar Pradesh[a]
Cocoa: Cameroon[a]
Coffee: Brazil: old areas[a]
Milk: England-Wales,[a] Greece,[a] California[a]
Eggs: United Kingdom,[a] United States[a]
Lamb: Australia,[a] United Kingdom[a]
Beef: United Kingdom,[a] West Germany[a]
Pork: United Kingdom,[b] Canada (east)[a]
Poultry: United Kingdom[a]

[a]Long-run elasticity.
[b]Short- and long-run elasticity.
[c]Pre-World War II.
[d]Post-World War II.
Unless otherwise noted, elasticities are short run.

Notes: As can be seen in Table B.1, in many cases several studies of a particular crop in a given area are available and may diverge in their reported results. In preparing this table an attempt was made to reconcile these differences by weighting the various studies according to several statistical criteria, such as the length of the time series, estimating methods employed, and so on.

Source: Compiled by the authors.

Bajra	Pearl or cattail millet; a cereal grass used for both human and animal food. Suitable for dry soils of low fertility.
Black gram	Urd bean; grown for human consumption as well as for fodder and for its soil-restorative properties. In the latter case the crop is plowed under as green manure.
Cassava	Several plants of the spurge family whose root stalks yield an edible starch; processed into tapioca.
Cumbu	Bajra.
Gram	A legume; also called chick-pea. The seeds can be eaten raw or cooked, or can be ground into flour.
Green gram	Mung bean; the seeds are edible. Also a forage crop and green manure.
Horse gram	Herbaceous plant with edible seeds primarily used for fodder.
Jowar	Durra; a grain sorghum.
Jute	A glossy fiber of either of two East Indian plants; chiefly used for making thread, twine, or burlap.
Kale	A type of cabbage with curled leaves.
Kenaf	An East Indian fiber used for rope-making.
Manioc	Cassava.
Millet	A family of small-seeded grasses cultivated for both human and animal consumption.
Pulses	A family of edible seed-bearing plants, such as peas, beans, and lentils.
Ragi	Finger millet; an East Indian cereal.
Rape	An herb of the mustard family; its seeds yield rape oil. It is also used for forage.
Sesamum	A tropical herb; its seeds are used for flavoring or ground into oil.
Sisal	An agave whose leaves yield a strong durable white fiber.
Sorghum	Originally a tropical cereal now grown also in temperate regions.
Vetch	An herbaceous plant cultivated for fodder and for its soil-restorative qualities.

Adesimi, A. A. "An Econometric Study of Air-Cured Tobacco Supply in Western Nigeria 1945-1964." Nigerian Journal of Economics and Social Studies 12 (November 1970).

Ady, Peter. "Supply Functions in Tropical Agriculture." Oxford Institute of Statistics Bulletin 30 (1968).

____. "A Note on the Use of the Nerlove Model." Farm Economist 12, no. 1 (1971).

Alibaruho, G. "Regional Supply Elasticities in Uganda's Cotton Industry and the Declining Level of Cotton Output." Eastern African Economic Review 6 (December 1974).

Almon, Shirley. "The Distributed Lag between Capital Appropriations and Expenditures." Econometrica 33 (January 1965).

Anand, Vinod. "Marketed Surplus, Income and Prices—A Case Study of Some of the Crops in Uttar Pradesh." Indian Journal of Economics 55 (July 1974).

Arak, Marcelle. "Estimation of Asymmetric Long-Run Supply Functions: The Case of Coffee." Canadian Journal of Agricultural Economics 17 (February 1969).

____. "The Price Responsiveness of Sao Paulo Coffee Growers." Food Research Institute Studies 8, no. 3 (1968).

____. "The Supply of Brazilian Coffee." Ph.D. dissertation, Massachusetts Institute of Technology, 1967.

Aromdee, Virach. "Can West Malaysia Become Self-sufficient in Rice by 1975?" Malayan Economic Review 14 (October 1969).

____. "Economics of Rice Trade Among Countries of Southeast Asia." Ph.D. dissertation, University of Minnesota, 1968.

Askari, Hossein. "Two Empirical Papers in Economic Development and International Trade." Ph.D. dissertation, Massachusetts Institute of Technology, 1970.

____. "The Supply Response of Sugar Farmers in the Philippines." Asian Economic Review 15 (April-June 1973).

____ and John Thomas Cummings, "Factors affecting Farmer Responsiveness to Price." Asian Economic Review 15 (August-December 1973).

____. "Output Price Response in Agriculture: An Evaluation." Indian Journal of Agricultural Economics 29 (1974).

____. "Supply Response of Farmers with Heterogeneous Land." Indian Journal of Agricultural Economics, forthcoming (1976).

____ and Bassam Harik. "Land Reform in the Middle East." International Journal of Middle East Studies, forthcoming.

Bacha, Edmar L. "An Econometric Model for the World Coffee Market: The Impact of Brazilian Price Policy." Ph.D. dissertation, Yale University, 1968.

Baer, Gabriel. A History of Land Ownership in Modern Egypt 1800-1950. London: Oxford University Press, 1962.

Bahadur, Tej and N. Haridasan. "A Note on the Price-Acreage Responses of Pulses in Andhra Pradesh." Indian Journal of Economics 52 (October 1971).

Balasubramaniam, M. "The Problem of Marketable Surplus in Indian Agriculture." Indian Journal of Agricultural Economics 16 (January-March 1961).

Bansil, P. C. "Farmer Response to Jute and Paddy Prices." A paper read at the 31st Annual Conference of the Indian Society of Agricultural Economics, abstracted in the Indian Journal of Agricultural Economics 26 (October-December 1971).

____. "Problems of Marketable Surplus." Indian Journal of Agricultural Economics 16 (January-March 1961).

Bardhan, Kalpana. "A Note on Price-Elasticity of Demand for Foodgrains in a Peasant Economy." Oxford Economic Papers 21 (March 1969).

____. "Price and Output Response of Marketed Surplus of Foodgrains: A Cross-sectional Study of Some North Indian Villages." American Journal of Agricultural Economics 52 (February 1970).

Bardhan, Pranab, and Kalpana Bardhan. "Price Response of Marketed Surplus of Foodgrains." Oxford Economic Papers 23 (July 1971).

Baritelle, John L., and David W. Price. "Supply Response and Marketing Strategies for Deciduous Crops." American Journal of Agricultural Economics 56 (May 1974).

Bateman, Merrill. "Aggregate and Regional Supply Functions for Ghanaian Cocoa 1946-62." Journal of Farm Economics 47 (May 1965).

____. "Cocoa in the Ghanaian Economy." Ph.D. dissertation, Massachusetts Institute of Technology, 1965.

____. Cocoa in the Ghanaian Economy: An Econometric Model. Amsterdam: North-Holland, 1968.

____. "A Supply Function for Columbian Coffee 1947-1965." A RAND Memorandum, Summer 1968.

____. "Supply Relationships for Perennial Crops in the Less-Developed Areas." In Subsistence Agriculture and Economic Development, edited by Clifton R. Wharton, Jr. Chicago: Aldine, 1969.

Behrman, Jere. "Econometric Model Simulations of the World Rubber Market 1950-1980." In Essays in Industrial Econometrics, Vol. III, edited by Lawrence R. Klein. Philadelphia: Economics Research Unit, Wharton School of Finance and Commerce, 1969.

____. "Monopolistic Cocoa Pricing." American Journal of Agricultural Economics 50 (August 1968).

____. "Price Elasticity of the Marketed Surplus of a Subsistence Crop." Journal of Farm Economics 48 (November 1966).

____. Supply Response in Underdeveloped Agriculture: A Case Study of Four Major Annual Crops in Thailand 1937-1963. Amsterdam: North-Holland, 1968.

____ and L. R. Klein. "Econometric Growth Models for the Developing Economy." In Induction, Growth and Trade: Essays in Honour of Sir Roy Harrod, edited by W. A. Eltis, M. F. Scott, and J. N. Wolfe. Oxford: Clarendon Press, 1970.

Berg, Elliot J. "Backward-Sloping Labor Supply Curves in Dual Economics—The Africa Case." Quarterly Journal of Economics 73 (1961).

Bhalerao, M. M., and Sant Lal. "Marketable Surplus in Maize." Indian Journal of Agricultural Economics 20 (July–September 1965).

Bhargava, P. N., and V. S. Rustogi. "Study of Marketable Surplus of Paddy in Burdwan District." Indian Journal of Agricultural Economics 27 (July–September 1972).

Blandford, David. "Some Estimates of Supply Elasticities for Nigeria's Cash Crops: A Comment." Journal of Agricultural Economics 24 (September 1973).

Boon-raung, P., J. S. Sharma, T. V. Moorti, and M. M. Wagner. "Supply Response for Groundnut in India." A paper read at the 31st Annual Conference of the Indian Society of Agricultural Economics, abstracted in the Indian Journal of Agricultural Economics 26 (October–December 1971).

Bose, Sailesh Kumar. "Problems of Mobilisation of the Marketable Surplus in Agriculture in India." Indian Journal of Agricultural Economics 16 (January–March 1961).

Brandow, A. E. "A Note on the Nerlove Estimate of Supply Elasticity." Journal of Farm Economics 40 (August 1958).

Brennan, Michael J. "Changes in Cotton Acreage in the Southeast: Implications for Supply Functions." Journal of Farm Economics 40 (November 1958).

Buttimer, D. J. "Supply Response in the Irish Dairy and Beef Herds 1953-1970: An Econometric Exercise." Irish Journal of Agricultural Economics and Rural Sociology 4, no. 1 (1972-73).

_____ and J. G. MacAirt. "Supply Response in the Irish Creamery Herd 1951-1970." Irish Journal of Agricultural Economics and Rural Sociology 3, no. 3 (1970-71).

Chan Kwong Wah, Francis. "A Preliminary Study of the Supply Response of Malayan Rubber Estates between 1948 and 1959." Malayan Economic Review 7 (October 1962).

Chen, Dean, Richard Courtney, and Andrew Schmitz. "A Poly-
    nomial Lag Formulation of Milk Production Response."
    American Journal of Agricultural Economics 54 (February 1972).

Clark, Ralph. "The Economic Determinants of Jute Production."
    FAO Monthly Bulletin of Agricultural Economics and Statistics
    3 (September 1957).

Colman, D. R. "A New Study of United Kingdom Cereal Supply."
    Journal of Agricultural Economics 21 (September 1970).

Cooley, Thomas F. Estimation in the Presence of Sequential
    Parameter Variation. Ph.D. dissertation, University of
    Pennsylvania, 1971.

____ and Stephen J. DeCanio. "Varying Parameter Supply Functions
    and the Sources of Economic Distress in American Agriculture,
    1866–1914." National Bureau of Economic Research working
    paper No. 57 (September 1974).

Cooley, Thomas F., and Edward Prescott. "An Adaptive Regression
    Model." International Economic Review 14 (June 1973).

____. "Estimation in the Presence of Stochastic Parameter Varia-
    tion." Econometrica 44, no. 1 (January 1976).

____. "Tests of an Adaptive Regression Model." Review of
    Economics and Statistics 55 (May 1973).

____. "Varying Parameter Regression: A Theory and Some Appli-
    cations." Annals of Economic and Social Measurement 2
    (October 1973).

Cummings, John Thomas. "Cultivator Responsiveness in Pakistan–
    Cereal and Cash Crops." Pakistan Development Review 14
    (Autumn 1975).

____. "Supply Response in Peasant Agriculture: Price and Non-Price
    Factors." Ph.D. dissertation, Tufts University, 1974.

____. "The Supply Response of Bangalee Rice and Cash Crop
    Cultivators." Bangladesh Development Studies 2 (October 1974).

____. "The Supply Responsiveness of Indian Farmers in the Post-
    Independence Period." Indian Journal of Agricultural Economics
    30 (1975).

Dahlberg, D. L. "Supply Responses for Wool in South Australia, 1949-61." Australian Journal of Agricultural Economics 8 (June 1964).

Dandekar, V. M. "Prices, Production and Marketed Surplus of Foodgrains." Indian Journal of Agricultural Economics 19 (July-December 1964).

Dantwala, M. L., ed. "Symposium on Farmers' Response to Prices." Journal of the Indian Society of Agricultural Statistics 22 (June 1970).

Dean, Edwin R. "Economic Analysis and African Response to Price." Journal of Farm Economics 47 (May 1965).

____. Supply Response of African Farmers. Amsterdam: North-Holland, 1966.

Dean, Gerald W., and Earl O. Heady. "Changes in Supply Response and Elasticity for Hogs." Journal of Farm Economics 40 (November 1958).

DeCanio, Stephen J. "Agricultural Production, Supply, and Institutions in the Post-Civil War South." Ph.D. dissertation, Massachusetts Institute of Technology, 1972.

____. Agriculture in the Post-Bellum South. Cambridge: MIT Press, 1974.

____. "Cotton 'Overproduction' in Late Nineteenth-Century Southern Agriculture." Journal of Economic History 33 (September 1973).

____. "Productivity and Income Distribution in the Post-Bellum South." Journal of Economic History 34 (June 1974).

____. "Tenancy and the Supply of Southern Cotton 1882-1914." A paper given at the Econometrics Conference in Madison, University of Wisconsin, April 1971.

Desai, M. B. "Rapporteur's Report on Problems in Marketable Surplus in Indian Agriculture." Indian Journal of Agricultural Economics 16 (January-March 1961).

Devi, P. Kamla. "Response of Acreage to Changes in Price: A Study in Madras State." Economic Weekly, September 19, 1964.

Duloy, J. H., and A. S. Watson. "Supply Relationships in the
    Australian Wheat Industry: New South Wales." Australian
    Journal of Agricultural Economics 8 (June 1964).

Eddie, Scott M. "The Role of Agriculture in the Economic Develop-
    ment of Hungary 1867-1913." Ph.D. dissertation, Massachusetts
    Institute of Technology, 1967.

El-Mir, Mohammad Raja'a. "Location Models for the World Rice
    Industry." Ph.D. dissertation, University of California
    (Berkeley), 1967.

Falcon, Walter P. "Farmer Response to Price in a Subsistence
    Economy: The Case of West Pakistan." American Economic
    Review 54 (Papers and Proceedings) (May 1964).

____. "Farmer Response to Price in an Underdeveloped Area:
    A Case Study of West Pakistan." Ph.D. dissertation, Harvard
    University, 1962.

Fisher, Franklin. A Priori Information and Time Series Analysis.
    Amsterdam: North-Holland, 1962.

____. "A Theoretical Analysis of the Impact of Food Surplus
    Disposal on Agricultural Production in Recipient Countries."
    Journal of Farm Economics 45 (November 1963).

____ and Peter Temin. "Regional Specialization and the Supply
    of Wheat in the United States, 1867-1914." Review of Economics
    and Statistics 52 (May 1970).

____. "Regional Specialization and the Supply of Wheat in the United
    States, 1867-1914: A Reply." Review of Economics and Statistics
    53 (February 1971).

____. "Regional Specialization and the Supply of Wheat in the United
    States, 1867-1914: A Reply." Review of Economics and Statistics
    54 (February 1972).

Ford, Derek J. "Long-Run Price Elasticities in the Supply of
    Kenyan Coffee: A Methodological Note." Eastern African
    Economic Review 3 (June 1971).

Frederick, Kenneth D. "Coffee Production in Uganda: An Economic
    Analysis of Past and Potential Growth." Ph.D. dissertation,
    Massachusetts Institute of Technology, 1965.

_____. "The Role of Market Forces and Planning in Uganda's Economic Development 1900-1938." Eastern African Economic Review 1 (1969).

Freire, Remy. "Price Incentives in Argentine Agriculture." Mimeographed. Development Advisory Service Report, Center for International Affairs, Harvard University (1966).

French, Ben C., and Raymond G. Bressler. "The Lemon Cycle." Journal of Farm Economics 44 (November 1962).

French, Ben C. and Jim L. Matthews. "A Supply Response Model for Perennial Crops." American Journal of Agricultural Economics 53 (August 1971).

Gardner, T. W. "The Farm Price and Supply of Milk." Journal of Agricultural Economics 15 (May 1962).

_____ and Rosemary Walker. "Interactions of Quantity, Price and Policy: Milk and Dairy Products." Journal of Agricultural Economics 23 (May 1972).

Ghoshal, Animesh. "Export Commodities and Economic Development: The Liberian Rubber Industry." Ph.D. dissertation, University of Michigan, 1974.

_____. "The Price Responsiveness of Primary Producers: A Relative Supply Approach." American Journal of Agricultural Economics 57 (February 1975).

_____. "The Supply Response of Liberian Rubber Farmers." Malayan Economic Review 19 (October 1974).

Goodwin, Richard M. "Dynamic Coupling with Special Reference to Markets Having Production Lags." Econometrica 15 (1947).

Griliches, Zvi. "Research Costs and Social Returns: Hybrid Corn and Related Innovations." Journal of Political Economy 66 (October 1958).

Gruen, F. H. et al. Long Term Projections of Agricultural Supply and Demand, Australia 1965 and 1980. Clayton, Victoria: Economics Department, Monash University, 1968.

Guise, J. W. B. "Economic Factors Associated with Variations in Aggregated Wheat Acreage in New Zealand 1945-1965." New Zealand Economic Papers 2, no. 1 (1968).

Gwyer, G. D. "Long- and Short-Run Elasticities of Sisal Supply." Eastern African Economic Review 3 (December 1971).

Haessel, Walter. "The Price and Income Elasticities of Home Consumption and Marketed Surplus of Foodgrains." American Journal of Agricultural Economics 57 (February 1975).

Halvorson, Harlow W. "The Response of Milk Production to Price." Journal of Farm Economics 40 (December 1958).

_____. "The Supply Elasticity of Milk in the Short-Run." Journal of Farm Economics 37 (December 1955).

Hanushek, Eric A. "Efficient Estimators for Regressing Regression Coefficients." American Statistician 28 (May 1974).

Hartman, David G. "The Egg Cycle and the Ability of Recursive Models to Explain It." American Journal of Agricultural Economics 56 (May 1974).

Herskovits, Melville J. The Human Factor in Changing Africa. New York: Knopf, 1962.

Higgs, Robert. "Regional Specialization and the Supply of Wheat in the United States, 1867-1914: A Comment." Review of Economics and Statistics 53 (February 1971).

Hill, Brian E. "Supply Responses in Crop and Livestock Production." Journal of Agricultural Economics 22 (September 1971).

_____. "Supply Responses in Grain Production in England and Wales 1925-1963." Journal of Agricultural Economics 16 (June 1965).

Houck, James P., and M. E. Ryan. "Supply Analysis for Corn in the United States: The Impact of Changing Government Programs." American Journal of Agricultural Economics 54 (May 1972).

Houck, James P., and Abraham Subotnik. "The U.S. Supply of Soybeans: Regional Acreage Functions." Agricultural Economics Research 21 (October 1969).

Huq, Sayeedul. "Jute Price Stabilization and Resource Allocation between Jute and Rice in East Pakistan." Pakistan Economic Journal 19, no. 2 (1968/69).

Hussain, Sayed Mushtaq. "Economic Development of the Agricultural Sector of an Underdeveloped Country with Special Reference to Pakistan." Ph.D. dissertation, University of California (Berkeley), 1968.

____. "The Effect of the Growing Constraint of Subsistence Farming on Farmer Response to Price: A Case Study of Jute in Pakistan." Pakistan Development Review 9 (Autumn 1969).

____. "A Note on Farmer Response to Price in East Pakistan." Pakistan Development Review 4 (Spring 1964).

Jabbar, M. A. "A Note on the Price Response Studies in Relation to Jute." Indian Journal of Agricultural Economics 27 (January-March 1972).

Jarvis, Lovell. "Cattle as Capital Goods and Ranchers as Portfolio Managers: An Application to the Argentine Cattle Sector." Journal of Political Economy 82 (May-June 1974).

____. "Supply Response in the Cattle Industry: The Argentine Case, 1937-38 to 1966-67." Ph.D. dissertation, Massachusetts Institute of Technology, 1969.

Jha, Dayantha. "Acreage Response of Sugarcane in Factory Areas of North Bihar." Indian Journal of Agricultural Economics 25 (January-March 1970).

Jha, Dayantha, and C. C. Maji. "Cobweb Phenomenon and Fluctuations in Sugarcane Acreage in North Bihar." A paper read at the 31st Annual Conference of the Indian Society of Agricultural Economics, abstracted in the Indian Journal of Agricultural Economics 26 (October-December 1971).

Jones, G. T. "The Influence of Price on Livestock Population over the Last Decade." Journal of Agricultural Economics 16 (December 1965).

____. "The Response of the Supply of Agricultural Products in the United Kingdom to Price and Other Factors: Including Consideration of Distributed Lags" (Part I), Farm Economist 9 (1961) and (Part II) 10 (1962)

Kahlon, A. S., and H. N. Dwivedi. "Interrelationships Between Production and Marketable Surplus." Asian Economic Review 5 (August 1963).

Kahlon, A. S., and Charles E. Reed. "Problems of Marketable Surplus in Indian Agriculture." Indian Journal of Agricultural Economics 16 (January-March 1961).

Kaul, Jawahar L. "A Study of Supply Responses to Price of Punjab Crops." Indian Journal of Economics 48 (July 1967).

Kaul, J. L., and D. S. Sidhu. "Acreage Response to Prices for Major Crops in Punjab—An Econometric Study." Indian Journal of Agricultural Economics 26 (October-December 1971).

Khan, Azizur Rahman, and A. H. M. Nuruddin Chowdhury. "Marketable Surplus Function: A Study of the Behaviour of West Pakistan Farmers." Pakistan Development Review 2 (Autumn 1962).

King, Gordon A. "Econometric Models of the Agricultural Sector." American Journal of Agricultural Economics 57 (May 1975).

Koyck, L. M. Distributed Lags and Investment Analysis. Amsterdam: North-Holland, 1964.

Krishna, Jai and M. S. Rao. "Dynamics of Acreage for Wheat in Uttar Pradesh—A Study in Supply Response." Indian Journal of Agricultural Economics 22 (January-March 1967).

Krishna, Raj. "Agricultural Price Policy and Economic Development." In Agricultural Development and Economic Growth, edited by Herman M. Southworth and Bruce F. Johnston. Ithaca: Cornell University Press, 1967.

____. "Cotton Production and Price Policy Since Independence." University of Delhi, Institute of Economic Growth, 1964.

____. "Farm Supply Response in India-Pakistan: A Case Study of the Punjab Region." Economic Journal 73 (September 1963).

____. "The Marketable Surplus Function for a Subsistence Crop: An Analysis with Indian Data." Economic Weekly 17 (annual number, February 1965).

____. "A Note on the Elasticity of the Marketable Surplus of a Subsistence Crop." Indian Journal of Agricultural Economics 17 (July-September 1962).

Krishna, Sushil. "Farm Supply Response in India: A Study of Four Major Crops." Tufts University, unpublished paper, 1975.

Krishnan, T. N. "The Marketed Surplus of Foodgrains: Is It Inversely Related to Price?" Economic Weekly 17 (annual number, February 1965).

____. "Role of Agriculture in Economic Development." Ph.D. dissertation, Massachusetts Institute of Technology, 1964.

Lipton, Michael. "Should Reasonable Farmers Respond to Price Changes?" Modern Asian Studies 1, part I (January 1967).

Madhavan, M. C. "Acreage Response of Indian Farmers: A Case Study of Tamil Nadu." Indian Journal of Agricultural Economics 27 (January-March 1972).

____. "Supply Response of Indian Farmers: A Case Study of Madras State." Ph.D. dissertation, University of Wisconsin, 1969.

Maitha, Joseph K. "Productivity Response to Price: A Case Study of Kenyan Coffee." Eastern African Economic Review 2 (December 1970).

____. "A Supply Function for Kenyan Coffee." Eastern African Economic Review 1 (June 1969).

Maji, C. C., D. Jha, and L. S. Venkataramanan. "Dynamic Supply and Demand Models for Better Estimations and Projections: An Econometric Study for Major Foodgrains in the Punjab Region." Indian Journal of Agricultural Economics 26 (January-March 1971).

Majid, Abdul. "Marketed Surplus of Agricultural Produce in Relation to Size of Cultivated Holdings." Agricultural Situation in India 15 (January 1960).

Mandal, G. C. "The Marketable Surplus of Aman Paddy in East Indian Villages." Indian Journal of Agricultural Economics 16 (January-March 1961).

Mandal, G. C., and M. G. Ghosh. "A Study of Marketed Surplus of Paddy at the Farm Level in Four East Indian Villages." Indian Journal of Agricultural Economics 23 (July–September 1968).

Mangahas, Mahar, Aida E. Recto, and V. W. Ruttan. "Price and Market Relationships for Rice and Corn in the Philippines." Journal of Farm Economics 48 (August 1966).

Mathur, P. N. "Differential Effects of Price Increases on Small and Big Cultivators—A Case Study." Artha Vijnuna 4 (1962).

_____ and H. Ezekiel. "Marketable Surplus of Food and Price Fluctuations in a Developing Economy." Kyklos 14 (1961).

Medani, A. I. "Elasticity of Marketable Surplus of a Subsistence Crop at Various Stages of Development." Economic Development and Cultural Change 23 (April 1975).

_____. "The Supply Response of African Farmers in Sudan to Price." Tropical Agriculture 47 (July 1970).

_____. "The Supply Response to Price of African Farmers at Various Stages of Development." Oxford Agrarian Studies 1 (1972).

Meilke, Karl D. "Nerlove's Theory of Adaptive Expectations: Confusion or Not?" Journal of Agricultural Economics 26 (September 1975).

_____, A. C. Zwart, and L. J. Martin. "North American Hog Supply: A Comparison of Geometric and Polynomial Distributed Lag Models." Canadian Journal of Agricultural Economics 22 (July 1974).

Merrill, William C. "Setting the Price of Peruvian Rice." Journal of Farm Economics 49 (February 1967).

Misra, B., and S. P. Sinha. "A Study of Marketable Surplus of Foodgrains in a Village in Bihar." Indian Journal of Agricultural Economics 16 (January–March 1961).

Mohammed, Ghulam. "Some Physical and Economic Determinants of Cotton Production." Pakistan Development Review 3 (Winter 1963).

Mubyarto. "The Elasticity of the Marketable Surplus of Rice in
    Indonesia: A Study of Java-Madura." Ph.D. dissertation,
    Iowa State University, 1965.

Mules, T. J., and F. G. Jarrett. "Supply Responses in the South
    Australian Potato Industry." Australian Journal of Agricultural
    Economics 10 (June 1966).

Muth, John F. "Optimal Properties of Exponentially Weighted
    Forecasts." Journal of the American Statistical Association
    55 (June 1960).

_____. "Rational Expectations and the Theory of Price Movements."
    Econometrica 29 (July 1961).

Nair, Kusum. Blossoms in the Dust. New York: Frederick A.
    Praeger, 1961.

Naqvi, S. "Problems of Marketable Surplus in Indian Agriculture."
    Indian Journal of Agricultural Economics 16 (January-March
    1961).

Narain, Dharm, Distribution of the Marketed Surplus of Agricultural
    Produce by Size-Level of Holding in India 1950-51. Delhi:
    Institute of Economic Growth, 1961.

_____. The Impact of Price Movements on Areas under Selected
    Crops in India, 1900-1939. Cambridge: Cambridge University
    Press, 1965.

Natarajan, B. "Problems of Marketable Surplus in Indian Agricul-
    ture." Indian Journal of Agricultural Economics 16 (January-
    March 1961).

National Council of Applied Economic Research. Long-Term
    Projections of Demand for and Supply of Selected Agricultural
    Commodities—1960/61 to 1975/76. New Delhi, 1962.

Nerlove, Marc. "Adaptive Expectations and Cobweb Phenomena."
    Quarterly Journal of Economics 52 (1958).

_____. "Distributed Lags and Estimation of Long-Run Supply and
    Demand Elasticities: Theoretical Considerations." Journal
    of Farm Economics 40 (February 1958).

____. *The Dynamics of Supply: Estimation of Farmers' Response to Price*. Baltimore: Johns Hopkins University Press, 1958.

____. "Estimates of Supply of Selected Agricultural Commodities." Journal of Farm Economics 38 (May 1956).

____. "On the Nerlove Estimate of Supply Elasticity: A Reply." Journal of Farm Economics 40 (August 1958).

____ and William Addison. "Statistical Estimation of Long-Run Elasticities of Supply and Demand." Journal of Farm Economics 40 (November 1958).

____ and Kenneth L. Bachman. "The Analysis of Changes in Agricultural Supply: Problems and Approaches." Journal of Farm Economics 42 (August 1960).

Nowshirvani, Vahid. "Agricultural Supply in India: Some Theoretical and Empirical Studies." Ph.D. dissertation, Massachusetts Institute of Technology, 1968.

____. "The Efficacy of the Market Mechanism in Traditional Agriculture: A Re-examination of an Old Controversy." Center Discussion Paper No. 106, Economic Growth Center, Yale University, 1971.

____. "Land Allocation under Uncertainty in Subsistence Agriculture." Oxford Economic Papers 23 (November 1971).

____. "A Modified Adaptive Expectations Model." American Journal of Agricultural Economics 53 (February 1971).

____. "A Note on the Elasticity of the Marketable Surplus of a Surplus Crop—A Comment." Indian Journal of Agricultural Economics 22 (March 1967).

Olayemi, J. K., and S. A. Oni. "Asymmetry in Price Response: A Case Study of Western Nigerian Cocoa Farmers." Nigerian Journal of Economic and Social Studies 14 (November 1972).

Olayide, S. Olajuwan. "Some Estimates of Supply and Demand Elasticity for Selected Commodities in Nigeria's Foreign Trade." Journal of Business and Social Studies 1 (September 1968).

____. "Some Estimates of Supply Elasticities for Nigeria's Cash Crops." Journal of Agricultural Economics 23 (September 1972).

Olson, R. O. "The Impact and Implications of Foreign Surplus Disposal on Underdeveloped Economics." Journal of Farm Economics 42 (December 1960).

Oni, S. A. "Econometric Analysis of Supply Response Among Nigerian Cotton Growers." Bulletin of Rural Economics and Sociology 4, no. 2 (1969).

____. "Production Response in Nigerian Agriculture: A Case Study of Palm Produce 1949-1966." Nigerian Journal of Economics and Social Studies 11 (March 1969).

Oury, Bernard. A Production Model for Wheat and Feedgrains in France 1946-1961. Amsterdam: North-Holland, 1966.

Owen, E. R. J. Cotton and the Egyptian Economy 1820-1914. London: Oxford University Press, 1969.

Paddock, Brian W. "Supply Analysis of Rapeseed Acreage." Canadian Journal of Agricultural Economics 19 (July 1971).

Page, Walter P. "Wheat Culture and Productivity Trends in Wheat Production in the United States, 1867-1914: A Comment." Review of Economics and Statistics 56 (February 1974).

Papaioannou, M. C., and G. T. Jones. "Supply Response for Cattle, Sheep and Goats in Greece 1952-65." Oxford Agrarian Studies 1 (1972).

Parikh, A. "Farm Supply Response: A Distributed Lag Analysis." Oxford Institute of Statistics Bulletin 33 (1971).

____. "Market Responsiveness of Peasant Cultivators: Some Evidence from Prewar India." Journal of Development Studies 8 (January 1972).

Parker, William N., and Judith Klein. "Productivity Growth in Grain Production in the United States 1840-60 and 1900-10." In Output, Employment and Productivity in the United States after 1800, Studies in Income and Wealth, Vol. 30. New York: Columbia University Press, 1966.

Parthasarathy, G., and B. V. Subba Rao. "Production of Marketed Surplus of Rice in the Deltas of the South." Agricultural Situation in India 19 (November 1964).

a

Pfanner, David E. "A Semisubsistence Village Economy in Lower
Burma." In Subsistence Agriculture and Economic Development edited by Clifton R. Wharton, Jr. Chicago: Aldine, 1969.

Poduval, R. N. "Economic Development and Marketed Surplus in
Agriculture." Agricultural Situation in India 13 (August 1958).

Powell, Alan A., and F. H. Gruen. "The Estimation of Production
Frontiers: The Australian Livestock/Cereals Complex."
Australian Journal of Agricultural Economics 11 (June 1967).

Prato, Anthony A. "Milk Demand, Supply, and Price Relationships,
1950-1968." American Journal of Agricultural Economics 55
(May 1973).

Rabbani, A. K. M. Ghulam. "Economic Determinants of Jute
Production in India and Pakistan." Pakistan Development
Review 5 (Summer 1965).

Rajagopalan, V. "Supply Response for Irrigated Crops in Madras
State, India." Ph.D. dissertation, University of Tennessee,
1967.

____ and V. Meenakshisundaram. "Travails of the Tea Industry—
An Economic Appraisal." Indian Journal of Agricultural
Economics 24 (October-December 1969).

____, A. Senniamalai, S. A. Radhakrishnan, and A. Kandaswamy.
"Price Elasticities—Methodological Issues with Reference
to Perennial Crops." A paper read at the 31st Annual
Conference of the Indian Society of Agricultural Economics,
abstracted in the Indian Journal of Agricultural Economics
26 (October-December 1971).

Rao, M. S., and Jai Krishna. "Price Expectation and Acreage
Response for Wheat in Uttar Pradesh." Indian Journal of
Agricultural Economics 20 (January-March 1965).

Rao, P. V. G. K. "Marketed Surplus and Agricultural Production—
A Case Study of a Village in U.P." Agricultural Situation in
India 20 (October 1965).

Rao, V. Sreenisvasa. "A Study of the Marketed Surplus of Food-
grains with Special Reference to Selected Villages in South
India." Indian Journal of Agricultural Economics 16 (January-
March 1961).

Raquibuzzaman, Mohammad. "Marketed Surplus Function of Major Agricultural Commodities in Pakistan." Pakistan Development Review 6 (1966).

Rathod, K. L. "Farmers' Aversion to Risk—A Case of Sugarcane in Western Uttar Pradesh." Indian Journal of Economics 53 (April 1973).

Reddy, J. Mahender. "Estimation of Farmers' Supply Response— A Case Study of Groundnut." Indian Journal of Agricultural Economics 25 (October–December 1970).

Robertson, C. A. "Supply Response to Price under Certainty, with Reference to the United Kingdom Egg Market, 1954 to 1966." Journal of Agricultural Economics 22 (May 1971).

Roy, Shyamal. "Farmers' Response to Price in Allocating Acreage to Jute in West Bengal." Journal of the Indian Society of Agricultural Statistics 24 (June 1972).

Ryan, Mary E., and Martin E. Abel. "Corn Acreage Response and the Set-Aside Program." Agricultural Economics Research 24 (October 1972).

____. "Oats and Barley Acreage Response to Government Programs." Agricultural Economics Research 25 (October 1973).

____. "Supply Response of U.S. Sorghum Acreage to Government Programs." Agricultural Economics Research 25 (April 1973).

Saab, Gabriel S. The Egyptian Agrarian Reform 1952–1962. London: Oxford University Press, 1967.

Saran, Ram. "Problems of Marketable Surplus of Foodgrains in India." Indian Journal of Agricultural Economics 16 (January– March 1961).

Satyanarayana, Y. "Factors Affecting Acreage under Sugarcane in India." Indian Journal of Agricultural Economics 22 (April–June 1967).

Sawhney, B. L. "Farm Supply Response: A Case Study of the Bombay Region." Asian Economic Review 10 (February 1968).

Saxena, B. S. "Problems of Marketable Surplus in Indian Agriculture." Indian Journal of Agricultural Economics 16 (January-March 1961).

Saylor, R. Gerald. "Alternative Measures of Supply Elasticities: The Case of Sao Paulo Coffee." American Journal of Agricultural Economics 56 (February 1974).

Schmitz, Andrew. "Canadian Wheat Acreage Response." Canadian Journal of Agricultural Economics 16 (June 1968).

Schultz, Theodore. "Value of U.S. Farm Surpluses to Underdeveloped Countries." Journal of Farm Economics 42 (December 1960).

Seth, G. R., and D. Singh. "Estimation of Marketed Surplus in India." Indian Journal of Agricultural Economics 16 (January-March 1961).

Shah, C. H. "Market Supply of Farm Products in a Growing Economy." Indian Journal of Agricultural Economics 16 (January-March 1961).

Sharma, K. L., and M. P. Gupta. "Study of Farm Factors Determining Marketed Surplus of Bajra in Jaipur District." Indian Journal of Agricultural Economics 25 (October-December 1970).

Shastri, C. P. "The Problems of the Marketable Surplus in Agriculture in Bihar." Indian Journal of Agricultural Economics 16 (January-March 1961).

Singh, R. D., and Dinkar Rao. "Regional Analysis of Supply-Price Relationship of Major Foodgrains in Uttar Pradesh." Indian Journal of Economics 53 (April 1973).

____ and P. R. Rao. "Determinants of Supply Behavior: The Case of Virginia Tobacco in India." Artha Vijnuna 16 (September 1974).

Singh, R. P., Parmatma Singh, and K. N. Rai. "Acreage Response to Rainfall, New Farm Technology and Price in Haryana." Indian Journal of Economics 54 (October 1973).

Sinha, S. N. "Marketable Surplus in Agriculture in Underdeveloped Countries." Economic Review 13 (April 1962).

Sinha, Surendra Prasad, and Benoy Nath Varma. "A Study of
    Trends and Variations in the Prices of Foodgrains in Bihar
    with Special Reference to Prices of Cereals between 1956 and
    1968." A paper read at the 31st Annual Conference of the
    Indian Society of Agricultural Economics, abstracted in the
    Indian Journal of Agricultural Economics 26 (October-December
    1971).

Srinivasan, M. "Problems of Marketable Surplus in Indian Agri-
    culture." Indian Journal of Agricultural Economics 16
    (January-March 1961).

Stern, Robert. "The Determinants of Cocoa Supply in West Africa."
    In African Primary Products and International Trade, edited
    by I. G. Stewart and H. W. Ord. Edinburgh: Edinburgh
    University Press, 1965.

_____. "Malayan Rubber Production, Inventory Holdings and the
    Elasticity of Export Supply." Southern Economic Journal 31
    (April 1965).

_____. "Price Responsiveness of Egyptian Cotton." Kyklos 12
    (1959).

_____. "The Price Responsiveness of Primary Producers."
    Review of Economics and Statistics 44 (May 1962).

Subbarao, K. "Farm Supply Response—A Case Study of Sugarcane
    in Andhra Pradesh." Indian Journal of Agricultural Economics
    24 (January-March 1969).

Subramaniam, S. R., S. Varadarajan, and K. Ramamoorthy.
    "Farmers' Supply Response." A paper read at the 31st
    Annual Conference of the Indian Society of Agricultural
    Economics, abstracted in the Indian Journal of Agricultural
    Economics 26 (October-December 1971).

Sud, Lalita, and A. S. Kahlon. "Estimation of Acreage Response
    to Price of Selected Crops in Punjab State." Indian Journal
    of Agricultural Economics 24 (July-September 1969).

Swerling, B. C. International Control of Sugar. Stanford, Calif.:
    Stanford University Press, 1949.

Swift, Jeannine. "An Economic Study of the Chilean Agrarian Reform." Ph.D. dissertation, Massachusetts Institute of Technology, 1969.

Taplin, J., and P. Smallhorn. "The Supply of Honey in Australia." Quarterly Review of Agricultural Economics 23 (April 1970).

Tobin, James. "Liquidity Preference as Behavior Towards Risk." Review of Economic Studies, February 1958.

Tomek, William G. "Distributed Lag Models of Cotton Acreage Response: A Further Result." American Journal of Agricultural Economics 54 (February 1972).

Tweeten, Luther G. "Econometric Models of the Agricultural Sector: Discussion." American Journal of Agricultural Economics 57 (May 1975).

_____ and C. Leroy Quance. "Positivistic Measures of Aggregate Supply Elasticities: Some New Approaches." American Journal of Agricultural Economics 51 (May 1969).

_____. "Techniques for Segmenting Independent Variables in Regression Analysis: Reply." American Journal of Agricultural Economics 53 (May 1971).

VanderTak, Herman G., and Jan De Weille. Reappraisal of a Road Project in Iran. Washington: International Bank for Reconstruction and Development, 1969.

Venkataramanan, L. R. "A Statistical Study of Indian Jute Production and Marketing with Special Reference to Foreign Demand." Ph.D. dissertation, University of Chicago, 1958.

Warriner, Doreen. Land Reform in Principle and Practice. London: Oxford University Press, 1969.

Waud, Roger N. "Misspecification in the 'Partial Adjustment' and 'Adaptive Expectations' Models." International Economic Review 9 (June 1968).

Weeks, John. "Uncertainty, Risk, and Wealth and Income Distribution in Peasant Agriculture." Journal of Development Studies 7 (October 1970).

Wharton, Clifton R. "Rubber Supply Conditions: Some Policy
    Implications." In The Political Economy of Independent Malaya,
    edited by T. H. Silcock and E. K. Fisk. Canberra: The
    Australian National University, 1963.

Wickens, M. R., and J. N. Greenfield. "The Econometrics of
    Agricultural Supply: An Application to the World Coffee Market."
    Review of Economics and Statistics 55 (November 1973).

Williams, R. L. "Jamaican Coffee Supply, 1953-1968, An Explora-
    tory Study." Social and Economic Studies 21 (March 1972).

Wise, John and Pan A. Yotopoulos. "The Empirical Content of
    Economic Rationality: A Test for a Less Developed Economy."
    Journal of Political Economy 77 (November-December 1969).

Witherell, William H. "A Comparison of the Determinants of Wool
    Production in Six Leading Producing Countries: 1949-1965."
    American Journal of Agricultural Economics 51 (February 1969).

Wittenberg, John. "Nerlove's Theory of Adaptive Expectations."
    Journal of Agricultural Economics 25 (September 1974).

_____. "Nerlove's Theory of Adaptive Expectations: A Reply."
    Journal of Agricultural Economics 26 (September 1975).

Wolffram, Rudolf. "Positivistic Measures of Aggregate Supply
    Elasticities: Some New Approaches—Some Critical Notes."
    American Journal of Agricultural Economics 53 (May 1971).

HOSSEIN ASKARI is Associate Professor of International Business and Middle Eastern Studies at the University of Texas in Austin.

Dr. Askari has written extensively in the fields of international finance, international trade, and economic development with special emphasis on economic development in the Middle East.

Professor Askari received his B.S. degree in civil engineering and his Ph.D. degree in economics from the Massachusetts Institute of Technology.

JOHN THOMAS CUMMINGS is Assistant Professor of International Business at the University of Texas in Austin.

Before joining the University of Texas faculty, Professor Cummings was Director for Economics, Lincoln Filene Center for Citizenship and Public Affairs, and Assistant Professor of Economics at Tufts University. He has authored numerous articles on agricultural economics, and on Middle Eastern economic development.

Dr. Cummings received both his M.A. and Ph.D. degrees in economics from Tufts University.

AFRICAN FARMERS: Labor Use in the Development
of Smallholder Agriculture
John H. Cleave

AGRICULTURAL DEVELOPMENT PLANNING:
Economic Concepts, Administrative Procedures,
and Political Process
Willard W. Cochrane

ECONOMICS OF THE GREEN REVOLUTION IN
PAKISTAN
Mahmood Hasan Khan

FOOD, POPULATION, AND EMPLOYMENT:
The Impact of the Green Revolution
edited by Thomas T. Poleman
Donald K. Freebairn

MERCHANTS AS PROMOTERS OF RURAL
DEVELOPMENT: An Indian Case Study
Paul A. London

THE AGRICULTURAL DEVELOPMENT OF IRAN
Oddvar Aresvik

THE AGRICULTURAL DEVELOPMENT OF JORDAN
Oddvar Aresvik

THE AGRICULTURAL DEVELOPMENT OF TURKEY
Oddvar Aresvik

THE STATUS OF BOLIVIAN AGRICULTURE
E. Boyd Wennergren
Morris D. Whitaker